D1521278

FLORIDA STATE
UNIVERSITY LIBRARIES

MAY  9  1996

TALLAHASSEE, FLORIDA

This is the first English translation of important writings on the Thirty Years' War by the great Soviet historian B.F. Porshnev. Little is known of the Muscovite contribution to the conflict and Paul Dukes – arguably Britain's senior historian of *ancien régime* Russia – has selected the most valuable areas of Porshnev's unparalleled archival research to fill a crucial gap in the literature of the seventeenth century. In placing this work in the context of Porshnev's larger undertaking, Professor Dukes's substantial introduction assesses Porshnev's critics and evaluates his contribution to our understanding of the Thirty Years' War and of relations between Eastern and Western Europe at the time. This significant reinterpretation of a fascinating period will interest both Russian specialists and historians working on one or more widespread areas of seventeenth-century European politics.

Muscovy and Sweden in the Thirty Years' War, 1630–1635

# Muscovy and Sweden in the Thirty Years' War, 1630–1635

B.F. Porshnev

*Edited by*
*Paul Dukes*
University of Aberdeen

*Translated by*
**Brian Pearce**

CAMBRIDGE
UNIVERSITY PRESS

Published by the Press Syndicate of the University of Cambridge
The Pitt Building, Trumpington Street, Cambridge CB2 1RP
40 West 20th Street, New York, NY 10011-4211, USA
10 Stamford Road, Oakleigh, Melbourne 3166, Australia

© Ekaterina B. Porshnev, Moscow, c/o Progress-Academia Publishers Ltd.,
Moscow

All rights reserved.

© Translation and Introduction, Cambridge University Press 1995

First published 1995

Printed in Great Britain at the University Press, Cambridge

*A catalogue record for this book is available from the British Library*

*Library of Congress cataloguing in publication data*

Muscovy and Sweden in the Thirty Years' War, 1630–1635/
Porshnev, B. F. (Boris Fedorovich), 1905–1972;
edited by Paul Dukes; translated by Brian Pearce.
   p.   cm.
ISBN 0 521 45139 6
1. Thirty Years' War, 1618–1648. 2. Russia – History – 1613–1689.
I. Dukes, Paul, 1934– . II. Title.
D271.R8P67 1996
940.2'4 – dc20   95–10293   CIP

ISBN 0 521 45139 6 hardback

D
271
R8
P67
1995

VN

# Contents

# Editor's introduction

Boris Fedorovich Porshnev was born in 1905 in St Petersburg. He graduated from Moscow University, and worked in Moscow in several institutions after some years of school teaching in Rostov-on-Don. From 1943 he was a senior research associate of the Institute of History of the Academy of Sciences, although he also taught at Moscow University. In 1940, he defended his doctoral dissertation on 'Popular Revolts in France before the Fronde (1632–1648)': published under the same title in 1948, it was awarded the State Prize in 1950 and, later, translated into both German (1954) and French (1963). A man of several passionate interests, ranging from social psychology to the yeti, Porshnev polemicised widely.[1]

*Muscovy and Sweden in the Thirty Years' War, 1630–1635* is Brian Pearce's translation of Chapters 4 to 8 of a work originally published in 1976. Although it clearly bears the stamp of the time and place in which it was written, the book retains much of its value as an essential part of its author's general thesis concerning the political relations of West and East Europe during the epoch of the Thirty Years' War. First broadcast to the wider academic community in a paper given at the International Congress of Historical Sciences in Stockholm in 1960,[2] this thesis was then due to be enlarged in a trilogy. Sadly, in 1972 Porshnev died before his plan could be fully realised: indeed, only one part, the third, came out in his lifetime – *France, the English Revolution and European Politics at the Middle of the Seventeenth Century (Frantsiia, Angliiskaia revoliutsiia i evropeiskaia politika v seredine XVIIv.)*, 1970.[3] The second part, which was to consider the crisis and break in relations between Western and

---

[1] See the obituaries in *Voprosy istorii*, No. 1, 1973, p. 218; *Novaia i noveishaia istoriia*, No. 1, 1973, pp. 219–221. Little of Porshnev's work has hitherto been translated into English, although see, for example, *Social Psychology and History*, Moscow, 1970.

[2] B. F. Porchnev [sic], 'Les rapports politiques de l'Europe occidentale et de l'Europe orientale à l'époque de la guerre de Trente Ans', *XIe Congrès International des Sciences Historiques, Rapports IV, Histoire moderne*, Göteborg-Stockholm, Uppsala, 1960, pp. 136–163.

[3] See Paul Dukes, 'Russia and Mid-Seventeenth Century Europe: Some Comments on the Work of B. F. Porshnev', *European Studies Review*, Vol. 4, No. 1, 1974, pp. 81–88.

Eastern Europe and their influence on the continental war in the 1630s, was foreshadowed by several articles but has yet to see the light of day. Even the first part was published posthumously, albeit after its preparation was completed by the author himself.

Chapters 4 to 8 of the first part, which have been renumbered 1 to 5 in this translation, constitute the heart of the book, while the original first three chapters may be seen as introductory, setting the scene for the drama to follow. However, although they have been excluded, they should not pass without any notice at all, and therefore a brief summary of them follows here. In turn, they are concerned with 'Europe', 'Germany' and 'Prologue to European War – the Counter-Reformation in Germany, 1617–1629'.

Sixteenth-century Europe confronted the old Imperial power of the Habsburgs in West and East with a newer national absolutism, especially in England and France, and the growth in influence of the Ottoman Empire and Muscovy. Internal strife, part social, part religious, impeded the resolution of international conflicts. The Peace of Augsburg of 1555, extending toleration to the Lutheran princes of North and North-East Germany, was motivated at least partly by the Imperial desire to devote a greater effort to the solution of foreign problems. From 1556 to 1582, the Holy Roman Empire's *Ostpolitik* was aimed at the reduction of the threat emanating from Muscovy and Ottoman Turkey, and this involved some diminution of the rivalry with Poland. An important moment was the outbreak in 1558 of the Livonian War, in which Ivan the Terrible attempted to break through the Imperial blockade to the Baltic Sea. By 1569–1570, a barrier had been erected against Muscovite expansionism consisting of Sweden, the newly united Poland–Lithuania and Ottoman Turkey. However, not all the action was against Ivan the Terrible: indeed, in 1572, there was talk of a Muscovite–Habsburg alliance against Turkey along with a two-way partition of Poland–Lithuania between the allies. But negotiations broke down over the question of Livonia. Meanwhile, to the west, the English, the French and the Dutch were all able in various ways to overcome the blockade that the Habsburgs would have liked to enforce in that part of Europe. Although the division of the Habsburg lands between Spain and Austria in 1555–1556 meant to some extent a division of labour, such problems as the maintenance of the 'road' along the Rhine and of stability in the Netherlands were of concern to both branches of the family.

By 1582–1583, Ivan the Terrible's grasp for the Baltic in the Livonian War had met with final failure, and the Tsar died in 1584. Boris Godunov met with little or no more success in 1590. In 1593, the Turks exerted new pressure up the Danube, and an Imperial envoy strove in that and the following year to establish a firm peace between Sweden and Muscovy so that the latter might combine with the Empire against the Turks. As before, however, the fate of Livonia proved to be a stumbling block. Godunov made another unsuccessful attempt for a foothold on the Baltic from 1600 to 1603, again vainly trying for the support of the Empire against Poland–Lithuania.

Now, Muscovite Russia was virtually to fall apart during the Time of Troubles, with intervention from both Poland–Lithuania and Sweden. A succession of Polish puppets was installed as tsars, and there was widespread social dislocation. However, Muscovy was saved from complete collapse by the rivalry between Poland–Lithuania and Sweden and more general European tension as well as by a patriotic revival culminating in the election as tsar of Mikhail Romanov in 1613. The new government made peace with Sweden at Stolbovo in 1617, and with Poland–Lithuania, after a final incursion, at Deulino in 1618. Meanwhile, having made a twenty-year truce with the Ottoman Turks in 1606, the Imperial Habsburgs were restrained by a threat of war with France and other difficulties from taking their hopes of expansion to the East any further. Along with the Spanish branch of the family, the Imperial Habsurgs were now poised for the commencement in 1618 of the Thirty Years' War.

Narrowing his focus, Porshnev suggested that German historians had put forward two principal theses about the Thirty Years' War: that it was the consequence of the Holy Roman Emperor's attempt to unify Germany; and that France – 'the eternal enemy' – exploited the tension between the Emperor and the princes to divide and weaken Germany even further. They had blamed the war, along with foreign enemies – especially France, for all the negative features of later German history. But Porshnev asserted that two counter-theses could be put forward: that the aggressors were in fact the Habsburg powers, especially the Empire; and that the war was largely concerned with the Imperial attempt to suppress the opposition to this aggression by the Protestant princes. Hostilities in Germany were in the first instance not so much because of intervention from outside as because of internal circumstances. There were four categories of contradiction: state, between the Empire and the princes; confessional, especially between Catholics and Protestants; national, involving principally Germans, Slavs and Hungarians; and social, between the classes. The first category was the most noticeable, and the last – the least, but their actual importance was the other way round.

Of course, the pretensions of the Emperor as defender of world order were huge, while the princes could make for themselves considerably lesser claims. Yet it could be said that the Emperor and the princes were two sides of the same feudal edifice, the material foundations of which, never strong, were now in the process of disappearing.

Leadership of the Reformation had come more from the princes than the burghers, and the confessional division of the Empire followed a pattern defined by the borders of the principalities rather than the disposition of the towns: to put it simply, the South was Catholic, the North-West was Calvinist, and the North-East was Lutheran. There could therefore never be princely unity, and even the principle introduced in 1555 by the Peace of Augsburg – *cuius regio, eius religio* (whoever's region, his religion) – could never be applied strictly.

The shortfall was to a considerable extent the consequence of the national question. There were age-old tensions between the Germans and the Slavs, while for Czechs and Hungarians, among others, freedom of conscience became the symbol of national independence. The Czechs and Hungarians were conscious of taking the brunt of Turkish aggression, and such awareness also contributed to the circumstance that the Austro–Czech–Hungarian Habsburg monarchy was not only the largest component of the Empire but also the main threat to its political balance.

The 'most national movement in the whole history of Germany' had been the Great Peasant War ending in 1525, with its participants ignoring frontiers, but this was also a class struggle. The continuance of such social struggle could be seen in the entrenchment of serfdom, a process stretching from after 1525 up to about 1650, after the end of the Thirty Years' War. Although it varied in its nature according to the basis of the peasant's position in the system of land ownership, there was a considerable amount of tension evident before 1618 and intensified by the taxation, billeting and pillage of the Thirty Years' War, which, although a European war, was fought largely in Germany. The extent of the terror was difficult to estimate with any degree of exactness, but there could be no doubt that the war could be characterised as 'a punitive expedition against the German peasants'. If Karl-Friedrich von Moser had been justified in his observation made a century or so later that each nation had its own basis for motivation – France: the honour of the monarch; Holland: trade; England: freedom; and Germany: obedience – the last of these was a consequence of the terror inflicted during the Thirty Years' War.

Turning to the Counter-Reformation in Germany from 1617 to 1629 as a prologue to war throughout Europe, Porshnev argued that there had been a persistent myth, encouraged by the Prussian school of historians, but accepted by many of their French and English colleagues, that the conflict as a whole had largely consisted of an attempt by the Habsburg Catholic–feudal reaction to dominate Europe, which had succeeded only in encouraging the intervention of foreign powers in Germany. To be sure, up to 1629, hostilities could indeed be characterised as centring around the Catholic reaction, but 1630 marked an important turning-point, and after that, hostilities continued basically between two coalitions. There were, as had often been accepted, four main periods in the Thirty Years' War: (1) the Czech–Palatinate, 1618–1623; (2) the Danish, 1625–1629; (3) the Swedish, 1630–1635; (4) the Swedish–French, 1635–1648. However, the greatest change of direction in the war was undoubtedly marked by the invasion of Pomerania by Gustavus Adolphus of Sweden in 1630.

The famous Defenestration of Prague in 1618 had not actually marked the war's outbreak, for Ferdinand of Styria, soon to become Holy Roman Emperor, had already in 1617 launched aggression against both the French and the Czechs. The Czech Revolt following the Defenestration had produced the first reverses for the Habsburg camp, but it had bounced back, with emphasis on the cause of the Counter-Reformation, and the growing realisation that the outcome of the war would depend largely on money and mercenaries.

In 1624, a saviour for the Imperial cause arose in the shape of Albrecht Wallenstein, a fantastic entrepreneur who managed to raise a considerable army, and then to put it to effective use. While France, England and the Dutch Republic held back from full involvement in the conflict, the efforts of Wallenstein and others took the Habsburg–Catholic forces to a zenith of success by 1628–1629. But then the activities of the French in Italy, and of the Dutch on land and sea were enhanced at the end of the Danish period of the war by the vigorous entry of the Swedes. This is where the translated chapters of Porshnev's book take up the story. The foregoing summary of the first three, introductory chapters has inevitably given emphasis to a fault detected by some readers of the full 150 pages or so of the original Russian text: over-simplification to the point of caricature of the complex realities of late sixteenth- and early seventeenth-century Europe. On the other hand, at the very least, the summary serves perhaps to make clear one of Porshnev's fundamental assertions, the neglect in much historical writing on the period under discussion of the part played by Eastern Europe, especially Muscovy, in the affairs of the continent as a whole.

Admittedly, vigorous assertion can lead to over-assertion, and other exaggerations in his argument are not difficult to find. Perhaps the most serious of them is his estimate of the extent of the subsidy given by Muscovy to Sweden through grain transactions (one calculation of the profit obtained in this manner by the Swedish Crown from 1629 to 1633 amounting to 160,000 reichsthalers as opposed to the sum of 2,400,000 reichsthalers arrived at by Porshnev[4]). On the other hand, again, while errors and misunderstandings should always be pointed out, at least some allowance must be made for the difficult circumstances in which a Soviet historian would be working in the 1970s. Furthermore, not even Porshnev's sternest critics would deny that he was making a worthwhile point, or rather enlarging upon a point already made by several other historians, although their work could at the same time indicate another of his faults – the tendency to claim a greater degree of originality for his work than it actually possessed. G. V. Forsten and D. Norrman,[5] to name but two, both foreshadowed the theses put forward in this book, even if not giving the same emphases, nor, to give Porshnev his due, making anything like as much use of the Russian archives as did he.

Going back even further into the past, indeed right back to the period that the book discusses, we might question the very possibility of originality in the work of any historian, at least in the sense that, if he or she is revealing some truth about the past, then this is not so much discovery as rediscovery. However, to look forward rather than back, his successors have been enabled by the contribution of B. F. Porshnev, added to that of others including those named above, to give a full consideration to problems of European history in the epoch of the Thirty Years' War. If Porshnev could first formulate his ideas on this subject during the years of the Second World War and then develop them and work towards the completion of his trilogy during the subsequent years of the Cold War, how much more should we be able to take advantage of the new opportunities for investigating the history of the entire continent of Europe that have opened up in the early 1990s. Further assessment of the role of individuals such as Alexander Leslie[6] and Jacques Roussel as well as further consideration of Porshnev's basic question – 'Is it possible to

---

[4] Lars Ekholm, 'Russian Grain and Swedish War Finances 1629-1633', *Scandia*, Vol. 40, 1974, pp. 101–103. Paul Bushkovitch, *The Merchants of Moscow, 1580–1650*, Cambridge, 1980, p. 158, writes that 'Nor was the amount of money involved in the sale and purchase of grain for the Smolensk War tremendous, when compared with the total turnover at Archangel . . . The grain sales by the treasury in the 1620s and 1630s to Sweden, which were partly an attempt to support the Swedish effort in the Thirty Years' War, were also not very large by Archangel standards, although the total of this activity in the years 1627–34 was larger than usual.' On the other hand, a work cited by Bushkovitch in support of this assessment also gives some indication of the importance to Sweden of the Russian grain trade. See A. Attman and others, eds., *Ekonomicheskie sviazi mezhdu Rossiei i Shvetsiei v XVIIv.: dokumenty iz sovetskikh arkhivov*, Moscow-Stockholm, 1978. No doubt, the final word on this subject has yet to be spoken.

[5] G. V. Forsten, *Baltiiskii vopros v XVI i XVII stoletiiakh (1544–1648)*, 2 vols., St Petersburg, 1893–4; David Norrman, *Gustav Adolfs politik mot Ryssland och Polen under Tyska kriget (1630–1632)*, Uppsala, 1943.

[6] See, for example, Paul Dukes, 'The Leslie Family in the Swedish Period (1630-1635) of the Thirty Years' War', *European Studies Review*, vol. 12, no. 4, 1982, pp. 401–404.

think of the history of one country on its own?'[7] – should now present fewer obstacles while losing none of their importance.

### Acknowledgements

In Moscow, to L. A. Nikitina for a copy of the book, and to K. B. Porshneva for facilitating translation rights. In Aberdeen, for help in preparing the typescript, to Cathryn Brennan, Cathy Fourie, John Hadden, Andrea Hannah, Alan McAdam and especially Gillian Brown and Sandra Williams; for advice on some aspects of the translation of the Author's preface, to James Forsyth; for advice on some aspects of the Introduction, to Howard Hotson; for proof-reading, to Alexeia Grosjean. Further afield in the UK, to Douglas Matthews for the index as well as to Brian Peace for the translation. A final acknowledgement, my own ultimate responsibililily for errors of omission (including Slavonic diacritical marks) and commission, wherever they may not be attributed to B. F. Porshnev himself, or his editor.

---

[7] For example, there could be further investigation of the international impact of the Smolensk War. Certainly, there was a series of pamphlets produced on this subject in both German and Spanish. See *Wahre und gründliche Relation . . .*, September 1633; *Fernere und gründliche Relation . . .*, [October 1633]; *Gründliche und wahre Relation . . .*, January 1634; *Gründliche und wahrafftiger Bericht . . .*, February 1634; *Glaubwürdige Zeitung . . .*, 1634; *Gründlicher Bericht . . .*, 1634; *Fröliche und gewisse Zeitung . . .*, 1634. They are located in the City Archive, Gdansk. And see *Las Continuas Vitorias . . .*, 1634; *Relacion Verdadera de la Insigne Vitoria . . .*, 1634, both located in the British Library. The most complete study in English is Geoffrey Parker, *The Thirty Years' War*, London, 1984.

# Author's preface

This book is part of a trilogy. The author's intention was that three monographs were to constitute a single study of the system of European states during the epoch of the Thirty Years' War. It has so happened that in 1970, the third, i.e. the chronologically concluding part – the monograph *France, the English Revolution and European Politics at the Middle of the Seventeenth Century*[1] – was published before the others. Now the first book is put in the hands of readers.

The theme of the second monograph in the trilogy, already basically prepared, is the crisis and rupture in relations between Western and Eastern Europe and also in the fortunes of the general European war. Its principal parts are: I. The peasant–Cossack rising in the Moscow state called the *Balashovshchina* (1633–1634);[2] II. The Peace of Polyanovka of 1634,[3] the crisis of Russo–Swedish relations and the Treaty of Stuhmsdorf of 1635,[4] the open entry of France into the war with the Habsburgs; III. The epic career of Jacques Roussel,[5] Catholicism, Protestantism, Orthodoxy

---

[1] A résumé of the work was already given by me at the XI International Congress of Historical Sciences at Stockholm in 1960. See *XIe. Congrès International des Sciences Historiques, Stockholm, 21–28 août 1960, Rapports, IV: Histoire moderne*, Uppsala, 1960, pp. 136–163; Russian translation – 'Politicheskie otnosheniia Zapadnoi i Vostochnoi Evropy v epokhu Tridtsatiletnei Voiny', *Voprosy istorii*, No. 10, 1960. However the completion of the work has been delayed for many years.

[2] Fragments have been published: 1. 'Sotsial'no-politicheskaia obstanovka v Rossii vo vremia Smolenskoi voiny', *Istoriia SSSR*, No. 5, 1957; 2. 'Razvitie "balashovskogo" dvizheniia v fevrale-marte 1634g.', *Problemy obshchestvenno-politicheskoi istorii Rossii i slavianskikh stran: sbornik statei k 70-letiiu akad. M. N. Tikhomirova*, Moscow, 1963.

[3] A fragment has been published: 'Na putiiakh k Polianovskomu miru 1634', *Mezhdunarodnye otnosheniia, politika, diplomatiia XVI–XVIIvv.: sbornik statei k 80-letiiu akad. I. M. Maiskogo*, Moscow, 1964.

[4] The theses have been published as papers delivered on: 1. 'Shvedskoe posol'stvo v Moskvu v 1634g.', *Tezisy dokladov vtoroi nauchnoi konferentsii po istorii, ekonomike, iaziku i literature Slavianskikh stran i Finliandii*, Moscow, 1965; 2. 'Stumsdorfskii mir 1635g.: ego istoriografiia i istoricheskoe znachenie', *Tezisy dokladov 4-i Vsesoiuznoi konferentsii po istorii Skandinavskikh stran*, Part 1, Petrozavodsk, 1968.

[5] A fragment has been published: 'Iz istorii russko-frantsuzskikh sviazei v epokhu Tridtsatiletnei voiny', *Frantsuzskii ezhegodnik, 1958*, Moscow, 1959. See also the special section 4 'V masshtabe individual'noi zhizni' in the concluding part of the book *Frantsiia, Angliiskaia revoliutsiia i evropeiskaia politika v seredine XVIIv.*

and Islam, the struggle for unity against Catholicism of the other Christian churches in the 1630s; IV. The position and role of Turkey in East and West European politics in the 1630s.

This summary of the second link in the trilogy is completely necessary here as a conceptual bridge between the book now presented and that which came out in 1970 and is concerned with the 1640s.

In the origin and outcome of the whole work a special part has been played by the theme of the role of Russia, i.e. of Russian diplomacy and the so-called Smolensk War (1632–1634) in the history of the Thirty Years' War. The author has taken upon his shoulders the whole unenviable burden of the discoverer ... My suggestion of the well-founded nature of a research project such as this has met with a sceptical attitude. I for my own part have not only seen the positive qualities of the theme, which have been confirmed by subsequent searches in archival and published sources, but have also been attracted in scholarly endeavours by that aspect which may be called discovery. To be sure, historiographical tradition has excluded and made appear improbable the combination of these two subjects. The maximum allowed by the conventional mould for the sixteenth and seventeenth centuries has been the study of the commercial links between Russian and Western merchants.

Of course, there could be no talk of the actual influence of the military-political power of the Muscovite state on Western Europe previously: therefore, it is easy to see that making such an encroachment on tradition and providing a solid foundation for my attempt has constituted a discovery. It arose in my mind during the process of lighting upon and comparing more and more new documentary data, but I cannot fail to mention that it was prompted during the years of the great historical clash between our country and Nazi Germany – the inheritor of everything reactionary that had accumulated over the many centuries of German history.[6] Just such a reappraisal of the 'Russo–German' historical theme during the stormy years of the war encouraged in particular a reconsideration of the problem of 'Russia and the Thirty Years' War' (and a number of other questions about Russia's place in the historical past among European political forces).

If a general title be thought necessary for my trilogy, I would adopt for such a purpose the heading for one of the introductory parts of the third book, namely: 'Is it possible to think of the history of one country on its own?' The epoch of the Thirty Years' War is here only a specific historical fact, serving as a kind of experimental material for appraising this

---

[6] See B. F. Porshnev, 'Zavoevatel'nye avantiury v istorii Germanii i gitlerovshchina', *Bol'shevik*, No. 14, 1943; B. F. Porshnev, 'Über die gewissen Tendenzen in der deutschen Geschichte', *Sowjetliteratur*, No. 1, 1947.

question. Consequently, on the plane of the system of European states in process of formation at that time under the heading could be put a subheading: 'From the example of the epoch of the Thirty Years' War'.

In order to correlate the idea of the 'system of states' with concrete historical reality, it is necessary as thoroughly as possible to point out the untruthfulness of the traditional, usual and unnoticed omissions and contradictions. Thus, in the third book I showed the falsity of the almost universally held opinion concerning the mutual indifference and gulf between the French Fronde and the English Revolution. However, it has turned out to be both a more complicated and more worthwhile task to fill in the gulf between the political history of Russia and the rest of Europe, in a word, 'to reunite Europe' as regards the second quarter of the seventeenth century. The word 'reunite' is used here by no means in the sense that would exclude the examination of antagonisms and conflicts but rather in the sense of a scholarly grasp of this subject in its entirety. The history of historical science has for various reasons involved a significant exclusion of Russian history from 'universal history', especially in such a relatively early period as that known as the fifteenth to the seventeenth centuries ... Overcoming the traditional isolation of Russia from Europe must necessarily mean revision and enhancement of the historian's methods themselves – especially those of the historian of international relations. Thus, theoretical and concrete researches clearly interact in the given case, with the rejection of the artificial division of historical science into 'universal' and 'national'.

Turning to the study of 'Russica', I have also met with certain specific methodological difficulties. In particular, here is one of them, sufficiently characteristic. Western historians do not at all consider it unscholarly when citing texts of the sixteenth and seventeenth centuries to somewhat modernise both the language and the orthography. This way of quoting from sources is generally acceptable, even in the historians' most academic publications. There are weighty reasons for this. What was the norm in earlier stages of history for one language or another has not disappeared completely and given way to new norms, but is preserved for a long time in poorly educated and peripheral social circles. Therefore, archaic texts are accepted by us unwillingly and haughtily: they are associated with contemporary archaisms and provincialisms. The image of the author of a text is transformed in our consciousness from 'old' to 'old-fashioned', and we condescendingly forgive him for a certain inadequate education, clumsiness and provinciality, or, on the other hand, too, a somewhat amusing affectation. But in fact, there was nothing of this within the linguistic culture of the text's own time. Western historians do not want their readers to have a sense of their ancestors as 'naive' – they translate their speech into the language of a member of the contemporary elite. Nobody sees in this a violation of the interests of historical science, and only philological specialists are interested in unaltered old texts. The stubbornness of devotees of 'Russica', justifying itself by academic propriety, renders the history of Russia of preceding centuries somewhat odd. Some scholars have noticed this psychological bias and have tried to alter the tradition of citation, thus substituting in the reader's perception an intelligent author for a quaint ancestor. And so M. N. Tikhomirov has arrived at the conclusion that it has become necessary to quote Old Russian texts in historical works (of course, we are not talking about philological editions) in translation into contemporary Russian language, but he has not met with understanding for this view ... To be sure, the translation of old texts into contemporary Russian demands that one does only what is absolutely necessary as well as with the greatest care, but what I have said explains why I associate myself with M. N. Tikhomirov (with whom I have discussed this question), and why I offer to the reader all quotations from Russian documents of the seventeenth century in a minimally modernised version or with the citation in brackets of parallel versions.

This textological question is only a small illustration of the many difficulties in the path of the historian restoring the place of Russia in the system of European states.

In this task, my choice of the period of the Thirty Years' War has not been accidental. It was the first pan-European war. At least, though having started as one of the 'wars of religion', it brought to the surface by the beginning of the 'Swedish period' profound political contradictions on a continental scale and attracted participants less and less characterised by their confessional tendencies. By that very fact the Thirty Years' War was very important for the historical elucidation of the idea of 'Europe'.

At the same time, it is necessary to recall that the Thirty Years' War was not an isolated or newly arisen historical phenomenon. It belongs in the complex of other, preceding armed conflicts which expressed in the political sphere the profound and radical processes of the genesis of capitalism within the womb of feudal Europe. Several deeply different wars preceded the Thirty Years' War and historically prepared for it or were merged with it. Above and beyond all others was the war of the Netherlands for independence from Spain. This war began with the Dutch Revolution and finished with the Peace of Westphalia. Another root was constituted by the armed conflicts which went on at the end of the sixteenth and at the beginning of the seventeenth century in the Mediterranean, where the key question was the struggle for control of that sea between Turkey and Spain, as well as Austria, the Italian commercial republics and France. Later, there was the complex armed struggle for the littoral of the Baltic Sea. And, finally, there were the armed clashes between Russia and Poland, mainly on the principal basis of the struggle for the territories of the Ukraine, Byelorussia and West Russia.

# 1 Muscovy and the entry of Sweden into the Thirty Years' War

## The diplomatic preparation

The years 1628–1629 were a turning-point in the Thirty Years' War. Its first phase had ended with almost complete victory for the Emperor and the Catholic reaction in Germany. All Europe was now faced with the danger that the Habsburgs' design of universal domination would be realised. The Polish–Lithuanian state was also closely associated with the Habsburg–Catholic bloc. The other states were alarmed by this developing aggression and in the 1630s we see them already united in a broad anti-Habsburg coalition which was to alter the course of the Thirty Years' War. Vague outlines of this future coalition were to be observed already in the 'Danish period' of the war (1625–1629), but two of its principal participants, France and Sweden, still at that time remained in the background.

It was precisely these two states, however, that were threatened with immediate dangers – France with strangulation in a ring of Habsburg possessions[1] which, under Richelieu, it had twice tried to break in Italy, in 1624 and in 1628 (the wars for the Valtelline and Mantuan succession), and Sweden with loss of its domination of the Baltic and establishment on the Swedish throne of the Catholic Sigismund III, by the hands of his kinsmen and allies the Habsburgs.

Richelieu emerged as the organiser of the European coalition against the Habsburgs. He had expressed the idea in 1624–1625 that the only way to bring down the Empire would be to make it fight a war on two fronts, to grip it between two armies, and, through the Dutch, he had tried to put that idea into effect, moving Denmark into Germany from the north-west and Sweden from the north-east. But at that time this plan miscarried owing to refusal by Gustavus Adolphus to begin a war with the Empire before he had concluded his war with the Polish–Lithuanian state for the

---

[1] Most scholars now reject the traditional thesis of German historians according to which Richelieu pursued an aggressive policy in the Thirty Years' War (cf. Beller, E., 'Recent Studies on the Thirty Years' War', *Journal of Modern History*, Vol. 3, No. 1, March 1931).

Baltic littoral (Livonia and Prussia). This long-standing conflict, which had died down in 1622–1624, flared up again in 1625.[2] Despite all persuasion, Gustavus Adolphus remained adamant in his refusal. This had the consequence of temporarily discouraging Richelieu, and contributed to his inclining even to seek a *rapprochement* with the Habsburgs. But he was soon obliged to realise that such a course would be fatal for France.

The key role in the development of the Thirty Years' War at the beginning of the 1630s fell to Sweden. Not so much because of its strength as because of its strategic position, Sweden had the power to decide the fate of Europe. England and Denmark had withdrawn from the game at the end of the 1620s. France possessed an excellent ally against Spain, namely the Dutch, but had no ally against the Empire, despite intense diplomatic efforts. The Ottoman Empire was too much taken up with Persian affairs, and French diplomacy failed to bring it in against the Empire, right down to the end of the Thirty Years' War.

Sweden was a different matter, because it had its own dream of striking at the Empire, due to the growing concern with which it followed the Habsburg–Catholic preparations for 'the rape of Europe'. Gustavus Adolphus, who had already 'taken away the sea', as he put it, from Muscovy (by the peace of Stolbovo in 1617) and was moving towards a similar result in his bitter war with the Rzeczpospolita, was now not merely hankering after the Pomeranian shore of the Baltic, which belonged to the Empire, but was also anxious about the Habsburgs, since they were preparing to deprive him of all his gains and even of his crown. In Gustavus Adolphus's own words, the Emperor was 'aiming at the very heart of the Swedish state'.[3]

However, to take the offensive against the Empire before he had concluded his war with the Rzeczpospolita would have been, in Gustavus Adolphus's opinion, a stupid move to make, as he told the English, Dutch and Brandenburger diplomats in 1626. The Swedish King was convinced that he would be able quickly to achieve a definitive defeat of the Poles.

In the Habsburg camp, though, they also perceived that possibility. Wallenstein was mortally afraid of Swedish intervention in the war in Germany. As early as the Brussels congress of the Habsburg coalition, in 1626, the decision was taken to give covert military help to Poland, so as to keep Sweden's forces tied up. From 1627 a substantial part of Wallenstein's army was stationed in Pomerania so that from there it could come to the aid of the Poles. Swedish vessels were set on fire in the

[2] The basic source for the history of this war is the work by I. Hoppe, the *Burggraf* of Elbing: *Geschichte des ersten schwedisch-polnischen Krieges in Preussen*, edited by M. Toeppen, Leipzig, 1887.

[3] Forsten, G., *Baltiiskii vopros v XVI–XVII stoletiiakh*, Vol. II, St. Petersburg, 1894, p.304.

Pomeranian ports. In 1629 a force of ten thousand men under Arnim's command operated in Prussia alongside Sigismund III's army, against the Swedes. Gustavus Adolphus's plan to end the war with Poland quickly was thus frustrated. But the Swedish King had already in 1628 been partly drawn into war with the Emperor when, in alliance with the Danes, he gave what help he could to the besieged Pomeranian port of Stralsund, against Wallenstein's army.

This event inspired Richelieu with fresh hope and reinvigorated his diplomatic efforts. To be sure, it proved impossible in the end to keep Denmark, which had been irretrievably beaten, within the anti-Habsburg coalition. Nevertheless, he strove by every means to keep up Denmark's spirits while at the same time applying himself to his main task – bringing Sweden into the war against the Empire.

That was still a task of exceptional difficulty. In the first place, Sweden lacked sufficient resources for paying and maintaining its armed forces: the state's coffers were empty. Richelieu could help with that problem by granting Sweden large subsidies from France's treasury. In the second place, it was necessary, at whatever cost, to reconcile Sweden and Poland: the situation in Europe brooked no further delay. But how was this result to be attained? Dutch and Brandenburger intermediaries had tried to bring it about in 1627 and 1628, and failed. Consequently, Richelieu was required to turn his diplomatic efforts to disentangling the very complicated contradictions in the far east of Europe. Unless he plunged into East-European politics he would be unable to solve the problem, of importance to all Europe, of organising an anti-Habsburg coalition.

Richelieu himself explained this in his memoirs. Gustavus Adolphus was 'a new rising sun' in North-Eastern Europe. The King of France

had taken note of this young prince with a view to trying to make use of him in order to divert, in due course of time, the Emperor's main forces and to prevent the Emperor from unjustly waging war in Italy and France, and to make him give up, through the terror and damage he would suffer, his design aimed at oppressing public freedom . . . Several princes of the Empire, wrongly despoiled of their states by the Imperial forces . . . look toward the King of Sweden in their wretchedness, as navigators look toward the North. But he was busy with war against Poland, and, although he lacked neither courage nor ambition, he needed to be freed from that enemy before making for himself another, such as the House of Austria was.[4]

Richelieu succeeded in accomplishing this task. In September 1629, through French mediation, a six-year truce was agreed between Sweden and the Polish–Lithuanian state. Gustavus Adolphus was free to move against the Habsburgs.

[4] Richelieu, *Mémoires* (Collection Michaud et Poujoulat, Vol. XXII, Paris, 1854), pp. 67–69.

Many historians consider this truce to be Richelieu's most brilliant diplomatic achievement. 'What an incomparable piece', Lamprecht exclaims, 'was this Swedish King on the chessboard of France's anti-Habsburg policy! If only his hands were freed so that his full strength was made available, he would be able, from an unsuspected corner, to cause the Emperor to find himself in check. Consequently, it was a masterly move of French diplomacy when, through its mediation, a six-year truce favourable to Sweden, was agreed on by Poland and Sweden in September 1629.'[5] Many such enthusiastic evaluations by historians concerning Richelieu's skill in connection with the truce of Altmark could be quoted.[6]

Unfortunately, West-European historians have stayed with this view. Yet the question arises here: what did this masterly move consist in, with what means did Richelieu succeed in solving the key task of European politics, namely, ending the Polish–Swedish war? One cannot confine oneself, as they do, to talk about Richelieu's 'cunning' or about some 'extensive connections' which he possessed in Poland. Let us try to throw light on this question.

The dispatches of Baron Charnacé, whom Richelieu sent into Eastern Europe at the beginning of 1629 on a mission of mediation, show that he encountered considerable difficulties. When, in 1627, the Dutch had sought to incline Sigismund III of Poland towards peace with Sweden, he was unwilling to hear of it on the grounds, as one dispatch tells us, that he had received 'great promises from the Pope, the Emperor and the King of Spain that they would render powerful aid to the Polish King'.[7] And in fact the Emperor did send Sigismund III an auxiliary corps for the war with Sweden, while the Spaniards supplied warships, and so on. True, Richelieu knew in 1627, from his informants in Poland, that the magnates and the Sejm were pressing for a quick peace with Sweden precisely because of this military aid from abroad, as they feared that Sigismund might, relying on such support, proclaim himself an hereditary and absolute monarch.[8] The Empire's open preparations to fight for domination of the Baltic also disposed part of Poland's merchant class and *szlachta* against the pro-Habsburg policy of Sigismund III and for reconciliation with Sweden. Charnacé, of course, had to base himself first and foremost on these oppositional sentiments, as we learn from one of the dispatches

[5] Lamprecht, K., *Istoriia germanskogo naroda*, Vol. III, Part 5, St. Petersburg, 1896, p. 516. [*Deutsche Geschichte*, Vol. V, Part 2, 1895, p. 726.]
[6] The main work on this is Cichocki, M., 'Medjacia Francji w rozejmie Altmarkskim', in *Polska Akademja umiejetnosci. Wydral hist-filojof. Rozprawy*, Vol. 67, No. 1, Cracow, 1928.
[7] *Akty i pis'ma k istorii baltiiskogo voprosa v XVI i XVII stoletiiakh*, ed. G. Forsten, fasc. II, St. Petersburg, 1893, p. 91.    [8] Ibid.

of his mission.[9] But the King's party nevertheless enjoyed undisputed predominance in Poland, and the French diplomat's intervention was incapable of altering this relation of forces. After having won a victory over Gustavus Adolphus in Prussia in June 1626, with the aid of the Imperial auxiliary troops, Sigismund III remained, as before, uninterested in peace.

As for Gustavus Adolphus, he too did not feel that he was weak, and in July he turned the tables on the Poles, in a small way, before Marienburg. The chief argument of the Swedish government against peace with Poland was set out with complete frankness by Chancellor Oxenstjerna in his reply to Charnacé's proposals for mediation: Sweden saw no certainty that the Poles would not use the truce for making war preparations, and then stab the Swedes in the back as soon as they began war with the Empire.[10]

These were the almost insuperable difficulties that Charnacé encountered in Eastern Europe. However, Richelieu possessed the key to the accomplishment of his task.

In order to understand how it was that Charnacé, in spite of everything, compelled Sigismund III to go over from uncompromising belligerency to compliant peaceableness it is enough to read the brief instructions that were given to him on 25 January 1629, when he set forth on his mission. The most important item in them was the point which indicated how Charnacé had to go about inclining the Polish King towards peace. The diplomat was to tell Sigismund III that, in offering to mediate for conclusion of peace, 'His Majesty [the King of France] is guided chiefly by the interests of the King of Poland, for if the Swedish King allies with the Muscovite [*unist avec luy le moscovitte*] which is his intention, so His Majesty has learnt, such an alliance can bring notable harm to the Polish King.'[11] This was Richelieu's idea: to frighten Poland with the prospect of a Swedish–Russian military alliance, a war with two enemies at the same time, even while the war with Sweden alone was proving hard to keep up. As we read in Richelieu's memoirs, Charnacé convinced the Poles that Louis XIII knew on good authority that the Tsar of Muscovy had decided 'to break the truce that winter and march a powerful army into Poland', so that Poland would have 'two strong enemies to cope with at the same time'.[12]

[9] *Relation de ce qu'a faict le S. Charnacé en Brandenbourg et en la trève entre les rois de Pologne et de Suède. Octobre 1629*, in *Akty i pis'ma*, fasc. II, No. 40, pp. 101–103.

[10] *Akty i pis'ma*, fasc. II, No. 56, p. 135: Forsten, *Baltiiskii vopros*, Vol. II, p. 279.

[11] 'Instruction et dépêsche baillée à Mons. de Charnassé allant en Allemagne. Du 25 Janvier 1629': Forsten, *Baltiiskii vopros*, Vol. II, p. 278.

[12] Richelieu, *Mémoires*, p. 70.

The information about the Moscow government's decision was no invention of Richelieu's but did accord, as we shall see, with the truth. Richelieu merely made vigorous use of information supplied to him by his brilliant international informants. But he was not content with that: he resolved to give active backing to the Muscovite's decision to go to war with Poland. After Baron Charnacé was sent to talk to Sigismund III in Prussia, Baron des Hayes de Courmesnin was sent to Moscow, to Tsar Mikhail Fedorovich, accompanied by an equally noble retinue.

Thus, Richelieu's 'masterly move' consisted of two parts, united by a single aim: (1) to tell the Polish government of Moscow's decision to break the truce of Deulino and (2) to send a special embassy to Moscow.

Let us analyse the reasons that could have compelled Richelieu to make such a seemingly unexpected move. We can point to three motives:

1. As far back as 1625 Richelieu contemplated sending an embassy to Moscow. This was recorded by the Dutchman Isaak Massa, who was intending at that time to accompany this mission, which, however, did not take place.[13] Formally, it was to have been a response to the Russian embassy of Kondyrev and Neverov which had come to France in 1615. Why was Richelieu thinking of Moscow in 1625, particularly? Doubtless because it was then, as we have mentioned, that he had a real hope of bringing Sweden into the war with the Empire. The logic of things demanded that the situation in Eastern Europe should in no way hinder Sweden from engaging in West-European affairs. In 1625, however, Richelieu's plans regarding Sweden were not fulfilled. It was natural that in 1629, when these plans were revived, there was reactivated along with them the idea of an embassy to Moscow.

2. In 1628 a group of French merchants who wished to form a company for trade with Muscovy presented Richelieu with a memorandum in which they set forth the principal problems affecting Franco–Russian trade. Among other things they proposed was that a response should at last be made to Kondyrev's embassy of 1615 – that an embassy to Moscow be organised. It is important to stress that one point in this memorandum cannot have failed to prompt Richelieu into thinking that a *rapprochement* between France and Muscovy might serve as a lever for political pressure on Poland. This point ran as follows: 'Besides the advantages that France can draw from these relations with Muscovy through trade, the King will become even more important among the Northern rulers and especially in the eyes of the Polish King, who, having no enemy more powerful than Muscovy, will henceforth hold back from promoting the interests of the House of Austria, since His Majesty [the King of France] can also harm

---

[13] *Tsentral'nyi gosudarstvennyi arkhiv drevnikh aktov (TsGADA), Dela gollandskie*, 1625, stb. 2.

him and render services to the Grand Duke of Moscow.'[14] This memorandum was doubtless among the preconditions for the embassy of Des Hayes de Courmesnin to Moscow in 1629, although it was not the immediate reason for the embassy.

3. There can be no doubt that the immediate reason for the embassies of Charnacé and Des Hayes was some news received in Paris of a very important political decision which had been taken in Moscow, namely, not to wait for the expiry of the truce with the Polish–Lithuanian state but to start a war with it at once, thereby helping the Swedes. This news doubtless did not come to Paris from Sweden, since the decision in question was first conveyed, confidentially, by the boyars to the Swedish ambassadors Monier and Bönhardt in March 1629,[15] and Richelieu already knew of it two months earlier, in January 1629, when he drew up his instructions for Charnacé, saying '. . . as His Majesty has learnt'.

We have succeeded in discovering another source of Richelieu's information – Turkey. The first person in Moscow who was told of the decision to break the truce with Poland was the Turkish ambassador, the Greek Foma Cantacuzene, who at once passed the news back to Turkey (1628). And in Constantinople, at the court of Sultan Murad IV, there were no secrets safe from those who were able to pay for them. First among the latter was France's permanent ambassador in Turkey, Césy. Extracts from his dispatches to Paris in 1620–1627, taken from the archives of the French Ministry of Foreign Affairs,[16] show that this French agent was very well informed concerning Moscow's policy, and, consequently, that the government in Paris knew about it. Unfortunately, Césy's dispatch of 1628, which is of most interest to us, has not been published and is apparently missing from the archives, so that we can only speculate about its content.

After carrying out a number of diplomatic assignments on his way to Germany, Charnacé arrived at Sigismund III's camp before Marienburg in the middle of July 1629. At that same time news was received there, from Denmark, of the mission of Des Hayes de Courmesnin, who had embarked at Dieppe on 6 June and arrived in Denmark on 29 June. His stay in that country was marked with great celebrations.[17]

Thus, both components of Richelieu's 'masterly move' influenced Sigismund III's policy simultaneously.

[14] *Recueil des instructions données aux ambassadeurs et ministres de France, Russie,* published by Rambaud, Vol. VIII, 1890, p. 23. Cf., also, Bezobrazov, P.V. *O snosheniiakh Rossii s Frantsiei,* Moscow, 1892, pp. 5–6.

[15] *TsGADA, Dela shvedskie,* 1629, *stb.* 2, *ll.* 275, 319, 353–354.

[16] *Akty istoricheskie, otnosiashchiesia k Rossii, izvlechennye iz inostrannykh arkhivov i bibliotek A.I. Turgenevym,* Vol. II, St. Petersburg, 1842.

[17] *Les voyages de M. Des Hayes de Courmesnin en Dannemarc, anrichis d'annotations par le sieur P.M.L.,* Paris, 1664.

Charnacé was at first received by the Poles in an unfriendly way. On the pretext of a dispute about titles and credentials he was not admitted to the King's presence. He was showered with reproaches because his sovereign, the King of France, while presenting himself as a friend of Poland, had at the same time sent Des Hayes to Moscow to stir up the Muscovite Tsar against Poland. Charnacé parried these reproaches with the prepared reply that the mission of Des Hayes to Moscow pursued solely commercial aims.[18] Special care was taken in Paris to lend verisimilitude to this story. Des Hayes de Courmesnin had in fact been given very extensive commissions regarding trade, as well as his political instructions. Furthermore, in the eyes of the public, his visit to Moscow was merely the French government's response to the above mentioned memorandum about difficulties being experienced in trade with Muscovy which had been presented to Richelieu by a group of French merchants in the previous year.[19] All of this deprived the Poles of any formal justification for reproaching the ambassador. But, of course, there was nothing to stop them speculating about the political content of Des Hayes's mission.

This mission and the information brought by Charnacé greatly disturbed the Polish government. But it did not yield at once. While Charnacé was being held up by endless altercations, a diplomatic trial-balloon was quickly flown towards Moscow. We know about this from a letter of Mikhail Fedorovich to Gustavus Adolphus. In July 1629 there suddenly appeared at the Russian frontier near Viazma two Polish envoys whose task was to restore diplomatic relations between Poland and Russia, which had been broken off in 1622. These envoys said that they were to be followed by a 'great embassy' from the Polish King. This was undoubtedly an attempt by Sigismund III either to ward off a blow or, at least, to find out for certain what the situation was. The second aim was definitely attained, for not only was the 'great embassy' not accepted, but the Muscovites refused even to talk with the envoys. They were refused audience in Moscow and ordered to quit the territory of Muscovy forthwith.[20]

At the same time Charnacé, having lost patience, left at the end of July for the Swedish camp, almost despairing of success. On 1 August, however, apparently just as the Polish envoys returned from Viazma, he was suddenly recalled, by an urgently worded letter, to the Polish camp, where he was graciously received by Sigismund III. All the diplomatic obstacles collapsed at once. Peace negotiations began on 6 August.[21]

[18] Richelieu, *Mémoires*, p. 71.    [19] *Les voyages de M. Des Hayes*, pp. 1–2.
[20] *TsGADA, Dela shvedskie*, 1630, *stb.* 2, *l.* 246.
[21] Hoppe, *Geschichte*, pp. 434–459; Richelieu, *Mémoires*, pp. 72–75.

In fact, nothing was left to Sigismund III but to trust Charnacé and agree to a truce with Sweden. Moreover, he now showed impatience for even greater speed and tractability in the negotiations. He agreed to leave Sweden, for the duration of the truce, in possession of almost all the Baltic coast that belonged to the Rzeczpospolita. The negotiations lasted through August, with military operations suspended, and in September 1629 they were crowned with the signing of the truce of Altmark.[22] It should be mentioned that the English intermediary Thomas Roe, who arrived at the end of August, tried to blacken his rival, Charnacé, in the eyes of the Poles by means of something that was actually to his credit, namely revelations concerning the Des Hayes mission to Moscow.

Gustavus Adolphus's agreement to the truce was obtained partly with the aid of that mission. Des Hayes's embassy strengthened the Swedish King's hope that the Russo–Polish antagonism would become active and so Sweden would be able, without fear, to embark on the great struggle with the Empire. It was with this prospect in mind that Gustavus Adolphus entered into the truce of Altmark. But he had already received, by then, without the help of France, Muscovy's promise to begin a war with Poland.

It was highly characteristic of the Richelieu school of diplomacy that while Charnacé was having to disavow Des Hayes, describing him as no more than a commercial agent, Des Hayes, in Moscow was having to disavow Charnacé and his mission in Poland. Since, in Richelieu's view, cessation of the war between Sweden and Poland did not suit the interests of Muscovite policy, Des Hayes assured the boyars that French diplomacy was not involved in any attempts at conciliation between the warring powers, neither those said to be prompted by Thomas Roe, the English ambassador in Poland, nor those which were ascribed to the Dutch. On the contrary, France was helping the Swedish war-effort.[23] It may be that it was in order to make the mutual disavowal by his two envoys seem more natural that Richelieu had assigned these roles to men who were irreconcilable enemies one of the other. Charnacé and Des Hayes continued their bitter political conflict in the years immediately following their missions in Eastern Europe, until Charnacé won the day. Des Hayes, having been found guilty of connections with the anti-Richelieu court party of Gaston of Orléans, ended on the scaffold in 1632.[24] This biographical episode deserves mention because it may account for the extraordinary reserve shown by the French memoirists and historians of

[22] For the text of the treaty see Hoppe, *Geschichte*, pp. 666–676.
[23] *TsGADA, Dela frantsuzskie*, 1629, kn. 2, ll. 115, 181, 227–229.
[24] Richelieu, *Lettres, instructions diplomatiques et papiers d'état*, published by M. Avenel, Vol. VIII, Paris, 1877, p. 82: Richelieu, *Mémoires*, p. 414.

the seventeenth century, including Richelieu himself, when discussing Des Hayes's mission to Moscow in 1629. And that, in turn, has caused later historians to neglect this very important fact in the diplomatic history of the Thirty Years' War – all the more because the French public records contain neither the instructions drawn up for Des Hayes nor any reports on his mission.[25]

It is significant that Louis XIII's letter to Mikhail Fedorovich, with which Des Hayes set out, was signed at Susa (in Northern Italy) on 22 April 1629,[26] that is, a few days after the signature there of the treaty between Savoy and France[27] and two days before the signing, also at Susa, of the Anglo–French peace treaty.[28] This was a moment of feverish and truly titanic activity on Richelieu's part. The negotiations between Denmark and the victorious Empire were nearing conclusion. Richelieu had failed to delay them any further. In May the peace of Lübeck was signed. Not a moment must be lost, for the dark cloud of Habsburg–Catholic aggression hung over Europe. At home Richelieu hastened to put an end to the struggle with the Huguenots (the *Edit de grâce* was issued in June 1629). In September 1629 came the truce of Altmark. And in June 1630 Gustavus Adolphus, freed from his conflict with the Polish–Lithuanian state, landed on one of the islands on the Empire's Baltic coast. The 'Swedish period' of the Thirty Years' War had begun.

One should not, however, exaggerate the part played by Richelieu in all of this. He himself remarks that France was unable to influence Muscovite policy.[29] Moscow's position in relation to the division of Europe into two coalitions, Habsburg and anti-Habsburg, was determined not by Richelieu's intrigues but by the entire preceding history of Muscovy's intercourse with Europe.

An historian of the Thirty Years' War who confines his attention to Western Europe might perceive the role played by Moscow in the history of the truce of Altmark as an involuntary one, as the mere coincidence in time of two series of events, a fortunate accident that Richelieu exploited. It would even seem more likely than not that when the Muscovite government decided to terminate the truce with Poland it failed to contemplate the consequences that its decision would entail for Europe.

On the other hand, though, common sense is against such a notion. It is beyond doubt that even the most short-sighted foreign policy of any state must take account of the strength not only of its neighbours but also that

---

[25] *Recueil des instructions*, p. 24.     [26] *TsGADA, Dela frantsuzskie*, 1629, *ll.* 11–12.
[27] During the War of the Mantuan Succession, in which the Duke of Savoy at first took the side of France's opponents (Editor) [i.e. the editor of the Russian original – Trans].
[28] Ending the war of 1627–1629 between these states (Editor) [see n. 27].
[29] Richelieu, *Mémoires*, p. 70.

of potential allies and adversaries. And Moscow had, in practice, grasped long since the elementary political truth that any change in its relations, say, with the Polish–Lithuanian state must affect, in one way or another, not only those particular relations but also the entire system of states which either sympathised with or were opposed to such a change. Also beyond doubt is the fact that seventeenth-century Muscovy sought to understand the system of European states as a whole and did indeed have a conception of this system. It was aware not only of the friends and enemies of the Polish–Lithuanian state but also of the enemies of those friends and the friends of those enemies.

We know that in the period of the Thirty Years' War the Embassies Department in Moscow had a staff of qualified interpreters for all the languages of Europe. Less well known is the fact that within the Department much painstaking work was already carried on to collect information from agents and all sorts of informants in every corner of Europe. From the reports sent to Moscow by the governors of Novgorod extensive summaries of the European press and other information were compiled.[30] Russian ambassadors also sent from abroad – from Sweden, for example – extracts from the local newspapers and other sources. All this material was, apparently, digested by the Embassies Department, as we see from a parchment roll of 1632 which has survived ('Translations from European newspapers and all other materials sent to Moscow'). But, even without looking into the records of the Embassies Department, the first historian who concerned himself with the role played by Russia in the history of the Thirty Years' War, G.V. Forsten, correctly observed: 'Those who think that nothing was known in Moscow about events in Western Europe are wrong. On the contrary, the great religious and political conflict which occupied Europe for all of thirty years was closely followed there.'[31]

In Moscow they also knew of the close relationship of alliance which existed between the Polish–Lithuanian state and the Empire, a relationship which, from the beginning of the Thirty Years' War took the form of open lending of military support by one to the other at critical moments. All of Europe's politicians knew that Sigismund III relied upon the powerful assistance he could expect to receive from the House of Austria.

Study of Muscovy's external relations in the 1620s convinces one that literally all the foreign ambassadors in Moscow who concerned themselves with the Polish problem – those of Turkey, Sweden, France and Holland – were agreed on one thing, namely that the Polish–Lithuanian state owed much of its strength to the help it received from the Empire. If the

---

[30] *TsGADA, Dela shvedskie za 20-40-e gody XVIIv.*
[31] Forsten, G., *Baltiiskii vopros*, Vol. II, p. 497.

international situation in Europe were to develop in such a way that the
Empire could no longer help the Polish–Lithuanian state, that state
would become weak and might be beaten. It will be shown that the actual
view of Polish–Imperial relations held by the Muscovite state was
identical with these considerations by foreign observers. However, let us
first adduce some illustrations of what has been said already.

Only three years after the truce of Deulino, in 1621, relations between
Muscovy and the Rzeczpospolita had grown so strained that they almost
reached the point of war, and alliance against the Poles was offered to
Moscow by both Gustavus Adolphus and the Turkish Sultan Osman II.
Typical were the arguments with which the Sultan's ambassador
Cantacuzene sought to win the Tsar's agreement to a joint campaign
against the Polish–Lithuanian state: 'It is known to you, great sovereign,
that in Germany there is a great conflict between the Emperor and the
Lutherans, so that he is now unable to help the Poles, and, on his part, the
Sultan has ordered the rulers of Transylvania, Wallachia and Moldavia to
attack the Emperor so that he will go on being unable to bring aid to the
Polish King.'[32] In 1621, however, the proposed coalition did not come about.

Gustavus Adolphus never ceased to dream of drawing Muscovy into
the war with Poland. In 1625 the Swedish government received a
dispatch from Moscow which informed them that certain boyars were
demanding that the Tsar make haste to declare war on the Poles.[33] It was
apparently in connexion with this news that at the beginning of 1626,
Gustavus Adolphus ordered his statthalters at Reval, named Bremen and
Ungern, to go to Moscow to negotiate. The instructions compiled for
them, which Forsten published, are extremely interesting. They start
from the correct observation that the Muscovite Tsar will not participate
on either side in the war between Sweden and Poland as such. Consequently
the ambassadors' task is to explain that, in fighting Poland, Sweden is
essentially fighting the Empire, which stands behind Poland. If the
ambassadors find that this view is received with understanding and
sympathy, they must then tell the Tsar of the grandiose plans entertained
by the Empire, and its ally Poland, for 'universal monarchy'. The sixth
paragraph of the instructions is devoted to this theme. What is projected,
it claims, is a partition of Europe in which the Empire will take Germany,
Italy, France, Spain, England, the Netherlands and Hungary while
Poland will take Russia, Sweden and Denmark. Catholicism will be
introduced everywhere, after which a crusade will be launched against
Turkey, whose territory will be divided between the Empire and Poland.

[32] Bantysh-Kamenskii, N., 'Perepiska mezhdu Rossieiu i Pol'sheiu po 1700 god', Part II –
*Chteniia v Obshchestve istorii i drevnostei rossiiskikh*, Moscow, 1862, Book IV, p. 29.
[33] Forsten, *Baltiiskii vopros*, Vol. II, pp. 207–208.

This is why, says the seventh paragraph, the Tsar should draw close to the enemies of Poland and the Empire; while the eighth paragraph advises him also to stir up the Tatars and the Zaporozhian Cossacks against the Poles.[34]

In Gustavus Adolphus's letter of 19 February, handed to the Tsar by the Swedish ambassadors, some of the ideas contained in the fifth and seventh paragraphs are developed in more detail. We will quote some passages from this letter translated into Russian in the records of the Embassies Department.[35] Gustavus Adolphus informs Mikhail Fedorovich that the Polish King 'has joined with the Roman Kaiser [the Emperor] and the Spanish King, and they design to uproot all Christian beliefs and establish everywhere in place of them their Popish religion, bringing under its sway all Christian states and the whole of Europe'. The relation of political forces in Europe is set forth briefly and, on the whole, quite correctly:

The Roman Kaiser, helped by the Kings of Spain and Poland, has subjected nearly all the apanage princes of Germany, eradicated their Evangelical Christian religion and deprived them of lands and people, making himself supreme ruler over all Germany. After this, the Roman Kaiser wants to help the King of Spain to conquer the States of Holland and the Netherlands, and also wants to help the King of Poland to become the ruler of the Swedish and Russian states. They have great hopes of accomplishing this aim, and many are already calling Wladyslaw emperor of all the Northern countries. The Roman Kaiser and the Kings of Spain and Poland think that they have now overcome all the rulers of Christendom. But the King of France, together with the great city of Venice and the Duke of Savoy, have formed a coalition against the above-mentioned powers, and in particular against the King of Spain, and raised up a great force against him in Italy. The King of England, too, along with the rulers of the Netherlandish states, have formed an alliance against the Kaiser and the King of Spain, and have sent to us, the great King Gustavus Adolphus, and to the King of Denmark, to ask us to join them in opposing the Roman Kaiser and his advisers. To this end the Danish King has gone to war against the Kaiser and now stands with a great army opposing him within Germany, having on his side many of the German apanage princes, who all support him. And in order that the Polish King may not go to the aid of the Kaiser we have now entered the land of Lithuania, so that he cannot help the Roman Kaiser, but the Kaiser and his advisers will be everywhere ousted and will not be able to realise the wicked design which they have formed against all Christian states.

Later it is stated that this design threatens Muscovy as well, 'if only they

[34] *Akty i pis'ma*, fasc. II, No. 26, pp. 80–83. All these points were set forth by Bremen and Ungern during their negotiations in Moscow (see *TsGADA, Dela shvedskie*, 1626, *stb.* 2, *ll.* 267–278, 334–340).

[35] Here and subsequently, so as to facilitate reading, we have brought the more archaic expressions used in Russian writing of the seventeenth century nearer to present-day Russian, used present-day spelling and given proper names in present-day transcriptions.

[the Catholic coalition] succeed in overcoming the others'. The Tsar is reminded how long and persistently the Poles have aimed 'to crush the Greek faith and persecute all who hold to it'. Consequently, in Gustavus Adolphus's view, it is incumbent on the Tsar 'to defend himself as other rulers are defending themselves, to act against the King of Poland and prevent him from helping the Kaiser. Then he [the Emperor] will forget to act against those rulers who stand by their beliefs and will give up his wicked design against our Christian Evangelical and Greek faiths.' For his part, Gustavus Adolphus goes on, 'we, with our allies,' will do everything to accomplish this common purpose: 'by which they will be exalted above the other rulers, so as to humble and abase those rulers before us'.[36] In other words, Muscovy was being invited to enter into an all-Europe coalition of powers aimed against Habsburg aggression, against the threat to their independence and their religion. The role assigned to Muscovy was to divert the forces of Poland from giving aid to the German Emperor, thereby facilitating victory by the allies over the Empire, after which the Empire would no longer be able to help the Poles with their own plans for conquest.

The Swedes' conception of the international situation was received in Moscow with complete understanding and sympathy, as is shown by the record of the negotiations and especially by the text of Mikhail Fedorovich's reply to Gustavus Adolphus (this is given by Forsten both in the Russian original and in the French translation which he found in the Stockholm archives).[37]

In the letter from Gustavus Adolphus, which was brought to Moscow by the Swedish ambassadors A. Monier and J. Bönhardt in March 1629, it was stated even more definitely than in 1626 that behind Poland stood another, mightier power, and if that dread power was not smashed Poland would become unbeatable. The power in question was the Empire. In the past year, said the letter, Gustavus Adolphus had all but overcome the Poles, so that he 'could have marched unhindered through all Poland with his army', had he not been prevented by the Imperial–Catholic forces which 'in great strength drew near and laid siege to the town of Stralsund', so that Gustavus Adolphus had been obliged to divert his forces in order to liberate Stralsund. Later in the letter the idea is developed in detail that the Swedes' war against the Emperor is more to the interest of Moscow than their war against Poland. 'The Pope, the Roman Kaiser and the whole House of Austria strive only to become masters of the whole world, and they are now very close to succeeding in this . . . It is certainly known to Your Majesty that the Roman Kaiser and

[36] *TsGADA, Dela shvedskie*, 1626, stb. 2, *ll.* 249–263.
[37] *Akty i pis'ma*, fasc. II, No. 27, pp. 83–84.

the Papists have brought under their rule most of the Evangelical princes in Germany.' As soon as the Emperor and the Catholic League ('the Kaiser and the Popish conspirators') 'overcome Sweden they will start to try and force the Russian people into submission and extirpate the ancient Greek faith'.[38] As we see, the Swedo–Polish war was pushed into the background, the foreground being assigned to the Habsburg–Catholic aggression, which might reach even to Moscow and the realm of Orthodoxy if not checked. In that case it would threaten Moscow from the direction of Poland.

After the signing of the Altmark truce the Swedish envoy Monier, who was sent specially to Moscow, explained that Gustavus Adolphus, who was without an ally, was obliged to fight not against Poland alone but against the combined forces of Poland and the Empire. He needed to untie his hands in Poland so as to get to work in Germany, as the French government was urging him to do. The instructions given to Monier, together with the memorandum which he handed to the Tsar and the boyars in Moscow, laid stress on the idea that the main danger to both Sweden and Muscovy consisted not so much in Poland itself as in the Empire, which stood behind Poland.[39]

Thus, the Swedish *démarches* in Moscow in 1626–1630, which were based on a broad and accurate view of international relations, put forward a special theoretical conception for Moscow's consideration, namely the unity of interest between Orthodoxy ('the ancient Greek faith') and Protestantism ('the Evangelical faith') in struggle against a common foe, aggressive Catholicism. To this conception the Swedes held consistently in their dealings with Moscow in subsequent years as well. King Gustavus Adolphus was killed, on 16 (6) November 1632, Mikhail Fedorovich was informed in a letter signed by twelve Swedish magnates, 'in the fight against the Papists for the Christian Evangelical and the ancient Greek faiths'.[40]

Since France was a Catholic power, when Richelieu sent Des Hayes de Courmesnin to Moscow he could not employ this ideological schema, but advanced a different basis for Franco–Russian *rapprochement* – not a religious basis but a purely political one, namely, the idea of the similarity between France and Russia as two great absolutist powers. 'These great sovereigns, the King of France and the Tsar's Majesty, are everywhere renowned and there are no other rulers so great and so powerful as they, and their subjects are all people who obey them in all things and do their rulers' will – not as it is with the English and the Brabanters [the Dutch?],

[38] *TsGADA, Dela shvedskie*, 1629, stb. 2, *ll.* 180–196.
[39] Forsten, *Baltiiskii vopros.*, Vol. II, p. 358: *TsGADA, Dela shvedskie*, 1630, *stb.* 2, *ll.* 124–152.
[40] Bantysh-Kamenskii, N., *Obzor vneshnikh snoshenii Rossii*, Vol. IV, Moscow, 1902, p. 159.

who do whatever they like.' 'The French obey their King just as the Russians obey and do honour to their Tsar.' 'The ceremonies and customs of the French Crown are alike and similar to those of the Russian state.' The international importance of France and Russia is similar too. In the West all monarchs and rulers look on the French King 'as if he were the Sun' and he occupies first place among them, while Russia's Tsar holds a comparable position in the East. 'Just as the Tsar of all Russia is head and protector of the Greek church in the Eastern countries, so the Most Christian King is head and upholder of the Roman Church in the countries of the West.' The same sort of ideas run through the memorandum handed by Des Hayes to the boyars and the Tsar.[41] The letter addressed by Louis XIII to Mikhail Fedorovich says: 'Although our realms are far apart and divided from each other by many different states with different measures and languages . . . we wish to maintain our firm, cordial friendship, and love, and true concord and reference [i.e., diplomatic relations] with Your Majesty . . . for the good and advancement of both our crowns and . . . that a treaty may be made to the benefit of us both.'[42]

This entire political conception was understood and reproduced in the Muscovite reply in this formulation: 'Our royal persons and powers, when allied, would hold the whole world in awe.'[43]

Des Hayes told Moscow that France was in friendly relations with all the states except those with which it was actually at enmity: 'King Louis is at enmity with the Kaiser and with the King of Spain . . . and he is at enmity with the King of Poland because that Monarch is helping the Roman Kaiser, King Louis's foe.' The House of Austria, and especially the Emperor, are 'friends' to the Polish King, who is himself 'kin to the Kaiser',

and they act in concert with Sigismund, the Polish King, and give him no little aid . . . And this they [the French] know for certain, that the Roman Kaiser is at one with the Polish King, they are friends, the Kaiser's daughter is to marry the heir to the Polish throne, and they help one another. And so let the Tsar's Majesty be in friendship and amity with his [the ambassador's] sovereign King Louis and stand together with him against their common enemies.

This amounted to nothing less than a proposal for a military-political alliance to be sealed by a treaty. To the boyars' question whether this meant that the French King might send troops, Des Hayes replied affirmatively. However, he stressed mainly the point that while France continued to combat the Emperor the Poles would not be able to receive help from him, and this was how the French King's help to the Tsar

---

[41] *TsGADA, Dela frantsuzskie*, 1629, *kn*. 2, *ll*. 162, 178, 176–175, 160.
[42] Ibid., *ll*. 11–12.    [43] *Recueil des instructions*, p. 29.

would be expressed. 'The Poles, who have allied themselves with the House of Austria and have long been hostile to the French King, are in great fear lest the Grand Duke [the Tsar] conclude this alliance [with France].' They 'will be checked and will not soon encroach upon our lands' when they hear of an alliance between France and Russia, for then 'no aid will be coming to the Poles from the House of Austria against the Grand Duke, since the Austrians will be fighting the French King'. Details are supplied regarding the causes and course of the war of the Mantuan succession in Italy, between France and the Habsburgs, and it is emphasised that France intends in the near future to intensify military operations against the Emperor, while the Emperor, on his part, intends, as soon as his war with Louis XIII is over, to divert all his forces to the assistance of Sigismund III.[44]

Des Hayes even linked commercial matters[45] directly with international political problems. The chief source of the financial power of the House of Austria, he said, was Spain's maritime trade with the Orient. If French merchants were given permission to go to the Orient (to Persia) by a land route through Muscovy, the Habsburgs would be deprived of their revenues, which would pass in their entirety to Muscovy and France.

It is necessary to check and prevent the Austrian Princes from profiting by trade with the Orient, for, as we have pointed out, they used the profits obtained from this source in the past year to hire many soldiers whom they sent to help the Polish King against the King of Sweden, and if the [Muscovite] sovereign does not stop them from engaging in this trade they will go on helping the Polish King. And it would be better if the [Muscovite] sovereign were to gain by this trade rather than that his enemies should be enriched by it.

If only French merchants were allowed free passage to Persia, the French state 'would begin to press hard on the House of Austria and take away their Eastern trade, which would diminish their strength so that they would not be able to help the Polish King.'[46]

Besides having the same enemies, France and Muscovy were also linked through having the same friends. Des Hayes expounded the friendly relations that prevailed between the French King and England, Holland and Denmark, and emphasised especially France's friendship with Sweden and Turkey. The ambassador mentioned that, on his way to Moscow, he had been splendidly received by Gustavus Adolphus. In the Tsar's minute on Des Hayes's memorandum handed to the boyars particular instruction was given to find out how 'the French [King] will

---

[44] *TsGADA, Dela frantsuzskie*, 1629, *kn.* 2, *ll.* 115, 155–160, 152, 176, 54–55, 228.

[45] The commercial aspect of these negotiations is dealt with in G. Zhordaniia's work, *Ocherki iz istorii franko-russkikh otnoshenii kontsa XVI i pervoi poloviny XVII v.* Parts I and II. Tbilisi, 1959.     [46] *TsGADA, Dela frantsuzskie*, 1629, *kn.* 2, *ll.* 178, 156.

help the Swede'. And Des Hayes quoted the number of soldiers that had already been sent from France to help Gustavus Adolphus and who were to be sent at that time. Special significance was accorded by Des Hayes, however, to the theme of Franco–Turkish and Russo–Turkish friendship. The French King 'is a friend of the Turkish Sultan . . . and the Sultan is also a friend of the Tsar's Majesty'. A French ambassador now resides in Constantinople and Louis XIII 'has ordered his representatives to help in every way those Russians and Orthodox whom they meet in Tsaregrad and give them all assistance they can'. The King of France is ready to order his men in Constantinople to render 'any other service the Tsar may require'.[47]

This particular reference to the Turkish problem was, it would appear, not accidental. Immediately after uttering those words Des Hayes unexpectedly broke off his address to the boyars (at their first meeting with him) and, according to the record, 'having remained silent for a moment, said that he had been ordered to speak of other matters as well, but would not speak of them now, as this would be tedious for the boyars'.[48] It is not hard to guess that Des Hayes's instructions ordered him, as was often done, to set forth at first no more than part of his proposal and to proceed to the most confidential matters and most candid discussions only if this first part proved to be well received. Des Hayes's hint evidently evoked two minutes by the Tsar in the handwriting of the council's secretary Efim Telepnev: 'The Tsar's Majesty wishes to be in friendship, amity and league with their [the French] sovereign and how this is to be arranged is to be subject to examination.' 'The sovereign and the patriarch[49] ordered that the ambassador be asked how friendship, counsel and unity [between France and Russia] could be strengthened.'[50] However, the trade negotiations stumbled on the question of allowing French merchants to practise their Catholic religion. Des Hayes was unable to guess that the Muscovite government would nevertheless, at the last moment, accept his minimum programme.[51] He did not show sufficient diplomatic far-sightedness and consequently departed without having finished saying what he had been ordered to say.

What was it that Richelieu had instructed his envoy to propose in Moscow? Forsten says, basing himself on documents in the Stockholm archives, that the task of Des Hayes de Courmesnin in Moscow was 'to propose that Mikhail Fedorovich join with Bethlen against Poland and

[47] Ibid., *ll.* 225–226, 161, 176–177.    [48] Ibid., *l.* 162.
[49] Filaret Nikitich (note by Editor) [see n. 27].
[50] *TsGADA, Dela frantsuzskie*, 1629, *kn.* 2, *ll.* 168, 179.    [51] See *infra*.

the Emperor'.[52] This is fully in conformity with the ambassador's significant stress on the Turkish problem, for Bethlen Gábor, the ruler of Transylvania and part of Hungary, was at that time a sort of vassal of the Sultan and without a favourable attitude on Turkey's part such an alliance would be out of the question. Richelieu was already informed of Muscovy's decision to enter into an alliance with Sweden. One may therefore surmise that Richelieu had a grand design to grip the Empire, from north, east and south, in an unbroken half-ring of his allies – England, Holland, Denmark, Sweden, Muscovy, Turkey and Transylvania – all of whom were, incidentally, hostile to Catholicism, though for different reasons. The eastern section of this half-ring had to take the form of an armed coalition of Sweden, Muscovy, Turkey and Transylvania.

This supposition is confirmed by the arrival in Moscow in May 1630 of the prominent French aristocrat Charles de Talleyrand (an ancestor of the famous diplomat Talleyrand and brother of the famous Count Chalais, whom Richelieu executed) with corresponding proposals. He came, to be sure, in the capacity of ambassador of Transylvania, not of France. But it is highly probable that Richelieu foresaw a distrustful attitude in Moscow towards proposals coming from Catholic France, and the possibility that Des Hayes's mission might fail for that reason, and therefore dispatched another envoy using Transylvania as intermediary. Richelieu employed similar procedures in his dealings with distrustful Protestant Sweden, too, acting, for example, through Brandenburg. On his way to Moscow and when he returned five years later from Russia (where, as we shall see, he had been arrested), Talleyrand told his travelling companions that he had been sent to Transylvania, Turkey and Muscovy by the King of France.[53] It is sufficiently revealing, likewise, that the French government took vigorous measures to rescue him from captivity while concealing its participation in those measures. In 1631 it persuaded the King of England and the Dutch Stadtholder to write to Mikhail Fedorovich on his behalf, and only in 1635 was an appeal made in the name of Louis XIII himself.

Judging by certain statements made by Talleyrand[54] and by the presence in his papers of the text of the Anglo–French peace treaty, we may assume that he was sent off from France at the same time as Des Hayes de Courmesnin. Jacques Roussel arrived simultaneously at Bethlen

[52] Forsten, *Baltiiskii vopros*, Vol. II, p. 278.
[53] Report by the escort Lopukhin, in *TsGADA, Dela vengerskie*, 1630–1631, *stb.* 1, *l.* 10. Olearius, Adam, *Opisanie puteshestviia v Moskoviiu i cherez Moskoviiu v Persiiu i obratno*, St. Petersburg, 1906, pp. 60–61, 183–184.
[54] *TsGADA, Dela vengerskie*, 1630–1631, *stb.* 1, *ll.* 166, 10, et al.

Gábor's court, with similar political projects,[55] and the Transylvanian ruler sent them both as his envoys to undertake very responsible negotiations in Turkey, Muscovy and Sweden.

On behalf of Bethlen Gábor, Talleyrand and Roussel propounded in Moscow a detailed plan for an East-European military coalition. This plan had been agreed by them on the road to Constantinople (evidence of this is provided by the credentials given them by the Grand Vizier, Rejeb Pasha), through the mediation of the Dutch ambassador in the Sultan's capital, Cornelius, the Patriarch of Constantinople, Cyril Lucaris, and, very probably (though, of course, this is not said) the French ambassador Césy.[56] In reply to the proposal for an alliance which he had received not long before from Mikhail Fedorovich, Bethlen Gábor says that he wants an alliance 'not in words but in deeds' so as to throw his forces against any foe jointly with the Muscovite Tsar, the King of Sweden and the Turkish Sultan.

And since these three great sovereigns – the Tsar's Majesty, and the Swedish King and their sovereign King Bethlen Gábor – are united and mean to act together against their enemies, and the Turkish Sultan Murad intends also, for his part, to oppose those enemies, nobody will be able to withstand these great forces. So as to secure and establish this beforehand, let good alliance be maintained. The enemies of these forces are the King of Spain, the Roman Kaiser and the King of Poland. So as to stand against them and take revenge for their enmity.

Further on it is said that Bethlen Gábor has fought long and successfully 'against the House of Austria' and that he counts on taking the throne of Poland from Sigismund III. Once more we find emphasised the statement which is most important for our theme, namely, that there is close political unity between the Polish–Lithuanian state and the Empire: 'Because of this the Polish King is afraid of their sovereign, King Bethlen Gábor, lest he on many occasions may press upon and overcome the House of Austria.' In other words, victories over the Empire would be dangerous to Poland, by depriving it of support. Finally come detailed calculations of how many soldiers Bethlen Gábor can put into the field, and some considerations are advanced regarding the projected coalition. It is proposed that, besides the Sultan and the King of Sweden (with whom Bethlen Gábor had close contact), his brother-in-law the elector of Brandenburg be brought into the alliance, since he has 'great power in men and money'.[57]

---

[55] Already in 1626 Gustavus Adolphus, in one of his letters to Bethlen Gábor, which was intercepted by the Poles, put forward the idea that what was needed was a combined attack by Sweden, Transylvania, Muscovy and the Crimean Tatars (vassals of Turkey) against Poland and the Habsburgs (see Forsten, *Baltiiskii vopros*, Vol. II, p. 204).
[56] *TsGADA, Dela vengerskie,* 1630–1631, *stb.* 1, *ll.* 167, 172–177.
[57] Ibid., *ll.* 160–164.

We have not quoted all these facts concerning various approaches by foreign powers in Moscow in order to create the impression that the international position of Muscovy in the conditions of the Thirty Years' War was imposed upon it and inspired by someone from outside. On the contrary, this position was quite independent. The examples adduced show merely that Moscow was not alone, that, in promoting indirectly the truce of Altmark and favouring Sweden's entry into the war with the Empire, Moscow's leaders proceeded from the same notions about the European situation that were widely held and considered self-evident among the other political leaders of Europe. What was said in Moscow by the ambassadors of Turkey, Sweden, France and Transylvania, however diverse, had a common foundation: these powers were already allies of Muscovy owing to the fact that they were enemies of the Empire, and the Empire was the principal ally of Muscovy's own principal enemy, the Polish–Lithuanian state. This completely concurred with Moscow's point of view, which was inspired by nobody's words but by long experience of Russo–Imperial and Russo–Polish relations.

There were no territorial disputes between Muscovy and the Empire, since Livonia had ceased to be an Imperial fief. No military clashes had occurred between the Tsar and the Emperor. Indeed, the Empire frequently acted as an intermediary when conflicts arose between Muscovy and its neighbours. But that was just the problem – that in the sixteenth century the Empire had assumed the role of guarantor of political stability in Eastern Europe, whereas at that time Muscovy, having emerged from under the Mongol yoke, could not fail to demand from its western neighbours return of the Russian lands they had seized in previous centuries. Particularly extensive were Muscovy's claims on the Polish–Lithuanian state. Consequently the Empire, in defending the status quo in Eastern Europe, was objectively defending the Rzeczpospolita against Muscovy. But the alliance between the Empire and the Rzeczpospolita became actively hostile to Muscovy during the period of Sigismund III's aggressive policy. It was not only that when the Poles openly intervened at the critical moment, behind the Pretenders in 1612, the hand of the Habsburgs reached out, over the heads of the defeated Poles, to grasp the throne of Muscovy. Later, after 1613, the Emperor refused *de jure* recognition to Mikhail Fedorovich as Tsar, which amounted to recognition of the claim of the Polish Crown Prince Wladyslaw by this 'intermediary', who did not shrink from rendering more than diplomatic aid to the Poles, in money and troops.

Whoever supported Wladyslaw's claim to the Muscovite throne was bound to be seen as an enemy by the government of Mikhail Fedorovich. It was on these grounds that diplomatic relations were broken off between

Muscovy and the Empire in 1613, though a brisk epilogue was performed in 1614–1616, after which no relations with the Empire were maintained by Muscovy throughout the duration of the Thirty Years' War.[58]

During all that period agents of the Empire in Moscow were treated not in accordance with diplomatic protocol but as agents of an enemy state. The Imperial ambassador Adam Dorno was arrested in 1613 and held in custody until his death in 1654. He was helped neither by his conversion to Orthodoxy nor by his appeals to the Emperor, which, of course, owing to the absence of diplomatic relations, were never transmitted. Still more significant was the arrest in 1630 of Charles de Talleyrand. He was arrested on suspicion of intending to go over to the Spanish King and German Emperor,[59] that is, as a secret agent of the Habsburgs who might reveal to them the plans for an East-European coalition while pretending to be working to weld this coalition. The statement contained in a much later letter of Louis XIII's, that Talleyrand was arrested on a charge of military espionage for Poland,[60] does not contradict the first explanation but is in full accord with it. Furthermore, when in 1632 Emperor Ferdinand II sought to renew diplomatic relations with Moscow his envoy was invited at the frontier to return whence he came, for the significant reason that he had arrived there through Poland and escorted by Poles, that is, in the capacity of an ally of Poland. Of no less significance, finally, was the fact that it was in 1654, when the Empire, beaten in the Thirty Years' War, was no longer able to help the Poles, that Muscovy decided to renew diplomatic relations with it.

Thus, all the facts testify that the hostility of Muscovy to the Empire was not direct in origin but was a reflection of its hostility to the Rzeczpospolita, with which it had very serious territorial and, after the Polish intervention, also political disputes. The logic of things, however, obliged Muscovy to regard as its friends in Europe not only the adversaries of Poland but also the adversaries of the Habsburgs. In 1615 Muscovy sent an embassy to France and in 1617 to England to ask for support against the Poles, because although neither France nor England was directly opposed to Poland, they could certainly be considered hostile, in one degree or another, to the Habsburgs. On the same bases friendly relations were strengthened in the 1620s between Moscow on the one hand, and Holland and Denmark on the other.

The truce of Deulino in 1618 did not eliminate the hostility between

[58] Bantysh-Kamenskii, *Obzor vneshnikh snoshenii Rossii*, Vol. I, Moscow, 1894, pp. 17–19. *Pamiatniki diplomaticheshikh snoshenii Drevnei Rossii s derzhavami inostrannymi*, Vol. II, St. Petersburg, 1852.
[59] *TsGADA, Dela vengerskie*, 1630–1631, *stb.* 1, *l.* 190.
[60] *Recueil des instructions*, pp. 35–36.

Muscovy and the Rzeczpospolita. In 1619 there returned from his nine years' captivity in Poland the father of Mikhail Fedorovich, the Patriarch Philaret (Filaret Nikitich), who became *de facto* head of the Muscovite state. Philaret saw as the most important task for Muscovy in the field of foreign policy the smashing of the Polish–Lithuanian state, so as to recover the lost West-Russian, Ukrainian and Byelorussian lands. He took account of the need, to this end, for smashing also the allies of the Polish–Lithuanian state – the entire Habsburg–Catholic camp in Europe. Philaret appears to have regarded the truce of Deulino as a mistake, and according to the Rostov Chronicle, urged that it be broken.[61] His reason was, of course, not 'resentment' against the Poles, but the broad international outlook he acquired while abroad, in Polish custody. As early as 1620–1621, under the vigorous leadership of Patriarch Philaret, Muscovy became one of the most actively anti-Habsburg powers in Europe. It not only entered into negotiations with Turkey and Sweden for a military alliance against Poland and, in autumn 1621, by decision of the *Zemskii Sobor*, sent an ultimatum to the Poles while at the same time assembling troops, but also sought allies against the Habsburgs in Western Europe. An embassy bringing a proposal for a political alliance was sent in 1620 to England, but the English were at that time still in thrall to a policy of 'appeasement' and woke up only in 1623, when they sent ambassadors to Moscow with the text of a treaty of alliance all ready for signing.[62] By that time, however, the favourable situation in Eastern Europe had already changed. The ambiguous attitude of France and England to the war raging in the Empire (in Bohemia and the Palatinate) was the incentive for the dispatch of Rodionov's embassy into Western Europe in 1621, nominally to find a bride for Mikhail Fedorovich but really in order to discover the answer to such questions as, for example, 'whom the French King is going to help, the Kaiser or the Count Palatine of the Rhine, or if he means to help neither'.[63]

The news from the West proved depressing. And in Turkey in May 1622 Sultan Osman II was murdered by the Janissaries, cutting short the war with Poland which he had begun (the Khotin campaign of 1621), and Gustavus Adolphus signed a truce with the Poles. Thus, the activity of the Muscovite state was paralysed: its only result in this period was a breach of diplomatic relations with the Polish–Lithuanian state (between 1622 and 1634). His lack of success in foreign policy seems to have

[61] Bantysh-Kamenskii, 'Perepiska mezhdu', Part III, p. 47.
[62] Liubimenko, I., 'Proekty anglo–russkogo soiuza v XVI i XVII vekakh', in *Istoricheskie izvestiia*, Issue 3-4, 1916.
[63] *Pamiatniki diplomaticheskikh snoshenii Drevnei Rossii*, Vol. II, St. Petersburg, 1852, pp. 1353–1365.

weakened the influence of Patriarch Philaret and facilitated the brief ascendancy at the Tsar's court of the previous boyar leadership, including the official Ivan Gramotin, who had collaborated with the Poles during their intervention and had arranged the truce of Deulino in 1618. Already in 1625, however, Sweden's informants told Stockholm of an attempt at a sort of *coup d'état* in Moscow, with a discontented group of boyars and courtiers raising the slogan of declaration of war on Poland. This was undoubtedly the Patriarch's party. Between 1626 and 1629 he held the conduct of all public affairs in his hands. Ivan Gramotin was replaced in the Embassies Department by the secretary of the Council, Efim Telepnev, an outstanding diplomat, and in the field of foreign policy there triumphed the principle of working to assemble an anti-Polish and anti-Habsburg coalition.

The international situation favoured this line. The approaching end of the Danish period of the Thirty Years' War made even more urgent for all the non-Habsburg powers of Europe the question of how to repulse Habsburg–Catholic aggression. More and more foreign ambassadors arrived in Moscow with every year that passed. But Moscow did not wait for any initiative from without; it determined for itself its place in the division of Europe into two camps. Here, for example is the instruction received as early as 1626 by the 'commissioners' sent to meet Swedish envoys who were arriving after a long interval. To questioning by the envoys as to the Tsar's relations with other sovereigns they were to reply that 'the English, Dutch and French Kings and the princes of the Netherlands and Holland' were in diplomatic and commercial relations with the Tsar: that relations with the Sultan of Turkey, the Khan of the Crimea and the Shah of Persia were particularly close: 'but that with the Kaiser our great sovereign, His Majesty the Tsar, has long had no communication', and 'as regards the King of Poland, he has himself stated through his envoys that he is hostile to our great sovereign, His Majesty the Tsar, and to Muscovy in general, and if there is not at the moment a state of war with the Polish King [it is only] because, earlier, by His Majesty's order, the boyars signed with the Polish lords' council a truce for a certain period of time.' (Struck out are these words: 'His Majesty will never forget the enmity towards him shown by the Polish King and his son, for their unjust conduct brought ruin upon Muscovy.') 'If they ask, regarding the Pope, whether His Majesty the Tsar has any relations with him, the commissioners are to say that His Majesty has not entered and will not enter into relations with the Pope of Rome, and the envoys themselves know that the Pope is an enemy to Orthodox Christians and is not concerned to promote goodwill among Christians.' Then follow instructions as to how to answer questions that might be asked about the subordination of the Tsar to the Greater Nogai Horde, of Kazyi's *ulus*, of the Circassian highlanders, of the Kumyks, and about the ordering of the Siberian realm. All this was important for Western politicians because it determined the ability or inability of Muscovy to pursue an active policy in the West.[64]

As we see, before any negotiations took place with the Swedes, Muscovy had a clearly defined position in the world system of states and peoples. All were divided into two categories, friends and foes, and to the latter category were assigned Poland, the Papacy and the Empire. This categorisation is reproduced in many other documents and in the entire practice of foreign policy by Muscovy at the end of the 1620s and the beginning of the 1630s. Diplomatic considerations introduced only insignificant nuances into what was put into writing. Thus, the instructions given in 1629 to the commissioners sent to meet the French ambassador Des Hayes De Courmesnin prescribe that he be told, if he asks, that the Tsar is in friendship with England, Denmark, Sweden and Holland, and especially with Turkey and Persia, but that 'relations have not existed for a long time' with the Empire and that the King of Poland, as is known to everyone, is himself hostile to Muscovy, for they will be dealing with the ambassador of a Catholic power.[65] In communications in 1628–1631 with Holland, which, though at war with the Spanish half of the House of Habsburg, was in a state of neutrality with the Empire, what was emphasised was Moscow's hostility to Spain. Moscow even sought an alliance with Holland on the basis that the Spaniards, who were as much enemies of Holland as the Poles were of Moscow, were allied to the Poles.[66] These nuances do not obscure but rather emphasise the fact that, in the last analysis, Muscovy determined its attitude to any European state in accordance with whether that state belonged to the Habsburg or the anti-Habsburg camp.

This was the basis, too, on which, at the end of the 1620s, Muscovy pursued an active policy aimed at assembling a coalition. Among the indirect results of this policy, not at all unforeseen, was the truce of Altmark, 1629.

In 1626 the foundation for an active policy, which had proved evasive in 1622, had still not been fully discovered. What reply should be given to Sweden's proposal of a military alliance? The result of the Swedish embassy proved indeterminate. On the one hand, Bremen and Ungern

---

[64] *TsGADA, Dela shvedskie*, 1626, *stb*. 2, *ll*. 50–55, 190–194. This same instruction was repeated for the reception of a second Swedish embassy in October 1626 (see ibid., *kn*. 19, *ll*. 81–85).

[65] *TsGADA, Dela frantsuzskie*, 1629, *kn*. 2, *ll*. 89–91.

[66] Report by A. Burg and J. van Veltdriel . . ., in *Sbornik Russkogo istoricheskogo obshchestva*, Vol. 116, St. Petersburg, p. 55 *et seq*. See also *TsGADA, Dela gollandskie*, 1628–1631.

found in Moscow complete understanding of the Swedish point of view and sincere desire for political co-operation against common foes. On the other, the direct proposal of a military alliance against the Habsburgs and the Rzeczpospolita was nevertheless rejected, for this reason: the Swedes' 'good counsel' to strike at the Poles at this favourable moment was received by the Tsar 'with love and cordial friendship, and he will think about how to take vengeance on the Polish King and his country for the wrongs done earlier, but at the present time of truce this cannot be done, because that [Deulino] peace treaty . . . was sealed by great ambassadors with hearts and oaths'. But this rejection is immediately followed by a sentence which hints at the possibility of an agreement, i.e., ending the Deulino truce ahead of schedule: 'but if some wrong, however slight, be committed by the King of Poland or his son, by the Poles or by Lithuania, then, although the period of truce be not expired, our great sovereign, His Majesty the Tsar, will be ready to take action, in advance of its expiry, against Poland and Lithuania, to punish their wrongdoing.' The boyars only kept silent before the Swedish envoys about the fact that there were already plenty of pretexts available for denouncing the Polish–Lithuanian state and that the *Zemskii Sobor* had solemnly proclaimed, as far back as 1621, that the Poles had violated the terms of the truce. Bremen and Ungern's proposals that the Tatars and the Tsar's Cossack subjects be stirred up against Poland, and the Zaporozhian Cossacks induced to repudiate their allegiance to the King of Poland, were also rejected on the same grounds.[67]

Of great interest is the problem of why the director of Swedish foreign policy, Chancellor Axel Oxenstjerna, on receiving the Russians' answer, at once dispatched another embassy (Rubtsov and Bönhardt) to Moscow. Apparently he decided to check whether Moscow's rejection of his proposal was due to the fact that the first embassy had offered Moscow not a Swedo–Russian alliance against the Polish–Lithuanian state but one by which Russia would have to deal with the Rzeczpospolita while Sweden dealt with the principal organiser of aggression, the Empire. Would things not go better if Moscow were to be promised simply a joint attack on the Polish–Lithuanian state? In fact, in Gustavus Adolphus's letter of 5 August 1626 and in the speeches made by the ambassadors on this occasion, nothing is said about general European problems, the Habsburg–Catholic menace or the Emperor's aid to the Poles. Gustavus Adolphus merely speaks of his successes in the war with the Polish–Lithuanian state, and against that background, puts forward this proposal: 'And if Your Majesty the Tsar wishes to take vengeance for that great

---

[67] *TsGADA, Dela shvedskie,* 1626, *stb.* 2, *ll.* 360–380, 289–322.

wrong which the Poles did to the land subject to you, Your Majesty cannot find any time for this better than the present, since the Tatars have invaded Poland from one side and we from another, and we hope that another great sovereign will now march into Lithuania from a third side.'[68] Ambassador Bönhardt told the boyars that it was in the interest of Muscovy to attack Poland at once before it made peace with Sweden.[69]

Were the Swedes justified in assuming that if they put the matter that way it would change Moscow's attitude? Not in the least. The ambassadors were told that the Tsar knew about the Poles' enmity and about the situation in which Poland was facing 'war from all directions', so that, if the Tsar wished, he could at once take vengeance on the Poles for all their previous hostility, but that, nevertheless, he 'would not make war on them', even though he was very pleased about Gustavus Adolphus's victories 'over their common foe, the Polish King', and would be glad if the Swede succeeded in 'conquering him completely and taking possession of his lands'.[70]

Thus, Moscow held back in 1626 from war with the Polish–Lithuanian state not because it was opposed to the concept of a coalition. On the contrary, they understood very well in Moscow that it would be necessary to fight not 'one against one' or 'two against one' but 'wall against wall'. The plain fact of the existence of a Polish–Imperial–Spanish coalition evoked the idea that this bloc must be opposed by another 'wall', another bloc, and that each member thereof must take on one of the opponents to the best of its ability. But the weakness of Muscovy's position in foreign affairs in 1626 lay precisely in the circumstance that it had no coalition. Its only ally would have been the Swedes, who were, in the last analysis, no less its enemies than the Poles, since Sweden had, not long before, deprived Muscovy of its Baltic Coast, which was as necessary to it as air. Muscovy would have had no cause to show more favour to the Swedes than to the Poles if the Polish King, backed by the Habsburgs, had not, as earlier, shown aggressiveness by laying claim to further Russian territory and to the Russian throne, whereas the Swedish King had, in the peace of Stolbovo, solemnly declared himself completely satisfied with his conquests and without any further claims on Russia. But what guarantees were there that all this was not just empty words, and Gustavus Adolphus's anti-Habsburg declarations as well – that Sweden would not turn on Muscovy when Muscovy was sufficiently involved in war with Poland? The only possible guarantee could be provided by the existence of a broader coalition. Muscovy would never have taken overt action if it had

---

[68] Ibid., 1626–1627, *kn.* 19, *ll.* 125–128.    [69] Ibid., *ll.* 176–182.
[70] Ibid., *ll.* 183, 159–160, 167–169.

been left to move against the Habsburgs side-by-side with Sweden alone. This was perfectly well understood, incidentally, by the Polish diplomats, and that was why Sigismund III, in his war with Sweden, showed no great anxiety regarding Moscow's position, until July 1629.

Consequently, the task before Patriarch Philaret from 1626 onward was actually to seek additional members of the desired coalition. Very close connexion was maintained with Sweden, even on the military plane, to the extent that they were able to circumvent the terms of the Russo–Polish truce. For example, in 1627, secret information was received in France from Poland to the effect that, under Gustavus Adolphus's command in Livonia, 'Muscovites' were fighting alongside the Swedes,[71] doubtless not without the government in Moscow being aware of this. However, attention was chiefly focused on attempts to find other allies. And it was in 1626 that a certain circumstance placed before Muscovy a real possibility to begin implementing an active policy of making alliances. That year saw the rise of a new wave of the 'price revolution' on the markets of Western Europe, in the form of a dizzy increase in the price of wheat,[72] whereas in Muscovy in the seventeenth century the price of grain, while fluctuating markedly, stayed low and, on the whole, even fell.[73] The difference in the level of prices attained by 1628, in a proportion of 1 : 10, which later went up to 1 : 20 and even higher, resulted in an extra financial, and with it political, potential for Muscovy, where the export of grain was a royal monopoly, and also for those states to which, as an ally, it supplied its grain.[74] What mattered was not so much the importance of this grain for consumers (since Muscovy did not export all that much, in absolute figures, and seventeenth-century Russian agriculture was not at all ready to serve as Europe's granary) as the monetary expression of this difference in prices. By supplying grain cheaply to its allies Muscovy was, in effect, helping them with money. And financial subsidies, in that period when the military mercenary's trade flourished, when with ready money one could hire international riff-raff in unlimited numbers, was equivalent to military aid. In this way, particularly, great possibilities for an active foreign policy opened up before Muscovy from 1626–1628 onward.

Where France was concerned, no *rapprochement* with that state was seemingly counted on in Moscow in view of the failure of the embassy of

---

[71] *Akty i pis'ma*, fasc. II, p. 91.

[72] See, e.g., Naudé, W., *Getreidehandelspolitik der europäischen Staaten vom 13. bis zum 18. Jahrhundert*, Berlin, 1896.

[73] See Kliuchevskii, V. O., *Russkii rubl' XVI–XVIII vv. v ego otnoshenii k nyneshnemy*, in *Soch.*, Vol. VII, Moscow, 1959. Cf. Lubimenko, J., 'Les marchands anglais en Russie au XVII siècle', *Revue historique*, Vol. 9–10, 1922.

[74] Many details of prices are given in Soom, A., *Die Politik Schwedens bezüglich des russischen Transithandels über die estnischen Städte in den Jahren 1636–1656*, Tartu, 1940.

1615 to bring results. As regards England, on the contrary, active attempts at *rapprochement* were made. Moscow's attention in 1627–1628 was mainly focused, however, upon Denmark, as the only country which had in its time fought, not indirectly but directly, not in words but in deeds, against the Empire. It had fought, moreover, principally on the basis of subsidies provided by England, Holland and France. The Muscovite state readily resorted to that way of achieving *rapprochement*, by offering Denmark a considerable quantity of grain not at the price at which the Tsar's treasury, with its monopoly, normally sold grain abroad but at a very much lower price.[75] The peace of Lübeck between Denmark and the Empire naturally aroused indignation in Moscow. The Danish ambassador who arrived in Moscow in June 1631 with a proposal for a treaty of alliance was informed that an alliance (and along with it continued access to Russian grain) would be possible only if the Danish King Christian IV agreed to be in good friendship not just with the Russian Tsar but also with 'the Tsar's good friend, King Gustavus Adolphus of Sweden' (who was at that time already at war with the Empire) – in other words, if he once more showed himself an enemy of the Empire. The matter ended with breaking-off the negotiations and 'great offence' given to the Danish ambassador.[76]

Besides the Danes, Moscow paid special attention to the Dutch, since they, too, were *de facto* at war with the Habsburgs, even if only with the Spanish branch. To the Dutch, besides grain, was supplied (partly free of charge) the chief 'strategic raw material' of that epoch, namely saltpetre.[77]

However, if we want to trace precisely how and when Muscovy came to find solid ground for a coalition, leading it to the decision to break the truce of Deulino, we must look not so much at these attempts to find allies in Western Europe, which, at the time with which we are concerned, the beginning of 1629, were not yet producing clear diplomatic results, as in a quite different direction, namely the development of Russo–Turkish relations.[78]

As we are not able to discuss this subject in detail here we will say merely that, precisely in 1627, a turn was observed in the policy of Sultan Murad IV towards that anti-Imperial and anti-Polish line which had been interrupted in 1622 by the murder of Osman II. And that same Turkish ambassador, the Greek Foma Cantacuzene, who in 1621 had won Moscow over to a coalition policy now, in 1627, brought similar proposals. They were received with pleasure in Moscow. Ambassadors

[75] More about the Russian subsidies *infra*.
[76] Solov'ev, S. M., *Istoriia Rossii s drevneishikh vremen*, book V, Moscow, 1961, pp. 148–149. Bantysh-Kamenskii, *Obzor vneshnikh snoshenii Rossii*, Vol. I, pp. 217–218.
[77] Report by A. Burg and J. van Veltdriel, in Solov'ev, *Istoriia*, Book V, p. 147.
[78] See Zabelin, I., 'Russkie posol'stva v Turtsii v XVII stoletii', in *Russkaya starina*, September 1877.

Yakovlev and Evdokinov were sent to Turkey to formulate a Russo–Turkish alliance. They took with them letters from the Tsar to Bethlen Gábor, the ruler of Transylvania (these were conveyed to him from Constantinople by the brother of the above mentioned Cantacuzene), which contained a proposal for diplomatic relations and a political alliance. They knew in Moscow about the close family and political ties between Bethlen Gábor and Gustavus Adolphus. In other words, in 1628, in connection with Turkey's new Western policy, there arose in Moscow the idea of forming an East-European coalition made up of Transylvania, Turkey, Muscovy and Sweden (which would have friendly relations with Denmark, Holland and England), directed against the Polono–Habsburg coalition. Moscow applied itself vigorously to realising this project and undertook definite engagements. When news of this development reached Richelieu it served, as we know, as an impetus to his dispatch of embassies to Eastern Europe (Charnacé, Des Hayes and Talleyrand) and, moreover, to the reflection in his thinking of that same idea of an East-European coalition.

The next link in the development of Moscow's position was the negotiation with the Swedish ambassadors Monier and Bönhardt, which took place in Moscow in March 1629.

After its repeated failure in 1626 the Swedish government had entertained no more thought of being able to break the truce of Deulino between Muscovy and Poland. But news of the anti-Habsburg activity of Muscovite diplomacy aroused hope in Sweden at the end of 1628 that it might obtain a large subsidy from Muscovy (as also from France) for the struggle against the Empire.

What aid was Gustavus Adolphus asking the Tsar to give him? The best, of course, would have been military action against Poland and the Empire, but since the Tsar did not wish to begin such a war until the truce with Poland expired, there was also another possible form of aid: aid 'to the public weal' in money or grain. Gustavus Adolphus asked permission to buy in Muscovy, for his 'great army', 50,000 quarters of rye. (Actually, this grain was not destined for the army but for the world grain exchange in Amsterdam, but the Muscovite government did not care in the least about that.) Permission to purchase the grain at the state's own price was given, and thereafter the Swedish ambassadors were told: 'Let your King simply write what food supplies he needs, and our great sovereign will let him purchase them, duty-free, in the year that the corn comes to ripeness.'[79] This already amounted to a military-political alliance. Monier and Bönhardt received what they had asked for. Quite unexpectedly,

[79]  TsGADA, Dela shvedskie, 1629, stb. 2, ll. 192–211: see also, on these negotiations, infra, pp. 46–48.

however, they were also given what had twice been refused to the Swedish ambassadors in 1626. The records of Monier and Bönhardt's visit to Moscow contain a document of exceptional importance, such as we do not usually have at our disposal in such cases – something like a record of the discussion of the Swedish proposals, held in the absence of the ambassadors in the Tsar's rooms, between the Tsar, the Patriarch, and the boyars and officials who were most fully in their confidence. This record shows the direct and close link between the decision to break the Deulino truce and the proposals for alliance which had recently come from Turkey. The plan to form an East-European coalition against the Habsburg coalition, which had arisen in 1627, here comes to fruition before our own eyes in March 1629. Here we find, too, the texts of the addresses which the boyars and officials were to deliver in reply to the Swedish ambassadors. The latter were to be told that the Tsar sympathised warmly with the Swedish King's intention to take upon himself the hardest part of the common task, namely, war with the Kaiser, and would enter into alliance with him to this end. The Tsar had decided 'to help your sovereign and the other Christian sovereigns of the Evangelical faith by all possible means, so that the evil design of the Emperor and the Papists may not succeed'. Besides giving the aid requested, they were also to promise that the Deulino armistice with Poland would be broken: 'Owing to the wrongs done by the Polish King and his violation of the peace treaty, the great sovereign does not want to wait until the term of the truce expires, but intends to go to war against him and to help your sovereign.'[80] This was the decision by the Muscovite government, mentioned more than once by us, which had very great importance for the course of the Thirty Years' War and for the fate of Europe.

As we see, this decision was taken not through Swedish inspiration but wholly as an independent development of Muscovite policy. Thereafter that policy's most important task was mediation to bring about *rapprochement* and the conclusion of a military alliance against the Habsburgs between Muscovy's southern neighbour, Turkey, (with its vassals the Crimea and Transylvania) and its northern neighbour, Sweden. Muscovite diplomacy was very active in this cause in 1630–1631: Turkish and Crimean envoys passed through Moscow on their way to negotiate in Sweden, while Swedish envoys passed through on their way to Turkey and the Crimea.

In Sweden and beyond its borders, especially in Germany, the news brought from Moscow by Monier and Bönhardt made a great impression. In his next message to Mikhail Fedorovich, Gustavus Adolphus said:

[80] Ibid.

'The King is especially glad that the Tsar of Muscovy . . . has promised to help the oppressed Protestants of Germany: many thousands of people have been comforted by this promise, and may Almighty God move the Tsar's mind and heart to carry out the promise he has given.'[81] From that moment, all through the Thirty Years' War right down to the Peace of Westphalia, Sweden widely advertised all over Europe its alliance with Muscovy, and in Moscow the Swedish resident agent Möller even made propaganda along this line: 'Gustavus Adolphus and his army are the advance wall of Muscovy, its vanguard regiment fighting in Germany for Russia's Tsardom.'[82]

As for the promise to begin war with the Polish–Lithuanian state without waiting for the truce to expire, the Muscovite government earnestly asked the Swedes 'that this matter be kept secret'. But we already know that Gustavus Adolphus and Oxenstjerna had agreed to the truce of Altmark precisely because they had been initiated into Moscow's secret decision and were assured that Poland's armed forces would soon be tied up in conflict with Muscovy. True, they were nevertheless afraid that the Swedo–Polish truce would meet with disapproval in Moscow. And, indeed, if the Muscovite government had only one aim, to fight against Poland along with Sweden, it would have to be admitted that by promising to break the Deulino truce it had merely harmed itself. In reality, however, although of course the Muscovite government would have been very glad to have Sweden as a direct ally against Poland, it had a much broader 'coalition' concept in mind and undoubtedly foresaw that a truce was bound to be made between Sweden and Poland when it urged Sweden to go to war with the Emperor. Consequently the truce of Altmark had no effect at all on Muscovy's position.

There are some grounds for supposing that when Des Hayes de Courmesnin arrived in Moscow at the end of October 1629, Muscovy already knew about the truce of Altmark, which had been signed a month earlier.[83] Des Hayes certainly knew, if not of the fact that the truce had been concluded, at least that the negotiations for it had gone well. He came back several times in his conversation with the boyars to the delicate question of a possible truce between Sweden and Poland, stressing each time that it was not France but only England and Holland that were trying to reconcile Poland and Sweden. Like Richelieu, he was mistaken in thinking that the truth about France's role in the Swedo–Polish

---

[81] Forsten, *Baltiiskii vopros*, Vol. II, pp. 358–359: *TsGADA, Dela shvesdkie*, 1630, *stb.* 2, *ll.* 138–139.

[82] Solov'ev, *Istoriia*, Book V, p. 136.

[83] But the complete text of the truce agreement was not supplied to Monier until the beginning of 1630 (see *TsGADA, Dela shvedskie*, 1629, *stb.* 3).

peacemaking had to be concealed in Moscow. The Muscovite government understood the situation a great deal more correctly, and more calmly, than they imagined. Des Hayes's expatiations were interrupted by an unexpected question from the boyars: 'If the Polish and Swedish Kings were to make peace, would that be to King Louis's advantage, and would it also be to the advantage of the rulers of England, Denmark and Holland?' This way of putting the question testifies to their clear appreciation of the essence of the matter: for all the anti-Habsburg powers of Europe it was extremely necessary that Sweden be freed from its war with the Polish–Lithuanian state. To this direct question, which called for an honest answer, Des Hayes gave no such response, thereby only weakening the Russians' confidence in him.[84]

Nevertheless, the Muscovite government was so keenly concerned to obtain one more partner for its anti-Habsburg policy that it agreed to giving most unusual and undesired concessions to France on commercial matters, since the French ambassador considered this a necessary preliminary condition for any political alliance. Solov'ev's mistaken idea that 'Courmesnin left [Moscow] without having obtained anything new'[85] was due to the fact that, in the Muscovite archive copy, Mikhail Fedorovich's letter to Louis XIII is given without its termination, which contained concrete points (i.e., this copy was made not from the final text but from a draft prepared before the definitive concessions had been decided on). The complete text of the reply is to be found in the French archives.[86] But the concessions met so fully the wishes of the French and attested so convincingly to Muscovy's goodwill that the text of his reply was published in Paris, in the government's annual *Mercure français*, quite justifiably under the significant heading: 'Treaty of alliance and commerce between Louis XIII, King of France, and Mikhail Fedorovich, Tsar of Muscovy'.[87]

The principal results of Des Hayes's negotiations, the political ones, were not entrusted to the paper. They concerned, first and foremost, the question of war between Muscovy and Poland. Des Hayes subtly wove into his conversations with the boyars items of information which were intended to show the Muscovites that the opportunity to attack Poland ought not to be missed. This was really unnecessary, since the question had already been firmly decided in Moscow. In the Tsar's minute on Des Hayes's memorandum we read that the boyars are not to reply to a question from the ambassador regarding relations between the Tsar and

[84] *TsGADA, Dela frantsuzskie*, 1629, *kn.* 2, *ll.* 225, 181, 227–229.
[85] Solov'ev, *Istoriia*, Book V, p. 145; cf. Bantysh-Kamenskii, *Obzor vneshnikh snoshenii Rossii*, Vol. IV, pp. 79–80.    [86] *Akty i pis'ma*, fasc. I, No. 123, pp. 295–298.
[87] *Mercure français*, Vol. 21, 1629, pp. 1022–1032.

the Polish King until they have definitely learnt from him 'whether the French King is at enmity with the Poles', and then 'the boyars are to say in reply that which has been said to the King of Sweden', i.e., they are to repeat to the French ambassador what Monier and Bönhardt had been told, namely, that the Tsar had decided not to wait for the term of the truce to expire but to go to war forthwith against the King of Poland. Des Hayes conveyed to Paris confirmation of this undertaking.[88]

Soon after Des Hayes left Moscow the Swedish ambassador Monier arrived with Gustavus Adolphus's excuses and explanations regarding the truce of Altmark. Contrary, however, to the fears entertained by the Swedish King (and by Richelieu), the truce caused no changes in the Muscovites' intentions. Monier was told that the Tsar was not angry with the King over the truce with Poland 'because it was made from necessity'. But let not Gustavus Adolphus suppose that the truce would guarantee him against a clash with the Polish forces. Sigimund III would now move against him in alliance with the German Emperor unless the Polish forces were kept occupied by another war. Consequently, the Tsar repeated, 'for his part he will not wait for the expiry of the truce but will act to take vengeance on the Polish King for his wrongdoing'. As we have seen, when Moscow was offered a coalition against Poland in 1626 it had not agreed to this, but now it decided on its own initiative to take its place in the anti-Habsburg coalition, and to do that precisely by distracting Poland's forces. 'And as soon as His Majesty the Tsar begins war against the Pole, our sovereign will be freer to go to war against the Kaiser', said Monier.[89] They realised quite well in Moscow that, without that guarantee, Sweden would not commit itself to war with the Empire. Furthermore, they appreciated that Sweden could not but fear a stab in the back, not only from the Poles but also from the Russians. Where were the guarantees that the Russians would not try to take advantage of the Swedish forces' involvement in Germany in order to recover from Sweden their lands on the shores of the Baltic? The only such guarantee could be a war between Russia and Poland which would pin down the forces of both contenders. And now this guarantee, war with Poland, had been promised to Monier in Moscow, regardless of the fact that Sweden had signed a truce with that country – even, as we see, just because of it – in order finally to prod Sweden into war with the Empire. The Tsar, the boyars told Monier, wants Gustavus Adolphus to bring the enterprise begun to a happy conclusion, with the crushing of his enemy.

Monier, had, of course, also been instructed to persuade the Tsar to act

[88] *TsGADA, Dela frantsuzskie*, 1629, kn. 2, *ll.* 55, 181, 226–227, 179–180.
[89] *TsGADA, Dela shvedskie*, 1630, stb. 2, *ll.* 203–204.

against Poland. If the Tsar began hostilities, the Swedish King promised him help in the form of arms, mercenaries and so on. On its side the Muscovite government encouraged Sweden to go to war with the Empire. In 1630 the Swedes were again permitted to buy 'prohibited goods' in Muscovy, free of customs duties and at prices lower than on the free market.[90]

Finally, there arrived in Moscow, as we know, the envoys of Bethlen Gábor – the Frenchmen Charles de Talleyrand and Jacques Roussel – to propose that same East-European coalition against the Habsburgs which was already so close to acceptance by the Muscovite politicians. It is not hard to guess how this proposal was received in Moscow. A formal reply was indeed not given. In a letter to the Turkish Vizier Rejeb Pasha it was said that while the Transylvanian envoys were in Moscow the Tsar had learnt that Bethlen Gábor had died, and so he had decided to put off replying until it became clear 'who would, by order of His Majesty Sultan Murad' become his successor. In reply, however, to Rejeb Pasha's request to be told what the Muscovite government's decision was on Bethlen Gábor's proposal, and the Vizier's statement that if it was positive (if it was 'good to put those matters into effect'), then Turkey was ready to act at once ('to commit itself to action'), he was informed directly that the envoy Roussel, 'answering the boyars closest to the throne, said what was pleasing to us, the great sovereign,' and so Roussel had been instructed 'to busy himself further about this matter', for which purpose he had been sent to Sweden.[91]

Roussel left Moscow for Sweden in July 1630. The ready-prepared plan for a simultaneous onslaught by Transylvania, Turkey, Muscovy and Sweden which he took with him would undoubtedly have served as the final impetus for Sweden to enter the Thirty Years' War if previous diplomatic events had not already provided sufficient cause. Roussel did not find Gustavus Adolphus in Sweden: he had thrown himself upon Germany not long before the envoy's arrival.

Gustavus Adolphus had, apparently, received Moscow's answer from Monier at the beginning of April 1630. By that time the sincerity of Richelieu's hostility to the Habsburgs had also become clear to the Swedish government, even though the Cardinal dragged out negotiations for a formal military alliance with Sweden. There could be no doubt, either, of the sincerely anti-Habsburg attitude of Muscovy, although, there too, things were carried to the point of a formal alliance and military action. Gustavus Adolphus and Oxenstjerna, the head of Swedish diplomacy, understood that they had first to prove the sincerity of

[90] See *infra.*, pp. 48–49.
[91] *TsGADA, Dela vengerskie*, 1630, *stb.* 1, *ll.* 173, 192, 196.

Sweden's own position. The next step in the creation of an anti-Habsburg coalition had to be the beginning of military operations by Sweden against the Empire. The final preparations for the expedition took about a month. On 19 May 1630 the ships set out from Sweden. Soon a 13,000-strong Swedish army headed by the King himself landed on one of the islands of the Empire's Baltic coast. War had begun. Not encountering at first any strong resistance, Gustavus Adolphus, after seizing the mouth of the Oder and linking up with the Swedish forces stationed at Stralsund, quickly reoccupied almost all of the Duchy of Pomerania, with its capital Stettin. Following these first brilliant successes, Gustavus Adolphus suddenly ceased his advance and, while fortifying his Pomeranian bridgehead, turned to using his other weapon, diplomacy.

## Russia's subsidies to Sweden

In the history of warfare the Thirty Years' War marks the highest point in the development of the mercenary system. In economic history this means that unprecedented masses of men were drawn into action through the power of money – in other words, the Thirty Years' War was a war of financial resources.

A specific feature of the Thirty Years' War was that the powers which possessed the greatest potential fought not so much overtly as covertly, through giving subsidies. They financed both large-scale *condottieri*, such as Mansfeld, who operated in Germany, and entire states which assumed the role of *condottieri*, such as Denmark and Sweden. Both Denmark and Sweden had, of course, their own reasons for seeing the Empire as a foe, but they were able to fight that foe only thanks to subsidies received from other states. Would it have been possible to speak of a whole 'Danish period' of the Thirty Years' War if, behind Denmark, there had not been brought to bear the power, financial and therewith political, of Stuart England? Behind Denmark, as we have seen, an entire coalition operated: Christian IV received subsidies not from England alone but also from Holland and France. But this coalition, leadership of which was claimed by Charles I of England, proved to be as brittle as the financial rights of the English Crown. In 1626 Christian IV was deprived of the Dutch and French subsidies, and in 1627 it became apparent that the English King was quite unable to fulfil his promises to Denmark. If Christian IV kept on fighting for another eighteen months, that was due to subsidies from Russia which have escaped the notice of West-European historians.

Sweden went to war against the Empire in June 1630. In every textbook one can read that Gustavus Adolphus fought, basically, with money which Richelieu began paying him in 1631 – one million Paris *livres*, i.e., about 400,000 reichsthalers, annually, on condition that he maintained in Germany an army of no fewer than 36,000 men. In fact, Sweden, whose original territory then supported a population no larger than 900,000, could not even think of waging independently a major European war. Commodity–money relations were so poorly developed in Sweden that even at the end of the sixteenth century the bulk of the state's revenues were received not in money but in kind.[92] A special sort of tax in kind was levied in the form of military service by Sweden's peasants (one recruit for every ten men), which distinguished the Swedish military system from that of other European states with more developed market relations. In the sixteenth century, under Gustavus Vasa, the Swedish army numbered about 15,000 men, of whom only 800 were German mercenaries, the rest being peasant conscripts. Later, however, from the end of the sixteenth century and especially under Gustavus Adolphus, continuous warfare necessitated expansion of the Swedish army. It numbered 30,000 men in 1619, 40,000 in 1623, 50,000 in 1628, 70,000 in 1630, and 147,000 in 1632.[93]

Now, despite Gustavus Adolphus's abolition of the privilege enjoyed by peasants on the landlords' estates, the number of recruits could not be increased significantly above the sixteenth-century level. Consequently, the relative weight in Sweden's army of the peasant conscripts rapidly diminished, and during the Thirty Years' War the overwhelming majority of Gustavus Adolphus's army consisted of German, Scottish and other mercenaries.[94] Along with this development the state's need for ready money to pay these mercenaries increased steeply. Under Gustavus Adolphus measures were adopted to replace the peasants' dues in kind by money payments, to introduce many indirect taxes, and to pursue a mercantilist trade policy. At the cost of overstraining economic possibilities and ruining a mass of peasant households, the Swedish state's revenues grew under Gustavus Adolphus at this rate: 600,000 silver dalers (thalers) in 1613; 1,200,000 in 1620; 2,000,000 in 1630; 3,189,000 in 1632.[95]

Yet military expenditure outran these revenues, so that the state debt increased year by year. In 1632 it came to 2,180,000 silver dalers. Naturally, the Swedish government's financial situation was seriously improved when it began to receive the annual subsidy from France of 400,000 reichsthalers. If we consider that in 1632 one reichsthaler was

---

[92] Berendts, E., *Gosudarstvennoe khoziaistvo Shvetsii*, Part I (*Istoriia gosudarstvennogo khoziaistva Shvetsii do 1809g.*), St Petersburg, 1890, p. 126.

[93] Ibid., pp. 195–200.

[94] In Gustavus Adolphus's army in 1632 there were only 13,000 Swedes and Finns (see *Istoriia Shvetsii*, Moscow, 1974, p. 190 – Editor). [See n. 27 *supra*.]

[95] Berendts, *Gosudarstvennoe khoziaistvo*, pp. 154–167.

equivalent to 1.6 silver thalers, i.e., that the French subsidy of 1,000,000 *livres* was equivalent to 640,000 silver thalers, we see that in 1631 it made up about a quarter of Sweden's state budget and an even larger proportion of the specifically military section of the budget. The idea that Sweden fought in Germany to a substantial degree on French money and was, in that sense, France's mercenary, is perfectly correct. For France, with its highly developed finances, the sum paid to the Swedes constituted an incomparably smaller relative amount (in 1631 no more than one-fiftieth of the entire state budget).

More rarely do historians mention England's subsidies to Sweden. Yet Charles I, during the period when he ruled without a parliament (1629–1640), still tried, especially at first, to play some sort of role, mainly covert, in the European war. Incidentally, in the records of Muscovy's Embassies Department for 1631, in the reports of the Russian envoys F. Plemiannikov and A. Aristov, who were sent to Gustavus Adolphus in Germany and, on their way, provided detailed information to the Muscovite government about the international situation in Europe, we twice come upon communications concerning aid rendered to the Swedes not only by the French King 'in money' but also by the English King 'in men' – 12,000 foot soldiers and 4,000 calvalrymen (in the second case only 6,000 foot soldiers are mentioned), hired by him 'out of his treasury' for service with Gustavus Adolphus.[96] This type of subsidy – not in monetary form but in that of a ready-for-use commodity – was also practised widely throughout the Thirty Years' War and did not differ in principle from the first-mentioned. In its amount however, if we are to judge by the figures given, the English subsidy to Gustavus Adolphus was not to be compared with the subsidy from France, and it was soon proved to be beyond King Charles's means.

Historians know also of one form of 'extraordinary revenue' received by the Swedish treasury which was of enormous importance for Gustavus Adolphus's war in Germany, but which they do not assign to the category of foreign subsidies. This is the Swedish Government's speculation in grain on the international market. The correspondence of Chancellor Axel Oxenstjerna during the first years of Sweden's participation in the Thirty Years' War abounds in references to grain. On 4 January 1631 he writes that, provided the state monopoly of the grain trade is maintained and strengthened, it will by itself supply sufficient additional revenue to

---

[96] *TsGADA, Dela shvedskie*, 1631, *stb*. 4. These dispatches constitute a valuable source for the history of the Thirty Years' War, especially since enclosed in one of them is an extensive selection from correspondents' reports in European newspapers for January–March 1631, at the end of which is this note: 'Read, 12 June 139 (1631) to the sovereign and His Holiness the Patriarch in the Chamber of the Cross.'

cover the entire state debt and restore Sweden's shaken credit. Yet he quotes, as we shall see, an extremely cautious figure: the grain trade will henceforth bring in to the treasury each year 'more than 300,000 reichsthalers' in net revenue.[97]

Sweden had a long tradition of state-run foreign trade. Receiving its taxes in kind, the government transformed them, to some extent, into money by selling the produce abroad. The sale of copper had also long been a state monopoly. On the basis of this experience a system of speculation in grain also developed in the seventeenth century. Sweden became master of almost the entire Baltic coast, and the Swedish government, not satisfied with the huge customs duties that it could exact from grain-export merchants in the Baltic ports, itself engaged in the buying up of cheap grain so as to sell this at a profit in the ports of Western Europe. (Sweden was the beneficiary of a privilege from Denmark for sending its exports through the Sound.) After 1626 Gustavus Adolphus held not only Ingermanland and Livonia but Prussia as well. In Königsberg, Pillau and Danzig he contented himself with levying duties on exported grain, but in Riga and Reval he organised direct purchase of grain. Owing to the prohibition of free export, prices of grain in these ports remained low and the Swedish government's factors were able to re-sell this commodity on the international grain market in Amsterdam at an immense profit, amounting in 1629 to as much as 40 reichsthalers per last, according to the calculations of Joost Nykerke, the Dutch author of a pamphlet published in The Hague in 1630, entitled 'A clear exposition or statement of measures for putting an end to the present high cost of grain and for developing our country's shipping'.[98]

This grain from Livonia and Courland was also frequently the source of the Swedish government's 'extraordinary revenue' from grain speculation. Swedish historians alone, who have studied the records, point to another source, namely, Russian grain exported through Archangel. Thus, Cronholm mentions that, in order to fulfil his military tasks, Gustavus Adolphus speculated in Livonian and Russian grain in Holland.[99] However, these two sources – Baltic grain and Russian grain – are not clearly differentiated, and the overall figures given for Swedish grain

---

[97] Quoted in Cronholm, A., *Gustaf II Adolf in Deutschland*, Vol. I, Leipzig, 1875, p. 182.
[98] Marquardus, J., *Tractatus politico-juridicus de jure mercatorum*, Frankfurt, 1662, pp. 634–640: cf. Naudé, *Getreidehandelspolitik*, pp. 362–364; Kordt, V., *Ocherk snoshenii Moskovskogo gosudarstva s Respublikoiu Soedinennykh Niderlandov do 1631g.*; *Sbornik Russkogo istoricheskogo obshchestva*, Vol. CXVI, St Petersburg, 1902, pp.CCXVIII–CCXXVI. [The title of Nykerke's pamphlet is: 'Klaer-Bericht ofte Aenwysinghe hoe ende op wat wijse de tegenwoordige dienke der granen sal konnen geremidieert werden, ende de Schipvaert deser Landen oergroot' – Trans.]
[99] Cronholm, *Gustaf*, p. 138.

operations in Holland are extremely incomplete and merely illustrative. It seems that the Swedish archives do not contain complete documentation which would show the whole course of the grain operations,[100] and the historian has to rely for the most part on scattered accounts by Swedish factors in Holland who were responsible for the final phase of the process, the sale of, and calculation of the net profit on, each particular consignment of grain. Cronholm quotes from these accounts for 1630 a few figures showing net profit (at the points where the grain was delivered and payment for it received), but addition of even these somewhat casual figures produces an impressive result – over 500,000 reichsthalers – and he comments: 'The revenues enumerated were all that Gustavus Adolphus had wherewith to strengthen his credit, and to which he was obliged to resort in order the ensure the maintenance of his army by covering the cost of recruiting, paying and transporting the soldiers.'[101] Cronholm assigns to the Russian grain a secondary place in these operations, as compared with the Baltic grain. The groundlessness of this idea can easily be shown, even without using Russian sources.

True, we cannot establish the quantity of grain that was exported by the Swedish government from Riga and Reval, since no duties were charged on this grain, designated as being 'for the Swedish army', so that the archives of Riga and Reval retained no figures for grain exports in the years that concern us. But we do know that, before the Swedish monopoly was enforced, about 13,000–14,000 measures of grain were exported every year from these two cities,[102] and that the people of Riga complained about the marked decline in grain exports under the Swedish monopoly. This decline must have been facilitated by the low prices at which grain was bought up there by the state monopoly and, especially, by the difficulty now encountered in conveying thither the Polish grain which had apparently accounted for a substantial proportion of the previous exports. As for the Russian grain, almost none made its way out any more by the Baltic route.[103] Finally, of the quantity of Baltic grain that the Swedes did manage to buy, a certain proportion was used 'in kind', to

---

[100] It is revealing that in 1634 the Swedish envoys Scheiding, Fleming and Gyllenstjern who came to Moscow for important negotiations connected with grain purchases (see *infra*) were given no precise figures by their government for the amounts and prices of grain purchases in previous years and were consequently obliged to ask for the necessary extracts to be made for them from the records in Moscow's government offices (see *TsGADA, Dela shvedskie*, 1634, *stb.* 2).

[101] Cronholm, *Gustaf*, pp. 140–182.

[102] Bienemann, F., *Ueber Rigas erste Deputation nach Stockholm*, Riga, 1894, p. 19. Riga exported 200,000 tons every year (the Amsterdam last was equivalent to 22.39 Riga tons), while Reval exported 120,000 tons (the Amsterdam last was equivalent to 24.66 Reval tons).    [103] Cf. Soom, *Die Politik*.

meet the demands of the Swedish Army stationed in Livonia, Prussia and Pomerania, since it was easier and cheaper to supply them with food from the Baltic ports. The Swedes could therefore export to the Dutch market hardly more than 5,000 lasts of Baltic grain, which could not provide them with even half of that figure of net revenue (over 500,000 thalers) which itself, as we have mentioned, is an extremely inadequate reflection of the reality.

Consequently we need to try and clarify, with the aid of the Russian archives, the actual share of *Russian* grain in Sweden's speculative operations in the first years of this state's participation in the Thirty Years' War. We must completely separate the question of speculation in Russian grain from that of speculation in Baltic grain: Sweden had access to cheap Baltic grain by right of conquest, whereas it obtained cheap Russian grain on a quite different basis.

In fact, the Muscovite government's presentation of Russian grain to the Swedish King was no different from a military subsidy, essentially similar to the French subsidy, and merely hidden in a particular commodity-form – which has also concealed it from researchers. The only Russian historian who paid attention to this fact, K. Iakubov, confined himself, unfortunately, to writing just a few words about it. Gustavus Adolphus, he says, 'derived considerable advantages' from his political closeness to Muscovy. 'He frequently asked, referring to the insufficient availability of grain in Sweden, for a delivery of Russian grain at the state's price. This grain was then re-sold by his agents in Holland, and the profit obtained went to strengthening Sweden's depleted finances. Thus the Thirty Years' War was, in a certain sense, waged with Russian money.'[104] E. Stashevskii, who studied the organisation of foreign purchases of grain in Russia under Mikhail Fedorovich,[105] offered no explanation of the Swedes' privileges and failed to note the significance of these facts for Western Europe.

Russian grain could function as a financial subsidy for two reasons. First, it was considerably cheaper than West-European grain, so that its re-sale on the West-European market brought a big money profit. Second, it was included among those 'forbidden goods' which were covered by the Tsar's monopoly of foreign trade, and could be supplied to one or other allied power, in greater or smaller quantities and at higher or lower prices, according to the will of the Muscovite government.

As mentioned earlier, the new wave of the 'price revolution' in Western

[104] Iakubov, K. I., 'Rossiia i Shvetsiia v pervoi polovine XVII veka', in *Chteniia v Obshchestve istorii i drevnostei rossiiskikh*, Book III, Moscow, 1897, p. ix.

[105] Stashevskii, E. D., *Ocherki po istorii tsarstvovaniia Mikhaila Fedorovicha*, Part I, Kiev, 1913, pp. 277–294.

Europe which rose during the 1620s reached its peak at the beginning of the 1630s. In particular, grain prices throughout Western Europe, which were reflected in the international grain market in Amsterdam as on a delicate barometer, showed, despite some fluctuations, a marked tendency to rise in 1620–1625 and even a feverish increase in 1626–1630.[106] The Thirty Years' War, in its first years, could not have failed to stimulate this aggravation of the 'price revolution'. The American silver which had to some extent been dammed up in Spain in the preceding years now once again gushed forth in a broad stream into Europe, through the wide-open sluices of the Spanish treasury and other channels, among which were the Dutch privateers who seized on the open sea the galleons of Spain and Portugal laden with treasure from the Americas and the Orient.[107] The colossal extent to which hiring of mercenaries went on involved a sharp increase in the number of buyers of this commodity, i.e., in the purchasing power of the European market for it, and in demand, primarily, for foodstuffs, while at the same time agricultural production was falling as a result of the devastation of the countryside, the extermination of part of the peasantry and the flight of peasants into the army or into the towns. In 1625–1626 trade relations were broken off between Spain, on the one hand, and France, England and Holland, on the other, and this contributed to a profound financial crisis in all of these countries in 1626. At the same time the Swedo–Polish war in Livonia, renewed in 1625, and the Swedes' invasion of Prussia in 1626 deprived the West-European market of a substantial proportion of the East-European (Polish, Baltic, Prussian) grain which had previously, through the Dutch, fed the countries of Western and Southern Europe, including Italy, Spain and Portugal. This closing-off of the Baltic trade area was due not only to the Swedes but also to the Spaniards, who insisted that their ally Poland cease to sell grain to the Dutch, and to Wallenstein, who in 1627 forbade any export of grain from the Baltic coast-lands.[108] As a result of all of this, Western Europe entered into a period of dearth and fantastically high prices for grain which lasted for several years, while in the parts of Eastern Europe thus cut off and deprived of outlets a fall in grain prices was even observed, beginning in 1625–1626.[109]

Under these conditions the Russian grain market, which, though

---

[106] Naudé, *Getreidehandelspolitik*, pp. 353–363.

[107] The records of the Embassies Department contain a translation of a Dutch leaflet (published in Amsterdam in 1628) which gives a detailed list of the gigantic gains resulting from one such operation (*TsGADA, Dela shvedskie*, 1629, *stb.* 2, *ll.* 99–109).

[108] Förster, F., *Albrecht von Wallensteins ungedruckte Briefe*, Vol. I, Berlin, 1828, nos. 75, 84, 128.

[109] Even grain prices at Danzig showed some reduction at the same time as prices in Amsterdam were rising rapidly (cf. Kordt, V., *Ocherk*, pp. CLXXVI–CLXXIX).

already cut off from the Baltic by the Swedes, retained an outlet through Archangel, became a centre of interest for all Europe. Its isolation from the Baltic trade proved to offer even a certain advantage to the Tsar's treasury, in that prices on Russia's internal market stayed low and the export of grain was a royal monopoly. The government's correspondence with the governors of Novgorod in 1628 vividly depicts a veritable assault by European smuggler-merchants upon this monopoly. With the help of their agents among the Russian population they, 'by theft, stealth and underhand dishonest practices', were buying up grain and sending it out through the Baltic ports. However, the government was vigorously combating this encroachment, employing a system of confiscation of goods, corporal punishment, imprisonment and so on.[110] Where the route across the White Sea was concerned, conditions were not at all favourable to smuggling, for in the north, grain was not locally grown but brought from other parts, and all of it passed through storage points, in Vologda and Archangel, that were easy to supervise. At Archangel the grain was loaded into foreign ships under strict supervision by responsible officials who required the exporters to show their 'letters of authority' from the Tsar, i.e., their permits 'to buy and send overseas' some defined amount of grain. Since it was not possible to get round the royal monopoly, foreigners laid siege to government circles in Moscow. Beginning in 1627–1628 there was no fending off of the petitions from European powers, especially Holland, for permission to buy substantial quantities of grain in Russia. In the first half of the 1620s a system of 'letters of recommendation' had been operated, by which a foreign government – the Dutch government, say – merely supported an application by some private merchant, but from 1627 the role of would-be buyers came to be filled mainly by the governments themselves, each authorising a particular factor or 'steward' to purchase a permitted amount of grain and load it into ships at Archangel. Each government strove to secure monopoly rights on Russia's grain. The amount of this grain available for export was not large, and competition between purchasers inevitably inflated the price. Since, from the commercial point of view, it did not matter to the Muscovite government who it sold its grain to, the rivals naturally resorted to political arguments, and the Muscovite government itself began to look upon the delivery of grain to this or that other government as a gesture of political friendship. Even when it charged the high monopoly price, as, for example, when selling to Holland, England and France, it nevertheless, with complete justification, regarded mere permission to purchase and export grain as, in itself, material assistance to

[110] *TsGADA, Dela shvedskie*, 1628, *stb.* I, *ll.* 1–16.

a friendly power, because it knew that this price, though high, was much lower than grain prices in Europe. What we see here, essentially, is to some degree, the concept of subsidy, which appears fully developed in the way that grain was supplied, to a limited extent, to Denmark but mainly to Sweden.

In general, the concept of subsidy occupied by no means the smallest place in the foreign policy weaponry of the government of Mikhail Fedorovich, or, more correctly, of Filaret Nikitich. Having started to prepare, soon after signing the Deulino truce of 1618, for renewed war with the Polish–Lithuanian state, it actively sought allies, and already in 1623 the French ambassador reported to Paris from Constantinople that Moscow was proposing to pay Turkey 400,000 thalers a year in return for participation in a war against Poland,[111] i.e., the same amount that France was later to pay Sweden. Ten years later Moscow agreed to pay Sweden, also for war against Poland, 100,000 thalers every month, i.e., 1,200,000 a year, or three times the amount of the French subsidy[112]. In other words, for the sake of striking a blow at the main enemy, the Rzeczpospolita, Moscow did not shrink from paying over to one ally or another a substantial amount of the cash which had been gathered with so much difficulty into the Tsar's treasury.

But it was not just a question of organising a direct blow at the Rzeczpospolita. They understood quite well in Moscow that Sigismund III's strength lay in support from the Papacy and the Habsburgs, that his aggression in North-Eastern Europe was only one sector in a mightier front of all-European aggression, led by the Empire and Spain. Consequently, the Muscovites saw all enemies of the Habsburgs in Europe as their allies. In 1626 the Dutchman Isaak Massa, in a memorandum to the States-General, wrote concerning the possibility of a *rapprochement* with Russia: 'Affairs of state are conducted in that country by the Tsar's father, the Patriarch, a skilful politician, who, as a result of his imprisonment in Poland, is an intransigent enemy of the Poles and knows well who are to be considered friends of Austria and Spain and who their enemies.'[113] Naturally, the German Emperor ('the Roman Kaiser') with his militant Catholic entourage ('with his Popish counsellors') figured as principal enemy after the Polish–Lithuanian state

---

[111] *Akty istoricheskie*, Vol. II, p. 424.

[112] See the correspondence on this question between Gustavus Adolphus and the Muscovite government: *TsGADA, Dela shvedskie*, 1631, stb. 8; 1632, stb. 2, 5. The plan already agreed on, whereby Gustavus Adolphus undertook to use the Russian money to raise a special army and send it from Germany against Poland was cancelled by the Swedish King's death and subsequent events. See *infra*. Chapter 5.

[113] Isaak Massa, *Histoire des guerres de la Moscovie (1601–1610)*, edited by M. Obolensky and A. Van der Linde, Vol. I, Brussels, 1866, p. 264.

where the Patriarch was concerned. And in order to smash him, or at least to divert his aggression, Filaret Nikitich considered it necessary to make very serious sacrifices, not only diplomatic but also material. Actual money had to be hoarded for the expenses of war with Poland, but the Russian treasury had at its disposal other potential resources as well that could be employed against the Emperor – first and foremost, grain.

In 1653, when, after the decline during the 1630s and 1640s, a new upturn in grain prices was discerned in Western Europe, the Swedish resident agent in Moscow, I. Rodes, described in these words the importance of this resource to the Tsar's treasury:

All over Russia grain belongs to His Majesty the Tsar and absolutely no private person is allowed to trade in it. Recently, when year after year has seen high prices, this trade has brought considerable revenue to His Majesty, especially in the last four years, when orders have been given every year to collect nearly 200,000 'quarters' (of grain), which have therefore been bought up throughout the country and conveyed from all ports to Vologda. In Kazan, Nizhny-Novgorod and surrounding regions, a 'quarter' costs 12–25 kopecks . . . in Iaroslavl, Rostov and Vologda regions 36–50 kopecks . . . Therefore, in Archangel, a 'quarter' cannot cost, allowing for all expenses, more than one reichsthaler.[114] Since then in the four years mentioned, they charged more than $2\frac{1}{2}$–$2\frac{3}{4}$ reichsthalers for a 'quarter', revenue from grain brought in more than a million reichsthalers to His Majesty the Tsar.[115]

Leaving aside the absolute figures that Rodes gives for 1653 we can see from his description a clear notion of the mechanism whereby state revenue was derived from the grain monopoly. This item in state revenue, which it was comparatively difficult to realise owing to Muscovy's lack of a sea-going fleet of its own, was in 1627–1634 partly employed by the government to serve the purposes of foreign policy. As has been mentioned, permission accorded to one or other state to purchase grain from the Tsar was a profitable privilege that was reserved exclusively for the European enemies of the Habsburgs (England, Holland, France). But in 1627 the Danish King Christian IV, who was engaged in overt war with the German Emperor, was given an absolutely exceptional right – to purchase 30,000 quarters of 'grain stocks' in Russia through a plenipotentiary (the Dutchman David Ruts), not from 'the Tsar's merchants' but directly in the domestic market, and to export this grain without paying any duty, i.e., at a very low price. In 1628 Christian IV again received

---

[114] The reichsthaler or yefimok [from Polish *joachymik* – Trans.] was nominally equivalent to 50 kopecks or half a ruble, but its exchange rate varied in the first half of the seventeenth century between 45 and 57 kopecks.

[115] 'Sostoianie Rossii v 1650–1655gg. po doneseniiam Rodesa', in *Chteniia v Obshchestve istorii i drevnostei rossiiskikh*, Book II, 1915, p. 159.

permission to buy 40,000 quarters on the same terms.[116] In other words, in these cases the Muscovite government 'conceded' or sacrificed in favour of the Danish King the sum which it could itself have received for such a quantity of grain exported. That this was seen as a war subsidy is plain in view of the sharp change of policy that followed the conclusion of peace between Denmark and the Emperor at Lübeck in 1629. The Muscovite government considered itself bound by the promise it made earlier to Christian IV, and therefore allowed him in 1630 to buy 25,000 of the 75,000 quarters previously agreed, but not on the same terms. He had to pay a high duty on the grain, and in the following year, 1631, such a high price was demanded that Denmark finally left the ranks of purchasers of Russian grain.

Since we are not able here to go into details about Denmark's grain purchases, let us turn to those made by Sweden. First of all we must see how this question was dealt with in the Russo–Swedish negotiations – as a commercial or a political matter; in other words, was it merely political utilisation of trade relations or was it open solicitation and conscious provision of political subsidies?

On 20 December 1627 Gustavus Adolphus sent a message to Mikhail Fedorovich asking permission to buy 10–12 shiploads of grain. In his reply of 1 March 1628 the Tsar gave permission for the Swedish plenipotentiary Beckman and the Dutch 'stewards' De La Dale and Ul'ianov to acquire 36,000 quarters 'for the Swedish King' on the same privileged conditions as had been granted to the King of Denmark. Unfortunately, neither of the letters has survived in the archives of the Embassies Department (they are merely mentioned in subsequent correspondence), and we do not know what political arguments may have accompanied Gustavus Adolphus's request and Mikhail Fedorovich's consent.

We can, however, form some idea of them from the similar negotiations which took place in the following year, 1629. The Swedish ambassador Monier, on arriving in Moscow, said in the Tsar's presence that when the latter should decide to take overt military action, 'the Roman Kaiser's evil design will be powerless and abated, so that many Christians

---

[116] See the 'extract' from the Department's records made in 1653 – *TsGADA, Dela shvedskie*, 1653, *stb.* 4, *ll.* 17–18. On how the Danes' grain purchases proceeded a special roll has been kept in the collection of 'departmental papers of olden times' (1630, No. 48), containing abundant documentation. For study of the entire history of these purchases plentiful material is contained in the *Dela datskie* for 1627–1633, and also in two publications by Iu. N. Shcherbachev: 'Datskii Arkhiv. Materialy po istorii Drevnei Russii, Khraniashchesia v Kopengagene' in *Chteniia v Obshchestve istorii i drevnostei rossiiskikh*, Book III, Moscow, 1897, and 'Russkie akty Kopengagenskogo gosudarstvennogo arkhiva' in *Russkaia istoricheskaia biblioteka*, Vol. XVI, St Petersburg, 1897.

who are suffering want in Germany and Denmark and who wish for and
seek help will be aided and rescued thereby'. But since it was supposed
that the Tsar would not act until the term of his truce with the Polish
King had expired, Gustavus Adolphus had resolved to go it alone, for
the time being, 'with all his power', because it was necessary 'to bring
help to those poor and oppressed people in Germany and Denmark', and
he merely asked the Tsar, without committing any formal breach of the
truce with Poland, 'to aid him peacefully, by making available either
money or some thousands of barrels of rye and other foodstuffs'.[117] Here
we see clearly expressed the idea of 'covert war' waged through subsidies.
It is very important that subsidies in the form of money and in the form
of grain are reckoned as equivalent one to the other. If authority were
given to purchase 50,000 quarters of grain, the ambassador went on,
'timely' aid could thereby be rendered not only to the oppressed
Christians in Germany already mentioned, but also to 'other kings,
princes and lords, against the Pope and the Roman Kaiser, and to check
the entire House of Austria and hinder their savage and bloody design.
They aim at nothing short of making themselves sovereign masters of
the whole world, and today (but may God not allow it) they are very near
to realising that aim.'[118] At the same time the ambassador requested that
no permission be granted for export of grain from Russia to any persons
who 'seek and plan thereby to strengthen the Roman Kaiser and the
Popish power'.[119]

The boyars returned this answer to the Swedish ambassador, on behalf
of the Tsar. 'His Majesty the Tsar knows certainly that the Roman Pope
and the Kaiser and the King of Poland and other rulers of the Roman faith
stand and plot in concert and pursue a grand design to obtain possession
of our Christian state and the states of your Swedish King and the Danish
King, and to turn them over forever to the Popish religion.' Therefore the
Tsar has decided 'to help in every way your sovereign and other Christian
states of the Evangelical faith'. To this end the Tsar will allow the
Swedish King, 'for his royal love and to help him', to purchase the
requested 50,000 quarters of rye, free of customs duties, and in future
years, 'if your sovereign King Gustavus Adolphus needs to purchase rye
and other foodstuffs', let him write how much he wants and, 'in the year
when the grain is harvested', the Tsar will permit him to buy this grain
free of customs duties, 'and he has sent his sovereign order and command

---

[117] TsGADA, Dela shvedskie, 1629, stb. 2, ll. 189–191. Archive materials relating to
Russo–Swedish negotiations about the purchase of grain have now been published in
the collection of documents entitled Russko-shvedskie ekonomicheskie otnosheniia v XVII
veke, Moscow and Leningrad, 1960.
[118] TsGADA, Dela shvedskie, 1629, stb. 2, ll. 192.     [119] Ibid., l. 211.

to all the cities of his realm, permitting rye and certain other grain to be sold without any hindrance'.[120]

And in fact, from the correspondence of the Muscovite government with the governor of Vologda which is included in the same roll of 1629, we can see that the government treated the Swedish grain purchases as a matter of great political importance. The Tsar's letter of 20 April explains to the governor that this grain is being made available to the Swedes 'for a present actual war, which war is now being waged in their country', and prescribes that this grain is to be taken from the amount which it had previously been ordered was to be bought for the Tsar ('and let not, according to our previous order, the grain for us be taken and sold'). In other missives to this address instructions are conveyed which report the Swedish ambassador's desire that the uniform Moscow measure be used, that no foreigners be allowed to be present when the purchases are made other than the authorised representatives of the Swedish King, and so on[121] – which, however, did not eliminate a number of 'obstacles' of which the Swedish ambassador complained in 1630, and to the removal of which the Muscovite government again applied itself very vigorously, even to the point of arresting the governor of Archangel.[122]

On the whole, however, the tone of the embassy of 1630 indicates great satisfaction on the part of the Swedish government with the subsidy they received: 'For such great love and good action the King's Majesty has ordered that much thanks be given to your Majesty [the Tsar].' But, as Sweden saw it, this was only 'the beginning' of the fulfilment of the Tsar's promise 'to defend the public weal in Germany', a promise which 'has brought comfort to many thousands of wretched souls'. To be sure, it was somewhat more difficult for Gustavus Adolphus to ask for a subsidy now than it had been in the previous year, because he had made the truce of Altmark with Poland. Ambassador Monier explained carefully that the Kings of France and England had promoted this truce so that Gustavus Adolphus might be able 'to take action for the public weal in the Kaiser's territory [i.e., in Germany] and offer resistance to the Kaiser and his Popish counsellors', and Gustavus Adolphus did not want to reject 'the advice of these great and powerful monarchs', having seen for himself 'for a long time what that Kaiser and his counsellors were doing and the need to overcome them and prevent the ruin and destruction of many states and countries'. Having signed the truce with Poland, Gustavus Adolphus intended, 'with the money and aid of those two kings and other great rulers who wish to help with money and men, to test his fortune in the

[120] Ibid. 1629, stb. 2, ll. 349–351, 357.    [121] Ibid. ll. 386–388, 420–477.
[122] TsGADA, Dela shvedskie, 1630, stb. 2, ll. 139–241, 250–259.

coming spring with a great army', and go to war with the German Emperor. First and foremost among the 'other great rulers' who were to help in this war, it was understood, was the Tsar, since he knew that the plans of the Empire and the Papacy included, by acting 'through Poland' to 'conquer and ravage the great Russian lands', to substitute Catholicism for Orthodoxy in Russia and to establish in that country their 'unbearably cruel rule'. Gustavus Adolphus therefore asked Mikhail Fedorovich, appealing to his friendship, to 'show in deeds his goodwill towards the public weal in Germany and render aid to the poor abused Christians by supplying rye', specifically by granting permission for the purchase of 75,000 quarters of it, and also 4,000 quarters of millet. Referring to this action as a 'sacrifice', the Swedish missive at the same time supposes that 'to Your Majesty this is a minor matter', and that, in general, 'no loss will be inflicted' on the Tsar's subjects (since it is all the same to them who is the buyer of their grain, the Swedes or the Tsar's mercantile agents). On the contrary, the missive goes on, in the long run the Tsar will 'profit and gain' from the transaction, while his enemies will suffer 'hindrance and loss', as anyone may understand if account be taken of the fact that 'Poland, the Kaiser and the Papists are united and agreed that both gain and loss will be common among them', and, 'in general, this aid in grain will, covertly, do harm to the Kaiser and the Polish King'. The Kaiser will be unable to help the Polish King, 'and as his Royal Majesty [Gustavus Adolphus] will wage war against the Kaiser, the great country and state of Your Majesty the Tsar will be protected'.[123]

This entire conception was received in Moscow with understanding and sympathy. In order that 'hindrance and loss' be inflicted on their common enemies the Tsar allowed the Swedish King, despite the failure of that year's harvest, to buy, free of customs dues, over and above what remained unbought from the permissions granted in previous years, 75,000 quarters of rye, together with, as a mark of 'friendship and love', not the 4,000 quarters of millet asked for, but 8,000, along with 200 barrels of resin and saltpetre 'wherever they may be found' (i.e., not to be taken from the state's reserves). And may your sovereign, said the written reply handed by the boyars to the Swedish ambassador, remain with ours 'in so great friendship and love and good counsel'.[124]

In the following year, 1631, the Swedish ambassador was already able, on his arrival in Moscow, to tell the Tsar of the victories won by Gustavus Adolphus over the Emperor in Germany and to expound the idea that if the Swedish King were not now 'waging war against the Kaiser, the Kaiser would have sent aid in men and money to the Tsar's enemy the

---

[123] Ibid., *ll.* 138–139, 133–135, 128–129, 143–148.    [124] Ibid., *ll.* 152, 254–259, 268.

Polish King and would long since have invaded Muscovy'. On these grounds the Swedish King again requested that he be helped in his campaign in Germany by means of supply of cheap grain. The ambassador was assured in Moscow that the Tsar wished to see the Swedish King succeed in 'overcoming the Kaiser', and he was again permitted to purchase 50,000 quarters without making any payment to the Tsar's treasury, it being specially emphasised in the official reply that 'His Majesty is doing all this for your royal sovereign out of friendship and love and to support his soldiers.' An order was sent to Archangel 'that the representatives of the Swedish King in Archangel be supplied with grain by all the King's agents in the city'.[125]

In 1632 Gustavus Adolphus again received authority to purchase 50,000 quarters of grain to enable him to continue his campaign in Germany. After the King's death, in the spring of 1633, the courier Steinmann brought to Moscow a message from twelve important magnates of Sweden, including De la Gardie, Gyllenhjelm, Gabriel Oxenstjerna and others, assuring the Muscovites that the war begun by Gustavus Adolphus would be continued. The magnates reminded the Tsar of 'that good friendship and benefaction which Your Majesty showed in relation to the war now being waged in Germany, in enabling us . . . to purchase stocks of grain . . . at as low a price as possible and to procure it and transport it from Archangel in our ships'. At present, the magnates went on, we 'have reason greater than before' to wage this war, for which the blame lies on the Emperor, the Polish King and the Papacy, and the Tsar, for his part, ought to be concerned 'to crush and sink them'. Therefore, the magnates hope that he will 'continue constant in his aid' and allow them 'to buy the grain in question'.[126]

Permission to purchase grain once more, in 1633, had been granted before this appeal was received. But so soon as 1634, after Muscovy's withdrawal from the Smolensk War (1632–1634) and the sharp change in its foreign policy,[127] a fresh subsidy was denied to the Swedes. Vainly did Queen Christina, in a letter of 21 May 1634, request permission, 'for the great interests we share', to obtain at least a smaller quantity of grain than in the previous years, 'because it will be a great help to our army fighting against the Kaiser and his counsellors', assuring the Tsar that 'our Royal Majesty maintains an army no smaller than before in Germany, fighting against the Roman Kaiser and his Popish and Jesuit counsellors'.[128] Mikhail Fedorovich's reply said that it was not possible to release any grain, owing to the failure of the harvest and the resultant high prices, but

---

[125] *TsGADA, Dela shvedskie*, 1631, stb. 7, ll. 212–217, 195.
[126] *TsGADA, Dela shvedskie*, 1633, stb. 6, ll. 10–12.    [127] See *infra*, Chapter 5.
[128] *TsGADA, Dela shvedskie*, 1634, stb. 2, ll. 173–176.

promised that permission would be given in subsequent years.[129] In fact, however, no further delivery of cheap Russian grain to Sweden was allowed until 1650.

Thus, the question of grain purchases was dealt with between Sweden and Muscovy not at all as a mere matter of trade relations. The question why Muscovy considered it advantageous to subsidise Sweden's war against the Empire has been answered already.

We have established that Russian subsidies in grain to Sweden during the Thirty Years' War were granted over a period of six years, 1628–1633. The purchasing of the grain was not organised always in the same way. In the first three years (1628–1630) it was somewhat anarchic: the Tsar merely allowed some individual designated by the Swedish envoys (a 'steward') to 'purchase grain along the banks of the Dvina and in other places, freely and without paying customs dues and to convey it to the town of Archangel'.[130] In particular cases certain districts were designated for the purchase of grain.[131] But the Swedes themselves, aiming to monopolise Russia's grain exports, urged the Tsar's government to bring a greater degree of organisation into its own monopoly. In 1629 they proposed to conclude a Russo–Swedish commercial treaty covering a period of four or five years, to be based on a clearing calculation that Russia would export 100,000 rubles' worth of agricultural produce every year, while Sweden would export metals and metal articles, including armaments, to the same value.[132] This project, which was realised in part, already assumed the need for the Tsar's purveyors to act as intermediaries between the Russian population and the Swedes. In 1631 the Swedes proposed to Muscovy something like a trade bloc directed against the Dutch – an agreement not to sell grain to the Dutch at a price below that to be agreed between Russia and Sweden.[133] The proposal was sympathetically received in Moscow, but what it eventually led to was a new system for buying up grain. From 1631 onward foreigners, including Swedes, received their grain directly from the quays at Archangel, from 'the Tsar's grain', and were not allowed to go buying within the country. The purchasing work was centralised in the hands of the Great Treasury, and merchants were nominated who had to find grain 'collectors' in the localities, these in their turn sometimes passing the order on to 'contractors'. During the winter 'the Tsar's grain' was stored in barns, and when spring came it was conveyed 'by the great river' to Archangel, where it

[129] Ibid., *ll.* 236–242.
[130] *TsGADA, Dela shvedskie,* 1629, *stb.* 2, *l.* 286.
[131] *TsGADA, Dela shvedskie,* 1630, *stb.* 2, *l.* 154.
[132] *TsGADA, Dela shvedskie,* 1629, *stb.* 2, *ll.* 194–195, 224–236.
[133] *TsGADA, Dela shvedskie,* 1631, *stb.* 8, *ll.* 103–104.

was to be delivered to the foreigners' warehouses.[134] However, the economic essence of Russia's grain subsidies to Sweden was not affected by this organisational reform. While grain was sold at Archangel to other foreigners at an arbitrary price determined by the Great Treasury, to the Swedish King it was supplied at cost price i.e., no dearer than it would have cost the Swedish buyer without the intervention of the Tsar's middlemen. The Tsar's decree of 1631 prescribed that grain should be supplied to the King of Sweden at Archangel 'and that the payment for this grain by the Swedish King's stewards to the sovereign's treasury in that city be at the same price which the grain cost the sovereign, together with the cost of carriage', 'at the same price, without increase, at which this grain was purchased together with the cost of its carriage to Archangel and all the victualling', without any duties having to be paid.[135] Similar procedures were observed in 1632 and 1633. It is possible to examine separately the nominal amount of these Russian subsidies to Sweden, or the 'concession', that is, what the profit and customs duty amounted to which the Russian government presented, so to speak, to Sweden by not imposing these charges, and what these subsidies actually amounted to, that is, the amount of net profit that the Swedish government made by re-selling the Russian grain on the Dutch market.

From the formal standpoint, only the former amount figured in the diplomatic negotiations. In 1634 and later the boyars frequently calculated before the Swedish envoys how much, in 1628–1633, 'our great sovereign lost' by selling this grain to the Swedish King without requiring customs-duties and 'at a lower price', 'at cost price'.[136] In return for this considerable 'concession' they asked for mutual most-favoured nation treatment and a supply of Swedish arms for the Russian army. In legal terms only this aspect of the subsidies mattered, even though the Muscovite government could not but be aware that it was giving the grain to the Swedish King for no other purpose than profitable re-sale. True, the Swedish envoys who explained so frankly the military-political significance of the subsidy strove with remarkable persistence to conceal the way in which Sweden used Russia's aid. They invariably asserted that the grain was needed immediately for feeding Sweden's 'great army', owing to harvest failure in Sweden, the lack of stocks of foodstuffs in Pomerania, Prussia, and so on.[137] In taking this line they fell into flagrant

---

[134] *TsGADA, Prikaznye dela starykh let*, 1630, *stb.* 48. Cf. Stashevskii, *Ocherki po istorii*, pp. 284–291.
[135] *TsGADA, Dela shvedskie*, 1631, *stb.* 7, *ll.* 195, 215–216.
[136] *TsGADA, Dela shvedskie*, 1634, *stb.* 2, *l.* 295.
[137] Cf. *TsGADA, Dela shvedskie*, 1629, *stb.* 2, *l.* 212; 1630, *stb.* 2, *l.* 143.

contradictions and resorted to very implausible fabrications. Thus, in 1629 the envoys alleged, in a special letter, that Gustavus Adolphus would have preferred the grain to be sent directly to Sweden across the Baltic Sea, but, since the season for doing that had been let pass, the grain should be dispatched through Archangel so that, 'after it had been bought, it might be conveyed to Holland', where Gustavus Adolphus, they said, had made an arrangement with some Dutch merchants for the grain to be transferred to him via Pomerania and Prussia.[138] All this was said in order to explain why the purchased grain was addressed for dispatch to Holland. Sometimes, carried away by their commercial calculations, the Swedish envoys spoke of the amount of 'loss' suffered by their King when it proved impossible to purchase all the grain allowed to them, but then, remembering suddenly, they would add something about 'the shortages in the stocks held by his great regiments'.[139] Ambassador Monier complained in 1630 that other foreigners besides the Swedes were buying grain 'and re-selling it to other states, but his sovereign King Gustavus Adolphus needed grain not to sell but to feed his soldiers', and, cleverly interweaving this falsehood with a truth, said, speaking for his King, that other sovereigns ask the Tsar for permission to buy and export grain 'at the instigation and on behalf of traders' who seek to profit by it – he alone has 'good cause and concern' aiming not at gain for himself but for the public weal.[140]

In reality Sweden had no need at that time for Russian grain *in natura*. Chancellor Oxenstjerna said in 1631 that Sweden was itself able to export seven thousand tons of grain every year.[141] If that had not been the case, supply to Sweden of Baltic grain would have been incomparably easier than supply of Russian grain through Archangel. True, the latter was cheaper, but it must not be forgotten that it had to be conveyed to Sweden via Amsterdam, where it could be sold at a much higher price, and so that would be just as impracticable, economically, as if the Swedish government were to buy the grain at the high Amsterdam price. What we have here are operations carried out by the government, not by private Swedish merchants and, let us repeat, this government did not use the Russian grain *in natura* either for feeding the population of Sweden or for feeding its army overseas. Essentially, the Swedish government was quite indifferent to whether it re-sold the grain or any other commodity. Thus, from the reports sent by Rodes to Queen Christina in 1650 we learn that the grain which Tsar Aleksei Mikhailovich had allowed him to export,

[138] *TsGADA, Dela shvedskie*, 1629, *stb.* 2, *ll.* 362–363.
[139] *TsGADA, Dela shvedskie*, 1630, *stb.* 2, *ll.* 141–142.    [140] Ibid., *ll.* 153, 145–147.
[141] Berendts, *Gosudarstvennoe khoziaistvo*, p. 166. The Stockholm ton (barrel) was equivalent to 0.8 of a Russian quarter.

allegedly for the needs of the Swedish army, could be obtained only at a price much higher than had been expected (by the Dutch contractors), 'so that less profit can be got from the grain this time owing to its high purchase price'. Consequently, Rodes proposed to spend the Swedish public money entrusted to him not on grain but on Persian raw silk, which could be bought cheaply in Russia and sold for a high price in the West. Altogether, the grain purchases clearly emerge in this correspondence on the plane of international financial operations, along with the acceptance of bills of exchange, dealings in foreign currency, and so on.[142]

The use for speculation of the grain that the Swedish King obtained from the Russian government was an open secret. The *Burggraf* of Elbing, Hoppe, in his chronicle of the Swedo–Polish war in Prussia, enters this piece of information under the date 1629: on 23 June the envoys who were sent to the Grand Duke of Muscovy in the previous year returned to Pillau with good news – the Grand Duke had authorised the King to buy 30,000 lasts (sic) of rye, 'for Swedish copper money and at an agreed price'. Thereby, Hoppe goes on, 'a service was rendered to the Swedes, for they intended to re-sell the grain for silver money, at a profit'.[143] The Dutch trader Nykerke in his pamphlet already mentioned, which was published in 1630, speaking of the revenues obtained by the Swedish King from re-sale of Baltic grain, adds: 'Besides this he has in the last two years bought from Muscovy a large quantity of grain which he has likewise re-sold to our people through his agents, at a great profit.'[144] In that same year, 1630, the Dutch envoys Burg and Veltdriel were instructed to inform Moscow that the Russian grain sold to the Swedes had ended up in the hands of Dutch merchants, and that therefore it would be more advantageous to the Muscovite government to sell it directly to the Dutch. 'As matters stood', said Burg and Veldtriel before the Tsar, 'only the profit remained with those who were authorised to buy the grain, while the grain itself was sent to the Netherlands.'[145]

---

[142] *Chteniia v Obshchestve istorii i drevnostei rossiiskikh*, Book II, Moscow, 1915, pp. 11–18 *et seq.*

[143] Hoppe, *Geschichte*, p. 409.

[144] Quoted in Naudé, *Getreidehandelspolitik*, p. 364.

[145] Report by A. Burg and J. van Veltdriel, pp. 61–62. The Swedish agent in Moscow, Möller, did not try to refute these exposures, and even supplied the Embassies Department with a copy of Nykerke's pamphlet, but he did put forward a counter-exposure: Gustavus Adolphus 'does not now offer grain to the Dutch at the same price as they previously purchased it in his country, and because of this the Dutch wrote to the King's selling agents and, having printed their letter, published it, saying in this book that they want to be given access to buy all the grain in the country of the Tsar's Majesty and thus to have the others in their power.' Möller emphasised that if this happened the profit would not be used by the Dutch government for its war with Spain but by the merchants for their own enrichment: 'This grain would be sent to Spain by the merchants, and the States and the Prince of Orange would know nothing about that source of profit to the merchants.' (*TsGADA, Dela shvedskie*, 1631, *stb.* 8, *ll.* 103–104).

These revelations, however, were nothing new to the Muscovite government and did not affect its subsequent allowance of grain to Sweden. Only in 1631 was a curious enquiry sent to Gustavus Adolphus: 'Why is the grain sold, and what price will he henceforth fix for grain in his own country?', to which, of course, no answer was returned.[146] But, through its envoys Plemiannikov and Aristov, sent to Sweden in 1630, the Muscovite government knew, in any case, about the colossal increase in the price of grain in Europe. The envoys reported that, according to Dutch merchants, in England and Scotland in the winter of 1630–1631 a barrel of rye cost 10 yefimki, but in the spring of 1631, owing to the increased supply, only six.[147] Thus, the Muscovite government was in a position to calculate, if only approximately, not only the dimensions of its nominal subsidy to the Swedish King but also those of the actual revenue which the latter derived from re-sale of the Russian grain. It was able, finally, also to compare the amount of aid it gave to Sweden with the amount of France's subsidy, for already in 1631 Möller possessed a precise figure for that subsidy: 400,000 large yefimki (reichsthalers) a year.[148]

Let us also try to make this calculation, basing our figures mainly on the 'memoranda' in the Muscovite government's departmental offices, which contain detailed summaries, covering several years, of the amount of grain allowed to the Swedish King, with the relevant conditions. These were compiled on several occasions and in several variants for the requirements of diplomatic negotiations with the Swedish envoys.[149] In these documents it is shown how much grain the King was allowed to buy in each year, how much was actually bought and 'sent off overseas' and how much was 'underbought' out of the permitted quantity, because 'underbought' grain was carried forward to the following year as an addition to the newly authorised amount. Shown also are the names of the Swedish 'stewards' who effected the purchases in various years, the price at which the grain was sold to them, and the price at which, in the same years, grain was sold to other foreigners. The last mentioned information is given only for 1631–1633, but not for 1628–1630 (owing to the change mentioned earlier, in the way the purchases were organised). It is merely stated, in summary fashion, that in 1628–1630 the Swedes bought grain 'at a low price – at eight altyns and ten altyns and four grivens, and at

---

[146] *TsGADA, Dela shvedskie*, 1631, *stb.* 8, *l.* 109.

[147] Ibid., *stb.* 4, *l.* 34. 'Barrel' or 'ton' was an international measure which varied from one country to another but was broadly identified by Rodes, Pomerening, Kilburger and other foreigners with the Muscovite quarter. Consequently, 10 yefimki per barrel was roughly equivalent to 200 yefimki, or about 350 gold gulden per last, which, on the whole, corresponds to what we learn from other sources.

[148] Ibid., *stb.* 8, *l.* 61; cf. *stb.* 4, *l.* 111.

[149] Ibid., *stb.* 7, *ll.* 189–195; 1634, *stb.* 2, *ll.* 288–316; 1653, *stb.* 4, *ll.* 16–28; 1653, *stb.* 4, *ll.* 16–28.

most, a poltina per quarter'.[150] To this was contrasted the price at which
grain was sold to other foreigners in the following year, 1631 ('at a ruble
and four grivens, and even at one-and-a-half rubles') from which this
difference is deduced: if grain had been sold to the Swedes in 1628–1630
at the price at which it was sold to other foreigners in 1631, 'there would
have been taken from them for the great sovereign, over and above the
price at which they bought this grain, a profit amounting to at least more
than 150,000 rubles, apart from customs duties'.

It remains for us only to pursue, using this not wholly exact procedure,
the calculation of the nominal subsidy ('concession') during the first three
years. We can, however, distinguish the differences in price, to some
extent, for that period. There is no doubt that in 1628 the purchase price
was lowest, since already in 1629 the Swedish envoys asked the Tsar to
forbid the population to demand more for a quarter of grain than 'the
market price had been' during the previous year – which request the Tsar
had to refuse, because in his state, 'from the beginning, no compulsory
prices had been laid down and to do so would be impossible'.[151] In a letter
of 1630 Gustavus Adolphus complained that in the previous year, 1629,
the purchasing of grain had gone well in Totma, Ustyug and other places,
but in Archangel, through the fault of the governor, who had allowed
competitors to enter the market, the price of grain had been inflated: a
quarter 'cost six altyns, and later stood at four grivens', the latter being
referred to, with indignation, as 'a great price'.[152] We shall therefore be
overstating rather than understating the actual prices if we put them, for
1628, as averaging about six altyns, in 1629 about ten, and in 1630 about
14 per quarter. As regards the 'conceded' customs duties, an 'extract' of
1634 gives for them an approximate and rounded up figure, for 1631–1633,
of 17 per cent (with selling price at 187,222 rubles, 'more than 30,000
rubles' would have been taken in customs duties). But Rodes's table[153]
provides the more exact figure of 17.5 per cent, made up of 12 per cent for
road and shipping charges at Archangel, 5 per cent for the 'great duty'
and 0.5 per cent for 'loading' at Kholmogory.

We have established what grain prices were on the Amsterdam
exchange mainly from the works of V. Naudé and V. Kordt. Out of
caution, however, for the period of the highest price, the autumn of
1630, we have reduced the price of rye from 462 to 400 and the price of
wheat from 612 to 500 gold gulden per last, taking into account the fact
that the entire mass of grain might not have been sold at the highest

[150] An altyn was worth six dengi, a ruble 200 dengi, or 100 kopecks, or ten grivny or two poltiny.
[151] *TsGADA, Dela shvedskie*, 1629, *stb.* 2, *l.* 288.
[152] *TsGADA, Dela shvedskie*, 1630, *stb.* 2, *l.* 141.
[153] 'Sostoianie Rossii v 1650–1655gg. po doneseniiam Rodesa', pp. 175–177.

price. The missing prices for 1632 and 1633 have been projected approximately on the basis of indirect data and tend to be understated. Prices of millet have been conventionally aligned with wheat prices. The cost of freight from Archangel to Holland has been taken to be four rubles per measure, since Rodes shows the cost of this freight for private cargoes as five rubles per last,[154] but for the Swedish government, contracting with the Dutch for entire shiploads, it must have been considerably less. We have equated a last in every case to be 19 quarters, as Burg and Veltdriel say that a last contained '19 or 20 Muscovite quarters', but they themselves, in practical calculations of prices, in five cases out of six take a last as equal to 19 quarters, and in only one case, for a rounded-up calculation without commercial significance, do they take 100,000 quarters as equalling 5,000 lasts.[155] Finally, the Amsterdam prices, expressed in gold guldens, have been translated into reichsthalers, and reichsthalers into rubles and *vice versa*, in the following proportions: one ruble equals two reichsthalers, or five silver guldens (florins), or 3.5 gold guldens. These proportions (which refer, of course, to units of account, not to actual coins, the relations between which, in weight, fluctuated round this nominal standard) have been derived from all the evidence given by contemporaries[156] and can be checked very precisely by translating them into French currency units in accordance with the excellent commercial dictionary for the seventeenth and eighteenth centuries compiled by Savary.[157]

The results of our calculations are shown in Table 1.1. Of course, despite all our endeavours to achieve accuracy, this table can only be roughly indicative, but, nevertheless, it does give an idea of what sort of figures are involved. The results obtained need correction in both directions, for overstating and understating. Above all, we need to take account of Cronholm's statement that Russian grain was sold in Holland at a lower price, so that what was received for it was reduced by as much as 16 thalers per last in comparison with the asking price – a statement which, to be sure, somewhat contradicts Cronholm's own words when he says that Gustavus Adolphus's agents freely granted loans in Stralsund and Lübeck on the mere notification that the Russian grain had been

[154] Ibid., p. 178.

[155] Report by A. Burg and J. van Veltdriel . . ., pp. 64–65, 126, 130, 133, 159. In his commentary on *Sochinenie Kil'burgera o russkoi torgovle*, Kiev, 1915, p. 380, B. G. Kurtz mistakenly alleges that Burg and Veltdriel assumed a last to be equal to 20 quarters practically everywhere. In 1711 (by the Julian calendar) a last of rye was equivalent to 16 quarters. (*Chteniia v Obshchestve istorii*, Book III, 1899, p. 316). In 1784, according to a commercial handbook (Ricard, S., *Handbuch der Kaufleute*, Vol. II, Greifswald, 1784, pp. 381, 393), a last meant 15 quarters.     [156] Cf. Kurtz, *Sochinenie*, p. 404.

[157] Savary, J., *Dictionnaire universel de commerce*, Vol. II, Paris, 1732, pp. 296, 568, 770, 1401, 1423, 1564, 1607.

Table 1.1. *Dimensions of Russia's grain subsidies to Sweden in 1628–1633*

| | 1628 | 1629 | 1630 | 1631 | 1632 | 1633 | Total |
|---|---|---|---|---|---|---|---|
| Permitted to be bought for the King of Sweden | 36,000 quarters | 50,000 quarters | 75,000 quarters of rye and 8,000 of millet | 50,000 quarters of rye and 1,469.5 of millet | 50,000 quarters of rye and 3,650 of millet | 50,000 quarters of rye and 2,880.5 of millet | 327,000 quarters[a] |
| Bought for the King of Sweden | 20,929 quarters (1,101.5 lasts) | 23,348.5 quarters (1,228.9 lasts) | 119,252.75 quarters[b] (6,277 lasts) | 61,469 quarters (3,235.2 lasts) | 54,423 quarters (2,864.4 lasts) | 52,880.5 quarters (2,783.2 lasts) | 332,302.75 quarters[c] (17,490 lasts) |
| At price (per quarter) | about 6 altyns | about 10 altyns | Rye: about 14 altyns. Millet: about 30 altyns | Rye: 25 altyns, 2 dengi. Millet: 1 ruble, 28 altyns, 2 dengi | Rye: 16 altyns, 4 dengi. Millet: 1 ruble, 28 altyns, 2 dengi | Rye: 16 altyns, 4 dengi. Millet: 1 ruble, 28 altyns, 2 dengi | – |
| Total amount | 3,767 rubles, 7 altyns, 2 dengi (7,534.5 reichsthalers/ yefimki) | 7,004 rubles, 18 altyns, 2 dengi (14,009 reichsthalers) | 53,926 rubles, 5 altyns, 1 dengi (107,852.5 reichsthalers) | 48,318 rubles, 6 altyns, 3 dengi (93,636.5 reichsthalers) | 32,139 rubles, (64,278 reichsthalers) | 30,328 rubles, 5 altyns, 5 dengi (60,658 reichsthalers) | 175,484 rubles, 1 altyn, 3 dengi (350,966 reichsthalers) |
| Selling price for other foreigners (per quarter) | | | Rye: 1 ruble, 13 altyns, 2 dengi Millet: 2 rubles | | Rye: 31 altyns, 4 dengi. Millet: 2 rubles | Rye: 28 altyns, 2 dengi. Millet: 2 rubles | – |
| Could have been received if sold at that price | 233,637 rubles, 11 altyns, 4 dengi | | | 86,943 rubles, 10 altyns | 55,534 rubles, 11 altyns, 4 dengi | 44,261 rubles | 420,376 rubles[d] |
| Could have been received in customs duties | 40,886 rubles, 18 altyns, 3 dengi | | | 15,215 rubles, 2 altyns, 3 dengi | 9,718 rubles, 17 altyns | 7,745 rubles, 22 altyns, 3 dengi | 73,566 rubles |
| Total dimension of the 'concession' to the King of Sweden | 209,825 rubles, 33 altyns (419,652 reichsthalers) | | | 53,840 rubles, 6 altyns (107,680 reichsthalers) | 33,113 rubles, 28 altyns, 4 dengi (66,227.5 reichsthalers) | 21,677 rubles, 25 altyns (43,355.5 reichsthalers) | 318,458 rubles (636,916 reichsthalers) |

| Price on the Amsterdam grain exchange in gold gulden (per last) | Rye: 250 Wheat: 280 | Rye: 300 | Rye: 400 Wheat: 500 | Rye: 300 Wheat: about 370 | Rye: about 200 Wheat: about 250 | Rye: about 150 Wheat: about 185 | — |
|---|---|---|---|---|---|---|---|
| Gross gain from sale of grain in Holland (in gold gulden) | 275,375 (154,210 reichsthalers) | 368,670 (206,455 reichsthalers) | 2,552,685 (1,429,504 reichsthalers) | 975,986 (546,552 reichsthalers) | 582,485 (326,192 reichsthalers) | 422,786 (236,762 reichsthalers) | 5,177,987 (2,899,675 reichsthalers) |
| Cost of freight (in reichsthalers) | 8,812 | 9,831 | 50,216 | 25,881 | 22,915 | 22,265 | 139,920 |
| Net profit from resale (in reichsthalers) | 137,864 | 182,615 | 1,271,436 | 424,035 | 238,999 | 153,839 | 2,408,788 |

*Notes:*

[a] This figure we also found in a document attached to roll 2 of 1634, p. 31: 'altogether, stocks of grain bought for their sovereigns King Gustavus Adolphus and his daughter, Queen Christina, from 136 [1625] to 142 [1631], 327,000 quarters.'

[b] This figure is the sum of the 47,722.50 quarters 'underbought' in 1628 and 1629 ('and this grain was in 141 [1630] entirely bought up') and the 71,530.25 quarters bought 'according to the figure of the new grant', i.e., the amount authorised to be bought in 1630, which was 83,000 quarters. The 'underbought' 11,469.75 quarters were bought up in the following year, 1631.

[c] This figure differs slightly from the total given in the memorandum of 1634, which is 337,807 quarters, as the latter takes account of 3,500 quarters sold in 1630, privately, to the Swedish ambassador Monier, along with another few hundred quarters. From the total permissions granted over the six years, the total actually purchased differs principally because in 1629 the Swedes obtained the right to buy 6,000 quarters extra, on the grounds that they had been given 'short measure' in the previous year, but the official documents clearly reject this pretext and do not deduct these 6,000 quarters from the amount bought in 1628.

[d] The differences between this sum and the sum for which the grain was actually sold thus amount to 244,093 rubles. This result is very close to the totals shown in the Muscovite officials' accounts. For 1628–1630, these accounts state, if the Swedish King's stewards had been charged as much as the foreigners were charged, 'there would have been taken' from them, in excess of what they actually paid, 'more than 150,000 rubles, apart from customs-duties' (1634, roll 2, p. 305) and for 1631–1633 this difference, again excluding customs duties, is calculated by them (p. 315) at 81,627 rubles, 26 altyns, 2.5 dengi (our figure is 74,952 rubles, 22 altyns, 4 dengi) which together (150,000 + 81,000) comes to over 230,000 rubles.

dispatched.[158] If, though, we accept the corresponding correction to our calculations, another correction serves to counterbalance it. We have not taken account of the Swedish treasury's profit from saltpetre and resin, supplied at what it cost the Russian treasury, nor have we taken account of the fact that the total purchases made in 1628 and 1629 included not rye alone but also a considerable amount of other products – linseed, buckwheat, barley, millet – the re-sale of which brought an incomparably higher level of profit than was the case with rye. Finally, we have not taken account of the 'leakage' of these more profitable products, in later years as well, into the general group headed 'rye'. Furthermore, in order to determine the actual revenue received by the Swedish treasury, we should have subtracted from our results that extremely big share which stuck to the hands of the factors, stewards and office-workers. But to this correction, in its turn, there is a no less substantial counterbalancing one. As we were able to observe in the letter of Hoppe, the *Burggraf* of Elbing, the Swedish treasury gained not only from the difference in grain prices, but also from the fact that in Russia it paid, if only partly, in copper money, whereas in Holland it was paid in silver.[159]

In Sweden one silver reichsthaler was equivalent, roughly, to 2.5 copper reichsthalers,[160] and the whole of this huge difference went to the treasury. Later, Sweden paid for the Russian grain partly in silver yefimki, but mainly in state-owned goods – copper plates, armour, cavalrymen's spiked helmets – for which it fixed a monopoly price,[161] though the cost of production was extremely low, so that the profit made on them was considerably increased.

Thus, we can provisionally assume that all our corrections more or less cancel each other out and that consequently our table does give an approximately true picture. In support of the assumption we can adduce one more piece of evidence: our results coincide fairly closely with the calculations made by the Swedish government itself in 1634. The instructions found by Forsten, which were given on 6 March 1634 to the envoys Scheiding, Fleming and Gyllenstjern who were being sent to Russia require them to ask the Tsar to help Sweden every year to the tune of 150,000 rubles (300,000 yefimki), for the war in Germany which was

---

[158] Cronholm, *Gustaf*, pp. 138–140. Cronholm's statement is refuted, it would seem, by the testimony of the Swedish resident agent in Moscow, Möller, that the Dutch received from Danzig only undried grain, 'and without the grain from Muscovy and Sweden they cannot exist, for they mix this kiln-dried and dry grain with the undried grain' (*TsGADA, Dela shvedskie*, 1631, *stb*. 8, *ll*. 103, 104).

[159] See, e.g., the report of Vnukov, government clerk at Vologda, on the course of the Swedish purchasing expedition in 1629 (*TsGADA, Dela shvedskie*, 1629, *stb*. 2, *ll*. 524, 525).

[160] Berendts, *Gosudarstvennoe khoziaistvo*, p. 254.

[161] *TsGADA, Dela shvedskie*, 1634, *stb*. 2, *ll*. 308–312.

indirectly important for Muscovy, but allow them to request, instead of aid in money, confirmation of Sweden's right to purchase grain as before.[162] The Swedes' desire to transform the Russian subsidies into money is easily understood: grain prices in the West had fallen. But what is more important is that even then the amount of the annual aid they received in Russian grain was estimated by the Swedes at 300,000 reichsthalers, that is, twice as much as our total for 1633, even though, of course, this was lower than our average annual total for the entire period of six years – 400,000 reichsthalers per annum.

The average annual totals given by our calculations are eloquent enough. The Muscovite state was waging a covert war against the Empire by providing Sweden with, on the average, a nominal subsidy of about 100,000 reichsthalers annually which was actually worth about 400,000, that is, not less than what was given to Sweden by France during that country's covert participation in the Thirty Years' War. Still more eloquent, however, than the average figures is the way this aid was distributed over the years. Half of the total amount of the six years' aid was actually concentrated in the one year 1630. The Swedish treasury received about 1,200,000 reichsthalers of real subsidy in that year, before the Franco–Swedish military pact (1631) and the French subsidies. It immediately becomes apparent why it was in 1630 that Gustavus Adolphus decided to begin his war with the German Emperor and why hope-intoxicated Oxenstjerna thought, at the beginning of 1631, that if things continued like this, Sweden could look forward to the brightest of prospects. It is understandable, too, that the reduction in the real amount of the Russian subsidies in the following years was bound to have a certain influence on Swedish policy, while their complete cessation in 1634 meant a serious blow for Sweden.

Let us ask, in conclusion, whether it was easy for Muscovy to grant these subsidies. Given the absence of precise data for Russia's state budget in these years we cannot compare the amount of the nominal subsidies with the total amount of the state's revenue.[163] It is only beyond doubt that for the Russian economy, which was at that time not at all adapted to the role of Europe's breadbasket, intensified purchase of grain constituted a heavy burden. Grain prices on the domestic market rose sharply in these six years, cost-price amounted at Archangel, as we have seen, to not more than 35–36 dengi in 1628, but in 1631 was already 152

---

[162] Forsten, *Baltiiskii vopros*, Vol. II, pp. 440–441.

[163] If, hypothetically, we take the size of Russia's state budget in the 1630s as being about one million rubles (cf. Miliukov, P., *Gosudarstvennoe khoziaistvo Rossii v pervoi chetverti XVII stoletii*, 2nd edition, St Petersburg, 1905, p. 74 *et seq.*), the nominal subsidies (100,000 yefimki per annum) amounted to approximately one twentieth of the state's expenditure.

dengi and in 1632 not less than 100 dengi a quarter. Thus, the burden of the subsidies to Sweden fell on the shoulders, mainly, of the urban population of Muscovy, for it was they who bought grain on the domestic market and they who paid with their incomes for the rise in the price of grain. If purchasing of grain for sending 'overseas' had not stopped in 1632, a wave of urban disorders and revolts would undoubtedly have arisen in Muscovy in the 1630s. Here was the first flash of lightning. On 18 June 1630 the 'stewards' of the Swedish King, Desmoulins and Ul'ianov, complained to the Tsar about the people of Archangel:

When we had loaded the stock of grain purchased for the King on to our vessels on 7 June, Dementii's men [Dementii Pogozhev was the governor of Archangel – Author] came in force, in great numbers, to the King's ships and began to beat the workmen and drive them off the ships, and, having seized and tied them up, flogged them and mortally wounded them and dragged them by force to the unloading office, we do not know why, where they robbed these workmen of ours of their money, and they want to kill us, and say . . . 'we have a hundred and fifty stout fellows here and can slaughter you foreigners'.[164]

Here we see in miniature what was to happen on a larger scale twenty years later. In 1650 Muscovy again gave permission to Sweden to export Russian grain, this time via the Baltic, and this brought about major revolts directed against the foreigners, and the Tsar's administrators along with them, in Novgorod and Pskov.

Let us sum up. Under the conditions of the Thirty Years' War, being a war fought with armies of mercenaries, the fighting potential of both the belligerent coalitions was determined to a very large extent by their ability to mobilise the largest possible quantities of cash. True, a certain role was played by the existence of a convenient, accessible market for recruiting soldiers and buying arms, and by the availability of military strategic materials (especially saltpetre). But the leading role belonged to cash. Governments could mobilise this if they resorted to credit, or by increasing the burden of taxation, or finally, by speculation on the international market. The latter method was especially possible owing to the differences in price-levels engendered by the uneven progress of the 'price revolution' in different parts of Europe. Under these conditions Muscovy, whose government was wedded to a broad coalitionist point of view in foreign policy, was able to render extremely substantial material assistance to the Swedes in their costly war. We can understand why in 1631 Gustavus Adolphus managed to deploy large-scale forces in Germany.

[164] *TsGADA, Dela shvedskie*, 1630, *stb.* 7, *l.* 1.

## 2   Gustavus Adolphus and the preparation for the Smolensk War

In the history of the Thirty Years' War the 'Swedish period' (1630–1635) has perhaps received more attention than any other, and yet it is this period which, in certain of its aspects, has remained most mysterious to historians. Many of the major factors in the conduct of the Swedish army in Germany have not been fully explained by modern historiography. Why did the Swedish expeditionary force land in Germany not after the conclusion of the treaty of alliance between Sweden and France (January 1631) but more than six months earlier, when Sweden was still on its own? Why did Gustavus Adolphus, after having established his bridgehead in Pomerania in the summer of 1630, wait for a whole year before plunging into the heart of Germany? There are plenty of pointers indicating what his reasons were, but no satisfactory explanation why they suddenly and all at once ceased to apply in the summer of 1631. Further, what in the final analysis, accounts for the famous 'zigzag lightning' – the impetuous and mysterious return of Gustavus Adolphus with his army in October 1632 from South-Western Germany, into which he had burst as a triumphant victor, back to the north-east of the country? And, finally, what were the reasons for the sharp change in the relation of military forces in Germany in the autumn of 1634, which led to the Swedes' defeat at Nördlingen, their subsequent loss of most of their conquests and, along with them, the princes who had been their allies? In short, what caused this unexpected collapse of the Swedish intervention in 1634–1635, which must inevitably have culminated in complete triumph for the Empire and Catholic reaction if France had not saved the situation by entering the Thirty Years' War itself in 1635?

The first of these difficult questions, about the reasons why Sweden took action at a time when it seemed to be isolated, has been partly answered in the previous chapter. We explained that Muscovy granted Sweden in 1629–1630 a large subsidy for war against the Empire and at the same time provided the Swedes with a guarantee in the form of a war against the Polish–Lithuanian state, without which Gustavus Adolphus's invasion of Germany would have been quite out of the question. Let us now try to show that the other riddles of the 'Swedish period' of the Thirty Years' War can be satisfactorily explained if we pay attention to the state of affairs in Eastern Europe, and especially to the Russo–Polish conflict in these years.

The legitimacy of this way of seeing the matter becomes clear if we consider that the entire history of the Thirty Years' War, so far as its strategy was concerned, was based on one principle only, namely, that anyone who found a second opponent somewhere in his rear was almost certainly doomed to defeat. Fighting two wars at the same time would have meant, above all, committing all one's forces to each of these wars, for the mercenary armies of those days, which to us seem extremely small, cost so much that they required exertion of the full financial strength of the state. And when a war was being waged with only half of a state's forces, the enemy's army might prove to have numerical superiority at the decisive moment – that numerical superiority which, in the epoch of the Thirty Years' War, a war of mercenary professional soldiers, was the principal factor in victory. But the specific feature of the Thirty Years' War consisted, essentially, not in the fact that having two fronts was dangerous – that has been true all through the history of war – but in the fact that it was comparatively easy to bring about the opening of a second theatre of military operations. Just because the mercenary armies were small, armed with fairly simple weapons, and multi-national in composition, it was not difficult by means of subsidies and diplomacy to create a second front in an enemy's rear.

The wisdom of the politicians and diplomats of any country in the age of this first all-European war consisted of making alliances with the neighbours of their neighbours. Europe was like a chessboard. Each state warded off the danger of being trapped strategically by creating that same danger for every one of its neighbours. Habsburg Spain and the Habsburgs' 'Holy Roman Empire' (Germany) formed, together, a deadly trap for France. But Spain itself was caught in a trap between France on land and Holland on the sea, while the Empire was caught between France and Sweden. Sweden, in turn, was also trapped: the Truce of Altmark in 1629 did not mean peace with the Polish–Lithuanian state and did not do away with the acute hostility that existed between Gustavus Adolphus and Sigismund III. But, then, the Polish–Lithuanian state itself was likewise trapped – between Sweden and Muscovy.

We shall not continue this series any further. What is important here is to emphasise its unity. All the links in the chain were strongly made. In 1630–1634, there was none of the states mentioned that was not actually fighting on two fronts at once, even if one of its opponents was distracted by some other state, and in the case of France, from time to time, even both opponents were distracted, and it waged only 'covert' war. But we can see that it was enough for just one of the links to be affected for the whole system to be rearranged. If, for example, Muscovy or some other state should fail to distract the armed forces of the Rzeczpospolita the latter would become a real threat to Sweden, which would be obliged to face towards the Rzeczpospolita and then the forces of the Empire would be free to fight France, and if France's armies were occupied with war against the Empire, that would enable Spain to begin operations against France, even if only with that portion of its forces that was not tied down by the Dutch. In short, Europe would have to assume more or less the aspect which it did in fact assume after 1635, in the 'Franco–Swedish' period of the Thirty Years' War.

Few contemporaries, of course, were able to grasp mentally this entire complex system of states. But European opinion did nevertheless link closely the course of events in Germany with the course of the Russo–Polish war. Even persons without much experience in politics could not but ask themselves why, when the Emperor was engaged in a duel to the death with the Swedish King, a struggle that was shaking all of Germany, his long-time faithful ally the Polish King failed to come to the aid of the exhausted Emperor – and receive the reply that the Polish King was unable to come to his aid because he was himself threatened with war, and later was actually made war upon, by the Muscovite Tsar. Already in 1629 there flocked to the Rzeczpospolita and to Muscovy from all corners of Europe the leaders of *lansquenet* regiments, enterprising *condottieri*, to offer their services, having been attracted by rumours that the term of the truce would soon run out and war was inevitable between the Polish–Lithuanian state and Muscovy.[1] In 1632–1634 one could hardly have found a grown man in Germany who had not heard about that war. It was in the 1630s that merchants and all sorts of travellers, stimulated by the increased interest in Muscovy that prevailed at that time in Europe, made their way thither with special eagerness, and publishers satisfied a demand for the first serious books about Russia, books that were up to the then level of

---

[1] See, e.g., the correspondence on this question between the Muscovite government and the governor of Novgorod, Prince D. M. Pozharskii, in 1629 (*TsGADA, Dela shvedskie, stb.* 1, *ll.* 264, 397, 410, 439). One of these *condottieri*, named Fritt, who had served the Swedish and then the Danish King, against the Emperor, and after that had served the Emperor against the Danish King, wrote offering to supply the Tsar with any number of mercenary soldiers and officers of all ranks: 'We [meaning himself and the four other knights who came with him] know full well that the state of peace between His Majesty the Tsar and the Polish King will come soon to an end and consequently His Majesty the Tsar will need soldiers [from the German Empire], since the Polish King now has several thousand such soldiers standing ready' (ibid., *l.* 411). The pleas of many dozen *condottieri* like this who in 1629–1634 offered their services to Muscovy are mentioned by E. Stashevskii in his *Smolenskaia voina, 1632–1634. Organizatsiia i sostoianie moskovskoi armii*, Kiev, 1919, pp. 19–38, 69–71, *et seq.*

scientific investigation.[2] In the European, especially the German, press, which was quite abundant, and avid for rumours and sensations, sometimes crudely polemical,[3] both in newspapers proper and in the innumerable broadsheets, pamphlets and booklets, throughout the period of the Thirty Years' War and especially in the 1630s, it is not unusual to come upon mentions of Muscovy. Much was written in particular about Poland. In the earliest historiography of the 'Swedish period' of the Thirty Years' war, in the writings of contemporaries who produced the first surveys of the Swedish campaign in Germany, such as Burgus,[4] Abelinus[5] and others, reference is made as a matter of course to the situation in the Swedes' rear – to the position of the Rzeczpospolita and the worries about Poland, that troubled Gustavus Adolphus and his successors. Likewise the two first scholars who in the seventeenth century devoted a stout folio to the history of Sweden's war in Germany – Chemnitz,[6] who was then the official Swedish historiographer, and Pufendorf[7] – assigned numerous pages to Swedo–Polish, and in that connection also to Swedo–Russian and even Swedo–Crimean relations, although of course, they neither gave nor tried to find explanations for the true interconnections of the events they describe.

[2] For example, in 1630 an Elzevir book appeared in Leipzig entitled *Russia seu Moscovia. Commentario topographico atque politico illustratae. Lugdunum Batavorum.* This small volume (the second half of it was devoted to the Khanate of the Crimea) contained a detailed compendium of geographical, historical and political information about Russia.

[3] See Beller, E. A., *Propaganda in Germany during the Thirty Years' War*, Princeton, 1940; Schöne, W., *Die deutsche Zeitung des Siebzehnten Jahrhundert in Abbildungen*, Leipzig, 1940.

[4] Burgi, P. B., *gennensis*, *De bello suecico commentarii, quibus Gustavi Adolphi, suecorum regis, in Germaniam expeditio, usque ad ipsius mortem comprehenditur*, Leodii, 1633. See pp. 10, 12–14, 86, 134, 137. This work was reprinted as an Elzevir in 1643 (*editio nova*). A French translation appeared: Burge, P., *gennois. Commentaires des guerres de Suède qui contiennent tout ce qui est passé de plus remarquable depuis la descente de Gustave Adolphe, roy de Suède, en Allemagne, jusques à sa mort*, Paris, 1653.

[5] Arlanibaeus, Ph. (J. Ph. Abelinus). *Arma suecica, hoc est vera et accurata descriptio belli, quod Gustavus Adolphus, suecorum, gothorum et vandalorum etc. rex, contra Ferdinandi II romanorum imperatoris, etc., exersitum in Germania hactenus gessit . . .*, 1631, see pp. 3–4, 9–10, 15–16, 51–52, 162–163, etc. There was a sequel: *Armorum suecicorum continuatio, in qua breviter describuntur, omnia ea, quae a serenissimo et potentissima rege Sueciae Gustavo Adolpho, et aliis principibus, protestantibus confederatis post pugnam Lipsensem, in Imperio Romano memorati digna gesta sunt*, Francofurti, 1632. See p. 17 *et seq.* And a further sequel: *Armorum suecicorum continuatio ultima*, 1634. Later, Abelinus included all this material in the second volume of his huge history of Europe in the seventeenth century, *Theatrum Europaeum*, which covers the years 1629–1632. (Frankfurt-am-Main, 2nd edition, 1679). On Swedo–Polish relations see pp. 81–86, 108–110, 571–583, 733–738. For the years 1634–1635 see Vol. III of *Theatrum Europaeum*, 1644. On these first historians of the 'Swedish period' of the Thirty Years' War, see Droysen, G., *Arlanibaeus, Godofredus, Abelinus, sive Scriptorum de Gustavi Adolphi expeditione princeps*, Berolini, 1864.

[6] Chemnitz, B. Ph., *Königlichen-schwedischen in Teutschland geführten Krieges*, Vols. I and II (1630–1636), Stettin, 1648.

[7] Pufendorf, S., *Commentariorum de rebus Suecicis libri XXVI ab expeditione Gustavi Adolphi regis in Germaniam ad abdicationem usque Christinae*, Ultrajecti, 1686 (quoted, *infra*, from the 1705 edition).

In later historiography, however, all this 'Eastern' side of the 'Swedish' period of the Thirty Years' War somehow imperceptibly disappeared from view. This development was facilitated both by German historians who misrepresented the history of the Thirty Years' War with nationalistic legends and tore it from its position in world history and by Swedish historians who were subject to their influence. In particular, the two-volume publication of documents on Gustavus Adolphus's war in Germany[8] which appeared in Sweden in the middle of the nineteenth century, and which provided the foundation for the relevant sections of the most important biographies of Gustavus Adolphus, by Droysen,[9] Cronholm[10] and, later, Fletcher[11] and others, directed historians' attention in a quite one-sided way towards the internal German setting of the Swedish campaign. The East-European situation, which actually had an important influence on the entire outcome of that campaign, was also passed over in almost complete silence in general works on the history of the Thirty Years' War which were written in the nineteenth century – e.g., by Gindely, Charvériat, Gardiner, Winter, Klopp and Ritter[12] – and in the twentieth century, culminating in Wedgwood's short book.[13]

The gap in this one-sided historiography of the 'Swedish period' of the Thirty Years' War was to some extent filled by the publication in 1901 of a special monograph by the Swedish historian Carl Wejle, on Sweden's policy towards Poland in 1630–1635.[14] Wejle researched thoroughly in the materials contained in Sweden's public records, particularly in the sections *Polonica*, *Muscovitica* and *Turcica* and in the correspondence of the Chancellor Oxenstjerna. Wejle's conclusions are in many ways dubious and inadequate, but it is, nevertheless, regrettable that this fundamental work had little influence on later writers, including

[8]  *Arkiv till upplysning om svenska krigens och krigsinzättingarnes historia. Tidskiftet 1630–1632*, Vols. I–II, Stockholm, 1854–1860.

[9]  Droysen, G., *Gustav Adolf in Deutschland*, Vol. I, Leipzig, 1869–1870.

[10]  Cronholm, A., *Sveriges historia under Gustav II Adolphus regering*, Vols. 1–6, Stockholm, 1857–1872: German translation, *Gustav II Adolf in Deutschland*, Vol. I, Leipzig, 1875.

[11]  Fletcher, C. R. L., *Gustavus Adolphus and the Struggle of Protestantism for Existence*, New York, 1890.

[12]  Gindely, A., *Geschichte des Dreissigjährigen Krieges*, Vols. 1–4, Prague, 1869–1882: Charvériat, E., *Histoire de la Guerre de Trente Ans*, Paris, 1878; Gardiner, S. R., *The Thirty Years' War 1618–1648*, London, 1874; Winter, G., *Geschichte des Dreissigjährigen Krieges*, Berlin, 1893; Klopp. O., *Der Dreissigjährige Krieg bis zum Tode Gustav Adolfs*, Vols. 1–3, Paderborn, 1891–1896; Ritter, M., *Deutsche Geschichte in Zeitalter der Gegenreformation und des Dreissigjährigen Krieges, 1555–1648*, Vols. 1–3, Stuttgart, 1889–1908.

[13]  Wedgwood, C. V., *The Thirty Years' War*, New Haven, 1939 [London, 1938: Penguin edition, 1957. – Trans.].

[14]  Wejle, C., *Sveriges politik mot Polen 1630–1635*, Uppsala, 1901. An important supplement to Wejle's research is a work which, though small, is entirely based on archive documents: Rettig, H., *Die Stellung der Regierung und des Reichstages Schwedens zur polnischen Frage, April 1634 bis November 1635*, 1916.

even Swedish ones. The book is, perhaps, best known to Polish historians.[15] However, in the eight-volume collective work on the wars of Gustavus Adolphus which was published by the Swedish General Staff and which constitutes an exemplary compendium of everything known to history about these wars,[16] the international context of the beginning of Gustavus Adolphus's German campaign is dealt with in a special chapter, the fourth in Volume V, in this way: first, the relations between Sweden and the German states; then, in some detail, Sweden's relations with Poland, Russia and Transylvania; and, finally, with France, Holland, Denmark and England. Sweden's relations with the Rzeczpospolita and Russia are described essentially as in Wejle's book. But Russo–Swedish relations in those years have been clarified by Wejle and his successors only to a limited degree, and reconstruction of the East-European international situation in the 'Swedish' period of the Thirty Years' War remains, in our view, still incomplete until *Russo–Swedish* relations are made the centre of our attention and until, besides the Swedish and Polish archives, the Russian archives have been drawn upon, especially the files of the 'Swedish section' of the Embassies Department.[17] It is precisely these documents, that is, the unpublished

---

[15] See, e. g., Czaplinski, W., *Wladyslaw IV wobec wojny 30-letniej*, Cracow, 1937 (*Polska Akademia Umietjetnosci. Rosprawy wydzialu historyczno-filosoficznego*, Series 2, Vol. 45, No. 3). Polish historians have to some extent clarified, from their angle, the history of Polono–Swedish relations in the 1630s. See, e. g., Szelagowski, A., 'Uklady Krolewicza Wladyslawa i dysydentow z Gustawem Adolfem w r. 1632', *Kwartalnik Historyczny*, Vol. 4, 1899; Krajewski, *Wladyslaw IV a korona szwedska* (*Bibl. Warszawa*, Vol 3, 1913); Godziszewski, W., *Polska i Moskwa za Wladyslawa IV*, Cracow, 1930.

[16] Sveriges Generalstaben, *Sveriges Krig 1611–1632*, Vols. I–VI, Supplementary vols I–II, Stockholm, 1936–1939.

[17] In G. Forsten's book *Baltiiskii vopros v XVI–XVII stoletiiakh*, Vol. II (St Petersburg, 1894), Russo–Swedish relations are described on the basis of material from the Stockholm archives only, without any use being made of the records of the Embassies Department in Moscow. K. I. Iakubov, in his *Rossiia i Shvetsiia v pervoi polovine XVII veka* (Moscow, 1897), used both the Stockholm and the Moscow archives, but the title of this book misleads the reader. The diplomatic and political relations between Russia and Sweden are hardly touched upon, and what is dealt with mainly is the question of the population of the borderlands and some other special subjects. N. V. Golitsyn's work, *K istorii russko-shvedskikh otnoshenii i naseleniia pogranichnykh s Shvetsiei oblastei (1634–1638)* (Moscow, 1903), merely publishes some documents of secondary interest from the Livonian archives. Finally in the appendix to E. Stashevskii's book *Ocherki po istorii tsarstvovaniia Mikhaila Fedorovicha*, Part I (Kiev, 1913), some really important diplomatic documents were published, but the principle on which they were selected is incomprehensible and no explanation is given. In the preface to another of his books, *Smolenskaia voina 1632–1534. Organizatsiia i sostoianie moskovskoi armii* (Kiev, 1919), Stashevskii says that he devoted a special instalment of his work to the reasons for the diplomatic preparation of the war for Smolensk, but this instalment never got into print. Some documents from the collection of Swedish files in the Embassies Department for the 1620s and 1630s were published in *Sobranie gosudarstvennykh gramot i dogovorov* and other publications of early texts, but they were so few in number that, generally speaking, one can regard this extensive and very rich collection of records as having remained

rolls in the Swedish and other files of the Embassies Department, that we have made the basis of what follows in the present work.

Are we not biased in attributing such great importance to Russia, specifically? The answer to that depends on how one estimates the importance of Poland and the Polish problem in Gustavus Adolphus's policy. Was Poland, in his eyes, a seriously dangerous enemy, when he invaded Germany? There can be only one answer: yes, it was. Let us recall that a struggle with the Rzeczpospolita had constituted the principal theme in the entire preceding period of Gustavus Adolphus's reign, dragging on, with varying success, over many years. Until 1628, inclusive, Gustavus Adolphus still remained convinced that the Polish–Lithuanian state was weak and that he would be able, after defeating it, to transform this country into a bridgehead for war against the Empire. But the Emperor's military assistance given to the Polish–Lithuanian state led in 1629 to a radical change of plan. In the words of the historian Bornhaupt, 'the war with Poland had to develop into war with the Emperor'.[18] Gustavus Adolphus was now convinced that victory over Poland could not be attained before victory over the Empire. This was why he concluded, in 1629, the truce of Altmark with the Rzeczpospolita, though this truce was highly unsatisfactory from his standpoint, and why in 1630 he occupied a different bridgehead for his war in Germany – in Pomerania and not, as he had previously intended, in Poland. After a war that had gone on for many years, Poland remained unbroken. How could Gustavus Adolphus not fear Poland now that he was taking on another war? As the authors of the fundamental work on Gustavus Adolphus's wars mentioned above correctly observe, 'since Sweden's forces were going to be tied up in Germany, the country's foreign policy must be guided by the need to neutralise Poland, on their eastern flank'.[19] If this proposition is correct, all that remains to decide is whether Swedo–Russian relations were central to the realisation of the given programme in foreign policy.

At first glance it seems that this was not at all the case. The Swedish historian Nils Ahnlund, author of a biography of Gustavus Adolphus, after correctly stating that for Gustavus Adolphus the 'arch-enemy' was still Sigismund III; that consequently, seeing Russia as 'a political factor of some weight', he sought to invite the Tsar to engage in a joint offensive against the Rzeczpospolita; and that, just because of the orientation of Muscovite policy towards a break with Poland, Russo–

almost wholly unpublished and little utilised by researchers.

[18] Bornhaupt, C. von, *Gustav-Adolf vor seinem Auftreten in Deutschland*, in *Velhagen und Klasings Monatshefte*, Vol. II, Berlin, 1894–1895, pp. 71–73.
[19] *Sveriges Krig 1611–1632*, Vol. V, Stockholm, 1938, p. 227.

Swedish relations 'grew steadily more friendly towards the end of the reign and were even cordial', nevertheless finds it necessary to make this reservation: 'These schemes, however, took a relatively subordinate place in [Gustavus Adolphus's] active and enterprising statesmanship: they remind us of his tentative attempts at collaboration with the Turks and Tatars, with which, indeed, they were often connected.'[20]

Wejle's view is the same. He puts on the same level all the measures taken by Gustavus Adolphus to safeguard Sweden against the Polish danger during his war with the German Emperor – his secret anti-Polish negotiations in 1628–1629 with the ruler of Transylvania, Bethlen Gábor, through a special envoy, Paul Strassburg, and various couriers; his intrigue in Constantinople in 1630 through the same Strassburg, and the Dutch ambassador Cornelius Haag, and other persons, with a view to deterring Poland by means of a Swedo–Turkish alliance; his exchange of embassies with the Crimean Khan in 1629–1632, with the intention of diverting the Crimean Tatars either against the German Emperor or against the King of Poland; his attempts in 1630–1631 to break the Zaporozhian Cossacks away from the Rzeczpospolita and raise them up against the Catholic King of Poland; and finally his animated anti-Polish dealings with Russia.[21] To these plans for creating an external threat to the Polish–Lithuanian state Wejle adds also Gustavus Adolphus's project to render the Rzeczpospolita incapable of external action by kindling domestic, religious and political strife within that country. But can one really consider all these plans to have been equally significant? No, because only one of them came to fruition: war between Russia and Poland. All the others remained at the stage of 'soundings'. Transylvania did not attack Poland. Turkey, absorbed with war against Persia, was unable to threaten Poland, even made peace with Poland in 1631, and only in 1633–1634 carried out some insignificant diversions. The Crimean Tatars, too, failed to fall either on the Empire or the Rzeczpospolita: on the contrary, they acted together with the latter against Russia. The Zaporozhian Cossacks did not respond to Sweden's appeals. Religious and political strife inside the Polish–Lithuanian state not only did not flare up, but, on the contrary, quite died down when (in 1632) Wladyslaw IV was elected King. Consequently, if we wish to study not unsuccessful schemes but historical realities, not the subjective plans of statesmen but the objective relations between peoples, we must put in the forefront the importance

---

[20] Ahnlund, N., *Gustav Adolf den Store*, Stockholm, 1932. There is a German translation, *Gustav Adolf*, Berlin, 1938, pp. 315–316, and here and *infra* our quotations are taken from this. [Quotations here given from Michael Roberts's translation – *Gustav Adolf the Great*, 1940, pp. 233–234 – Trans.]    [21] Wejle, *Sveriges politik*, pp. 8–14.

of the Russo–Polish 'Smolensk War' in 1632–1634 for the history of the Swedish campaign in Germany.

When, in the spring of 1630, Gustavus Adolphus at last decided to launch his invasion of Germany he already knew of the death (in November 1629) of his brother-in-law Bethlen Gábor, and consequently of the collapse of the entire diplomatic structure which Paul Strassburg had erected with such labour and skill.[22] In Constantinople he was assured of co-operation from the Grand Vizier at the Court of Sultan Murad IV, and from the Patriarch Cyril Lucaris, but he received no actual promises of Turkish military action against Poland. When the Crimean Khan's ambassador Haydar Bey came, via Moscow, to Stockholm in October 1629, though he brought the Khan's agreement to a treaty of mutual assistance against the German Emperor, he promised nothing definite.[23]

On the other hand, Gustavus Adolphus had, in the spring of 1630, official confirmation of Tsar Mikhail Fedorovich's promise to begin war against the Rzeczpospolita in the near future.[24] This news was brought to Stockholm from Moscow at the beginning of April by the Swedish ambassador Anton Monier. He had been instructed to speak to the Tsar about a joint onslaught on the Catholics, by Russia on the Polish–Lithuanian state and by Sweden on the Emperor, in the event either that the Emperor helped the Poles or the Poles 'secretly' helped the Emperor, since Sweden and Russia willy-nilly had need of each other. As Wejle puts it, Monier received 'a reply that coincided completely with the ideas

[22] The dispatches of Strassburg and of another secret plenipotentiary of Sweden, Farensbach, were published, from the originals in the Stockholm archives, in a book by a Hungarian historian: Szilagyi, S., *Bethlen Gábor és a sved diplomáczia*, Budapest, 1882, pp. 53–75. Cf. Wibling, C., *Sveriges förhållende till Siebenburgen 1623–1648*, Lund, 1890, chapter I, 'Gustav II Adolf och Bethlen Gábor', pp. 1–37. Cf. also a communication received by the Embassies Department in Moscow in 1629: 'The Swedish King has sent the nobleman Farensbach, through Holland, France and Hungary, to Bethlen Gábor, to persuade Bethlen Gábor to make war on Poland.' (*TsGADA, Dela shvedskie*, 1623, *stb.* 2, *l.* 72.) After Bethlen Gábor's death all these plans connected with Transylvania fell into the background, and instead, as the authors of *Sveriges Krig* say, 'the greatest threat of encirclement of Poland came from Russia', and Russia thenceforward held first place in Gustavus Adolphus's anti-Polish projects (*Sveriges Krig 1611–1632*, Vol. V, p. 223).

[23] *TsGADA, Dela shvedskie*, 1629, *stb.* 4 (journey of the Crimean embassy of Sweden); 1630, *stb.* 4 (journey of the embassy from Sweden through Moscow in May).

[24] The promise had been given already in the spring of 1629 (see *supra*, p. 31) but in February 1630 Ambassador Monier said in Moscow that, until then, Gustavus Adolphus 'had not known' whether the Tsar had 'decided in his mind' that this war was necessary, while at the same time the Polish King was preparing for it. The reply stated that 'His Majesty the Tsar is firmly resolved' and is preparing immediately to take revenge 'on the Polish King and the entire Rzeczpospolita' for the injuries they have done to him, and to foil their evil plan, without waiting for the truce of Deulino to expire, since 'of what use is the truce when the Polish King has not kept his word'.

of Gustavus Adolphus'.[25] The King apparently assured himself, by other than diplomatic means as well, of the seriousness of Muscovy's decision to go to war with the Rzeczpospolita. As early as the end of 1629 he sent Alexander Leslie to Russia on a mission to obtain military information.[26] Having arrived in Moscow on 22 January 1630 (a fortnight earlier than ambassador Monier), Leslie offered his services to the Tsar, familiarised himself with the state of Russia's army and war plans, submitted his first proposals for reorganising the Russian regiments on the Swedish model[27] and, we may suppose, returned to Gustavus Adolphus in good time, in March.

In one way or another, by March/April 1630 Gustavus Adolphus knew that Muscovy was going to fight Poland. That immediately brightened the political horizon for him. Signing the truce of Altmark with Poland in September 1629, when he was not quite sure of Russia's position, he agreed to the inclusion in the treaty of a special Article 20 which provided for the beginning of peace negotiations between Sweden and the Polish–Lithuanian state during the period of the truce, through mediation by the Elector of Brandenburg. In other words, he accepted the idea that, in order to fight against the Emperor in Germany, he might have to agree to any peace at all that could be got with Sigismund III, even to the point of admitting the latter's right to the Crown of

[25] Wejle, *Sveriges politik*, p. 8. Actually Monier declared before the boyars, for example, that 'if your sovereign [Mikhail Fedorovich] does not begin war with the Polish King, then our sovereign [Gustavus Adolphus] will find it hard to stand against the Kaiser, because the Kaiser is helped by the King of Spain, the Pope and the King of Poland'. The boyars, in return, urged the Swedish King 'to understand and take firmly to mind' that unless the Polish King was forced to fight the Tsar it would be 'impossible to make him break with the Kaiser or refrain from helping him'. (*TsGADA, Dela shvedskie*, 1630, *stb.* 2, *ll.* 204, 244).

[26] Leslie's mission was prepared for by the transfer in 1629 of a group of officers from the Swedish army to the Russian. The Russian government would not accept them unless they had orders from the Swedish government. Among them there came in June Leslie's nephew Jacob Wemyss, who announced that his uncle would soon arrive, on his return from an embassy to England (*TsGADA, Dela shvedskie*, 1629, *stb.* 1, *ll.* 266, 397 *et seq.*). All this business began with Leslie handing to a Russian merchant named Glazkov, in Stockholm, a letter addressed to Mikhail Fedorovich asking the Tsar to obtain from Gustavus Adolphus leave for him to enter the Russian service. The Tsar wrote to Gustavus Adolphus accordingly, and only then did the King send Leslie to Russia with complimentary letters of recommendation. Colonel Leslie arrived accompanied not only by six servants but also by a whole staff: two captains, three lieutenants, an ensign, a clerk and a 'master-gunner', namely, the artillery engineer Julius Coyet, who was to apply himself energetically to organising the production of cannon in Russia. The Tsar received Leslie as soon as he arrived in Moscow and gave him generous presents (see Tsvetaev, D., *Protestantsvo i protestanty v Rossii do epokhi preobrazovanii*, Moscow, 1890, p. 372; Stashevskii, *Smolenskaia voina*, p. 70.

[27] In June–July 1630 recruitment was already under way for the first two Russian regiments of the foreign type, which were entrusted for training to Leslie's men (see Stashevskii, *Smolenskaia voina*, pp. 63–64).

Sweden or of returning to him Livonia and Prussia, which had been occupied by the Swedes. These peace talks were on the point of beginning, in Danzig, when on 8 April Gustavus Adolphus suddenly wrote to Chancellor Oxenstjerna to say that he saw no need for negotiations with the Rzeczpospolita, even if the Polish King were to renounce his claim to the Swedish throne. From then on he regarded negatively the idea of peace with Poland. War with the Emperor was decided on and at the same time an instruction was issued to the effect that Article 20 should be regarded as a dead letter.[28] The Polish–Lithuanian state, held fast by Muscovy, was now incapable of striking at the Swedes' rear. And Muscovy not only had a treaty of peace with Sweden but would in any case be tied up with this Polish war.[29]

Gustavus Adolphus was so confident regarding the Russo–Polish war that immediately after the Crimean embassy had left Sweden, in May, he sent an envoy, Benjamin Baron, to the Khanate with a special task to perform, namely to get the Tatars to refrain from attacking Poland (since that enemy was already paralysed) but, instead, to undertake a diversion through Transylvania against the Emperor. This plan proved to be both unreal, since Transylvania refused to allow the Tatar host to pass through its territory,[30] and mistaken, since the Tatars were soon to turn their weapons *against Russia*. Here, however, what interests us is that it was a symptom of Gustavus Adolphus's confidence that there was going to be

---

[28] Wejle, *Sveriges politik*, p. 7. Oxenstjerna, commenting in his own way on this instruction in a memorandum of 30 April 1630, formulates thus the new tasks of Swedish policy in relation to the Rzeczpospolita: instead of making peace with that state, draw closer to Poland's Protestants and create 'factions' in Poland in Sweden's interest (*Handlingar rörande Skandinaviens historia*, Vol. XXIV, Stockholm, 1840, pp. 196–197).

[29] 'Before he left for Germany Gustavus Adolphus directed those who were remaining in Sweden to work for friendship with the neighbour to the East [Muscovy] while at the same time maintaining vigilance, even to the point of a certain degree of readiness to fight' (*Sveriges Krig 1611–1632*, Vol. V, p. 229).

[30] Benjamin Baron left Moscow for the Crimea on 11 February 1631 and returned through Moscow to Sweden only on 14 February 1632, accompanied by a new Crimean ambassador, Nurali Ulan, whose task was to explain to Gustavus Adolphus that the Khan was unable to fight the Emperor but, when Sweden went to war with the Rzeczpospolita, he would willingly hurl his forces against the Polish King. On its return journey in 1633 the Tatar embassy was arrested by the Muscovite government, which was already at war with the Crimea, and only after several months was it released as a result of an appeal by Sweden (see *TsGADA, Dela shvedskie*, 1630, *stb.* 5; 1632, *stb.* 3; 1633, *stb.* 9 and 10). Not finding Gustavus Adolphus in Sweden, Nurali Ulan and his companions went on to Germany. According to information in the Stockholm archives they did not find him among the living and returned without having had an audience with the monarch (Wejle, *Sveriges politik*, pp. 10–11), but Chemnitz (Chemnitz, *Königlichen-schwedischen*, Vol. I, pp. 422–423) states that this embassy was received by Gustavus Adolphus before Nuremberg on 13 August 1632. Pufendorf writes of the arrival in Sweden in 1633 of a Tatar embassy which had come through Transylvania (Pufendorf, *Commentariorum*, Book V, para. 109, 'Legatio tatarica', p. 129), but this is evidently a mistake.

war between Russia and Poland, at the moment when he was making his final preparations for invading Germany.

Before leaving Sweden Gustavus Adolphus also sent to Moscow his trusted Johan Möller. The latter's task was to take a diplomatic message to the Tsar and to organise the export of the Russian grain subsidy from Archangel. He was actually an important specialist in military matters and when, later, he became Sweden's permanent resident agent in Moscow, he obtained permission to supervise the training of Russian troops, openly took upon himself the function of instructor in military engineering and fortification ('as His Royal Majesty did this in Germany'), and so on.[31] However, when he arrived in Novgorod at the beginning of June 1630 in the capacity of a mere diplomat, Möller met with failure. The Tsar's letter to the governor of Novgorod said that he was to be allowed to proceed, 'with a guard', through Vologda to Archangel only if his mission was to purchase grain. He was politely refused permission to go to Moscow, on the made-up excuse that there was an epidemic in Sweden. Accordingly, Möller sent back to the King the diplomatic message he had brought and himself went to Archangel: only in October did he get to Moscow.[32] The reason for this insulting treatment was that, at the beginning of June 1630, the Muscovite government had not yet received the reply it expected from Turkey concerning the project for a joint offensive against Poland. Until the coalition had taken shape Muscovy preferred not to commit itself to any further obligations to Sweden, wishing to confine its role to 'covert war'.[33] However, a favourable reply from Turkey arrived before June was out, and in October the Muscovites began to prepare a 'great embassy' to Gustavus Adolphus. Consequently, when Möller reached Moscow he was surrounded by marked signs of attention and the government endeavoured, with striking concern, to satisfy all the requests he presented, even those of a personal nature.[34]

But the Swedish government and, *a fortiori*, Gustavus Adolphus in Germany were informed of all that only in 1631, and when Gustavus Adolphus's letter to Mikhail Fedorovich was returned unanswered by Möller from Novgorod, this must have aroused serious alarm among the Swedes as to Russia's intentions. This was why Gustavus Adolphus, having occupied Pomerania as his bridgehead, but seeing now that Russia

---

[31] *TsGADA, Dela shvedskie*, 1631, *stb.* 8, *ll.* 65, 70, 106.
[32] *TsGADA, Dela shvedskie*, 1630, *stb.* 6, *ll.* 2–4, 17–20, 51–63.
[33] It was in March 1629 that, for the first time, the Swedish envoys in Moscow, Monier and Bönhardt, were promised that Russia would attack Poland (*TsGADA, Dela shvedskie*, 1629, *stb.* 2, *ll.* 275, 319, 354). A definite time for military operations to begin was not laid down in negotiations with Sweden before the beginning of 1631.
[34] *TsGADA, Dela shvedskie*, 1630, *stb.* 6, *ll.* 90–194.

was not following up his invasion of Germany by attacking Poland, and that, therefore, he must be in danger of a stab in the back from that quarter, made no move to advance further into Germany. Instead, he took one vigorous measure after another to establish military and diplomatic contact with Muscovy and urged it to go to war. In July, apparently, he sent Colonel Alexander Leslie to Russia again. Leslie arrived in Moscow in August or September 1630 accompanied by sixty-two persons, some of whom were members of his family. He addressed the Tsar and the Patriarch with fervent demonstrations of the need to begin war against Poland forthwith and, at the same time, with proposals not only to reorganise the Russian army on the Swedish model but also to hire entire regiments of foreign soldiers. Let us mention, in passing, the curious mistake made by E. Stashevskii, D. Tsvetaev and other Russian historians in treating Leslie as an obscure *condottiere* who had come from the West in search of work and was eventually russified in the Tsar's service. In fact, Colonel Alexander Leslie, was the son of that Alexander Leslie, Scotsman, whom the *Encyclopaedia Britannica* rightly describes as one of the most outstanding soldiers of the first half of the seventeenth century. In his youth Leslie senior took part in the Dutch War against Spain, then he became close companion-in-arms of Gustavus Adolphus, a hero of the Thirty Years' War. In 1636 he was a field-marshal in the Swedish army; he then commanded the Presbyterian army in Scotland and was one of the principal figures in the English Civil War, whose repute as a military leader rivals that of Cromwell.[35] Alexander Leslie junior emerged as the reformer and one of the chief commanders of the Russian army during the Smolensk War. There can be no doubt that he played this role on the direct instructions of Gustavus Adolphus. Already at the time of Leslie's first visit to Moscow, in February 1630, Ambassador Monier proposed officially, on behalf of his king, to have sent from Sweden to Moscow not only political intelligence but also military commanders and arms and ammunition for the Russian army, and this offer was accepted.[36] Among the foreign 'immigrants' in Russia

[35] In my article, 'Gustaf Adolf i podgotovka Smolenskoi voiny', *Voprosy istorii*, No. 1, 1947, p. 62, I treated as unsolved the question of the two Scotsmen named Alexander Leslie who were among the commanders of Gustavus Adolphus's army. Was the Alexander Leslie who came to Moscow in 1630 that famous Alexander Leslie who is regarded as one of the most outstanding soldiers of the first half of the seventeenth century, or was he some other Scotsman with the same name? This question was clarified by D. Norrman in his *Gustav Adolfs politik mot Ryssland och Polen under Tyska kriget 1630–1632*, Uppsala, 1913, p. 64. It was Alexander Leslie junior who arrived in Moscow in 1630 with a great number of relatives and accompanied by an important group of Scottish officers. [In fact, neither Porshnev nor Norrman was correct about the two Alexander Leslies, who were not closely related. See editor's introduction, n. 6.]

[36] *TsGADA, Dela smolenskie*, 1630, *stb.* 2, *ll.* 138, 248, 249.

in 1630 the principal place was held by officers (*nachal'nye or prikaznye liudi*), including officers who either came from the Swedish army or (mostly Scots) were personally associated with Leslie.[37]

Strictly speaking it would be wrong to consider that they reorganised the Russian army on the Swedish model: the Swedish military school of Gustavus Adolphus was to a very great extent a pupil of the Netherlands bourgeois revolution. Leslie senior was one of those professional soldiers who brought its lessons to Sweden, just as he did, later, to revolutionary England. It can be said that they were the military instructors of Gustavus Adolphus and of Cromwell. Together with the officers associated with him, Leslie junior tried to reconstruct the Russian army on the Dutch model. In September 1631 the Polish military governor, Gosiewski, received a spy's report that there were in Moscow already several 'regiments of the Dutch type', and during the siege of Smolensk Moszkorzewski wrote that it was necessary to fight against the Muscovite army 'in the Netherlandish fashion'.[38]

Gustavus Adolphus's art of war was, however, connected also with some purely Swedish innovations. These were, especially, light cannon such as had not been seen before in Europe. They greatly contributed to his breath-taking successes in Germany. And it was highly characteristic that Gustavus Adolphus made a present of this military novelty to Muscovy even before he went into Germany. The artillery expert, Julius Coyet, who arrived with Leslie in January 1630 knew the secret of how to cast light cannon and it was not long before the Muscovite government responded to his request by assigning to help him 'in the new matter of cannon' the craftsmen he needed (a blacksmith, a wheelwright, a turner and a man skilled in the casting of shot).[39]

In June 1631 Johan Möller passed on in Moscow the urgent advice of

---

[37] Stashevskii, *Smolenskaia voina*, pp. 35–36 *et seq.* The Scottish historian A. Steuart found in the records of Scotland's Privy Council the 'birthbrieves', confirmations of noble origin, which were obtained in the 1630s by these comrades of Alexander Leslie junior – important military specialists who formed, to use Steuart's word, his 'coterie' (Steuart, A. F., *Scottish Influences in Russian History from the End of the 16th Century to the Beginning of the 19th Century*, Glasgow, 1913, pp. 40–42). Two documents from the same archive witness to the activity of an agent of Alexander Leslie's. On 28 March 1633 Captain James Forbes petitioned for royal authority to recruit 200 men in Scotland for the Russian service, under the command of Sir Alexander Leslie. On 1 May 1633 an order for the engagement of this number of men was granted to Sir Alexander Leslie of Auchintoul, Knight, 'general colonel of the foreign forces of the Emperor of Russia' (ibid., p. 34). Later on there were a number of persons in Russia with the name Leslie, including Alexander junior (ibid., p. 40).

[38] Stashevskii, *Smolenskaia voina*, pp. 84, 174.

[39] *TsGADA, Dela shvedskie*, 1630, *stb.* 10, *ll.* 18, 48. In 1632 the arms factories at Tula and Kashira were founded by another emissary of Gustavus Adolphus, 'the Swedish King's steward' Vinius (Yelisei Ul'ianov), who, like Coyet, was of Dutch nationality.

his King that this was the best moment for an attack on the Rzeczpospolita, and also that the Tsar should provide himself for this purpose with 'many cannon and other armaments, the cannon being neither heavy nor bulky'.[40] But Gustavus Adolphus was not impatient, and at this same time another courier was on his way to Mikhail Fedorovich whose charge Leslie, who met him, set forth in a letter: the King wished to send the Tsar 'cannon made on the same light pattern as those which Master Julius Coyet has cast in Moscow'. Leslie explains the tactical advantages of light cannon and asks the Tsar to decide this question, taking account of the fact that Gustavus Adolphus has already 'in the current war won victories with these light cannon, and with this invention has been able to travel a great distance, and we expect that he will be able to advance even further'.[41]

The Muscovite government agreed to these requests and counsels from Gustavus Adolphus while still keeping its political distance.[42] It conferred numerous commands in the Russian army upon foreign officers sent from the Swedish army. It soon instructed its envoys Plemiannikov and Aristov to purchase in foreign countries a large quantity of muskets, carbines, pistols, swords, helmets, and so on, of the same pattern as those used in the Swedish army.[43] Leslie's plan was adopted almost completely in the form in which he presented it. Leslie himself was authorised to return abroad to engage, 'as quickly and as best may be', for the Tsar's service three (later changed to four) regiments of experienced *lansquenets* with the appropriate complement of commanders, subject to the same conditions of payment and service as applied in the rest of Europe.[44] When Leslie left, in February 1631, along with the Russian envoys Plemiannikov and Aristov, he was given, besides the cash he needed for

[40] *TsGADA, Dela shvedskie*, 1631, *stb.* 8, *l.* 64.

[41] *TsGADA, Dela shvedskie*, 1630, *stb.* 10, *ll.* 168–169: cf. 1631, *stb.* 2: the arrival of the Swedish courier Johan von Stenberg, brother-in-law of Coyet. Besides passing on this proposal about the cannon, Coyet had to do what he could to supervise the work of Yelisei Ul'ianov and Desmoulins in levying and sending off the Russian grain 'for the King of Sweden'.

[42] Cf., e.g., the sharp rebuff administered in 1630 to Swedish attempts at diplomatic familiarity: an extract made from treaties to show that the Tsar of Muscovy 'never wrote and does not write to the King of Sweden as "brother"' (*TsGADA, Dela shvedskie*, 1630, *stb.* 11, *l.* 5).

[43] *TsGADA, Dela shvedskie*, 1631, *stb.* 4. On the delivery of various purchased weapons in December 1631 to January 1633, see *stb.* 11 of 1631.

[44] E. Stashevskii mistakenly contrasts the plan put forward by the Scot Leslie with the plan of the Holsteiner Von Dam, submitted on 18 January and accepted at the end of February 1631 (Stashevskii, *Smolenskaia voina*, pp. 74–81). Von Dam was an assistant and, so to speak, a deputy to Leslie. When Leslie was away, Von Dam, together with Leslie's father-in-law, Unsing, wrote the reports sent from Moscow to Gustavus Adolphus (see *Akty i pis'ma k istorii baltiiskogo voprosa v XVI–XVII stoletiiakh*, edited by G. Forsten, Vol. II, St Petersburg, 1893, p. 129). They also received the soldiers hired by Leslie and the weapons he bought.

hiring men and making purchases, also 100,000 yefimki 'in letters' (i.e., bills of exchange) for Amsterdam merchants, from foreign merchants in Moscow.[45] The regiments began to arrive only at the end of 1631. It must be mentioned that Stashevskii propounds a quite mistaken conception that the hiring of foreign regiments, advocated by Leslie, produced bad results owing to refusal by Gustavus Adolphus (and also by the King of Denmark) to permit recruitment of troops in his own territories. Stashevskii supposes that the Muscovite government, knowing that the German *lansquenets* were demoralised and worthless, deliberately refrained from mentioning Germany in its mandate to Leslie and prescribed that if he did not succeed in raising all the men he needed in Sweden he should go further in search of recruits, to Denmark, Holland and England, but that circumstances compelled him, despite his instructions, to hire the bulk of his *lansquenets* in Germany. Actually Leslie advised, in his plan, that Gustavus Adolphus be asked 'that, for friendship's sake, he allow His Majesty the Tsar to hire men in his Kingdom and in those parts of Germany which are at present under him', and this same formulation was reproduced in the Tsar's letter to Gustavus Adolphus which was sent with Leslie. The Tsar asks the King, 'for the sake of our friendship and love to allow Colonel Alexander Leslie to hire soldiers in His Majesty's Kingdom and in the German lands that are now held by him'.[46] Stashevskii's entire notion is based on a misunderstanding. Gustavus Adolphus did not forbid Leslie but, on the contrary, helped him to do what he himself had, through Leslie, advised the Muscovite government to do, namely, to exploit for the strengthening of the Muscovite army those markets in Germany for mercenary soldiers that were then under Swedish control.

It is very characteristic that, both in the mandate given to Leslie and in the Tsar's message to Gustavus Adolphus, the Muscovite government expressed the wish that these arms be purchased, so far as possible, directly from the Swedish treasury; that the soldiers be hired, for preference, from among those 'good, keen men . . . who are at present serving his Royal Majesty as mercenaries'; and that Gustavus Adolphus release 'colonels, captains, lieutenants and other commanders who are now serving in the Swedish army but wish to go and serve in Muscovy'.[47] The King could not, of course, satisfy this request fully, to the detriment of his own army, but such an idea would never have arisen unless the

---

[45] *TsGADA, Dela shvedskie*, 1630, *stb.* 10; 1631, *stb.* 3; cf. *Sobranie gosudarstvennykh gramot i dogovorov*, Vol. III, Nos. 81–88; E. Stashevskii (*Smolenskaia voina*, pp. 71–83, 88–108) analyses in detail the story of the hiring of these foreign regiments, with their composition, conveyance to Moscow and organisation.

[46] *TsGADA, Dela shvedskie*, 1630, *stb.* 9, *l.* 139; *stb.* 10, *l.* 2.

[47] *TsGADA, Dela shvedskie*, 1630, *stb.* 9, *ll.* 108,139; *stb.* 10, *l.* 25.

Muscovites were sure that Gustavus Adolphus saw the Russo–Polish war as a branch of his own military operation.

While securing for himself, by all these means, a certain degree of influence in the Russian army, Gustavus Adolphus nevertheless realised that it was not on military circles but on the Russian government that it ultimately depended when Muscovy would declare war on the Rzeczpospolita. Remaining, against his will, still inactive on his Pomeranian bridgehead, he never stopped thinking of ways to speed up the sluggish progress of events in the East. He found the solution to this diplomatic problem only at the end of October and the beginning of November 1630. More precisely, the solution was then brought to him by one of the most original and interesting diplomats of that time, the Frenchman Jacques Roussel,[48] who passed, as Hungarian (strictly Transylvanian) ambassador, through Constantinople and Moscow to Sweden and handed to Gustavus Adolphus in Pomerania letters from Bethlen Gábor (who was dead by that time), the Sultan of Turkey, the Khan of the Crimea and the Tsar of Muscovy.[49]

Jacques Roussel, son of a citizen of Châlons and brother of a well-known Calvinist preacher, was a typical man of the late Renaissance period – fashionably educated and a man of the world, yet at the same time a fanatical adherent of Calvinistic Protestantism. He was a confederate and confidant of the leader of the French Huguenots, the Duc de Rohan. Roussel's activity embraced France, Poland, Savoy, Mantua, Venice, Transylvania, Turkey, Muscovy, Sweden, Germany and Holland. He gained the complete trust of Bethlen Gábor, Gustavus Adolphus and Patriarch Philaret, and played in the 1620s and the early 1630s no small part in the practical realisation of a political task of enormous importance, the welding together of an anti-Habsburg coalition, and also in attempts to put into effect a plan to unite all the non-Catholic Christian Churches which had been conceived at that time in anti-Catholic ecclesiastical and political circles. He visited distant Moscow several times, as Bethlen Gábor's ambassador, as Gustavus Adolphus's plenipotentiary, and, on the last occasion, in 1633, as plenipotentiary of the States-General of Holland. In this final stage of his career Roussel particularly stressed the

[48]  In my article 'Moskovskoe gosudarstvo i vstuplenie Shvetsii v Tridtsatiletniuiu voinu' (*Istoricheskii zhurnal*, 1945, No 3, p. 20) I wrongly described Roussel as a Swede. Biographical information on Roussel is to be found in the writings of French memoirists.
    A special section ('On the plane of one individual's life') is devoted to Jacques Roussel in the concluding part of our study, *Frantsiia, Angliiskaia revoliutsiia i evropeiskaia politika v seredine XVIIv.*, Moscow, 1970, pp. 339–354.

[49]  Wejle, *Sverige politik*, p. 19. Roussel left Russia through Novgorod on 24 July 1630 and on 20 August set sail from Vyborg to Sweden (*TsGADA, Dela shvedskie, stb.* 3, *ll.* 40, 42). See also (1630, *stb.* 8) the letter of recommendation given him for Gustavus Adolphus by Mikhail Fedorovich on 6 July 1630.

commercial aspect of his activity. He worked persistently and patiently to realise a grand project for opening up to Europe's merchants a route through Russia (down the Volga and across the Caspian Sea) to the Persian market. Calvinist piety was in him merged, quite in the spirit of the age, with tremendous cupidity. He became extraordinarily rich. In 1636 Roussel was in Constantinople, and there, through some epidemic that was raging, he met his death. He was only forty years old. Although Roussel was certainly not free from some of the traits of an adventurer, he won from Gustavus Adolphus, as from a number of other important statesmen, great respect for his wisdom and his political ideas. Together they worked out a plan which, in Ahnlund's words, 'surprised Europe',[50] to announce Gustavus Adolphus's claim to the throne of Poland, which, owing to Sigismund III's senility, must soon be vacant.

From subsequent letters of Roussel to Mikhail Fedorovich and Patriarch Philaret we see that Roussel had already discussed and worked out this project with them during his secret talks in Moscow,[51] though what he had been sent to do was to explain to them a plan for obtaining the Polish Crown for Bethlen Gábor.[52] (It was while Roussel was in Moscow that Bethlen Gábor's death became known.)[53] The project for setting Gustavus Adolphus on the throne of Poland was, clearly, a component of that 'grand design' which had been discussed at the Patriarch's residence in June 1630 and to which Roussel often alludes in his letters. But Gustavus Adolphus was also prepared for taking this step. He knew from his envoy Strassburg, when the latter returned to Sweden to report at the

[50] Ahnlund, *Gustav Adolf*, p. 32. [Quotation from Michael Roberts's translation, p. 244 – Trans.]

[51] In his first communication about the negotiations with Gustavus Adolphus (29 January 1631) Roussel writes: 'And furthermore I spoke alone with the King's Majesty about that good matter of Your Majesty the Tsar's and discussed privily with him your wish and desire. And only after that was it established that it is necessary to direct and organise the will of the Polish lords' council in favour of His Majesty King Gustavus Adolphus, since they all as one desired the late King Gábor, of blessed memory, if by God's will he had come into Poland with his army at the end of 1629' (*TsGADA, Dela shvedskie, 1630, stb. 3, l. 2*).

[52] Judging by the speech made by his envoys in Moscow, Bethlen Gábor counted on three factors: (1) the military strength of himself and his allies; (2) a favourable attitude on the part of the Sejm ('the lords' council') towards him and towards the idea of union between Poland and Hungary; (3) the grumbling which, as he supposed, from historical precedents, would rise up from the Poles against their King if he began a war of which they did not approve (*TsGADA, Dela vengerskie, 1630, stb. 1, ll. 162–163*).

[53] While still at the court of Bethlen Gábor, Roussel showed himself a warm supporter of Gustavus Adolphus. He definitely favoured the Swedish King and made a secret pact with his envoy, Strassburg. The latter furnished Roussel not only with letters of recommendation to Gustavus Adolphus but also with plenary powers to act in Turkey and Russia in Gustavus Adolphus's interests and in his name (Wejle, *Sveriges politik*, pp. 12–13).

beginning of 1630, that, before he died, Bethlen Gábor had written to the magnates of Poland warmly recommending Gustavus Adolphus as their King. Chancellor Oxenstjerna was already in favour of Gustavus Adolphus's candidature and now, along with Strassburg, set himself to kindle religious strife in Poland by all available means. Through Ulrich, the *Burggraf* of Riga, Gustavus Adolphus dealt secretly with the leader of the Protestants in Lithuania, Prince Krzysztof Radziwill.[54]

However, what actually took place was quite different. After raising Roussel to high court rank and on 5 November furnishing him with splendid credentials and extensive plenary powers, Gustavus Adolphus sent the Frenchman as his special ambassador to the Polish magnates and senators – to the Polish 'republic', ignoring the King. Roussel was to make open propaganda for the advantages of a union between Poland and Sweden, and for Gustavus Adolphus as defender of Polish liberties against the 'usurpation' by Sigismund, who intended to secure, while he was still alive, the election of one of his sons as King. After going to Elbing, at the end of November, to see Chancellor Oxenstjerna, who was astonished at this move but submitted to the King's will, Roussel in December 1630 established himself in Riga and Dorpat, from where he sent couriers to Poland with letters addressed to the magnates and the Sejm. Later he had these letters printed, along with anti-Habsburg appeals and the credentials Gustavus Adolphus had given him, and circulated them widely in Poland. Frightened, the Protestants of Poland and Lithuania, whom he had addressed (including Radziwill, of course) began to disavow any connection with the Swedes, and noblemen publicly tore up Roussel's broadsheets in which Gustavus Adolphus was extolled, or else sent them to angry King Sigismund. In April 1632 Roussel's courier Mavius, who tried to meet the Polish nobility after a session of the Sejm, barely escaped with his life.[55] All Europe was truly amazed at this unprecedented way of conducting politics.[56]

Roussel was seen as the prime culprit for the failure of Gustavus Adolphus's claim to the Polish throne; 'To the same degree', says Wejle, 'that Gustavus Adolphus's policy towards Poland had been successful before the conclusion of the truce of Altmark, it was unsuccessful during the term of that truce.' His 'fundamental plan, to stir up internecine strife in Poland, take the throne from Sigismund's heirs, or at least to force them to renounce their claims on Sweden, failed utterly. Roussel merely alienated from Gustavus Adolphus the oppositional groups in Poland, who had exposed their intentions too early to their opponents, when it

[54] Wejle, *Sveriges politik*, pp. 12–16.    [55] Ibid., pp. 19–33.
[56] Cf. Arlanibaeus, *Theatrum Europaeum*, Vol. II, pp. 571–572.

was still necessary to work in profound secrecy through Radziwill.'[57] But was that really Gustavus Adolphus's 'fundamental plan'? On 22 April 1631 he himself wrote to Oxenstjerna that the question of the Polish throne did not interest him in the least.[58] And, indeed, could this shrewd politician have failed to understand that in no circumstances had he any chance of getting by peaceful means a majority in the Polish Sejm? When we bring together the documents for his Polish and his Russian policies, they support a different idea, namely, that, in reality, his fundamental plan consisted in stimulating Muscovy to go to war with the Polish–Lithuanian state. After all, he was drawn towards a much more attractive aim than the Crown of Poland – the conquest of Germany, perhaps the Imperial Crown.[59] And the only obstacle in his path to that aim was the Rzeczpospolita's freedom to act against him. In the very days, at the beginning of November 1630, when Roussel was being sent to Poland with so much publicity, Gustavus Adolphus instructed Monier, in absolute secrecy, to go to Moscow with a new plan for defeating the Rzeczpospolita, of which more will be said later. The degree to which these two missions formed one whole is obvious from the fact that Gustavus Adolphus sent both of the instructions he had drawn up, the one to Roussel and the one to Monier, the former being dated 8 November and the latter 11 November, along with Roussel, apparently, to Chancellor Oxenstjerna, for the latter's information. The Chancellor's reply, dated 17 January 1631, criticising both instructions, confirms once more, incidentally, the impression that at that time Oxenstjerna held somewhat aloof from the King's Russian and Polish policy, either not understanding it fully, or not knowing the whole of it. In any case, though, it was clear to Oxenstjerna that the principal task not only of Monier but also of Roussel was to 'bring about war by Russia against Poland'.[60] Roussel's instructions ordered him to proceed from Poland to Moscow.

---

[57] Wejle, *Sveriges politik*, pp. 64–65.

[58] Ibid., p. 39.

[59] Cf. the analysis of the ultimate aims of Gustavus Adolphus's campaign in Germany in N. Ahnlund, *Gustav Adolf*, pp. 393–401. For a description of these aims, no-one has hitherto paid attention to the following passage in an unpublished letter from Gustavus Adolphus to Mikhail Fedorovich, from Stettin, 21 June 1631 (in the translation of the Embassies Department): 'And may Your Majesty the Tsar maintain good hope in Our Royal Majesty that Our Royal Majesty will help Your Majesty the Tsar against the Polish King: although not all of Germany has yet been subjected to Our Royal Majesty, we wish to show Our great Royal friendship and love to Your Majesty the Tsar'. This is followed by permission to recruit 5,000 soldiers in Pomerania, Mecklenburg and Prussia for the war with Poland and to transport them through Sweden, to export purchased armaments free of customs duties, and so on (*TsGADA, Dela shvedskie*, 1631, *stb*. 4, *l*. 133.)

[60] *Arkiv till upplysning om svenska krigens . . . historia*, Vol. II, p. 157.

What did Roussel and Gustavus Adolphus have in mind? They had decided to bring pressure to bear on the Muscovite government by using its own trump card. In offering, through Roussel, the Polish Crown to Gustavus Adolphus, the Muscovite government doubtless calculated that if the Swedish King accepted, he would then launch an attack on the Polish–Lithuanian state (as Bethlen Gábor had been about to do). He would in that case need to ask for a military alliance with Moscow, and so Moscow would be able to dictate its territorial and political conditions to the future King of Poland.[61] But Gustavus Adolphus had now, with the aid of that same Roussel, shifted the emphasis to the question of agreement by the Polish lords to his election as king and thereby frightened Moscow with the possibility that he might obtain the Crown of Poland by peaceful means, without resorting to military pressure and, consequently, without Muscovite help. Moreover, Muscovy would in that event, face as neighbour a powerful Polono–Swedish state, without having managed to recover any of the territory it had lost in the Time of Troubles and the Polish intervention. Clearly, the news of Roussel's mission was bound to make Moscow move quickly to declare war on Poland. And that was what happened.

Roussel applied himself very energetically, in December 1630, to the fulfilment of both parts of his mission – the subordinate, Polish one, and the principal, Russian one. It would seem that, among other things, he was responsible for the appearance in Moscow in December 1630 of provocative 'reports' about an impending attack by the Poles ('by Lithuanians and Russian criminals from among the borderland peasantry')[62] which evoked serious war alarms: a decree from the Tsar on transition to a state of war was issued in nineteen towns, a special inspection was carried out to check the readiness for defence of the border fortresses, and a series of emergency measures were undertaken by the Ordnance Office.[63] Connected with this alarm, no doubt, was also the sudden adoption, on 20 December, of all of Alexander Leslie's proposals for hiring foreign

[61] This is confirmed by the mandate given later to the Russian ambassadors Pushkin and Gorikhvostov when they were sent to Sweden in 1632 in order to conclude an alliance (see *infra*, Chapters 3 and 5).

[62] This supposition is based on the fact that in another case of the appearance of similar 'news', soon after this one, the clues lead straight to Roussel. In February 1631 he sent a man from Dorpat to the Russian frontier post near Pskov with a letter addressed to the Tsar, and this man gave at the frontier post a detailed account of the numbers and disposition of the Lithuanian troops who, so he said, were soon going to attack Pskov under the command of Wladyslaw. This time, the Muscovite government ordered two or three intelligence agents to go the frontier, disguised as merchants, to check on 'the Lithuanian reports', and soon received reassuring information as to the falsity of the story (*TsGADA, Dela shvedskie*, 1631, *stb.* 5, *ll.* 2–5, 14–15, 21–22).

[63] Stashevskii, *Smolenskaia voina*, p. 283.

regiments, proposals which had long been awaiting reply.[64] But Roussel made his big move in January 1631, when he sent from Dorpat to Mikhail Fedorovich and Patriarch Philaret a report of his meeting with Gustavus Adolphus, of his new high appointment as the King's plenipotentiary representative 'to everyone in Poland', in connection with the opening of the Sejm in Warsaw, and of his decision to remain for the moment in Riga and send to the Sejm only two couriers with invitations to the magnates to come to Riga for negotiations regarding Gustavus Adolphus's candidature to the throne of Poland. To this report were attached copies of the credentials given to Roussel by the King and of the letter from Gustavus Adolphus to the Polish magnates (the Castellan of Cracow, etc.), dated 5 November, Stralsund.[65] Roussel's report arrived at Pskov with an accompanying letter from the Swedish governor of Livonia, Johan Skytte,[66] requesting the governor of Pskov, in view of the importance of the matter, 'to have this letter conveyed at once [to Moscow] by direct courier travelling day and night without stopping'.

Gustavus Adolphus's manoeuvre proved to be quite precisely calculated. Roussel's report made a powerful impression in Moscow, as is clear if we compare dates. Literally on the day after it arrived a certain matter was settled which had been dragging on for several months. Although Turkey's engagement to strike at the Rzeczpospolita in the early spring of 1631 had reached Moscow as long before as June 1630, and the Muscovite government firmly intended to act simultaneously with Turkey, it had not considered it necessary to hasten to tell Sweden about this. The embassy of Plemiannikov and Aristov to Gustavus Adolphus, which had been ready since October 1630, kept on being postponed while information was being gathered in concerning the Swedes' military operations in Germany. On 16 January 1631 the Tsar's regular instruction to the governor of Novgorod, Prince D.M. Pozharskii, required him secretly to find out, abroad, what was happening in Sweden and at the war front,

---

[64] To judge by a special letter from Gustavus Adolphus to Mikhail Fedorovich dated 28 February 1631 (from Altenstadt in Pomerania), Leslie had even written to the King that he was not being employed in Moscow, and was poorly paid. Gustavus Adolphus asks that Leslie either be paid the same amount as was received by other colonels in the Swedish army or else released, 'because here in the Kaiser's country able colonels are needed for the service of Our Royal Majesty' (*TsGADA, Dela shvedskie*, 1631, *stb.* 8, *l.* 51). From a roll of the Embassies Department it is clear that even before this letter was received, Leslie's business was suddenly activated in the second half of December 1630. At the request of Prince Cherkasskii, Leslie presented a memorandum of previous discussions, and this was followed on 30 December by an order from the Tsar and the Patriarch to prepare, on the basis of the memorandum, all the documents that Leslie needed for his mission (*TsGADA, Dela shvedskie*, 1630, *stb.* 10, *ll.* 1–13).

[65] *TsGADA, Dela shvedskie*, 1630, *stb.* 3, *ll.* 1–6, 29–30. Roussel's letter is wrongly dated January 1630 instead of 1631.

[66] On Skytte and his activity as Swedish governor of Livonia, see Liljedahl, R., *Svensk förvaltning i Livland 1617–1634*, Uppsala, 1933, Ch. XI, pp. 524–539.

where Gustavus Adolphus was, 'and whether he is negotiating with the Polish King, and if so about what'.[67]

On 25 January 1631, however, immediately on the receipt of Roussel's report, the mandate for Plemiannikov and Aristov was signed; on 29 January a letter to the Swedish King received the Tsar's signature; and on 30 January Plemiannikov, Aristov and Leslie left Moscow in haste. They took with them that which Gustavus Adolphus wanted so ardently. The ambassadors, after expounding before him a brief history of Russo–Polish relations since the Time of Troubles, were to stress that the Tsar had already broken the truce of Deulino and had refused, in the previous year, to receive envoys from Poland, and then to say in the name of the Tsar: 'and now we, the great sovereign, for the many injustices committed by King Sigismund, wish to stand against him and intend to send against him in the spring [deleted and replaced by 'soon'] an army led by our boyars and commanders'.[68]

Alexander Leslie also received diplomatic messages from the Tsar for the English King Charles I, for the Danish King Christian IV, for the Dutch Stadtholder Frederick Henry of Orange and for the States-General of the Netherlands. In all of these messages, as also in the one sent to Gustavus Adolphus, after the list of 'injustices' by Sigismund III there appears one and the same formula, which is of great importance for our understanding the Muscovite government's conception of international affairs:

And it is known to us that Crown Prince Wladyslaw wants to invade our realm of Muscovy, to destroy our realm and our Christian faith and to introduce and establish his own accursed heretical Popish religion, according to the wish of the Pope of Rome and the counsels of the Kaiser, the King of Spain and the King of Lithuania [i.e., Sigismund]. And we, the great sovereign, in view of the many injustices committed by them, do not intend to suffer the Polish King [Sigismund] and the Polish lords' council [the Sejm] until the expiry of the Truce.

As we see, war against the Polish–Lithuanian state is here publicly explained before Europe as indirectly war against the whole Habsburg–Catholic camp. In informing the above-mentioned princes of his intention to begin hostilities in the spring of 1631, Mikhail Fedorovich asks them for help in hiring soldiers and purchasing armaments.[69] Thus,

---

[67] *TsGADA, Dela shvedskie*, 1630, *stb.* 9, *ll.* 46–47.

[68] Ibid., *ll.* 96–106. Here mention is also made of the embassy sent in the previous year from Sultan Murad IV to say that 'in the spring' he would send a great army against the King of Poland – 'and we shall go against the Polish King along with him' (l. 103). Approximately the same phrase appears also in the letter written by Mikhail Fedorovich to Gustavus Adolphus (ibid., *ll.* 127–145).

[69] *TsGADA, Dela shvedskie*, 1630, *stb.* 10, *ll.* 51–69 (letter to Christian IV), 70–85 (letter to Charles I), 86–97 (letter to Frederick Henry of Orange), 98–111 (letter of the Netherlands States-General). All these letters, like the one to Gustavus Adolphus, are dated 29 January 1631.

this was an open and formal declaration of war on the Rzeczpospolita.

But whatever haste the ambassadors and Leslie might make, they met obstacles on their way to Sweden and from Sweden to Germany. Four whole months passed before they could bring this precious news to Gustavus Adolphus.

In the meantime the King grew more and more worried. True, in January 1631 he had at last signed at Bärwalde a treaty of alliance with France, but he could not advance further into Germany. News reached him of Polish military preparations which might be directed against Sweden even without formal violation by the Polish–Lithuanian state of the truce of Altmark. Thus for example, on 8 January 1631, Ulrich, the *Burggraf* of Riga, reported that 'the Emperor has been trying to get permission to recruit an army in Poland in order to strike with it at the Swedes' rear in Germany'.[70] Indeed in 1631 all Europe knew that Sigismund, in accordance with the treaty of mutual assistance made in 1621 with Emperor Ferdinand II, had granted him freedom to recruit and organise troops on the territory of the Rzeczpospolita, while rejecting, however, his request that he should go to war immediately against Sweden.[71]

But Gustavus Adolphus had already prepared a counter to all these threats. We mentioned earlier his recent instruction to Monier in November 1630.[72] This was the second half of the project which Roussel had proposed to Gustavus Adolphus, with the aim of hastening Russia into war with Poland. Roussel's own mission was to act as the stick, Monier's as the carrot. It was solely owing to Monier's slowness and Roussel's impetuousness that the two parts of a single plan failed to synchronise: Monier had reached Moscow only on 15 May 1631, three-and-a-half months after the Russian embassy had set off to visit Gustavus Adolphus.

Monier was an important Swedish military man. When, later, the Muscovite government invited him to take command of a regiment, he refused, referring to the appointment he had been given in the Swedish army.[73] His mission was also partly military in character and was secret in

---

[70] Wejle, *Sveriges politik*, p. 18.

[71] Describing Sweden's situation in the spring of 1631, Burgus writes: 'The Polish King, being bound by a treaty with the King of Sweden and not able to offer anything to the Emperor, was unable to go to war, but nevertheless allowed the Emperor to recruit in his realm as many soldiers as he wanted' (*De bello suecico*, 1633, p. 134).

[72] Cf. the proceedings of the Swedish Council of State, 26 January 1631, on the sending of Monier to Moscow (*Svenska riksrådets protokoll: Handlingar rörande Sveriges historia*, series 3, Vol. 2, 1880, p. 53).

[73] *TsGADA, Dela shvedskie*, 1631, stb. 8, *ll.* 228–229.

the highest degree.[74] It served, so to speak, as the next step in the development of Leslie's mission.[75] In accordance with his instructions Monier was to propose to the Tsar and the Patriarch, on behalf of the King, something very similar to what they had wished to get from Gustavus Adolphus, through Roussel – an invasion of Poland from the west coinciding with Russia's invasion from the east – but this with a substantial amendment. The army making this invasion, though it would be raised in Germany (on the German territories occupied by the Swedes or their allies) and would even be under the personal command of Gustavus Adolphus, would be paid for by Russia.[76]

The complete text of the memorandum that Monier handed to the Tsar has not been preserved, but its content is reproduced, in part, in later correspondence and so we can form some idea of it. First, the ambassador gives fervent thanks to the Tsar on behalf of Gustavus Adolphus ('he bowed deeply') for his 'great friendship' expressed in the permission given for several years past to buy in Russia 'a good quantity of rye'. 'Esteeming highly' this aid, and asking that it be continued, Gustavus Adolphus 'has been concerned as to how he might repay it' and at last has found a way. Just as Mikhail Fedorovich helped him against the Emperor, so he has decided 'to help, in thought and deed, your present action against the Polish King'. Considering 'that the Polish King obliges the Kaiser in all respects and seeks to do him good; not only has he released officers of his to serve the Kaiser, he has allowed the Kaiser to recruit soldiers in his territory', Gustavus Adolphus thinks that he will

[74] On his arrival in Moscow Monier told the officials that, besides dealing with matters that were public, he was 'to speak privately with the sovereigns', and so it was proposed that at his public reception by the Tsar he should say nothing but merely hand over his speech in written form and sealed. The Tsar's reply was conveyed to him secretly, without it being known to anyone, even in the Embassies Department, apart from the secretary to the Council (F. F. Likhachev), by whom the text of this reply was pasted into 'a secret ambassadorial roll' which has not come down to us (see *TsGADA, Dela shvedskie*, 1631, *stb.* 7, *ll.* 140, 189). It should be mentioned that some unknown forces tried, successfully, to penetrate the secret of this reply: *ll.* 269–282 of the roll indicated relate that, during his departure from Moscow, at Khimki, the sleigh of the member of Monier's embassy who was carrying the documents was robbed, and a few days later all the documents, sealed and wrapped in 'a horse-cloth', were thrown on to the road and were brought to the Embassies Department in Moscow by a peasant who found them. A special courier was sent to catch up with Monier and return them to him.

[75] Monier did not find Leslie in Moscow but, after leaving the city on 7 June, he apparently went 'to have a drink' with Leslie's father-in-law, Unsing, who was living at Khimki (evidently with his daughter, Leslie's wife). It was when they were leaving that place that the sleigh, lagging behind, was robbed. Had Monier been tempted by someone's curiosity, while he was in Leslie's house, to show the Tsar's secret reply?

[76] For an account of the instructions given to Monier see Forsten, *Baltiiskii vopros*, Vol. II, pp. 364–366: Wejle, *Sveriges politik*, p. 9.

not be violating the truce between Sweden and Poland if he behaves in the same way as the Polish King and 'in like manner renders support' to the Tsar. 'It will be a great advantage to your Majesty the Tsar to raise a great army in the part of Germany which His Majesty [of Sweden] has conquered and to strike at Poland from that quarter.'[77] The Tsar is then advised, specifically, to engage 10,000 foot soldiers and 3,000 cavalrymen, a force which Gustavus Adolphus undertakes personally to organise and lead.[78] In return, he requests that no separate peace be made between Russia and Poland.[79]

Wejle notes correctly that if this plan had been implemented 'it would have made more certain the Russians' success in their war with Poland, while at the same time ensuring complete peace of mind for Gustavus Adolphus regarding possible Polish intervention against him'.[80] Oxenstjerna saw the plan as a mere ruse on the King's part. Analysing the instruction given to Monier in the letter quoted above, he writes that, to the best of his understanding, this consisted of three points:

(1) to draw the Muscovites into war with Poland; (2) to obtain money for Your Royal Majesty on the pretext of recruiting soldiers in Germany for Russia's benefit; (3) to secure continuation of the grain purchases. All three points [he goes on] are what the present situation needs, and I hope very strongly that Monier handled this business wisely and achieved something good. The security of Sweden and of your Royal Majesty requires that Poland be not left free from danger on the side toward Muscovy, and if Muscovy really does declare war, our affairs will go well and both sides will respect us.[81]

The sources confirm that the price which Gustavus Adolphus later asked from Moscow would indeed have enabled him, at the same time, to replenish his treasury, but the plan for an attack on Poland from the west was, nevertheless, not just a 'pretext'. Oxenstjerna himself admits, with some doubt: 'If this recruiting in Germany for the Grand Duke's needs is undertaken, Roussel will have much to discuss with me about it. He himself wants to advance this affair as much as possible.'[82] Roussel, the initiator of the whole plan, did indeed see it as something real, and wished to keep the conduct of it in his own hands. Gustavus Adolphus had the same attitude towards the plan. The authors of the work we have mentioned, *Sveriges Krig 1611–1632*, are inclined to reproach Gustavus Adolphus with thoughtlessness for his enthusiasm for Roussel's plan, and to praise the sober wisdom of Oxenstjerna. 'Roussel had ready a plan of the sort that adventurers of that period scattered around and which Oxenstjerna assessed with the coolest sobriety.' They proceed here from

[77] *TsGADA, Dela shvedskie*, 1631, stb. 8, ll. 220–222.    [78] Ibid., *stb.* 7, *l.* 287.
[79] Ibid., *stb.* 8, *l.* 68.    [80] Wejle, *Sveriges politik*, p. 9.
[81] *Arkiv till upplysning on svenska krigens . . . historia*, Vol. II, p. 157.
[82] Ibid.

the traditional view that all Roussel's schemes concerning Poland were foolish. They also attribute to Monier a disastrous influence on the King, for having persuaded him to carry out Roussel's plan despite the Chancellor's opposition.

Vainly did Oxenstjerna warn that the proposed recruiting on behalf of the Russians would only involve Sweden in the Russo–Polish war, whereas Sweden's role should have been merely to 'sit quietly during that situation . . .' and not be provoked by the Poles. The danger from Russia could have been averted without resorting to these adventuristic methods. However, Gustavus Adolphus held firmly to the notion of diverting the Rzeczpospolita by means of this plan, and zealously asserted that it did not flout international law.[83]

To us, on the contrary, it seems that Oxenstjerna's view was very short-sighted, and the plan by Roussel and Gustavus Adolphus considerably more far-seeing, even though risky. After all, the Russo–Polish war was not yet a reality. In the absence of a serious contribution from Sweden the thing might not come off. Because he realised that this was so, the King, disregarding Oxenstjerna, urged Roussel and Monier on.

After sending, in February 1631, another report to Moscow about his mission in Poland, in March Roussel himself appeared on the frontier, at the head of a magnificent embassy. The accompanying letter from governor Skytte introduced Roussel as 'a great ambassador, than whom none greater has been seen for a long time', and said that he was bringing a secret 'oral mandate from the Swedish King concerning matters most needful to the King and to the state of Russia'.[84] Owing to his earlier activity in Poland Roussel was allowed to go to Moscow only under great suspicion[85] and after much delay, especially as he carried no document in writing from Gustavus Adolphus.[86] However, he was followed by a fresh communication from Skytte which told how the King had 'sent couriers' to him at Riga at the beginning of April. Roussel was 'ordered to go to Moscow in all haste, travelling day and night', with the 'necessary matters' that had been entrusted to him, 'so that he may soon return

---

[83] *Sveriges Krig 1611–1632*, Vol. V, pp. 229–230.

[84] *TsGADA, Dela shvedskie*, 1631, stb. 5, *ll*. 42, 48.

[85] In February already the governor of Novgorod had been ordered, after he had sent spies into Livonia disguised as merchants, to instruct them, among other things, 'to find out secretly in Riga what Roussel was up to' – 'what task he has been given'. When the embassy arrived in Moscow its members were treated in an unusual manner. The responsible officials were told that anyone who came to where the embassy was housed, wishing to talk to the ambassador or his men, should be 'kept from the embassy's residence', seized, and sent to the Embassies Department, but this was to be done 'in such a way that the ambassador may not know about it or suspect it' (ibid., *ll*. 15, 120–121).

[86] There is an interesting instruction in the handwriting of the Patriarch Philaret: 'As the sovereign wills, but it seems to me that he should be allowed in without delay: why should he come here without the King's knowledge? So he should be let through at once. And I think he has come with some great matter' (ibid., *l*. 45 ob.).

without fail to the King's Majesty, bringing a good reply'.[87] Gustavus Adolphus was definitely feeling nervous. When he got to Moscow Roussel had absolutely secret talks with Prince Ivan Borisovich Cherkasskii, who was the close confidant of the Patriarch and the Tsar.[88]

From subsequent correspondence we can establish that Roussel, anticipating the slowcoach Monier, himself set forth the plan for recruiting soldiers for an attack on Poland from the west and concentrating them 'in the Silesian land', and also offered his services for the conduct of this recruitment.[89] This was the moment when Roussel began to oppose the recruitment of foreign regiments in Germany that Leslie was committed to. Taking into account, apparently, the limitations of the Russian treasury and also those of the German mercenary market (perhaps his own interests, as well), he demonstrated in every way, in letters sent to the Tsar thereafter, that the 'assembling' of troops by Colonel Leslie 'is not appropriate and will obstruct Your Majesty's design', that foreign regiments in the Russian service might turn traitor and go over to the Polish commander Gosiewski and that 'those Germans who are recruited' should be sent against Poland not from the Muscovite but from the Silesian side.[90] In addition, Roussel discussed with I.B. Cherkasskii all the problems of the coming war with Poland and also the Russo–Swedish alliance. The information he obtained, which was of immense value to Gustavus Adolphus, Roussel conveyed to the King later, in July, through Oxenstjerna.[91] But Roussel brought no official reply in writing, just as he had not taken any letter from Gustavus Adolphus. Loaded with rich gifts from the Tsar and surrounded with care and attention, Roussel left Moscow for Riga on 13 May,[92] two days before Monier reached Moscow. Roussel had, thus, prepared the way for Monier's negotiations, so that the latter was able to receive the Tsar's official reply to Gustavus Adolphus's plan.

---

[87] Ibid., *ll.* 147–148.

[88] The record of these talks has not been preserved. It must have been kept by Prince Cherkasskii, 'but in the Embassies Department nothing was known of this, because Jacques Roussel came about a great and secret matter' (Ibid., *ll.* 166–167).

[89] Ibid., *stb.* 9, *ll.* 3–19.

[90] Ibid., *stb.* 10, *ll.* 5, 29, 48. Roussel later offered to act as go-between for Muscovy with Prince Christian of Anhalt, who agreed, in return for better payment, to take command of the foreign troops recruited by Muscovy (ibid., 1632, *stb.* 8). But by that time the Smolensk War was in full swing.

[91] He sent this report from Riga on 17 June and it was received by the King, along with Oxenstjerna's letter (of 12 July) not earlier than the end of July 1631 (Wejle, *Sveriges politik*, p. 24).

[92] On 26 May Roussel set out from Pskov, by water, taking with him an ambler from the Tsar's stable and a sleigh covered with a sky-blue cloth which had not been given him outright but only lent for the journey from Moscow to the frontier (*TsGADA, Dela shvedskie*, 1631, *stb.* 5, *ll.* 187 *et seq.*).

What did this reply say? In Wejle's words, the King's proposal 'gave the Tsar great satisfaction'.[93] It was indeed accepted readily and in full, with only insignificant adjustments. Thus, the Muscovites did not want to include any cavalry in the forces they hired, preferring to hire a further 5,000 infantry and to send their own cavalry to the agreed place of assembly. The answer given to Gustavus Adolphus's request that Muscovy should not conclude a separate peace with the Polish–Lithuanian state took the form not only of agreement but of a hint that, perhaps, as a result of the war, there would be no question of either peace or truce with Poland's King – i.e., that the Crown of Poland might fall to Gustavus Adolphus himself. Finally came a request to be told the area from which the Swedish King intended to attack the Rzeczpospolita (through Livonia or through Germany) and the cost of this enterprise.[94] Monier left Moscow on 7 June 1631, but it was not until August that Gustavus Adolphus learned of the success of his mission and received the Tsar's secret message. Among other things, this message confirmed Muscovy's undertaking to begin war against Poland in that same year, 1631, though the date of the attack was put off from spring to 'summer'.[95]

Gustavus Adolphus was evidently worried by Monier's slowness, if we are to judge not only by his sending, in March 1631, the courier to Roussel already mentioned, telling him to make haste and get to Moscow, but also by his formal appointment (on 3 March) of a new ambassador to Moscow, Johan Möller, with the same mandate that Monier had had. Möller was sent 'in place of Anton Monier', who had travelled too 'protractedly', whereas his replacement undertook to deliver the King's letter within four weeks. The new ambassador was to remain at his new address in Moscow in order to deal with all 'matters both public and secret'.[96] It must be realised that Möller had, only a short time before this, in February 1631, gone from Moscow to Pomerania to see Gustavus Adolphus and was the first to bring him the news, joyful even if still unofficial, of Muscovy's preparations for war. Back again in Moscow at the beginning of June 1631 (a few days before Monier left), Möller related that he had 'for three weeks gone every day into His Majesty's chamber and talked to His Majesty about this realm [i.e., Muscovy] and about his secret information, with great zeal'. Besides the King, 'the Royal Chancellor Oxenstjerna knows about the secret matters of which he spoke to His Majesty the Tsar, but no-one else knows of them'.[97] All this gives

[93] Wejle, Sveriges politik, p. 10.
[94] TsGADA, Dela shvedskie, 1631, stb. 8, ll. 222, 68.    [95] Ibid., l. 68.
[96] Wejle, Sveriges politik, pp. 15, 57–58.    [97] Ibid., pp. 57, 16.

an impression of truth – with, however, the reservation made earlier concerning the role of Oxenstjerna.

Möller prefaced the exposition of his secret business with some information about international affairs which, though tendentious, was not without foundation. Among other things he spoke of the intention of the Polish King and the Sejm to seek peace with Sweden and Muscovy. A Polish envoy had already been sent 'to discuss peace' with Gustavus Adolphus, who, however, was not disposed to believe their 'deceptions'. The Poles had asked the German Emperor to arbitrate in their peace negotiations with Muscovy, and he had already sent, through the Rzeczpospolita, a great embassy to Moscow. Möller himself had met on the road two couriers whom the Emperor had sent on ahead, and had by cunning got all this out of them.[98] Furthermore, Möller told of Gustavus Adolphus's capture of many German cities, stressing significantly that 'these cities of the Kaiser's are close to the Polish King's realm, and they are all now held by his Prince, King Gustavus Adolphus'.[99]

Möller did not develop in any detail the plan to attack the Polish–Lithuanian state from the German direction, since Anton Monier had already, before him, 'completed that matter', but provided a number of supplementary facts. He passed on the military advice and instructions of Gustavus Adolphus and his general opinion that if Mikhail Fedorovich wanted 'to hire Germans and attack Poland from the German side', at the same time as Russian 'warriors go in from their side', the unexpectedness of this would cause the Rzeczpospolita to suffer inevitable defeat. In view of the action of the Polish King in supplying the Emperor with two regiments commanded by Polish colonels, which meant that he had already broken the truce with Sweden, Gustavus Adolphus would, 'from love of His Majesty the Tsar, transfer to him two regiments of his own soldiers, with good commanders'. Moreover, he was ready to go to war himself if the Poles gave him occasion: 'and if the Poles were to meet the Germans with large forces and the Germans were hard-pressed, the latter might withdraw into those places which are now under the Swedish King, and he would be glad if the Poles were to cross the frontier in pursuit, thereby breaking the truce.'[100]

As we see, the military genius of Gustavus Adolphus was involved in earnest in the elaboration of this strategical plan. Still more important for the King, though, was the diplomatic plan for a Swedo–Russian alliance. He instructed Möller to say: 'If His Majesty the Tsar could see into my heart he would perceive how great is my goodwill towards him' – and he

---

[98] An Imperial embassy actually arrived, accompanied by a Polish escort, at the Russian frontier in the following year, 1632, but was not admitted.

[99] *TsGADA, Dela shvedskie*, 1631, *stb*. 8, *ll*. 19–20, 15–16.    [100] Ibid., *l*. 64.

was even prepared to 'stand to the death' with Mikhail Fedorovich and his successors.[101]

The more favourably Möller's further negotiations progressed in Moscow, the more did he put forward fresh tempting proposals, evidently following instructions. These included a proposal for purchasing various armaments at a low price directly from the Swedish King's stores and a broadly conceived mercantilist plan to transfer craftsmen to Russia from the West in order to enrich the Tsar's treasury. All this, however, was of secondary importance when compared with the cautious sounding out of the most delicate matter in Möller's conversation with Prince Cherkasskii on 15 July. The ambassador expressed the opinion that, if the Tsar went to war against the Polish King ('to take White Russia from Poland') it would be good 'to induce the Zaporozhian Cossacks' to do likewise.[102] If we put this together with an earlier statement of his on behalf of Gustavus Adolphus – ' it would be good that there should be such ties between two great sovereigns that neither of them would make peace with the Polish King separately from the other'[103] – his line of thought becomes clear. In agreeing not to conclude a separate peace one necessarily foresees, if only in outline, a future joint peace treaty. Gustavus Adolphus was letting it be understood that he did not object to cession from the Rzeczpospolita to Muscovy of Byelorussia and the Zaporozhian Ukraine. We have seen already that the Muscovite government hinted in its reply sent with Monier (and, significantly, repeated to Möller) that there might not be any need to make peace or truce with a third party, 'the Polish King'. Through a diplomatic haze we perceive sketched before us the outlines of that agreement between Russia and Sweden, which, in the following year, 1632, the Muscovite government proposed to Sweden, without disguise or concealment, in accordance with the project developed by Roussel.

There can be no doubt that as long before as 1630 Roussel had agreed on the general lines of this scheme for a Russo–Swedish alliance, in separate talks with Mikhail Fedorovich (or, more probably, the Patriarch) and with Gustavus Adolphus. The Muscovite government would never have agreed to, and still less would itself have proposed, Gustavus Adolphus's candidature to the throne of Poland unless it could count on his support for the return of the extensive Russian territories which had been seized in the past by Lithuania and Poland.

However, the dimensions and composition of these territorial transfers could not have been understood by Roussel at the outset. About

[101] Ibid., *ll*. 63, 67.   [102] Ibid., *l*. 106.   [103] Ibid., *l*. 65.

Smolensk and adjoining districts there was no need for argument.[104] Roussel's whole attention was focused at first on the Zaporozhian Ukraine. The question of Byelorussia came up later. Roussel must have heard this demand by Muscovy for the first time in July 1630, and he brought it to Gustavus Adolphus's notice in October/November of that year. As regards the Ukraine, there are grounds for thinking that when Bethlen Gábor was making his plans to seize the Crown of Poland, he reckoned on receiving approval and military help from Muscovy in exchange for ceding the Zaporozhian Ukraine. It was in 1629 that the Orthodox Cossacks of Zaporozhe, who naturally leaned towards Muscovy, again rose in rebellion against the Poles. This event provided a real foundation for such a plan. From a common source, Bethlen Gábor, this idea reached, on the one hand, Gustavus Adolphus through ambassador Strassburg, and on the other, the Tsar and the Patriarch through ambassador Roussel. Already in 1630 Gustavus Adolphus was instructing Skytte, the Governor of Livonia, to do everything possible to stir the Cossacks to revolt against Poland.[105] Roussel apparently spoke about this with Patriarch Cyril of Constantinople, when he was in Turkey, and later discussed the Zaporozhian question in detail during his first visit to Moscow, as we see from the extracts that have survived of the letter to the Tsar and the Patriarch which he sent from Vyborg, on the way back, immediately after his departure.[106]

In the next letter, written after his audience with Gustavus Adolphus, Roussel talks again and in a very significant way about the Zaporozhian

---

[104] When Roussel was in Moscow for the second time he accepted from Prince Cherkasskii some diversionary or intelligence-gathering tasks in relation to Smolensk. In July and October 1631 he reported, through his secretary Wassermann, whom he sent from Riga to Moscow, that 'the design directed at Smolensk', connected with the use of some secret 'light-using device', was effected by employing two trusted persons sent to the governor of Smolensk, Gosiewski, on the pretext of presenting an official request from Sweden regarding some Swedish prisoners of war who were allegedly held in Smolensk. Roussel promised to inform the Tsar on his next visit to Moscow also about other 'unfailing' means he had conceived 'in order that this place Smolensk may be returned to Your Majesty'. Meanwhile, in October Wassermann brought to Moscow some very precise information about the fortifications and garrison of Smolensk, the sentiments of the inhabitants in favour of passing under Muscovite rule, and the advisers and personal entourage of the governor of Smolensk (*TsGADA, Dela shvedskie*, 1631, *stb.* 10, *ll.* 3, 30, 34–40, 54–55).     [105] Wejle, *Sveriges politik*, p. 25.

[106] Roussel writes that Sigismund III has for forty years been inciting the Cossacks to make raids into Turkish territory, and Sultan Murad IV should be told about this. 'I know', he goes on, 'that Your Majesty is well aware . . . And therefore Your Majesty the Tsar will see that you ought not to issue any reprimand about our intention. Also, if Your Majesty allows, I will labour night and day to persuade the Zaporozhians to go to war and involve them in this cause, but they will need all manner of help to ensure that this war does not break off' (*TsGADA, Dela shvedskie*, 1630, *stb.* 3, *ll.* 28 and 21).

Cossacks.[107] At this time he began to make preparations for sending two agents of his, l'Admiral and Des Grèves, through Moscow to the Cossacks. However, Skytte, the governor of Livonia, and also, apparently, Oxenstjerna opposed this move, although Roussel referred to instructions he had received from Gustavus Adolphus.[108] Not until June 1631 was he able, taking advantage of Skytte's absence, to send his men off, supplied with letters to the Tsar, asking for help with their mission, and to the Zaporozhian Cossacks, calling on them to continue their struggle against Poland, proposing an alliance and assuring them that Gustavus Adolphus saw it as his task to defend the Greek faith against the Papists.[109] The Muscovite government readily co-operated with this mission, placing an escort and interpreters at the disposal of Roussel's agents. It was itself prepared to give support to the Zaporozhians' struggle. According to the statement, which deserves attention, made in a printed Polish broadsheet of 1631, the Tsar and the Patriarch had in 1630, on learning that the Zaporozhians had begun war against the Rzeczpospolita, sent envoys to them and were intending shortly themselves to attack the Polish–Lithuanian state. The Tsar's commanders and boyars and all his forces had been made ready for an onslaught on Vitebsk and Polotsk, and for besieging Smolensk and even Kiev, but at that time the Polish government managed to pacify the Cossacks, and Moscow had to put off its intended action.[110] This unfavourable political situation explains also the complete failure of the mission of l'Admiral and Des Grèves. The new Hetman of the Zaporozhians, Kulaga, handed them over to the Polish Crown's Hetman, Koniecpolski, who forwarded them to Warsaw. From there the Polish Chancellor, Zadik, sent them on to Oxenstjerna, with a protest against this attempt to make propaganda among the Cossacks, in violation of the Swedo–Polish truce. Oxenstjerna was obliged to excuse himself at great length, alleging that Roussel had exceeded his authority. At the same time Roussel, for his part, was extolling the mission, and he even published (in 1632) his letter to the Cossacks.

If we consider that Gustavus Adolphus seriously assigned to Roussel the task of inclining the Poles in favour of his candidature, then we must argue that by his mission to the Cossacks Roussel finally ruined the

[107] He promises 'to write about the secret matters, and these matters will rejoice Your Majesty the Tsar, and it would be fit that Your Majesty the Tsar should unfailingly call on the Zaporozhian Cossacks, so that they...' (*TsGADA, Dela shvedskie*, 1631, *stb.* 5, *l.* 12.).
[108] Wejle, *Sveriges politik*, pp. 24–26. For the correspondence between Roussel and Moscow about the sending of the two agents see *TsGADA, Dela shvedskie*, 1631, *stb.* 5.
[109] Ibid., *stb.* 9.     [110] Ibid., *stb.* 10, *ll.* 42–43.

project. In reality, however, Roussel was trying to do something different. He strove to establish a practical link between the Cossack revolt and Moscow and thereby to predetermine the question of the transfer of the Zaporozhian Ukraine from Poland to Muscovy. An abstract promise to hand over to Muscovy the territory of the Zaporozhian Ukraine after Gustavus Adolphus had been crowned King of Poland would have had an untrustworthy sound about it. But if Mikhail Fedorovich were actually linked with the rebel Cossacks, he would be obliged, in defence of the success he had already obtained *de facto*, to go to war at once against the Polish–Lithuanian state.

We are now in a position to evaluate the plan of Gustavus Adolphus and Roussel as a whole. In his letter of 7 October 1631 Roussel spelt out the choice unambiguously. 'Eventually Poland will fall into the hands of my King either by force or in friendship'.[111] It is understandable that, if matters went the latter way, Muscovy would not only have played no part, it would have suffered a major political setback. How Roussel impressed this danger upon Muscovy can be seen, for example, from the fact that on the same day, 22 June 1631, when he signed his instructions to l'Admiral and Des Grèves, he also signed an order to his secretary, Wassermann, to inform Moscow of the success of his dealings with the political leaders of the Rzeczpospolita – Gosiewski and, especially, Lew Sapieha, who had already sent to Riga, for negotiations about the Swedish King's candidature, his plenipotentiary, Colonel Korf.[112] At the same time, however, this revealed to the Muscovite government another possibility – that Gustavus Adolphus might get Poland not 'in friendship' but 'by force', if Moscow would agree to go to war. In that case the Swedish King would contribute to the defeat of the Rzeczpospolita by striking a simultaneous blow from Germany (in the Tsar's name to, be sure, and using his money), and would cede to Muscovy the eastern part of the Rzceczpolita.[113]

---

[111] Wejle, *Sveriges politik*, p. 29.

[112] Whom, Roussel observes in his letter, You, Most Holy Patriarch, 'know very well' (ibid., pp. 2, 7). Three months later, in his next letter, sent with Wassermann, Roussel again lays stress on the success of his dealings with the Polish and Lithuanian dissidents and even encloses a letter from Lew Sapieha (ibid., p. 33).

[113] Oxenstjerna was not let fully into the plan, but knew enough about it to participate in bringing pressure on Moscow by the 'carrot and stick' method. Thus, in one of Leslie's reports sent on his way to Moscow (at the beginning of June) the concluding part, as we can easily make out from the context, was written either by Oxenstjerna himself or on his instructions. It had become known to the Swedish Chancellor that the King of Poland and that country's senators had decided to seek the conclusion of a 'permanent peace' with Sweden, 'but they made along with it this proposal – to try their fortune by going with all their power against Russia. But His Majesty King Gustavus Adolphus wants no such peace as that. After the Swedish King had taken the city of Frankfurt, the princes and estates of Silesia wrote to His Majesty to ask him to come with his army into Silesia,

The Muscovite government was as frightened by the first possibility as it was willing to co-operate in the second. This line in foreign policy was in no way imposed upon it by Sweden. On the contrary, it is not difficult to assure oneself from Roussel's letters that, essentially, he just put into Gustavus Adolphus's hand a weapon that he had received in Moscow from the hands of the Patriarch. He did not reveal immediately the entire design to Gustavus Adolphus. In a letter sent with Wassermann in July 1631 Roussel wrote to the Patriarch that he was soon going to see Gustavus Adolphus again 'in order to explain clearly to His Royal Majesty the matter about which I spoke with His Majesty your sovereign'.[114] It turned out that a Russo–Swedish military alliance against the Rzeczpospolita was only a minimum programme planned in Moscow ('the nearer matter', 'a military alliance against the common foe'), which could be put into practice even if a certain maximum programme, 'the higher matter', were not realised.[115]

Thus, Moscow's agreement to Gustavus Adolphus's proposal was not forced upon it. The only dispute between them concerned the timing of the Muscovite attack, and on that point nothing could shake Moscow, since it wished firmly to wait until it could launch an offensive jointly with Turkey.

What was forced was, rather, strange as it may seem, Gustavus Adolphus's claim to the Polish throne. He had no means of bringing about a Russo–Polish war other than to adopt Roussel's plan in its entirety. Once the King needed Poland to be caught up in war with Russia he had, willy-nilly, as we have shown, both to proclaim publicly his desire to be elected by the Sejm and secretly to agree to winning the Polish Crown with Russia's aid. He had also to occupy Poland's throne lest, after his victory, it should fall to the Tsar: that would have constituted too dangerous a rear for the Swedes. Consequently, gaining possession of the Crown of Poland, which Gustavus Adolphus did not want, proved to be a necessary condition for victory over the German Emperor, the aim towards which he strove so ardently.

During a whole year, from June 1630 to July 1631, Gustavus Adolphus undertook no large-scale operations from his bridgehead in North-Eastern Germany.

What is the explanation for this? Perhaps Richelieu, looking to the future, was already afraid of encountering a rival in the struggle for the

---

where all gates would be opened to them.' Earlier in this report it is mentioned that as a result of his capture of Frankfurt-am-Oder, 'the Silesian, Moravian and Bohemian lands lie open' to Gustavus Adolphus, and the Polish King 'is now powerless and His Majesty the Tsar can take vengeance on him for his enmity' (*TsGADA, Dela shvedskie,* 1630, *stb.* 10, *ll.* 195–199).    [114] Ibid., *l.* 5.    [115] Ibid.

Rhine, and secretly opposed a Swedish offensive? So it has sometimes been thought. But, however complicated were Gustavus Adolphus's relations with Richelieu, who tried to impose upon this fiery defender of Protestantism in Germany an alliance with the German Catholic League and its leader Maximilian of Bavaria, they were never such as to account for the passivity of the Swedish army through a whole year.

The view taken by historians amounts to this, that Gustavus Adolphus, having without difficulty obliged Bogislaw, the last Slav Duke of Pomerania, to accept a treaty of alliance, and having then acquired part of Mecklenburg thanks to the support of its dukes, who had been driven out by Wallenstein, was unable to advance further than Pomerania and Mecklenburg simply because he lacked the consent of the neighbouring princes of Germany. Only two or three minor territorial princes and a few cities, including Magdeburg, declared for him, but both of the Protestant electors whose realms barred the road into the heart of Germany – Brandenburg and Saxony – were unwilling even to hear of an alliance with the Swedish King against the Emperor. At the end of February 1631 these electors held the 'Convention of Leipzig', a gathering of Protestant princes and cities of Germany, at which it was resolved to maintain neutrality (with a favourable attitude towards Denmark), and alliance with Sweden was rejected. In vain did Gustavus Adolphus deploy his diplomatic skills – now humbly ingratiating himself with his brother-in-law Georg-Wilhelm, the Elector of Brandenburg, now bringing his troops up to the Elector's frontier and even seizing Frankfurt-am-Oder. Under the influence of his Catholic minister, Schwarzenberg, Georg-Wilhelm remained immovable. Only when the Imperial Catholic forces under Tilly and Pappenheim burst into his territory and began to threaten his uncle's possession, Magdeburg, did he agree to accept limited aid from Gustavus Adolphus. After Magdeburg had, nevertheless, been taken and horribly ravaged by Tilly's forces (10 May 1631), Gustavus Adolphus was asked to quit Brandenburg, but, relying on the support of the people, who were angered by Tilly's atrocities, the King compelled the Elector to enter into an alliance with Sweden. In the same way the Elector of Saxony was forced by Tilly's reckless aggression to seek alliance with Sweden. In order to make the Elector abandon his neutrality, Tilly invaded Saxony, and only then did Johann-Georg, fearing a wave of Catholic reaction in his realm, turn his back on the Emperor and join up with Gustavus Adolphus. In this way the gates into Germany were flung open. Following Brandenburg and Saxony, other Protestant principalities also placed themselves under the Swedish King's protection. After destroying Tilly's army on 17(7) September 1631 at Breitenfeld, near Leipzig, Gustavus Adolphus was able almost without opposition to march into Western and Southern Germany.

That is how one may briefly summarise the essential content of the many volumes which have been written on this theme, mostly by German scholars. It is not hard, however, to perceive the one-sidedness and contradictoriness of this German version of events. Apparently, Gustavus Adolphus was neither victor nor conqueror in Germany. It was not he who broke the stubborn opposition of the two Electors but only unwise Tilly. The initiative in all these events came exclusively from the German princes and commanders. The Swedish King did not invade Germany but merely waited until he was allowed in. That this view cannot represent the whole truth of the matter is obvious if we bring two facts together. How was it that Gustavus Adolphus could smash Tilly's mighty army if he could not exert military pressure either on Saxony, which had only an insignificant army, or on Brandenburg, which hardly had one at all?

All that we have written earlier helps us to understand more correctly the conduct of Gustavus Adolphus during the first year of the 'Swedish' war. It is not enough to say that he was awaiting Moscow's decision and doing all he could to hasten that decision. With his usual inexhaustible energy he was at the same time trying by other means to protect his rear against the Polish danger. If we examine the content and the tone of his negotiations with Georg-Wilhelm of Brandenburg,[116] we see that Gustavus Adolphus specifically assigned to Brandenburg the role of shield against Poland for when the Swedish army should advance into Germany.[117] For this purpose it was clearly necessary to make a friend of the Elector of Brandenburg and to ingratiate oneself with him rather than use armed threats, for an ally acquired by force must always be unreliable (as later proved to be the case with Saxony). While the friendship of Brandenburg (strengthened by Swedish garrisons) was needed by Gustavus Adolphus in order to keep Poland at bay, an unfriendly attitude by that state would, in the event of an attack by Poland, amount to catastrophe – inevitably, a coalition would be formed, embracing the Rzeczpospolita, Brandenburg and Denmark. In other words, we can affirm that Gustavus Adolphus's policy towards Brandenburg must be seen as of a piece with the whole series of attempts and projects already mentioned for solving the Polish problem – for moving Transylvania, the Crimean Khanate, Turkey, etc.

---

[116] Cf. Helbig, K. G., *Gustav Adolf und die Kurfürsten von Sachsen und Brandenburg 1630–1632*, Leipzig, 1854.

[117] This is reflected even in Alexander Leslie's report to Moscow in which he gives a valuable review of Gustavus Adolphus's campaign in Pomerania and his relations with Brandenburg (*TsGADA, Dela shvedskie*, 1630, stb. 10, *ll.* 172–175).

against the Rzeczpospolita. The Brandenburg project proved to be no more realistic than all the rest were, apart from the one concerning Russia. Georg-Wilhelm of Brandenburg, stupid and cowardly, allied himself with the drunkard Johann-Georg of Saxony, and the more politely and pleadingly Gustavus Adolphus appealed to them, the more did these two put on airs and dig their heels in. But as soon as the King, having received the news of Moscow's decision to go to war, no longer needed their alliance against Poland he 'spoke so brusquely' first to one and then to the other that they both suddenly became submissive and changed their 'political convictions'.

In fact, Gustavus Adolphus's entire conduct in Germany during this year appears in a new light when we relate it to his gradual receipt of news from Moscow. The King did not remain idle all the time, confining himself to manoeuvres and skirmishes: sometimes he threw himself, so to speak, upon the enemy, the spirit of battle took possession of him, but caution then got the upper hand and he again reined in, like a war-horse, his army which was the best in Europe. Thus, in January 1631, he dashed into Mecklenburg, routed two units of the Emperor's army at Greifenhagen and Garz, and then stopped. In April 1631 he fell upon Frankfurt, crossed the Oder and stopped again. At the beginning of June he laid siege to Berlin and forced Elector Georg-Wilhelm to ally with him, but did not exploit the opening to the West thus created. At the end of June and the beginning of July he came down upon Tilly, inflicted several severe blows on his army, but then allowed him to get away. Only on 17(7) September 1631 did Gustavus Adolphus strike at Tilly's main forces near Leipzig, wipe them literally from the face of the earth and, without stopping, begin his astonishing march across Germany. Each of these military threats was preceded by the King's receipt of some important news from Moscow. Did not each of these serve psychologically like an electrical impulse spurring Gustavus Adolphus to action? To explain his behaviour in Pomerania we need, of course, to take account of all the factors and the entire international situation, especially the complex political situation in Germany.[118] To reduce everything to the Polish factor alone would be to fall into one-sidedness. In order, however, to correct an opposite form of one-sidedness, a scholar has the right, and is even obliged, to give preponderant attention precisely to that factor which has hitherto been overlooked and to see to what extent he can, with its aid, explain the actions of Gustavus Adolphus, in so far as each of them was followed soon by one of the military events listed above, and each of

---

[118] See Helbig, *Gustav Adolf*: Boëthius, S. B., *Svenskarne i de nedersachsiska och westfaliska kustländerna juli 1630 – november 1632. Till lelysning af Gustav II Adolfs tyska politik*, Uppsala, 1912.

these military thrusts was preceded by the King's receipt of one of the dispatches from Moscow we have mentioned. Let us try to refine and test this hypothesis.

We mentioned earlier that it was at the beginning of 1631 that Johan Möller first brought to Gustavus Adolphus, direct from Moscow and the Russian government, the news of Muscovy's warlike intentions and preparations. After several months of stagnation in Pomerania this news, which brightened the international horizon, cannot but have given heart to Gustavus Adolphus. It naturally inspired him to launch his invasion of Mecklenburg, but it was, nevertheless, insufficient to justify a general campaign in Germany, if only because it had not taken the form of an official communication in writing, and to that extent failed to correspond to the new plan for Russo–Swedish co-operation which had been worked out with Roussel in November. As we have seen, Gustavus Adolphus spent three weeks instructing Möller in the spirit of this new plan and then sent him back to Russia.

In February the Russian envoys Plemiannikov and Aristov arrived in Stockholm, together with Alexander Leslie. Although, owing to the climatic conditions, they themselves were unable to cross the sea to Germany in sufficient pomp until May,[119] a request to receive the envoys and an explanation of their mission was at once sent to Gustavus Adolphus by the Swedish government. He received this communication not later than the last ten days of March. And it was at the end of March that he attacked Kolberg and on 13(3) April that he took Frankfurt-am-Oder. But it would, of course, have been foolish of him to develop his offensive any further before he had face-to-face talks with the Russian envoys, and so he returned to his waiting attitude and to diplomatic dealings with the Elector of Brandenburg.[120]

The latter, seeing that Gustavus Adolphus was not pushing on or threatening him, and taking this to be a symptom of weakness, put to the King at the beginning of May, at the instigation of Saxony, the arrogant demand that he immediately quit the Brandenburgers' fortress of Spandau, which the Swedes had occupied. The dispute over this demand went on for a month, and on 7 June Gustavus Adolphus experienced one of his most disagreeable days, when he was obliged to withdraw the Swedish garrison from Spandau. Then something unusual happened which military historians have been unable to explain clearly. Two days later, Gustavus Adolphus appeared with his army before the walls of

---

[119] Cf. the minutes of the Council of State for 11 February, 26 March, 16 April, 5 and 7 May 1631 (*Svenska riksrådets protokoll*, Vol. II, pp. 58, 72–73, 79, 84, 86).

[120] The most detailed account of Gustavus Adolphus's military and diplomatic operations in this period is given in Cronholm, *Sveriges Krig 1611–1632*, Vol. IV, pp. 107–164.

Berlin, aimed his cannon at the Elector's palace, declared all previous agreements null and void, and forced Georg-Wilhelm, who was out of his mind with fear, to sign, on 11 June, a treaty by which he presented his fortresses and granted military subsidies to the Swedes for the entire duration of the war.[121] It has been thought that Gustavus Adolphus had been infuriated by the news of the destruction of Magdeburg. But the event can be explained more simply. On 1 June the Russian envoys at last arrived at the King's court in Stettin. At first they thought of going to meet the King 'at the front', but then they were persuaded to await his speedy return, and a courier set out to bring the news of their arrival to Gustavus Adolphus. The courier apparently met the King immediately after he had abandoned Spandau. Without losing a minute, the King changed all his plans and pointed his army towards Berlin, while the courier went back to Stettin bearing an apology which explained that, 'owing to certain great matters', he had returned to his troops and would be back at his court in Stettin later than he intended.[122]

On 14 June Gustavus Adolphus, having successfully concluded those 'great matters', was back in Stettin and receiving Plemiannikov and Aristov with exceptional ceremony. Newspapers described in detail the magnificence of the embassy and the friendly atmosphere of the audience accorded to it. They also speculated and repeated rumours concerning the subject of the negotiations and the purpose of the recruitment of troops being carried out by Leslie (one of these newspapers was sent via Möller to Moscow). Some asserted that the Tsar was offering Gustavus Adolphus help against the Emperor, others, that the King was promising to help the Tsar against Poland.

The official Swedish communiqué stated (undoubtedly so as to mislead Poland) that the Tsar wanted to send Gustavus Adolphus troops and money. How various the reports that circulated were can be seen from the way that all the contemporary writers mentioned earlier – Burge and Abelin, Chemnitz and Pufendorf – describe and discuss the Muscovite embassy quite differently one from another, evidently relying on different sources.[123] Gustavus Adolphus's written reply to Mikhail Fedorovich, dated 21 June 1631 and handed to the ambassador, shows the frank

---

[121]  Ibid., Vol. IV, pp. 316–317.

[122]  See the translation of 'reports' from a German newspaper of 19 June 1631 (*TsGADA, Dela shvedskie*, 1631, *stb.* 8, *l.* 148). Cf. also, ibid., *stb.* 4, *ll.* 172–193 – the embassy's formal report on its work.

[123]  Burge, *gennois*, p. 137; Arlanibaeus, *Arma suecica*, pp. 162–163, *Theatrum Europaeum*, Vol. II, p. 413; Chemnitz, *Königlichen-schwedischen*, Vol. I, p. 173; Pufendorf, S., *Commentariorum*, Book III, Section 18, p. 47. The last-mentioned writer deals most thoroughly with the negotiations: Gustavus Adolphus 'was desirous of kindling war between the Poles and the Russians, which would always be of service to him as a measure of precaution against both of them'.

satisfaction with which he had received the Muscovite government's promise to begin war against Poland 'in the spring'. The King is ready to support the Tsar with advice and action. He again urges him to 'beware' of the designs of the Polish–Habsburg–Catholic camp[124] and states his readiness to help in every way with the hiring and transporting of soldiers, the selecting of experienced officers, and the purchase of arms and supplies, going into detail about all these matters. In a special enclosure Gustavus Adolphus 'bows deeply' before the Tsar's 'great friendship' – his permission to purchase Russian grain – and asks that this aid be continued in the future. He values it all the more highly 'because Your Majesty the Tsar wishes to begin a war and it is therefore needed by you'.[125] And, immediately after signing these documents, Gustavus Adolphus sets off from Stettin to join his army and attack Tilly's forces.[126] But could the King not check his impulse this time too? After all, Plemiannikov and Aristov had not brought him any answer to the plan for an attack on the Rzeczpospolita from two sides: they were even quite ignorant of the plan, as was Leslie. In that sense their visit brought Gustavus Adolphus a certain amount of disappointment, or, at least, required that he draw upon a fresh reserve of patience. He had been preparing to carry out his promise since the beginning of April. After the taking of Frankfurt-am-Oder he had at once sent his best general, Gustav Horn, with several thousand men (cavalry and infantry) into Silesia, to the Polish frontier. In July Horn was recalled from Silesia and Alexander Leslie senior appointed commander of the group of forces at Frankfurt-am-Oder and on the Silesian frontier.[127]

There can be no doubt that Gustavus Adolphus intended to employ this group for an invasion of Poland through Silesia, using Frankfurt as its base, when Muscovy went into action and when the bulk of the Swedish forces had already advanced into Germany.

We know already just when it was that Gustavus Adolphus received at last the news that Moscow had agreed in principle to his war-plan. The first report came at the end of July or the beginning of August: Roussel's account of his journey to Moscow passed on by Oxenstjerna. But this was unofficial. The official reply, sent through Möller, reached Gustavus

[124] 'Our Royal Majesty is well aware of the evil intention of the Kaiser and the Pope to press upon the great state and land of Your Majesty the Tsar through Poland, to conquer it and crush the ancient Greek faith, installing in its place their evil false Popish belief and idolatry' (*TsGADA, Dela shvedskie*, 1631, stb. 4, *ll.* 132–133).
[125] Ibid., *ll.* 127–142. These replies were delivered to Moscow on 3 November 1631 by Aristov. Plemiannikov fell ill in Stettin and died there in July 1631.
[126] *Sveriges Krig 1611–1632*, Vol. IV, pp. 368–397.
[127] Chemnitz, *Königlichen-schwedischen*, Vol. I, p. 192; cf. p. 228 (Article 41 – Acta des General-Major Leslé am Oderstrom).

Adolphus at the very end of August, as we can see from his letter to Oxenstjerna dated 29 August.[128] This time, all the King's energy which had been accumulating for a year and had with difficulty been held in check burst forth with tremendous force. Gustavus Adolphus impetuously left the camp at Werben where he had just succeeded in concluding a treaty of alliance with Landgrave Wilhelm of Hesse-Cassel and hurled himself upon Saxony. Elector Johann-Georg, in mortal terror, surrendered his army and his country to the King without making the slightest objection and finding a plausible excuse in the 'offences' committed by Tilly, while he himself fled from his army to distant Eilenburg, there to drown his fright in wine. And on 17(7) September Gustavus Adolphus won his great battle in Germany, at Breitenfeld.[129] At once, without any delay, he advanced with incredible speed through Thuringia and Franconia to the Rhine, and sent the Saxon army on an outflanking march through Moravia and Bohemia.

But on the eve of Breitenfeld and after it, Gustavus Adolphus's thoughts turned again, not without anxiety, towards far-off Russia. Only a week before the battle he wrote new instructions for Monier, making his plan more precise, as the Muscovite government had asked. On 30 August, when the King was 'with the great regiments', Gustavus Adolphus's letter to Mikhail Fedorovich also received his signature. This letter promised all manner of services and recommended to the Tsar a new confidential agent, Gilius Koner.[130] Immediately after his victory at Breitenfeld he dispatched to Moscow with extraordinary haste a special courier whose task was to convey , through Monier, the joyful news and also to assure the Tsar that he had sent one of his generals into Silesia to prepare an invasion of Poland.

To analyse these new *démarches* and the reasons for the postponement of Russia's offensive until 1632 would take us beyond the framework of this chapter.

---

[128] Wejle, *Sveriges politik*, p. 10. In the words of the authors of *Sveriges Krig 1611–1632*, 'the friendliness of relations with Russia appeared even more clearly when Monier returned from Moscow in August' (Vol. V, p. 230).

[129] *Sveriges Krig 1611–1632*, Vol. IV, pp. 428–523.    [130] See *infra*, Chapter 3.

# 3    The conflict concerning the Russo–Swedish alliance in 1631–1632

Only comparatively recently has the history of Russo–Swedish relations during the 'Swedish' period of the Thirty Years' War attracted close attention on the part of historians either in Sweden or in the USSR. The subject had, of course, been dealt with earlier in historical works, but far from fully.[1] Almost simultaneously, and independently of each other, D. Norrman in Sweden and the present writer in the USSR tried to compile, as far as possible, exhaustive surveys of the available sources and also applied themselves to the abundant unpublished material in the archives.

Norrman's book (in Swedish) *Gustavus Adolphus's Policy Toward Russia and Poland during the War in Germany (1630–1632)* appeared in 1943.[2] It is a highly conscientious and competent résumé of all the facts to which the author had access. Without this work no-one can henceforth succeed in studying international relations in Eastern Europe in the period of the Thirty Years' War. However, Norrman, though he made very thorough use of the Swedish archives, was unable to use the corresponding Russian archives, and apparently was even unaware of what an abundance of material relating to the subject that interested him was to be found in the records of Muscovy's Embassies Department. The Russian historians on whose works Norrman relied (V.O. Kliuchevskii, G.V. Forsten, *et al.*) had made no use at all of these records and evidently left him with the impression that they did not exist.

The present writer began in 1945 to publish a series of articles on Russo–Swedish relations in the period in question. Under wartime and immediately post-war conditions I was unable to obtain Norrman's book in good time and use his material in these articles.[3] I used only those data from the Swedish archives relating to this subject which had been quoted

---

[1] See, e.g., Palmstierna, C.F., *Utrikesförvaltninges historia 1611–1648 (Den svenska utrikesförvaltninges historia)*, Uppsala, 1935.

[2] Norrman, D. *Gustav Adolfs politik mot Ryssland och Polen under Tyska kriget (1630–1632)*, Uppsala, 1943.

[3] This applies also to the preceding chapters of this work, which are based on these articles [note by editor of Russian original].

by his predecessors (Wejle, Cronholm, Ahnlund, Paul, etc.) and the published Swedish sources.

In this chapter, as in the foregoing ones, I have based my argument on unpublished material in the archives of the Embassies Department in Moscow. Now, however, I am in a position to compare this, step by step, more fully than before, with what is in the Swedish sources, thanks to the work of my Swedish colleague D. Norrman in revealing and systematically studying them.

The Russo–Polish Smolensk War (1632–1634) and the 'Swedish period' of the Thirty Years' War in Germany (1630–1635) are two phenomena which have seemed to historians to be quite isolated one from the other. Yet, as we discover from the archives, especially from those of the Russian Embassies Department, these two wars interacted closely. If we study the connection between them we begin to understand much better the history of both.

What did that connection consist in, if we are to sum the matter up in a few words? For Sweden it was vitally necessary that Russia tie up, that is, distract from Sweden, the armies of the Rzeczpospolita. Without that condition, war against the German Emperor would have been out of the question for Gustavus Adolphus, since, for reasons both economic and political, the Rzeczpospolita remained Sweden's 'Enemy Number One'.[4] As for Muscovy, the main aim of its foreign policy in the period of Patriarch Philaret's rule was to recover the Ukraine, the Smolensk region and Byelorussia from the Rzeczpospolita. This aim dictated the necessity of a temporary military-political alliance with Sweden, however profound the contradictions might be with that state, which had taken away Russia's Baltic possessions. Concretely, the Russian government expected the following from the alliance with Sweden. First, a victory for Gustavus Adolphus in Germany would result in isolation of the Rzeczpospolita, since the Habsburgs' Empire was its chief external support, its bulwark and, to a certain extent, the source of Sigismund III's aggressive policy. Second, through the agency of such a first-class military power as Sweden then was, the Russian government could obtain, for its war against the

---

[4] When he was already in Germany, in 1630–1631, Gustavus Adolphus gave very great attention to news about Poland, seeing the Polish question as the basis for his foreign policy. Chancellor Oxenstjerna sent him from Prussia systematic information about the Polish–Lithuanian state, as did also Johan Skytte, the Swedish governor of Livonia. The unpublished correspondence of Johan Skytte, Jakob De La Gardie and others shows how very closely indeed the Swedes followed in 1630–1631 the military preparations in the Rzeczpospolita, the purchasing of the munitions and recruitment of the soldiers, which, though intended for use 'against the Muscovites', might, as we find it put in this correspondence, 'prove quite useful to the Emperor'. Measures were taken to ensure that, in that case, Polish troops would not be able to force their way into Germany through Marienburg and Prussia (see Paul, J., *Gustav Adolf*, Vol.III, Leipzig, 1932, pp. 40, 41).

Rzeczpospolita, mercenary soldiers and commanders, military specialists and the most up-to-date armaments. Reliance on foreign mercenaries was apparently necessitated by the still extremely uneasy social situation prevailing in Muscovy after the peasant war at the beginning of the seventeenth century. Third and finally, it was assumed that, when Gustavus Adolphus had entered Germany, he would direct some of his forces from there against the Rzeczpospolita, so that the latter would be crushed between two fronts – Russian, to the east, and Swedish to the west (or more correctly, between three fronts, as it was assumed that Turkey would also attack from the south).

It was this question of a blow to be struck at the Rzeczpospolita from the west, from Germany, simultaneously with the Russian blow from the east that constituted a very difficult question in the negotiations between Sweden and Muscovy. Both the Muscovite government, on the one hand, and Gustavus Adolphus, on the other, understood that profound interests of Swedish policy required that Sweden play its part in carrying out this plan. Without this, indeed, any result of a clash between Russia and Poland would be to Sweden's disadvantage. In particular, a victory for Russia would mean that the Swedish army would then have in its rear a neighbour not less but more to be feared than the Rzeczpospolita.

Equilibrium between the armed forces of Russia and Poland was also dangerous, for at any moment this might impel the two sides to conclude an armistice or a peace that would be disastrous for Sweden. There is no need to speak of the danger to Sweden that a victory for Poland would entail. On the other hand, if the Swedes were to attack Poland from Germany at the same time as the Russians attacked from the east, the result would be that Gustavus Aldolphus acquired the Crown of Poland and dominion over that country, while Muscovy gained the eastern possessions of the Rzeczpospolita, namely, the Ukrainian, Byelorussian and West-Russian lands. An agreement to this effect had been sketched already in the Russo–Swedish negotiations in 1630–1631, but detailed arrangements and provisions for co-ordination still remained to be seen to.

From the standpoint of sound logic, Sweden could not avoid this agreement once it had been decided to go to war against the Emperor in Germany. The King, personally, was well aware of the inexorable logic of the situation that had come about. They were sure of that in Moscow. In Stockholm, however, in the oligarchical Council of State, and in Chancellor Oxenstjerna's circles, other hopes persistently reigned, hopes that were short-sighted and ill-founded – that it would be enough to set Poland and Muscovy against each other and then let them fight it out between them. Sweden, they thought, need only maintain a position of non-intervention. Then both sides would find it necessary to fear and 'respect' Sweden.

Clearly this idea could appeal only to those who failed to look into the near future and did not see, for example, that the Russo–Polish war might come to an end before the Swedes had concluded their campaign in Germany. In one way or another, this short-sighted view was held by influential circles and by Chancellor Oxenstjerna himself. Gustavus Adolphus, who was more far-sighted, was obliged to conduct his negotiations with Moscow to a certain extent over the head of the Swedish state machine, resorting to a kind of 'personal royal diplomacy', merely informing Oxenstjerna, and consulting him only for form's sake.[5] Oxenstjerna shared that hostility towards Russia which, resulting from the Swedish intervention in Russia during the Time of Troubles, was a characteristic of the Swedish aristocracy of the period. In 1615 he wrote to De la Gardie: 'there can be no doubt that, in the Russians, we have neighbours who are disloyal but also mighty, whom it is impossible to trust owing to their innate perfidy and falsity sucked in with their mothers' milk, but who, because of their strength, are feared not only by us but also by many others among their neighbours, as we well remember'.[6] This fixed idea of Oxenstjerna's about the 'perfidy' and 'barbarism' of the Russians, which merely reflected the bad conscience of the Swedish aristocracy, who had seized Russia's Baltic provinces, prevented the Chancellor from understanding and supporting Gustavus Adolphus's policy towards Russia and Poland, which was dictated by new historical conditions. Norrman concludes that Axel Oxenstjerna did not go along with the King in his resolute Eastern policy:[7] he 'did not realise the profound significance of Gustavus Adolphus's offer to Russia',[8] 'the Chancellor's distrust of Russia went very deep, and in Gustavus Adolphus's Russian policy in these years he preferred to go his own way'.[9] Accordingly, the Polish problem also

---

[5] Historians are revealing more-and-more thoroughly the divergences between Gustavus Adolphus and Axel Oxenstjerna during the war in Germany. On the one hand, these differences concerned economic provision for the war. The King demanded more and more money from the Chancellor, and the disputes between them over this became acute (see Sörensson, P., 'Ekonomi och Krigföring under Gustav II Adolfs tyska fälttåg 1630–1632', *Scandia*, 1932, p.300: Ahnlund, N., *Axel Oxenstierna intill Gustav Adolfs död*, Stockholm, 1940, p.589). In particular, Oxenstjerna did not appreciate Gustavus Adolphus's reckoning on the resources of Russia or on trade with Persia through Russia (Norrman, *Gustav*, p. 138) and, apparently, was unaware of the actual sums that accrued to the King through the sale of Russian grain in Holland: he thought that in 1630–1631 Gustavus Adolphus was covering the enormous costs of the war by means of loans contracted in Holland at high rates of interest (Lorentzen, T., *Die Schwedische Armee im Dreissigjährigen Kriege und ihre Abdankung*, Leipzig, 1894, p. 22), whereas these loans were secured on the receipts from Russian grain in the Amsterdam exchange (see Chapter 1).
[6] Quoted in Norrman, *Gustav*, p. 77.
[7] Norrman, *Gustav*, p. 76.    [8] Ibid., p. 72.    [9] Ibid., p.49.

became a subject of protracted argument between Chancellor and King.[10]

In the spring of 1631, Gustavus Adolphus put to the Tsar and the Patriarch, through Roussel, Monier, and Möller, his confidential proposals regarding the organisation of a blow to be struck at the Rzeczpospolita from the west, from Germany, by Swedish troops (but with Russian money). These proposals were accepted in principle by Moscow. The Russian government's affirmative reply, accompanied by some supplementary questions, reached Gustavus Adolphus at the end of August 1631, in North-Eastern Germany, where he had been for over a year already, unwilling to start a thorough-going war against the Emperor's forces until the Polish problem had been cleared up.

There can be no doubt that Gustavus Adolphus's decision to launch, at last, a general offensive in Germany was connected with his receipt of Russia's reply signifying agreement in principle on the main question. Only a week before the battle of Breitenfeld, on 30/31 August 1631, in the midst of intensive military preparations, the King wrote further letters to Moscow, one addressed to Monier, and the other to Möller, to be passed to the Tsar and the Patriarch as quickly as possible. This signified confirmation of the agreement on joint action against the Rzeczpospolita and adjustment of the plan in accordance with the requests from the Muscovite government.

Monier wrote to the Tsar from Stockholm on 28 September 1631 that Gustavus Adolphus wanted to send him to Moscow again, to continue the negotiations, but, as he was ill, and as 'it did not seem good' to the King to send anyone else 'on these affairs', he had ordered Monier 'to inform Your Majesty the Tsar about them by letter'. First, Monier says that Gustavus Adolphus is 'greatly pleased' with the Tsar's reply and 'wishes, from the heart, that the time will come when he can show in action his goodwill and love to Your Majesty the Tsar'. That time was drawing near. Answering the Muscovite government's question as to whether he

[10] Ibid., p. 41. The irreconcilable divergence between them on questions of the Russo–Swedish military alliance against the Rzeczpospolita is revealed also in the last work of the greatest authority on the reign of Gustavus Adolphus, N. Ahnlund, mentioned above (Ahnlund, N., *Axel*, p. 603 *et seq.*). Even sharper, though, were those disagreements with the man who directly held all the threads of Swedish policy towards Russia and Poland, namely, the Swedish governor of Livonia, Johan Skytte. He was even less anti-Polish than the Chancellor, being closely connected with a section of the Polish–Lithuanian magnates (Norrman, D., *Gustav*, p. 24). It is understandable that Oxenstjerna and Skytte did all that they could, for example, to hinder the activity of Jacques Roussel, who personified direct contact between the political plans of the Muscovite government and of Gustavus Adolphus. This situation found reflection also in the fact that the King tried to reduce to the minimum his consultation with the Chancellor (who was in Prussia to serve as a link between the King, fighting in Germany, and the Council of State in Stockholm) and himself wrote from Germany to the Council of State very infrequently – once in three or four months.

proposed to strike at Poland from Livonia or from Silesia, Gustavus Adolphus said that it was not possible for him 'to strike at Poland from the Livonian frontier . . . because this would mean open violation of the peace treaty'. An offensive against Poland from Germany, however, particularly from Silesia, would be expedient for both diplomatic and strategic reasons. Addressing himself to the Patriarch (whom he had already informed of Gustavus Adolphus's victories in Germany), Monier explains the strategic aspect:

And this truly – if His Majesty the Tsar sends such an army through German territory into Poland, under good field commanders, he will do more harm to the enemy in four or five months than he could do in a year from the Russian side, since in Upper Poland these forces will strike at the enemy's heart and take them by surprise. His Majesty the Tsar and Your Holiness can think and consider about this – it will be to your advantage and profit.

Gustavus Adolphus, he adds, is so well disposed towards Muscovy 'that truly it may be hoped that in good time all manner of friendship will flow from His Royal Majesty'.

This tone, this proposal that they 'think and consider', was due to the fact that Gustavus Adolphus was at the same time advising the Muscovite government of the extremely burdensome material conditions on which his enterprise would depend – calculated, undoubtedly, on what was needed for a thorough defeat of the Rzeczpospolita, but also, perhaps to the same extent, on replenishing Sweden's treasury. The King rejected the Muscovites' wish that only infantry be recruited in Germany, with the necessary cavalry to be sent from Russia to the place and at the time to be agreed. He insisted on his original variant, namely, that the army in Silesia should be made up of 10,000 infantry and 2,000 cavalry, with the addition of artillery and the necessary arms. 'If Your Majesty the Tsar will agree to raise a good army of 10,000 foot and 2,000 horse in the place named in Germany, from there they can easily enter the enemy's country, so that they are taken by surprise – and this cannot be done without foreign cavalrymen and without guns and other weapons of war.' For all this no less than 80,000 rubles would be needed, 'every month'. If the Tsar agrees to this, let him send 'his officials with the money' to conclude an agreement with the leaders of the mercenary troops, 'with the commanders and officers'. (Incidentally, the circumstance which Gustavus Adolphus proposes, that the Russian plenipotentiaries talk directly and settle up with the commanders of the regiments and units, quite refutes the suspicion that he was chiefly guided by financial interests, as Oxenstjerna supposed.) Gustavus Adolphus, for his part, promises as before, 'to take care of these troops and seek out suitable officers for them'. If, however, the Tsar does not agree to this proposal, let him count on the Swedish King's 'goodwill' and 'always remember his unchanging friendship'.[11]

The letter which Gustavus Adolphus sent out at the same time to Möller, Sweden's permanent representative in Moscow, for transmission to the Tsar, was more-or-less identical in content.

It is not possible to send the troops in from Livonia because it was laid down in the truce that the King of Sweden would not send troops through Livonia or from Sweden or Finland, but nothing was said about not sending them from Germany, because Poland did not suppose that the King would think of making war from German territory. But the Polish King had aided the enemies of the Swedish King and so his Majesty the Tsar will understand that His Royal Majesty has no cause to be ashamed of planning to attack Poland.

Thus, Gustavus Adolphus found both judicial and moral justification for an onslaught on Poland from Silesia. At this point he repeats his basic organisational and strategical idea, his advice to the Tsar to raise 10,000 infantrymen and 2,000 cavalrymen in Germany 'and with these men strike at Upper Poland thereby striking at the heart of Poland', and doing that country 'great harm'. Later comes a divergence from the letter sent through Monier – the only such divergence, but one of importance. In Möller's letter it is said that the troops in question will cost '100,000 rubles each month' – not 80,000, as in the letter sent through Monier. This increase of 20,000 rubles can have only one explanation – the letter to Möller was evidently sent off by the King not at the same time as the one to Monier, but *after* the victory at Breitenfeld, which Gustavus Adolphus thought enhanced his military credit.[12] The King tells the Tsar, through Möller, that if he agrees to the Swedish conditions, he should 'soon' send 'his officials with the money, and His Royal Majesty wishes to give good officers of his to that force and to take care of it himself and indicate the points from which it is to enter Poland and how to act there so as to please His Majesty the Tsar'. Gustavus Adolphus ordered Möller, in any case, to ask, and, without delay 'to notify him, so that His Royal Majesty may be correctly informed' (1) 'at what date and in what places His Majesty the Tsar wishes to begin the war against Poland', and (2) whether the Tsar is going to recruit the army in question in Germany.[13]

Along with all these commissions Möller handed over Gustavus Adolphus's letter (written, 'with the great regiments' of the Swedish King, 'in the Kaiser's country', i.e., Germany, on 30 August 1631), sending with it his man Gilius Koner, to be temporarily in the Tsar's service, and at the same time offering to perform any services the Tsar

---

[11] *TsGADA, Dela shvedskie*, 1631, *stb*. 8, *ll*. 219–229.

[12] In a later message to Mikhail Fedorovich, in 1632, Gustavus Adolphus himself gives, without any explanation, the figure 100,000 rubles.

[13] *TsGADA, Dela shvedskie*, 1631, *stb*. 8, *ll*. 230–232.

may have need of.[14] In this way Gustavus Adolphus sought to strengthen his bonds with Muscovy, adding yet another link to the many that existed already.

This, then, was what engaged the mind of the Swedish King, these were the cares that troubled him on the eve of the decisive step in the development of his German campaign – on the eve and immediately after the greatest battle he won in this war, the battle which flung open before him the gates to the rest of Germany.

Running ahead of events, let us quote right here Moscow's reply to this message from Gustavus Adolphus, although observance of chronological order would require an interval. For some reason (later we shall see that this may have been a conscious effort by Axel Oxenstjerna and the Swedish state machine) these messages were greatly delayed in transmission. Not until the end of November did the Swedish courier bearing both the letters of Anton Monier, from Stockholm, to the Tsar and the Patriarch, and the King's instruction, from Germany, to his representative in Moscow, Johan Möller, reach the Russian frontier, and it was 7 December when he arrived in Moscow. The Russian government's answer to the Swedish King was seen as a matter of exceptional state importance, deciding the question of war, in full alliance with Sweden. This is clear from Möller's dispatch to the Chancellor and the King on 21 January 1632, telling them that the Tsar had held a six-weeks-long council with his boyars and representatives of the clergy, on the matter of Gustavus Adolphus's proposal that an army be recruited in Germany. Eventually the proposal was strongly approved and it was decided to assemble this army. What presented special difficulty, it seemed, was the financial aspect of the business. Möller says at this point that, for the expenditure connected with this plan, the Tsar will endeavour to raise 800,000 rubles (1,600,000 reichsthalers or yefimki) from Dutch and English merchants, and expresses the hopes that these money problems facing the Russian government will facilitate their agreement to the purchasing of Russian grain by Sweden.[15]

Only on 16 January 1632 did the Tsar and the Patriarch receive Möller and hear officially 'the letters of Anton Monier and the speech of Johan Möller', after which they ordered that a letter be written to Gustavus

[14] Ibid., *ll.* 233–234.
[15] Norrman, *Gustav*, pp. 85–86. Only much later and indirect evidence has survived (in the form of a mention by the English ambassador in Russia, Carlisle, in 1667) that the Russian government did actually approach England at this time with a request for a loan, and received 40,000 reichsthalers (Ilovaiskii, D.I., *Istoriia Rossii*, Vol.II, Part II, Moscow, 1899, p. 323). In the main though, as is clear from Möller's statement, it was a question of raising loans not from foreign governments, but from foreign merchants trading with Russia.

Adolphus and a reply sent to Monier: the task of answering Möller was entrusted to Prince Cherkasskii. The Tsar's letter to Gustavus Adolphus was signed on 19 January 1632.[16]

Prince Cherkasskii's answer to Möller mentioned, among other things, the difference between the figure of 80,000 rubles a month given by Monier and that of 100,000 rubles given by Möller. But it is quite clear from the Tsar's letter replying to Gustavus Adolphus that the Muscovite government had already decided to agree even to the higher of these two figures, however great a burden that might put upon Russia's treasury. That would have meant 1,200,000 rubles a year, or 2,400,000 yefimki (reichsthalers) – though, as we have seen, it was supposed that the affair could be over and done with in a few months. The Muscovite government possessed by this time some experience in the hiring of German *lansquenets*, knew the usual European rates of payment to mercenaries, and could therefore easily calculate that the amount asked for by Gustavus Adolphus was in excess of the expenditure required, though not by very much.[17]

Consequently, Moscow's reply to the King expressed agreement to pay the sum stated while at the same time asking for details on what it was to be spent on, so as, apparently, at least to prevent any fresh increases being proposed in the future.

This reply said: 'We, the great sovereign, Our Majesty the Tsar, accept it as a token of great love from your Royal Majesty that Your Royal Majesty wishes to concern yourself with this matter, and we, the great sovereign, wish to hire those soldiers and will send officials with money, but at present Our Majesty does not know to what place they are to be sent.' Gustavus Adolphus is asked to tell the Tsar quickly where the

---

[16] It was included, verbatim, in Prince Cherkasskii's answer to Möller. As regards the Tsar's letter to Monier, this was confined to the statement that a reply dealing with the substance of the matter had been sent directly to Gustavus Adolphus (*TsGADA, Dela shvedskie*, 1632, stb. 2, *ll*. 25–27).

[17] Norrman gives this calculation: Gustavus Adolphus spent in Germany in 1630–1632 about 3 reichsthalers a month for each foot soldier and about 5 for each cavalryman. Accordingly, if we include expenditure on victuals and fodder, the mercenary army should have cost about 73,000 reichsthalers a month (an infantry regiment 8,525 reichsthalers, a cavalry regiment of a thousand horses 9,496 reichsthalers, artillery in conformity with the norms of firearms in the Swedish army, not less than 10,000 reichsthalers a month). For a period of six months, that would have come to 438,000, and for a year 873,000 reichsthalers. Consequently, if he received from Russia 200,000 reichsthalers a month, Gustavus Adolphus would have made 127,000 a month, i.e. 762,000 reichsthalers in six months and 1,524,000 reichsthalers in a year. For comparison, he shows that the Prussian customs duties, which Axel Oxenstjerna called grains of gold, contributed only 13,400 reichsthalers a month to the war in Germany (Norrman, *Gustav*, pp. 145–148). However, Norrman's calculation greatly underestimates the cost of maintaining the army: e.g., for some reason he fails to take adequate account of the high pay received by the commanders.

officials are to report, and also, 'in what city the soldiers are to be assembled, whatever place Your Royal Majesty may appoint'. The reply asks also that the Tsar be told 'how many thousand yefimki a month will be needed for these mercenaries, and for how many months this sum will have to be sent, and what cannons, gunpowder and lead the mercenaries will have, together with particulars of the cost in each case, so that Our Majesty the Tsar may be informed of all this'. For its part, Moscow replies to the question about the date for its offensive: 'Our boyars and commanders, with many soldiers, with Russian and German mercenaries and with many Mirzas and Tatars from Kazan and Astrakhan will be sent by us, the great sovereign, into the country of the Polish King in the present year, 1632, in the summer, as soon as the grass has grown sufficiently for the horses to be fed'.[18] Finally, in Prince Cherkasskii's reply to Möller, it was agreed to accept Gilius Koner into the Tsar's service and to carry out as far as possible the other practical projects of Gustavus Adolphus communicated through Möller.[19]

What was in this secret correspondence between Gustavus Adolphus and the Muscovite government about the plan to attack the Rzeczpospolita from the east and the west at the same time?

We are convinced that both parties had a very positive attitude to the plan discussed and definitely wanted to put it into effect. The basic problems concerning strategy and finance had been settled. We can say that the secret Russo–Swedish military alliance, the main outlines of which had been shaped through Roussel's work, was already literally on the eve of final formulation when Gustavus Adolphus began his dizzying 'zigzag lightning' advance into the depths of Germany and the Muscovite government was completing its preparations for war with the Rzeczpospolita.

There is no need here to dwell at length upon the question why the Muscovite government again postponed the date for beginning hostilities: having first promised to move in the spring of 1631, then in summer 1631, it now put off the date to spring 1632, but in fact began the Smolensk campaign only in August 1632. There were, at bottom, three reasons for these postponements. First, the incompleteness of military preparations, i.e., the reorganisation of the army, the assimilation of new weapons, the accumulation of necessary stores, and the strenghtening of the western border fortresses. Second, the unfinished state of negotiations with Turkey, about a military alliance against the Polish–Lithuanian state. And, third, the fact that negotiations with Sweden itself had not been brought to conclusion.

---

[18] *TsGADA, Dela shvedskie,* 1632, *stb.* 2, *ll.* 20–24.    [19] Ibid., *ll.* 27–32.

At the moment of the battle of Breitenfeld, that is, on the 17 (7) September 1631, Gustavus Adolphus still did not know officially that Moscow's attack on Poland had been put off to the following spring, but he certainly could have guessed that this was so, since the summer of 1631 had already ended and there was no news yet of the beginning of a Russo–Polish war. This may be the solution to what at first sight seems strange, the fact that, after promising Moscow that he would personally prepare and lead the attack on Poland from Silesia, Gustavus Adolphus moved, immediately after the battle of Breitenfeld, in the opposite direction, far into the west and south-west of Germany. It is quite probable that he took this decision in view of the postponement of the Polish business until the following year, and meant to have returned to Eastern Germany by that time.

The King undoubtedly did hesitate regarding the priority of war with the Emperor or war with the Rzeczpospolita even after he had occupied the Pomeranian bridgehead. We mentioned earlier that in the spring of 1631, at the beginning of April, when Gustavus Adolphus was expecting that the Russo–Polish war would begin and Moscow would agree to his proposals, he sent into Silesia a group of infantry and cavalry under the command of his outstanding general Gustav Horn. True, we may see in the appointment of that particular general also an expression of the will of Chancellor Oxenstjerna and his circle to keep all these matters under their control: Gustav Horn was Oxenstjerna's son-in-law. On the other hand, it is not impossible that Gustavus Adolphus himself was trying, by this appointment, to reconcile the Chancellor to his plans. He apparently sought to make the Muscovite government understand the purpose of this Silesian group. Among the 'reports' which Möller had from time to time to pass on secretly in Moscow there once figured a statement that the Poles were trying to recruit mercenaries in Silesia, especially in Breslau, 'it is not known whether for Moscow or against the Swede: but the Swedish King has sent into Silesia his general Gustav Horn, with 15,000 soldiers, and as the Silesian princes have submitted to him, he will at once strike at the Pole, because the Polish King wants to help the Kaiser by sending him several thousand Zaporozhian Cossacks'.[20] In the last phrase it is not hard to recognise a favourite argument of Gustavus Adolphus's which we have already met more than once, giving, in his view, moral justification for his attack on Poland. Undoubtedly, Gustav Horn's group remained in Silesia from the beginning of April to the end of July 1631 in expectation of the Russo–Polish war which Moscow had promised to Gustavus Adolphus. This group was also, probably, that 'notable army'

[20] TsGADA, Dela shvedskie, 1631, stb. 8, ll. 188–189.

with 'a good field commander' which it had been proposed should be paid with the Russian money and which, from Silesia, was to have struck Poland 'in the very heart'. If those events had taken place then, i.e., in the summer of 1631, Gustavus Adolphus would probably have put off his march into the depths of Germany until the final defeat of Poland, since he believed, as we have seen, that, if attacked from west and east simultaneously, the Rzeczpospolita was certain to be routed in a few months. The Pomeranian bridgehead would in that case have served as an unexpectedly available means for carrying out what Gustavus Adolphus had for so long considered the immediate task of Swedish policy and which he had only recently put aside in order to fight in Germany – the task of finishing with the Polish–Lithuanian state so as thereafter, with a safe rear, to march into Germany.

But at the end of July 1631 Gustavus Adolphus recalled Horn from Silesia, with 4,000 men. Evidently, he had realised by then that the Russo–Polish war would not begin in the summer of 1631. To be sure, the King did retain on the Silesian frontier a reduced body of troops under the command of Alexander Leslie, his most outstanding general, a future field-marshal, who, moreover, unlike Horn, would not only not be influenced by Chancellor Oxenstjerna's opposition to the plan for a military alliance with Russia, but would undoubtedly do his utmost to realise that plan, since one of the leaders of the offensive to be launched from the Russian side would be his son, Colonel Alexander Leslie junior.

When, at the end of August, Gustavus Adolphus received at last, through Monier and Möller, the heartening news that Moscow had agreed to his military-strategic plan in its entirety, he could not but realise that, in the nature of things, fulfilment of the plan had been postponed to the following summer. Nevertheless, the King could be free from fear, during the interval, of a stab in the back from the Rzeczpospolita. As we have seen, Muscovy had almost formally declared war on Poland, before all Europe, and there were plenty of reports of alarm and military preparations in the latter country. Clearly, the Polish King was, in these circumstances, in no position to take the initiative in the war with the Swedes. Hence, war against the Emperor gradually resumed first place in Gustavus Adolphus's plans for the immediate future.

For an historian who knows how long the Thirty Years' War was to last it is not easy, psychologically, to imagine how in 1631 it seemed to be moving rapidly towards its *dénouement*. There can be no doubt, though, that Gustavus Adolphus was convinced, especially after his defeat of the Imperial army at Breitenfeld, that he would be able to end the war with the Emperor, for all practical purposes, before the summer of 1632, and then turn his attention to the Polish problem – hence the furious tempo of his operations in Germany after Breitenfeld. Let us recall the confidence with which he wrote, in June 1631, from Stettin to the Tsar, replying to the latter's request 'that Our Royal Majesty help your Majesty the Tsar against the Polish King', that 'although all Germany has not submitted to Our Royal Majesty, we nevertheless wish to show Our great Royal friendship and love for Your Majesty the Tsar'.[21] These words reflect the complete assurance that subjugation of 'all Germany' was a matter of the near future. Gustavus Adophus was not alone in thinking this. 'On the encounter between Tilly and Gustavus depends the entire future of Germany', the Papal Nuncio had written shortly before the battle of Breitenfeld.[22] Victory for the Swedes in this encounter ought, it would seem, to have determined the outcome of the entire war, since the defeated party could not yet count on any reserves. In this connection Marx, in his notes on Schlosser's *World History*, also observed that after the battle of Breitenfeld 'the war would have soon have been over, but for the base conduct of the *Kur-cur* [i.e., the Elector of Saxony – B.F.P.] and the treachery of his general Arnim'.[23] In that battle, which was not only of all-German but of all-European importance, producing political echoes in faraway places, there clashed not only the two strongest armies of that age but also, embodied in them, the two coalitions into which Europe was divided. That France was subsidising Sweden was well known. Contemporaries were inclined to overestimate the amount of England's subsidies. The extent of Russia's aid was least known, but instead was a subject for fantasy. According to French reports from Germany, Gustavus Adolphus had increased the size of his army before Breitenfeld 'not only by receiving reinforcements from Sweden, but also through the help given by the Tsar of Muscovy, the report of whose death has not been confirmed'.[24] In one sense or another this was the first battle in a truly all-European war, and in it the anti-Habsburg coalition achieved indisputable superiority.

Actually, the battle of Breitenfeld signified defeat not merely for some chance elements but for the main forces of the Empire, and with that the sweeping away of the successes which the Emperor and the Catholic League had gained at the end of the preceding period. Tilly's army had been reinforced not long before by a substantial contingent of Imperial forces brought back from Italy. Tilly approached Leipzig with a host of about 40,000. The Swedish army numbered no more than 21,000, but

21   *TsGADA, Dela shvedskie,* 1631, *stb.* 4, *l.* 133.
22   Forsten, G. V., *Baltiiskii vopros v XVI–XVII stoletiiakh,* Vol.II, St Petersburg, 1894, p. 352.
23   Marx, K., 'Chronological Extracts', in *Arkhiv Marksa i Engel'sa,* Vol.VIII (1946), p. 208. [Marx's abusive word, '*Kur-Köder*', is made up of 'Kur', for *Kurfürst,* i.e., Elector, and '*Köder*' – nowadays spelt '*Köter*' – meaning 'cur' – Trans.]
24   Forsten, *Baltiiskii vopros,* p.351.

was incomparably better armed and trained. To these were added between 18,000 and 20,000 Saxon recruits – who, to be sure, fled at the very beginning of the battle. The fight near Leipzig went on for five hours and ended with the almost complete annihilation of Tilly's army. He lost over 10,000 men, all his artillery, all his colours and his wagon-train, and narrowly escaped losing his own life.[25] The Imperial and Catholic army was literally destroyed, and along with that went the myth of its invincibility. When the news of this crushing defeat reached Vienna, they went mad with despair in the Emperor's capital. Gustavus Adolphus wrote to Sweden, in great joy: 'Fortune shone upon our armies . . . After a stern and stubborn four-hour fight we defeated freedom's foe, put him to flight and destroyed him as he fled helter-skelter from the battlefield.'[26]

After this dizzying victory, Gustavus Adolphus advanced at great speed and almost unopposed, through Thuringia and Franconia, into Western Germany, to the Rhineland, and then into Bavaria and the Habsburgs' hereditary territories, while the Saxon army led by Arnim was sent off on an outflanking march through Moravia, Lusatia and Bohemia.

However, this bound into the depths of Germany did not mean that Gustavus Adolphus had forgotten about Poland and Russia. He simply thought that he had some months at his disposal, a little short of a year, before the time would come to move against Poland. He did not cease to think about distant Muscovy when he turned his face towards the Rhine and the West. We have already had occasion to express the view that the above-quoted instruction to Möller was sent *after* Breitenfeld. We also possess another document which was unquestionably sent by the King to Moscow after the battle. This was Gustavus Adolphus's own report of the victory.

Immediately the battle was over, and directly from the vicinity of Leipzig, besides the message to Sweden, two triumphant accounts were sent, with details of the trophies captured, the number of casualties and so on – one to France, to King Louis XIII, the other to Russia, to Tsar Mikhail Fedorovich. Both of these allies celebrated this victory as a success for 'the common cause', to use Gustavus Adolphus's own expression. The Swedish courier bringing this message arrived in Moscow extraordinarily quickly, on 27 October, and that same day Möller reported to Prince Cherkasskii, on the King's behalf:

[25] Sveriges Generalstaben, *Sveriges Krig 1611–1632*, Vol. IV, Stockholm, 1938, pp. 428–523. On the battle of Breitenfeld, see also these special monographs: Opitz, W. T., *Die Schlacht bei Breitenfeld am 17 September 1631*, Leipzig, 1892, and Wangerin, E., *Die Schlacht bei Breitenfeld am 7 September 1631. Eine Quellenuntersuchung*, Halle, 1896 (Thesis).

[26] Forsten, *Baltiiskii vopros*, p. 353.

By Divine grace and His Royal good fortune, God gave him victory over the Kaiser's men. He beat the great commander named Tilly on September of this year 1631 at the city of Leipzig, which belongs to the Elector of Saxony, and harried the enemy for seven miles, and in this battle 20,000 were killed, and the great commander Tilly himself received a wound from which he died . . . [This supposition was not confirmed – B.F.P.]. Two days before his defeat, this Tilly occupied the city of Leipzig, and 6,000 of the Kaiser's men are now therein, but Gustavus Adolphus expects that they will yield themselves to the victor's mercy.

He went on to tell of the capture of twenty-eight cannons and the army's entire wagon-train, and of the great number of prisoners from the Emperor's infantry who 'could not get away'. A force of 6,000 cavalry, accompanied by Tilly's wife 'went off to the town of Wolfenbüttel, and the King has sent 16,000 soldiers to lay siege to that town', and thinks that the besieged, having no stores, will surrender. Three thousand men went to the town of Halberstadt 'and wanted to sack it', but Gustavus Adolphus sent troops to besiege the place and all these men surrendered to him and were to serve him henceforth. In this battle the King took prisoner the Duke of Holstein and sent him to Dresden. The communication ends with an extremely interesting forecast, which reflected Gustavus Adolphus's intentions: 'Those Electors and free Princes who do not belong to the Popish faith have all chosen the King of Sweden as their champion, and the King has now set forth against the Kaiser and the Pope and, with God's help, wishes to root out the Popish faith.' That was Gustavus Adolphus's dream after his first triumph in Germany!

As though acting on his own initiative, but undoubtedly following instructions, Möller expressed the wish that the Tsar and the Patriarch should, in honour of such a victory by their ally and friend, cause a 'volley' to be fired in Moscow, i.e. that guns be fired in salute, something which, apparently, had not been done before in Russia. It is interesting that Möller argued for this to be done not only on the grounds that all (?) Gustavus Adolphus's other friends and enemies of the 'Papists' had done this but also from a purely political consideration relating to the Polish problem. Such a salute, he said, was needed 'so that the enemy, the Polish King, hearing it, may be greatly frightened and the friendship between our states may be plain'.[27] In other words, as he set off westward, Gustavus Adolphus wanted Moscow to demonstrate, by yet another public action, its alliance with him and, along with that, the war-danger threatening Poland, since there were, as yet, no actual military operations.

The Muscovite government not only acceded to the request but, seizing the initiative, celebrated the victory at Breitenfeld as a real triumph for its own policy.

<hr />

[27] *TsGADA, Dela shvedskie*, 1631, *stb.* 8, *ll.* 185–188.

The Stockholm archives contain several descriptions sent from Moscow of this impressive celebration. A letter from Henrich Von Dam and Tobias Unsing to Gustavus Adolphus, dated 6 November 1631, tells how the Tsar, the Patriarch, and their counsellors, on learning of the King's victory, 'were not only very pleased and glad but, on 2 November His Majesty the Tsar went with several thousand people to a field outside the city and ordered that a joyous salute be fired from one hundred guns, inside and outside the city, in order to show how heartily glad he was at the news'. A more detailed account, destined for the public, is headed 'A true account of the triumph held by the Grand Duke of Moscow, within and without that city, in special honour of the Swedes, on the occasion of the victory won by His Royal Majesty near Leipzig. Moscow, 14 November 1631.' This gives a detailed description of the salute and the military parade in Moscow, and also of the ringing of church bells and public prayers, and, finally, the popular festival in which 60,000 persons took part.[28] Möller informed Gustavus Adolphus of the solemnities, the salute and the parade, which 'no one in this country remembers having happened before'. The Tsar 'ordered thanksgivings to be held in the churches, and then he ordered his troops to assemble in several groups outside Moscow, to form-up and to shoot from their big guns and muskets in honour of the victory won by the King of Sweden over his enemies. 'Never', adds Möller, 'has any victory been so celebrated in Moscow.'[29]

By such rejoicing, of course, the Muscovite government wished to mark not another's victory but its own. The Patriarch and his circle saw the Swedish King's successes against the German Emperor as a direct success for Russian policy, as the fulfilment of a plan which had been thoroughly matured in Moscow. Gustavus Adolphus's victory must have seemed the first, but, perhaps, decisive step on the road to recovering the West-Russian, Ukrainian and Byelorussian lands from the Rzeczpospolita. It seemed that the key to accomplishing this great political task was already in their hands. There was indeed something to rejoice about.

At the same time this was a demonstration aimed at the Poles. And it made a big impression on them. The salute in Moscow evoked much anxiety in the Rzeczpospolita, to the very great satisfaction of the Swedes. The Swedish governor, Johan Skytte, who watched developments in Poland from Riga and Dorpat, reported on them in a series

[28] *Akty i pis'ma k istorii baltiiskogo voprosa v XVI–XVII stoletiiakh*, fasc. II, St Petersburg, 1893, no. 54, pp. 129–130.
[29] Ibid., no. 55, p. 131; Forsten, *Baltiiskii vopros*, Vol. II, p. 367.

of letters, to the Count Palatine Johann Kazimir on 9 December, to Jacques Roussel on 16 December 1631, and to others.[30]

Long before Gustavus Adolphus received the Muscovite government's positive response to his proposals he had the answer to this question from his Chancellor, Axel Oxenstjerna. At the same time as he sent those proposals to Russia, on 29 August 1631, that is, even before the battle of Breitenfeld, the King had embodied them, along with his entire plan, in a letter to the Chancellor in which he asked for advice on how most diplomatically and effectively to implement this plan – to face the Rzeczpospolita with war on two fronts, 'so that the Poles may be unable to fall upon us when we are mainly occupied with this war in Germany and so that they may not recover their breath during the time of truce [with Sweden]'.[31] Oxenstjerna did not hasten to reply and only on 13 October sent Gustavus Adolphus the opinion he asked for. With all proper outward respect for the King's design, the Chancellor essentially indicated a negative view of it. He proposed to put off a definitive discussion of the question until he could meet the King in person. As we know, Oxenstjerna held a quite different view on what Sweden's East-European policy should be. He knew, to be sure, from Möller's dispatches, of the favourable attitude of the Muscovite government, especially Patriarch Philaret, toward Gustavus Adolphus and Sweden.[32] But he was opposed to an alliance with Russia, because he had no faith in its reliability or firmness. More precisely, he and most members of the Council of State wanted only an alliance from which Sweden would get all the benefits while giving nothing in return and committing itself to nothing. The plan for an attack from two sides on the Rzeczpospolita meant that, in the event of failure by the army, hired with Russian money, which was to operate from Germany, the Swedes would have to come to its aid, and so Oxenstjerna was against the proposal for this army to be hired by the Russians.[33] He considered that 'the German War', which entailed enormous economic difficulties, called for a concentration of all Sweden's forces, and also that Sweden should build a powerful navy which would dominate the whole of the Baltic Sea.[34]

Oxenstjerna was aware, of course, of the threat from the Rzeczpospolita to the Swedish army in Germany. In June 1631 he wrote to Gustavus Adolphus about Warsaw's secret dealings with Vienna, aimed against Sweden and threatening a denunciation of the truce between Poland and

[30] Paul, *Gustav Adolf*, p.38.
[31] *Rikskanzleren Axel Oxenstjernas skrifter och brefvexling*, Vol.II, Part I, p.738.
[32] Norrman, *Gustav*, pp. 72–73.    [33] Ahnlund, *Axel*, p. 603.
[34] Norrman, *Gustav*, p. 77.

Sweden.[35] But the Chancellor thought there were two factors which might hold the Poles back from breaking the truce. On the one hand, they would not take such a step while Gustavus Adolphus was winning victories in Germany: only if he were to suffer some reverses might they become a danger to Sweden. As proof, Oxenstjerna told the King that, a few days before the battle of Breitenfeld, a false report of a Swedish defeat reached Warsaw, and Sigismund III at once ordered his commanders to begin preparations for war. The news of the Swedes' victory brought chagrin, for it ruined the Poles' hope of easily recovering Prussia and Livonia, and a section of Poland's magnates at once began calling for a permanent peace to be concluded with Sweden, no matter what the price to be paid.[36] On the other hand, in Oxenstjerna's view the Poles would not break the truce with Sweden so long as Russia was threatening them with war, and so long as such a war lasted, for they certainly did not want Sweden drawn into it. On the contrary, realisation of Gustavus Adolphus's plan would, in Oxenstjerna's view, either draw him inexorably into the war between Russia and Poland or else make him fall out with the Russians if he failed to let that happen. Consequently, Oxenstjerna considered that Sweden ought by every means to urge the Russians to break their truce with the Rzeczpospolita, while Sweden itself should strictly observe its own truce with that state.[37]

Accordingly, Oxenstjerna stressed the notion of 'honour' in relations with the Rzeczpospolita and, in consequence, of the 'dishonourableness'

---

[35] Ibid., p. 75. The term of the truce did not run out until 1635. The Swedish military–publicistic propaganda publications issued in Germany, which appeared anonymously under the direction of C.L. Rasche (collected and edited later, for France, by Spanheim, under the title *Le soldat suédois descript les actes guerriers . . . de son Roy*, Rouen, 1634), made frequent mention of attempts by the court of Vienna to turn for military aid to the Rzeczpospolita, on the basis of the 1621 treaty. But Warsaw refused the Emperor's request again and again 'from fear of Muscovy', i.e., from fear of finding itself simultaneously at war with the Swedes (in Germany), and with the Russians. 'There [in Poland] they were very frightened', said the Swedish propaganda, 'that the slightest cause of discontent given to the King of Sweden might cause him to stir up the Tatars and the Muscovites, together, against Poland, while she was busy elsewhere.' Nevertheless the ruling classes of Vienna persistently spread rumours among the people about the thousands of Cossacks who were only awaiting the Polish King's order to butcher the Swedes (*Le soldat suédois*, pp. 430–433 [pp. 296–297, see n. 73 – Trans.]). Austrian sources confirm that Ferdinand II's advisors and commanders, including Wallenstein, persistently solicited from the Rzeczpospolita in 1631 and 1632 the sending of at least 6,000 to 10,000 Cossacks, for the war against the Swedes (*Fontes rerum Austriacarum*, Vol. LXV, Section 2, pp. 178, 231, 233). Evidence to the same effect is also given by Polish sources (Zhukovich, P. N., *Seimovaia bor'ba pravoslavnogo zapadnorusskogo dvorianstva s tserkovnoi uniei*, Vol. VI, 1912). Gustavus Adolphus tried, for his part, to win the Zaporozhian Cossacks' support for the Swedish cause.

[36] Letters from Axel Oxenstjerna to Gustavus Adolphus, 29 September and 13 October 1631.

[37] Letter from Axel Oxenstjerna to Gustavus Adolphus, 13 October 1631.

of a military alliance with Muscovy.[38] Furthermore, he exerted pressure on the King by protracted discussions about the internal and external situation of the Rzeczpospolita and by passive opposition to his claim to the Polish Crown. Thus, right down to the end of September 1631 he was assuring Gustavus Adolphus that no signs were apparent of any war preparations in Poland, i.e. that the Rzeczpospolita was trying to avoid war and seeking peace with the Russians. Only on 29 September 1631 did he inform the King, for the first time, that the Poles were being obliged to begin preparations for war.[39] At the same time he took care to emphasise that Crown Prince Wladyslaw's prospects of getting the Polish Crown were improving, while Gustavus Adolphus's chances were not great. He knew well that the Swedish King counted not on being elected but on being able to bring about civil war in the Rzeczpospolita, so as to prompt the Muscovite government to invade as soon as possible and occupy the West-Russian, Byelorussian and Ukrainian lands, and so as to obtain an excuse for himself to break the truce with the Rzeczpospolita and invade its territory. As against the 'caution' advised by the Chancellor in the matter of the Polish succession, Gustavus Adolphus considered that there was no point in standing on ceremony, nothing to be gained by waiting: everything could be won. Although obliged to agree with the King in words, in fact the Chancellor had no sympathy with his ideas and set himself against the whole design.[40]

The Chancellor's opposition found expression above all in delay in dealing with the matter of raising an army in Germany with Russian money. The essence of his reply of 13 October 1631 to Gustavus Adolphus's question was that the project should be postponed, that Sweden ought not, for the present, to run the risk involved in the proposal the King had made to Moscow, but they should resume consideration of the project later.

This attitude on the Chancellor's part justifies us in suspecting that he may have had a hand in the three-months' hold-up of the King's

---

[38] 'It was clear to Gustavus Adolphus from the start that any and every means must be used to weaken Poland, whereas persons like Axel Oxenstjerna and, to some extent, Johan Skytte, thought it wiser to use only such means as accorded with the Swedes' ideas of honour in politics' (Norrman, *Gustav*, p. 22). In reality, the idea of honour was not the motive in Oxenstjerna's foreign policy, but merely a pretext for opposing a Swedo–Russian alliance.

[39] Letters from Axel Oxenstjerna to Gustavus Adolphus, 12 July, 8 September, 29 September 1631. The Chancellor well knew, of course, that Muscovy's preparations for war against Poland were discussed in the Sejm in January 1631 and the senators decided officially to announce a general call-up of the militia in the Grand Duchy of Lithuania in order to frighten Muscovy (Zhukovich, *Seimovaia bor'ba*, p. 105). The Rzeczpospolita's preparations for war with Muscovy had not ceased since then.

[40] Ahnlund, *Axel*; Norrman, *Gustav*, pp. 52, 62, 74.

proposals to Moscow, which did not reach the Russian capital until December. From the practical standpoint, the Chancellor's most immediate task, given his views, was to ensure that the Russo–Swedish project should not be put into effect at once, in the autumn of 1631, so that thereby the matter would have to be put off until the spring or summer of 1632. Had Gustavus Adolphus's messages, sent through Monier and Möller, reached the Muscovite government without delay, then a favourable reply could have been sent already at the end of September or in October and the alliance formed *de facto*, and then, consequently, Russia could have begun operations on the eastern frontiers of the Rzeczpospolita, while Gustavus Adolphus held the Poles in check on the western frontier. While assuring Gustavus Adolphus, on the one hand, that the Rzeczpospolita was not yet getting ready for war with Muscovy, and so must have information that there were no war preparations under way over there, the Chancellor may, on the other hand, have been taking indirect measures to prevent Muscovy from beginning operations in 1631. Monier was sent from Germany, not to Moscow but to Stockholm, where the Council of State heard his report only on 23 September. The Council could not change the King's instructions, but after Monier had reported, he did not go on to Moscow in person, but was obliged, on the pretext of illness, to convey the message entrusted to him in written form. Monier signed his letters to the Tsar and the Patriarch in Stockholm on 28 September, but the Swedish courier with these letters and with Gustavus Adolphus's similar instructions to Möller did not arrive in Russia until more than two months later. Clearly, dispatch of these messages had been deliberately delayed. To prevent Monier from interfering with this delay he was honourably removed from Stockholm by being appointed, on 24 October 1631, governor of Gripsholm.[41]

Removing Anton Monier, who enjoyed the personal trust of Gustavus Adolphus and also of the Tsar, or, more precisely, of the Tsar's father, who had asked that the King empower Monier to continue their secret negotiations, was undoubtedly in line with the Chancellor's policy. At the same time he and Johan Skytte began a furious onslaught on Jacques Roussel, seeking to discredit him in the eyes of the King and of the Council of State, and thereby to eliminate him, as well, as an independent person engaged in working for a Russo–Swedish alliance and enjoying the trust of both sides. Once Roussel had been got out of the way the only link remaining would be the Swedish representative in Moscow, Johan Möller, who had to communicate with Gustavus Adolphus through Skytte or Oxenstjerna and was therefore subject to supervision by them.

[41] Norrman, *Gustav*, p. 72.

The thing was, to cut any direct line of communication between Gustavus Adolphus and Moscow apart from possible correspondence by letter with the Tsar and the Patriarch. Letters, after all, could be held up for a long time! In fact, while Oxenstjerna delayed his own reply to the King's inquiry about Russian affairs for two months, thereby deleting the whole business from the agenda of the year 1631, the Russian government's reply, apparently owing in no small measure to the Chancellor's effort, reached Gustavus Adolphus only after nine whole months, at the end of May 1632. Thereby Oxenstjerna safeguarded his King's 'German war' from any distracting, extraneous plans.

Gustavus Adolphus's expedition into the depths of Germany also might have been brief if he had not run up against difficulties there which were not of a narrowly military, but of a socio-political character. The class struggle in Germany (and in Bohemia) at the time of the Swedish invasion is a special subject[42] and here it is enough for us merely to mention it as a cause of the unforeseen prolongation of that campaign. It may also partly explain the well-known 'zigzag lightning' of Gustavus Adolphus – his incomprehensible turn back from South-Western Germany, where he was already within reach of the Imperial capital, Vienna. Our task here consists, however, in pointing out another reason for that zigzag.

For a while, Gustavus Adolphus seemed to forget Polish and Russian affairs, being immersed in the abyss of Germany's political, estate and class contradictions. In fact, though, the King simply considered that he possessed a reserve of free time for his Eastern policy, a sort of interval. While it lasted he could appease his Chancellor with seeming compliance. Actually, Gustavus Adolphus never forgot about Russia during this period.

It was in these months that he read the lengthy description of Muscovy compiled by Johan Skytte's son, Bengt, who had been sent there to study the country and its language: *Relatio Moscovitica Dni Benedicti Skytte Baronis . . ..* In Paul's words, this was a very extensive report on the geography and the relations, internal and external, of Muscovy, and its economic resources, with numerous ethnographical observations on the Russians and their neighbours. This report was sent to the King from Dorpat on 16 September 1631 and so came into his hands while he was campaigning in deepest Germany.[43]

---

[42] This is examined later, in Chapter 4.

[43] Paul, *Gustav Adolf*, p. 37. We may consider it beyond doubt that Johan Skytte carried out Gustavus Adolphus's order to study Russia and prepare specialists on the country. It was then, in the autumn of 1631, on the orders of Johan Skytte that at Nyenskans (on the site where St Petersburg was later to be built) a special school was founded in which, among other subjects, the Russian language was taught (Liljendahl, R., *Svensk förvaltning i Livland 1617–1634*, Uppsala, 1933, p. 478, n. 7). Carrying out the King's wish (as we see from Skytte's letter to Gustavus Adolphus dated 24 February 1632), in 1631–1632 Skytte

Because this work by Skytte junior and his brothers' reports (Jakob's work, *Relatio de Russia 1632*, may also have been sent to the King in Germany) were not published, it is hard to say whether they contained wholly accurate information or reflected Johan Skytte's political outlook. However, Geijer quotes this extract: 'They [the Russians] say that they love the Swedes more than others, but they also fear them more, and think that no-one can compare with them in the art of war: especially since they have learnt of His Majesty's successes, exceeding all expectations, won in Germany against the Papists, whom they hate.'[44]

While in Germany Gustavus Adolphus frequently also received dispatches from Johan Möller, via Johan Skytte or Axel Oxenstjerna. Thus, having been ordered by the King to discover the reasons for the delay in the Russo–Polish war, Möller reported on his talks with Prince Cherkasskii (who explained the delay by the lack of Tatar reinforcements and German mercenaries). Möller conveyed, among other things, his impression that the Tsar, personally, was more inclined towards a peaceful settlement with Poland. The Patriarch, on the contrary, had even expressed a desire to correspond privately with Gustavus Adolphus, who replied (12 November 1631), through Möller, that, although this would be unusual, he agreed.[45] Möller wrote to the King also about the preparedness of the Russian army and about the diplomatic negotiations that were going on in Moscow with other powers (for instance, with Denmark), about Poland's war preparations, as described to him by Cherkasskii, and about the purchasing of Russian grain.[46]

sent into Russia, one after the other, his three sons, Bengt, Johan and Jakob, and his nephew Lars, with instructions to make a thorough study of the country set out in a special document: *Instructio filio meo carissimo Benedicto Skytte in Moschoviam tendenti praescripta* (it is preserved in the Swedish public records along with a copy of Bengt Skytte's report sent to the King). The reports by Skytte's three sons (*Relationes Moscoviticae Iohannis, Benedicti et Jacobi Skytte*) are to be found also in the Palmsköld collection of documents (Vols. 97, 186) at Uppsala (Wejle, C., *Sveriges politik mot Polen 1630–1635*, Uppsala, 1901, p. 34 ; Paul, *Gustav Adolf*, p.37 ; Norrman, *Gustav*, p. 111).

[44] Geijer, E. G., *Svenska folkets historia*, Stockholm, 1926, p. 421.

[45] Norrman, *Gustav*, pp. 79, 84.

[46] On 2 February 1632 (could it be 16 April?), having learnt that the Tsar had given permission for the Swedes to buy 50,000 quarters of rye in Russia and that the Russians wanted to buy 10,000 muskets from Sweden, Gustavus Adolphus instructed Möller to propose to the Tsar that, in return for the stated quantity of rye, Sweden should supply the stated number of muskets (at 2 reichsthalers apiece) and also 5,000 cuirasses (at 5 reichsthalers apiece) and 2,000 pistols (at 10 reichsthalers apiece). If the Tsar reckoned to receive 1 reichsthaler for a quarter of rye, then, out of the 65,000 reichsthalers due for all this weaponry, part would cover the cost of the rye (50,000 reichsthalers), while the rest would make up for what had been left unpaid in the past. Should this proposal be rejected, Möller was to offer to pay for the rye by means of a bill of exchange on Holland, where it would be honoured by the Swedish representatives, the Falkenberg brothers. If this proposal was also rejected, Möller was to ask the Tsar to wait for payment for the rye until it arrived in Holland, after which the money (from the proceeds of the sale) would

Though the nature of the sources quoted above compelled us to personalise somewhat the political line of Gustavus Adolphus and that of the Chancellor, in reality they both relied, of course, on influential social forces and were their mouthpieces. While Axel Oxenstjerna expressed the views of the majority of Sweden's aristocratic oligarchy, Gustavus Adolphus based himself on the military section of that oligarchy, his distinguished field-marshals and generals. We have already mentioned that the King entrusted the fulfilment of his plan for an offensive against Poland from the west, first to Gustav Horn and then to Alexander Leslie. The third soldier on whom his choice fell was one of the most outstanding commanders of the Thirty Years' War, General (later, like Alexander Leslie, Field-Marshal) Herman Wrangel.

As a member of Sweden's Council of State, Wrangel must have been informed of Gustavus Adolphus's proposals to Russia not later than 23 September 1631, when Johan Möller reported to the Council on his mission. Wrangel thereupon immediately told the Tsar, through Johan Bökman[47], that he was ready to lead Russia's army of mercenaries against the Rzeczpospolita in an attack on Great Poland.[48] There can be no doubt that this proposal had either been agreed already with Gustavus Adolphus

immediately be sent from there. Finally, in extremity, Möller was to propose to Bökman, who had been sent to take charge of the transport of this grain, that he should himself obtain and pay the money, which would be repaid to him in Holland by the Falkenbergs (Norrman, D., *Gustav*, pp.112–113). This instruction shows that Gustavus Adolphus was hard pressed for money and that the speculation in Russian grain in Holland was carried out under his immediate direction (as a result of which the Swedish archives do not contain any complete figures for the huge sums that the King obtained by this means for 'the German War'). In reply, Möller reported, through Oxenstjerna, that Bökman had not arrived in Russia, that the proposal for a transaction without payment in cash, by supplying Russia with arms, had been accepted only as regards a supply of 2,000 cuirasses (the Russian government was evidently no less hard pressed for ready money), but that the Tsar had agreed to let the grain go for 20 rubles a last and to postpone payment until the winter – promising, at the same time, to allow purchase of the same amount of grain in 1633 (Forsten, G. V., *Baltiiskii vopros*, Vol. II, p. 369). However, Möller was now given a fresh instruction: to try to get the price of the rye reduced still further (Norrman, D., *Gustav*, p. 113). In the archives of the Embassies Department Möller's negotiations on this question, on 17 and 25 June 1631, are recorded obscurely. All that is of interest to us here is that Möller, when sending one of his men at once to convey the Russian's reply to the King, explains this action in a statement made to the Embassies Department that Gustavus Adolphus had 'ordered him to write frequently', and emphasises that he has been entrusted not with mere commercial dealings but with matters of importance to both states, 'about which my gracious King and sovereign specially ordered and instructed me with great care '(*TsGADA, Dela shvedskie*, 1631, *stb.* 8, *ll.* 71–76, 100–101).

[47] He had been nominated ,with Gustavus Adolphus's agreement (during the embassy of Plemiannikov and Aristov), as Muscovy's permanent representative in Stockholm, but he died soon after in Amsterdam. Monier recommended his brother Melchior, but the Russian government did not confirm the appointment (see *TsGADA, Dela shvedskie*, 1633, *stb.* 13).    [48] Norrman, *Gustav*, p. 88.

or else sanctioned by him later. We shall see, *infra*, that it was to Field-Marshal Wrangel that in 1632 he entrusted the preparation of this operation.

For their part, Russian ruling circles showed unremitting interest throughout Gustavus Adolphus's campaign in the German interior, in the position of Sweden and the course of the war. A review of the information that flowed, through a variety of channels, into the Embassies Department would show how fully the Muscovite government was kept posted in these years on the main events both in the war in Germany and in the political life of all the countries in Europe. The Tsar and the Patriarch asked Johan Möller to supply them with fresh news every week, which was, of course, not possible in the conditions of those days. Möller made a special request to Skytte to send him regularly the news from Germany and Poland.[49] The Russian government received particularly abundant and important information thanks to Jacques Roussel, both through the agents he sent to them and during his stay in Moscow.[50]

Material connexion between Muscovy and Sweden (or more correctly with the Swedish army in Germany) was effected at that time, on the one hand, by the dispatch from Archangel of many vessels laden with grain and groats, which, as we know, constituted a kind of subsidy for the prosecution of 'the German war', and also with saltpetre and pitch (strategic materials),[51] and, on the other hand, by the flow that had begun, through Narva, of soldiers hired in Germany and other countries, together with commanders and specialists of various kinds, as well as arms and armour of different sorts which the Russians had purchased abroad.[52] The hiring and purchasing was undertaken, as we recall, under

[49] Letters from Möller to Skytte in September and to Oxenstjerna, 11 October 1631.

[50] *TsGADA, Dela shvedskie*, 1631, *stb.* 9 and 10, *stb.* 4, 7, 8. From Roussel came also a selection of political information from the European press: 'Translations from European gazettes and various other news sent to Moscow' (*TsGADA, Prikaznye dela starykh let*, 1632, *stb.* 65). All this material shows that Roussel's clandestine activity and the information he furnished was viewed with particular confidence by the Muscovite government and regarded as a direct expression of close allied relations with the Swedish King.

[51] Even the Swedish Council of State, which had no precise notion of the actual size of these subsidies in money terms, included in its estimate of revenue for 1631: from the copper ore monopoly – 430,000 reichsthalers, from the Prussian and Livonian customs (duties on exports of grain) – 40,000 reichsthalers, from state trading operations in (Russian) grain – 255,000 reichsthalers, foreign subsidies additionally needed – 1,000,000 reichsthalers (Wittrock, G., *Svenska handelskompaniet och kopparhandeln under Gustav II Adolf*, Uppsala and Stockholm, 1919, p. 139).

[52] See *TsGADA, Dela shvedskie*, 1631, *stb.* 3, 4, 11. The whole story of the arrival in Russia of the mercenary regiments and purchased weaponry, their transport and distribution and, finally, their use in war, has been told very fully in the book, already referred to, by E. Stashevskii, *Smolenskaia voina 1632–1634: Organizatsiia i sostoianie moskovskoi armii*, Kiev, 1919. In the historical literature (see, e.g. Paul, *Gustav Adolf*, p. 38; Vainshtein, O. L., *Rossiia i Tridtsatiletniaia voina 1618–1648*, Moscow and Leningrad, 1947, pp. 99–100), we often find confusion between this recruitment of troops to form part of the

direct control by the courtier, Fedor Plemiannikov, the clerk Aristov, and Colonel Alexander Leslie. Plemiannikov died at Stettin in July 1631, Aristov arrived in Moscow on 3 November 1631,[53] and Leslie junior returned to Russia in January 1632, doubtless to share with the country's rulers much oral information about the situation of the Swedish army.

The loyalty of Muscovy to its duty as Sweden's ally was subjected in this period to a number of tests, and it passed them. Such a test was, for example, the appearance in Moscow in July 1631 of an embassy from the Danish King Christian IV with a proposal for an alliance. Despite the previous friendly relations between Russia and Denmark,[54] protracted negotiations first in Moscow and then, in 1632, in Copenhagen, ended without result, and even with rupture, in so far as the Danish diplomats' aim was to weaken the Swedo–Russian alliance, and the Russians would agree to making an alliance with Denmark only on the categorical condition that Sweden be included in such an alliance.[55] While the Danish embassy was still in Moscow, Jacques Roussel sent out information about tension in relations between Denmark and Sweden.[56] In September 1631 the Embassies Department told Johan Möller about the negotiations

Russian army in the Smolensk War and the plan to use Russian money to hire troops for an attack on Poland from the west, from Germany. Although both plans had been approved by Gustavus Adolphus and by the Muscovite government and were manifestations of the Russo–Swedish alliance, they were separate from each other in time and in organisation. Let us recall that Jacques Roussel had even counterposed them, insistently warning the Russian government that mercenary troops sent into Russia might go over during battle to the side of the Rzeczpospolita (which did happen to some extent), whereas with an army operating from Germany, under Swedish command, this was less possible. Axel Oxenstjerna, on the contrary, had no objection to the former plan but vigorously opposed the latter.

[53] He brought various agreements which had been concluded (*TsGADA, Dela shvedskie*, 1631, *stb.* 4, *ll.* 162–171). For the embassy's report, see ibid, *ll.* 172–193.

[54] Although Christian IV refused to allow Alexander Leslie junior to recruit soldiers in Denmark for the Russian service, he did allow him to bring troops he had hired and military equipment he had bought through the Sound without paying dues.

[55] See the diary and despatch of the Danish envoy Malte Juel, edited by E.N.Shchepkin, in *Letopis' istoriko-filologicheskogo obshchestva pri Novorossiiskom universitete*, Vol. XII, Odessa, 1905; Shcherbachev, Yu. N., 'Russkie akty Kopengagenskogo gosudarstvennogo arkhiva', in *Russkaia istoricheskaia biblioteka*, Vol. XVI; by the same author, 'Datskii arkhiv. Materialy po istorii drevnei Rossii, khraniashchesia v Kopengagene' in *Chteniia v Obshchestve istorii i drevnostei rossiiskikh*, Book III, 1897 ; Fridericia, A., *Danmarks ydre politiske Historie i Tider fra Freden i Lybek til Freden i Kjöbenhavn (1629–1660)*, Vol. I, Copenhagen, 1876, p. 197 *et seq.*

[56] 'The Danish King shares his thoughts with Sigismund and Ferdinand and gives himself to the House of Austria, out of hope that Ferdinand will give his daughter's hand to the King's eldest son, and he [Christian IV], on this account, obliges my sovereign [Gustavus Adolphus] to keep troops stationed on the Danish frontier, so that his forces in Germany are diminished – failing to recall how Ferdinand often struck at him and his subjects and nearly drove him out, but my King in those days saved his Crown for him, although Ferdinand urged my King to take what was left from him and destroy him, and that would have been quite possible, if only he had wanted to do it' (*TsGADA, Dela shvedskie*, 1631, *stb.* 9, *l.* 14).

with the Danes and asked him urgently to inquire of Gustavus Adolphus 'whether it was necessary to him' to be included in a 'perpetual treaty' with the Danish King, and, since the negotiations were to be continued in Copenhagen, to request him to send thither a 'reliable man' to work together with the Russian embassy.[57] In his reply, Möller evaluated Russia's policy towards Denmark as 'a great glory' to the country's sovereign.[58] He immediately wrote to Gustavus Adolphus,[59] who in November answered with a request that the Tsar be told that an alliance with Denmark would be undesirable and dangerous. The Russian embassy, passing through Sweden on their way to Copenhagen, had talks with the Swedish Council of State, and on arrival in the Danish capital linked up with the Swedish ambassador, Fegraeus, as Möller had advised in his reply to the Embassies Department.[60]

Another test occurred in connexion with negotiations between the Swedes and the Tatars. At the end of 1630 there arrived in Moscow a Swedish envoy named Benjamin Baron, on his way to the Khanate of the Crimea, which, owing to illness, he did not reach until July 1631. While in Moscow he, being a man well in the confidence of Gustavus Adolphus, carried on secret negotiations with the Embassies Department. From one of his subsequent letters it emerges that he was ascertaining whether the Russian government would support with active diplomatic pressure (in the form of a special embassy) on the Rzeczpospolita, Gustavus Adolphus's candidature to the Polish throne in the event of the death of Sigismund III.[61]

---

[57]  *TsGADA, Dela shvedskie*, 1631, *stb.* 8, *ll.* 126–128. On 16 September the Tsar sent a letter to Gustavus Adolphus with similar content, describing the negotiations with Denmark (ibid., *stb.* 8, *ll.* 132–138). Roussel had been informed of this on 13 September (Ibid., *stb.* 10, *ll.* 16–17).

[58]  Ibid., *stb.* 8, *ll.* 129–130.

[59]  *Akty i pis'ma*, Vol. II, No.55.

[60]  Norrman, *Gustav*, pp. 113–114. *TsGADA, Dela shvedskie*, 1631, *stb.* 3, *l.* 130. On the Swedo–Danish negotiations at the beginning of 1632 and the Swedes' reproofs to Christian IV for 'conspiring' with the Russians, see Paul, *Gustav Adolf*, Vol. III, pp. 50–51.

[61]  *TsGADA, Dela shvedskie*, 1630–1631, *stb.* 5. Baron had arrived in Novgorod, with an embassy of sixteen persons, already at the end of May 1630 (along with Johan Möller, who was on his way to Archangel), but owing to quarantine and other hindrances he reached Moscow only at the end of December. He brought a letter from Gustavus Adolphus giving thanks for the Tsar's permission for purchase of grain to maintain Sweden's war in Germany – 'and in this Our Royal Majesty perceives Your Royal Majesty the Tsar's sympathy with the oppressed and persecuted Christians in the Kaiser's country whom Our Royal Majesty is now helping'. 'Such neighbourly friendship on the part of Your Royal Majesty the Tsar', Gustavus Adolphus is 'ready and willing and glad to requite in whatever way is pleasing to Your Majesty the Tsar' (ibid., *ll.* 141–144). Baron set forth the message from Gustavus Adolphus orally and in deepest secrecy when he was received by the boyar M. B. Shein and the secretary F. F. Likhachev, 'and what he said to them about secret matters of state', we read in the roll, 'is recorded in a special note, which secretary F. Likhachev keeps in a chest' (ibid., *l.* 150). The same applied 'to the reply on the secret matters which was given to Ambassador

The purpose of Baron's mission to the Crimea was, first, to obtain from the Khan a similar promise to exert pressure on the Polish elections to the advantage of Gustavus Adolphus, and, secondly, to incite the Khan, in return for a handsome subsidy, to launch an offensive either against the Rzeczpospolita or against the Emperor (through Transylvania, whose consent the King undertook to ensure).[62] Having successfully accomplished his mission, Benjamin Baron set off back home, through Moscow, in January–February 1632, bringing a letter to Gustavus Adolphus from the Khan, Jan-Bek Giray, and accompanied by a Crimean embassy to the Swedish King. However, a conflict now arose. It had been arranged to reward him richly with sables and conduct him with honour to the frontier, but he flatly refused to tell the Embassies Department anything about his talks in the Crimea.[63] The concern felt by the Russian government is fully comprehensible, for it was itself counting on the help of 50,000 Tatar (Nogai) troops in its war with the Rzeczpospolita and at the same time was alarmed by renewed Tatar raids, which made that prospect doubtful.[64]

This behaviour by Benjamin Baron was absolutely incompatible with the ideas of the Muscovite government, especially the Patriarch, about relations between allies. It was decided to let Baron and the Crimean embassy proceed but at the same time to send a complaint about him to Gustavus Adolphus, with a request for information about Baron's negotiations in the Crimea. A letter to this effect was signed by the Tsar on 3 March 1632 and handed to Möller for transmission to the King.[65]

Profiting by the opportunity, the Patriarch also wrote, that same day, a personal letter to the Swedish King – an event without precedent in Russian diplomatic practice.[66] This letter was a sort of Patriarchal

Benjamin': it was 'removed [from the roll] and put in a chest by the secretary' (ibid., *l.* 162). Baron sent this reply to Sweden by courier. Before that, however, on being taken ill, Baron wrote on 2 February 1631 a memorandum for the Embassies Department which has survived and sheds light on the content of the negotiations (ibid., *l.* 171).

[62] This is clear from the letter of Jan-Bek Giray to Gustavus Adolphus of 2 December 1631 (*Acta literaria Svecia*, 1723, Vol. III, pp. 445–446). See Rühs, D. F., *Geschichte Schwedens*, Vol. IV, Halle, 1810, pp. 277–367; Cronholm, A., *Sveriges historia under Gustav II Adolfs regering*, Vol. V, Part II, 1871, p. 172; Norrman, *Gustav*, pp. 120–123.

[63] *TsGADA, Dela shvedskie*, 1632, *stb.* 3.

[64] Novosel'skii, A. A., *Bor'ba Moskovskogo gosudarstva s tatarami v pervoi polovine XVII veka*, Moscow, 1948, pp. 204–210.

[65] *TsGADA, Dela shvedskie*, 1632, *stb.* 3, *ll.* 104–113. Even earlier, on 29 February, Möller had written to the Chancellor Oxenstjerna about the clash with Baron, and also, evidently, to Skytte, who informed the King about it on 21 March 1632 (Norrman, *Gustav*, p.118).

[66] This is mentioned in a special minute by the Embassies Department on the draft: 'Before this letter from the great sovereign the Most Holy Patriarch Filaret Nikitich of Moscow and all Russia nobody had written to the Swedish King about such matters' (*TsGADA, Dela shvedskie*, 1632, stb., *l.* 126).

blessing on the friendship and alliance between the two Princes, of Russia and Sweden. Filaret Nikitich wishes Gustavus Adolphus good health and well-being, 'and that between us, great sovereigns, friendship and love may be increased, and moreover, we rejoice that God has given you victory and mastery [deleted: over your enemies] over our common enemies, and in future years we will stand together with you against your enemies in so far as Almighty God will help us.' Then follows the complaint about Baron's conduct, which is accompanied by this conception of relations between allies: 'You, Your Royal Majesty, as a friend of our son the great sovereign, His Majesty the Tsar, will not keep any dealings secret from him, and our son the great sovereign, His Majesty the Tsar will keep no secrets from you, and will take counsel together with you regarding our common foe the Polish King.' The letter ends with an expression of love now and in time to come.[67]

This letter and the Tsar's were sent (either by Möller or without his knowledge) direct to Gustavus Adolphus in Germany by hand of a courier who was a Russian interpreter named Lewa Menin. He evidently managed to break through the blockade by which Oxenstjerna screened off his King from Russia. Gustavus Adolphus entrusted him, at the end of June 1632, with transmission to Moscow of an oral account of Baron's negotiations in the Crimea and of written replies to the letters from the Tsar and the Patriarch – also to the letter of 19 January 1632,[68] his response to which was awaited with particular eagerness in Moscow.

In this connexion we are obliged to leave aside yet another important sphere of diplomatic activity, in which the interests of Muscovy and Sweden were interlaced and where the durability and sincerity of their alliance and the unity and co-ordination of their plans were put to the test, namely, their dealings with Turkey.[69] Here we shall restrict ourselves to remarking that, despite the importance that the Russian government ascribed to Turkey's participation in the forthcoming war with the Rzeczpospolita and all the efforts made to include Turkey in the coalition with Muscovy and Sweden and ensure an invasion of the Rzeczpospolita from the south by the Turkish army simultaneously with blows by the

---

[67] Ibid., *ll.* 115–125.    [68] Norrman, *Gustav*, p. 119.

[69] On the mission of the Swedish envoy Paul Strassburg to Turkey and Transylvania see *Monumenta Hungariae Historica*, Series 1, Vol. 2, Budapest, 1873 ; Rühs, *Geschichte*; Wibling, C., *Sveriges förhållende till Siebenbürgen 1623–1648*, Lund, 1890; Paul, *Gustav Adolf*, Vol. III, pp. 38–40. On Muscovy's dealings with Turkey in 1631–1632 there are plenty of documents in the Embassies Department ('*turetskie dela*') which have not yet been published or systematically analysed by anyone. These materials are partly quoted by N. A. Smirnov (*Rossiia i Turtsiia v XVI–XVII vv.*, Moscow, 1946), and A.A. Novosel'skii (*Bor'ba Moskovskogo*). A brief survey of Russian and foreign publications is given in Vainshtein, *Rossiia*, pp. 149–157.

Russian army from the east and the Swedish army (more precisely, the Swedo–Russian army) from the west, the actual course taken by events showed that this part of the plan played, nevertheless, no decisive part in Russian policy. Muscovy began the Smolensk War regardless of the absence of a Turkish invasion, and ended it in 1634, regardless of the attack on the Rzeczpospolita by a large Turkish army. All this, however, calls for detailed analysis. Here it suffices to say that, through Roussel[70] and other channels, the Russian and Swedish governments kept each other informed, to some degree, about their respective *démarches* in Constantinople.[71]

The biggest test of the firmness of the line of alliance with Sweden which the Russian government had adopted was provided, of course, by its relations with the Rzeczpospolita during this period of waiting.

Although there were profound territorial contradictions between Muscovy on the one hand and both Sweden and the Rzeczpospolita on the other (especially after the Polish and Swedish intervention at the beginning of the seventeenth century), Muscovy's principal task in foreign relations in this period was to reunite with the basic Russian lands the West-Russian territories and the Ukraine and Byelorussia which had been torn away from them. Only after this task had been accomplished, even though not completely, in the reign of Aleksei Mikhailovich, did the Russian state turn its attention, under Peter I, to the struggle to recover the Baltic countries. The objective historical situation made it impossible at that time to maintain any sort of good neighbourly relations with the Rzeczpospolita, a multi-national state which held Russians, Ukrainians and Byelorussians under oppression by Polish feudal lords. Consequently, until Russia had reclaimed its territory, the contradictions with Sweden had to be put in the background and a close alliance formed with that state. The Patriarch staunchly promoted that line in foreign policy. Numerous active measures were taken by the Rzeczpospolita to break up the Russo–Swedish alliance. There were attempts at *rapprochement* now

---

[70] Jacques Roussel was closely associated with Paul Strassburg when they met at the court of Bethlen Gábor. In November 1630 Axel Oxenstjerna, Jacques Roussel and Paul Strassburg met at Elbing before the last-named set off for Constantinople (Norrman, *Gustav*, p.40). There can be no doubt that when Roussel was in Moscow in March–April 1631 he spoke about Strassburg's mission, just as in June 1632 he told Moscow of the instructions with which the Swedish envoy Benjamin Baron was going to the Crimea (*TsGADA, Dela shvedskie*, 1631, *stb*. 9, *l*. 13). At that same time Roussel was petitioning for his own secret agent to be allowed to go through Moscow to Turkey (and also to Moldavia and Transylvania). In short, Roussel was *au fait* with Sweden's dealings with Turkey, and kept Moscow posted.

[71] For example, a letter from Mikhail Fedorovich to Gustavus Adolphus of 20 June 1632 told of the embassy of Pronchishchev and Bormosov to Turkey (*TsGADA, Dela shvedskie*, 1632, *stb*. 4, *ll*. 2–3).

with Sweden, now with Muscovy. As early as the beginning of April 1631 a 'Lithuanian courier', Adam Orlik,[72] was sent to Moscow on a mission unknown to us. But after receiving Gustavus Adolphus's proposals for war and accepting them (April–May 1631), all attempts at diplomatic *rapprochement* made by the Rzeczpospolita were rebuffed by Moscow in a most resolute fashion. Especially significant was the episode of the non-admission into Muscovy of the ambassador from Emperor Ferdinand II, who came through Poland to Dorogobuzh in March 1632 with the aim of mediating between the Rzeczpospolita and Muscovy, and thereby getting the latter to refuse to help Gustavus Adolphus in his war against the Emperor.[73] Russian envoys subsequently explained to Gustavus Adolphus that this ambassador was not admitted because he arrived at the frontier accompanied by Polish–Lithuanian noblemen and had been sent 'by common design of Kaiser Ferdinand and the Polish King Sigismund'. Although it was later acknowledged that the ambassador really did emanate from the Emperor (and was not an impostor from the Rzeczpospolita as they thought at first in Moscow), even if that had been precisely known, the Tsar and the Patriarch would not have allowed him to come to Moscow: 'because the Kaiser is an enemy to you, our friend, and what relations can we have with him?' The Tsar and the Patriarch, 'strengthened in their perpetual friendship and love for the King's Majesty of Sweden, ordered that the ambassador from the Kaiser be refused entry, because the Roman Kaiser is an enemy to the King's Majesty, and that ambassador, instructed by the Kaiser and the Polish King, wanted to practise deception in Moscow', so as to find out about the alliance and dealing of the Tsar and the Patriarch with the Swedish King and so as 'to do all manner of evil' and 'make much trouble'.[74]

On 15 July 1632 there arrived at the 'Polyanovka barrier' a Polish

[72] *TsGADA, Dela shvedskie*, 1631, stb. 3.

[73] Documents concerning this episode were published in *Pamiatniki diplomaticheskie snoshenii Drevnei Rossii s derzhavami inostrannymi*, Vol. III, St Petersburg, 1853, pp. 1–84. Cf. Niccolo Sacchetti's report from Vienna, 15 November 1631, regarding the dispatch of this embassy, which was included by G. V. Forsten in *Akty i pis'ma k istorii baltiiskogo voprosa*, Vol. I (St Petersburg, 1889), p.321. The Swedish propaganda publication mentioned *supra* stated that the Emperor's ambassadors Arnoldin and Count Mörsberg had been sent to Warsaw 'to be present on behalf of the Emperor at the election of the King of Poland [at the meeting of the Sejm in March 1632], but, seeing that that affair was going to take a long time, went on to Muscovy, with a view to negotiating with the Grand Prince in accordance with the commission they had from Vienna, while the Poles were deciding on the date for the election' (*Le soldat suédois descript les actes guerriers, merveilles de nostre temps, plus que très-généreuses et très-héroiques . . . de son Roy*, Rouen, 1634, p. 590). [In the British Library there is another edition of this work, entitled *Le soldat suédois ou histoire véritable de ce qui s'est passé depuis l'avenue du Roy de Suède en Allemagne jusqu'à sa mort*, and the page numbers of Porshnev's quotations will be given for both editions – in this case, p.407 – Trans.]

[74] *TsGADA, Dela shvedskie*, 1632, stb. 6, *ll.* 73–74, 125–129.

envoy named Marcin Koszyca, with a retinue. He represented the Archbishop of Gniezno and the Sejm. He too met with refusal of access to Moscow and an enumeration of the Rzeczpospolita's 'acts of injustice' towards Russia.[75]

At the same time the Russian government was fully and actively backing Gustavus Adolphus's Polish policy. This found expression particularly in its dealings with Jacques Roussel, whose official signature to his letter to Moscow was 'ambassador of His Majesty [the King of Sweden] to the Poles'. From his headquarters, which were sometimes in Dorpat and sometimes in Riga, Roussel was indeed vigorously at work in the Rzeczpospolita. He sent his couriers and agents to political figures there and received theirs in return, he circulated printed proclamations supporting Gustavus Adolphus's candidature to the Polish throne, acting both covertly and overtly, and by both bribery and kindling the spirit of militant Protestantism among the Polish–Lithuanian magnates and *szlachta*.[76] Roussel thought it necessary to keep the Russian government informed about all his more important activities in the Rzeczpospolita and about the news that reached him from there.

Thus, on 22 June 1631, he sent to Moscow from Riga two men from among those many agents and collaborators whom he somehow was amazingly capable of drawing into his service and who were always around him in great numbers. This time the persons concerned were two Frenchmen, fervent Calvinists both – Captain Pierre l'Admiral and Ensign Jacques Des Grèves.[77] In historical writings their mission has been associated only with their passage through Russia to the Zaporozhian Cossacks to appeal, unsuccessfully, to the latter to take action in support of Gustavus Adolphus. In reality, however, they had extensive commissions to carry out for Roussel in Moscow. Our attention is caught, among the documents in this roll, by the fact that the whole mission appears as something previously agreed on and discussed in the Russian capital. The letter of credence addressed to the Tsar and the Patriarch which Roussel gave l'Admiral and Des Grèves recommends them as persons who have been sent 'in accordance with the wish of Your Majesty the Tsar and according to my word and my declared desire . . . to work for the

---

[75] The authorities at Dorogobuzh were told that the envoy was not to be received, 'and no good can be expected from him, nothing but trouble and wrong actions, just as from the one who called himself the Kaiser's ambassador, and much harm and deception is to be expected from their senators' (*TsGADA*, *Dela polskie*, 1632, stb. 2, *l.* 17).

[76] On Roussel's doings in Poland see: Wejle, *Sveriges politik*, pp. 18–34; Cichocki, M., *Medjacia Francji w rozejmie Altmarskim*, Cracow, 1928, pp. 148–164; Szlangowski, A., 'Uklady Krolewicza Wladislawa i dyssidentoow z Gustawem Adolfem w r. 1632', *Kwartalnik Historyczny*, Vol. 4, 1899, pp. 685–700; Zhukovich, *Seimovaia bor'ba*, Vol. VI, pp. 142–156.    [77] See *supra*, p. 95.

well-being and extension of your realm'. And at the same time their mission was yet another confirmation of the fact that Gustavus Adolphus 'has one heart with you, great sovereigns, concerning all matters relating to the Jesuits and the Poles'.[78] We note also that Roussel (not only in this instance but in all his correspondence with Moscow after his first visit) constantly uses conventional expressions which had doubtless been agreed on in Moscow and with the King in order to designate and distinguish two tasks, different though interconnected, of the Russo–Swedish alliance: 'the higher matter' and 'the nearer matter'. We undertake, *infra*, decipherment and analysis of the 'higher matter'. As for the less conspiratorial 'nearer matter', both the context and the frank commentaries leave us in no doubt that this was a code for 'military combinations against the common foe, the Polish King'.[79]

Roussel declares in the instructions he gave to l'Admiral and Des Grèves that only Gustavus Adolphus's victories in Germany have derailed plans for a joint offensive by Emperor Ferdinand II and King Sigismund III against Muscovy, through Pskov and Smolensk. To demonstrate concretely what horrors would await the population of Muscovy if that had happened, 'a thousand times more terrible than at the hands of the Tatars', Roussel describes vividly the sacking and destruction by the Imperial troops of the city of Magdeburg (which had stood out 'for freedom on earth, and for the Evangelical faith, and for my Lord the King'). The enemy would already 'have entered your realm had he not been hindered by the victory that God gave to my Lord the King'. 'The many wondrous victories' of Gustavus Adolphus, 'over our common foes', 'have overturned and ruined' the design of the Emperor and the Polish King against Muscovy. 'So that Your Majesty knows that my Lord the King, with his army, forms an advanced wall for you, and that he is fighting at the head of these troops as a vanguard regiment for the realm of Russia.' Consequently, having learnt what 'great power' the Swedish King commands, by reason of his victories, the Tsar and the Patriarch will pray for the success of his arms and strive to help him, and still more strongly 'will see how desirable is that treaty for secret and direct unity about which I spoke with Your Majesties'. It is important to be ready to overcome the enemy at the first encounter. The Tsar must be on the alert all the time and not let himself be taken by surprise.[80]

This German–Polish army destined for an attack on Muscovy was also, according to Roussel, intended to serve Sigismund III's internal political

---

[78] *TsGADA, Dela shvedskie*, 1631, *stb.* 9, *ll.* 35–36.
[79] In June 1631 Roussel wrote about 'the secret treaty', 'the friendly alliance' of the Russian Tsar and the Swedish King and about the war they had 'agreed' to wage 'against the Polish Jesuits', as the pre-condition 'for the foundation of the higher matter' (ibid., *l.* 16).
[80] Ibid., *ll.* 3–6.

purposes. On arrival in Poland it was to help him force the Sejm to elect, during the King's lifetime, his son Kazimir as successor on the throne. This plan, however, had been frustrated by Gustavus Adolphus's victories and also by those in Poland who were 'on the side of good' (among those Roussel named, were Lew Sapieha and Krzysztof Radziwill). Sigismund III and the Jesuits had been plainly informed that if they were to speak of such things in the future, then, before they could carry out their plan, the Swedish King Gustavus Adolphus would be invited into the Rzeczpospolita and elected King. This had forced Sigismund III to retreat and to give a written undertaking not to raise again the question of the succession or the coronation of a new King while he, Sigismund, was still alive. Thus, Roussel goes on, everything is at present going 'to the advantage and desire of those who hold to the good side'.

Roussel ridicules the claims of Kazimir and Wladyslaw to the Polish Crown, because 'things are not going their way': as had been agreed when he was in Moscow, that crown was to fall to the lot of Gustavus Adolphus. While, on the one hand, speaking of the military weakness of the Poles and of their violation of the truce with Sweden by sending Cossack regiments into Germany to fight the Swedes, Roussel, on the other hand, tells the Muscovite government about the visit of his secret agent to the Sejm in Warsaw, his dealings with his supporters in the Rzeczpospolita, his distribution among the magnates and dissemination in the Sejm of his 'letters' and 'broadsheets', both printed and handwritten, in favour of Gustavus Adolphus's candidature and intended to stir up conflict in Poland between Protestants and Catholics.[81]

Having in this way fully informed the Muscovite government of his activity as Gustavus Adolphus's envoy to the Poles, Roussel asks the Tsar and the Patriarch to send him, through his agents l'Admiral and Des Grèves, an answer in writing, 'giving your decision about the recruitment of troops and assembling of this army in Silesia, according to the project which I put forward, and which was conveyed to you by old Ivan, the true and good interpreter, so that I may serve you, in this matter, great sovereigns, when I go to my lord the King'. Roussel explains that Prince Cherkasskii has not answered him yet, giving as his reason that no news

---

[81] *TsGADA, Dela shvedskie*, 1631, *stb.* 9, *ll.* 9–13. The not altogether clear ending of this 'article' leaves the impression that, on his last visit to Moscow, Roussel had promised to put the Russian government in touch with the Polish–Lithuanian dissidents, and was now excusing himself for having failed in that task. It is interesting that at this same time the Patriarch's secret informant on Polish affairs, 'Anatolii Muzhilovskii, monk of Pechersk Monastery', gave warning of war preparations in the Rzeczpospolita directed against Muscovy and offered to act as go-between in bringing over to the Tsar's side 'Krzysztof Radziwill, the hetman of the Lithuanian Principality, from whom secret information might also be obtained' (ibid., *ll.* 77–82). Evidently the Muscovite government and the Polish–Lithuanian dissidents were each sounding the other out, but this produced no noticeable political effects.

has so far been received from Leslie, Plemiannikov and Aristov, who had been sent to Gustavus Adolphus ('and until we have heard from them there can be no talk about so great a matter'). By now, probably, 'complete information' has arrived from them, so that the sovereigns will be pleased to write their decision regarding the plan[82] and also regarding the conclusion with Gustavus Adolphus of a secret treaty of friendship and about the agreed military operations against 'the Polish Jesuits'. 'And [this great matter] can soon be accomplished because my lord the King now has control of the route through Silesia.' Roussel asks that he be entrusted with 'the performance and fulfilment of this matter' and assures the Tsar and the Patriarch that his master is ready to carry out any requests which they may put to him.[83]

In this context the mission of l'Admiral and Des Grèves to the Zaporozhian Cossacks is seen as one of the links in Gustavus Adolphus's Polish policy. The Russian government's co-operation in this mission was a manifestation of its loyalty towards the Swedish King. Roussel stresses very significantly the importance of establishing a direct link between Gustavus Adolphus and the Zaporozhians, and declares that Russia and Sweden together will bind them more firmly than Russia could on its own : 'two belts together will hold them more strongly than one'. It will be easier to control the Cossacks after 'they have pledged themselves to both Majesties'.[84] Roussel's instructions to l'Admiral and Des Grèves and the text of Gustavus Adolphus's letter to the Cossacks present the Swedish King as defender of 'the Greek faith' and of Cossack liberties against Polish oppression. The secret articles raise the questions of support by the Cossacks for 'the election of His Majesty to the Polish Kingship' and of their 'dispatch into the Kaiser's country on His Majesty's service', in return for good pay.[85] One can well understand that it was not a light matter for the Russian government, which had long been carrying on secret negotiations with the Cossacks and which knew about the letters sent to them by the Patriarchs of Jerusalem and Constantinople, urging them 'to give allegiance to the ruler of Moscow', to hand over this initiative to the King of Sweden. Nevertheless, it supplied l'Admiral and Des Grèves with a letter of its own to the Cossacks and made great efforts to ensure the success of their mission and to prevent possible complications with the re-election of the Hetman which had just taken place, a change of direction by the leaders of the Orthodox Church in the Ukraine, and

---

[82] As we know, the plan was officially adopted by the Russian government only on 16 January 1632.

[83] *TsGADA, Dela shvedskie*, 1631, *stb.* 9, *ll.* 15–17.

[84] Ibid., *ll.* 7–8.

[85] Ibid., *ll.* 20–32. Roussel's envoys in Moscow had to petition the Tsar and the Patriarch 'to find a way to bribe the Archimandrite of Kiev, Pyotr Mogila, to help my lord the King [to the throne of Poland]' (ibid., *l.* 14).

concessions made by the Polish government to the Cossacks' leaders. It was no fault of the Russian government that the gallant Frenchmen left in Kiev their trusty escort Grigory Gladkii (the secret go-between for Moscow with the pro-Muscovite leaders of the Ukraine), who had instructions ('so as to protect these envoys without fail from those Cossacks who serve the King [of Poland], so that no harm may come to them') to prevent the envoys from meeting the Cossacks. They went straight, accompanied only by an interpreter, to Kanev, to see the new Hetman of the Zaporozhian Host, Kulaga – who handed them over to the Polish government.[86]

In one way or another, the embassy of l'Admiral and Des Grèves to Moscow was a clear demonstration of the unity of Swedish and Russian policy towards the Rzeczpospolita.[87] Exactly a month later, on 22 July 1631, Roussel sent another envoy to Moscow, his 'faithful secretary'

[86] *TsGADA, Dela shvedskie*, 1631, stb. 9, *ll*. 35 *et seq*. The opinion is widely held among Swedish historians that the whole enterprise of the mission of l'Admiral and Des Grèves to the Zaporozhian Cossacks was frivolous and proof of Roussel's light-mindedness. On the contrary, the ground for it had been prepared long and thoroughly, but the situation had altered for the worse a very short time before: Roussel could not be aware of that, and even in Moscow they were not fully in the picture. Even in this unfavourable situation, however, an acute conflict broke out in the Cossacks' 'council', when the 'broadsheets' of the Swedish King and the Tsar were read out. According to an eye-witness, 'the lesser people among [the Zaporozhians] all were for serving you [the Tsar] and defending the Cossacks and the Christian faith here from oppression by the Poles, but the better people among them, who sided with the Poles, overpersuaded them, and those broadsheets and the foreigners were sent to Hetman Koniecpolski' (*Akty Moskovskogo gosudarstva*, Vol. I, St Petersburg, 1870, no. 328). The movement among the broad masses of the Zaporozhian Cossacks in 1629–1630, supported by the rest of the Ukrainian peasantry, for union with Russia, was the prologue to the war of national liberation in 1648–1654, and their desire to link up with this growing socio-historical force testifies only to the perspicacity and realism of such politicians as Jacques Roussel and the Patriarch of Constantinople, Cyril Lucaris. (On the international significance of the Ukrainian people's fight for national liberation, see Porshnev, B.F., *Frantsiia, Angliiskaia revoliutsiia i evropeiskaia politika v seredine XVII v*, Moscow, 1970, pp. 261–276.)

[87] Besides the questions mentioned, Roussel sent with these envoys: (1) information about the mission of his man ('the engineer') to Polotsk and Smolensk on the pretext of searching for Swedish prisoners (*TsGADA, Dela shvedskie*, 1631, stb. 9, *l*. 13): (2) information about Denmark's foreign policy (see *supra*): (3) a statement that, at the command and desire of Prince Cherkasskii he has hired draughtsmen to prepare quickly 'a large map of your realm and all the neighbouring ones round about', including especially a well-surveyed depiction of the Polish kingdom, which map could be ready within four months (ibid., *l*. 17): (4) a request to be sent various wild animals, to serve as gifts to distinguished Poles who cannot simply be bought with money from Sweden's treasury (ibid., *l*. 19): (5) an exposure of the measures taken by the Jesuits for releasing Charles Talleyrand from his Russian prison, with a request to be sent the papers taken from him by Talleyrand (ibid., *ll*. 18–19): (6) a proposal to send two translators from Latin (ibid., *ll*. 17–18). This roll contains a wealth of information about political events in the Rzeczpospolita and war preparations there, supplied mainly by Grigorii Gladkii on his return to Moscow in October 1631. As regards the points listed, Prince Cherkasskii replied in a letter to Roussel on 13 September that permission to go to the Zaporozhians had been given to l'Admiral and Des Grèves; that point four could not be met; that point five had been seen to; and that point six was considered desirable (ibid., *stb*. 10, *ll*. 13–14).

Christian Wassermann.[88] This man had just returned from the Rzeczpospolita, where he had had talks with the magnates. It was his task to report
to Moscow in detail on the positions of Lew Sapieha, Radziwill and
Gosiewski and on their mutual relations and differences in connexion
with the approaching death of Sigismund III. From the instructions
given to Wassermann by Roussel and from the record of Wassermann's
conversation with Prince Cherkasskii it is further clear that the line of
action taken by Roussel in the affairs of Poland–Lithuania had been, to a
certain extent, agreed beforehand in Moscow. Wassermann reported, for
example, that two agents of Roussel's were living with Sapieha and
Gosiewski respectively in order to carry out that task about which
Roussel had spoken in confidence with Prince Cherkasskii.[89] Together
with plentiful information about political events in the Rzeczpospolita,
the preparations being made there for war with Muscovy, the condition
of the armed forces and political attitudes, Wassermann was to present
once more (with references to Gustavus Adolphus) the argument for the
rulers of Muscovy to try and 'buy the support of the Zaporozhian
Cossacks and incite them to armed action' against the Polish King,
because, in that case, 'the entire power of our foe will be drawn to that
front', i.e. will be distracted into conflict with the Cossacks (as was
actually to happen in 1648–1653).

After spending a month and a half in Moscow (from 9 August to 22
September 1631), Christian Wassermann returned to Roussel in Riga.
Prince Cherkasskii sent Roussel thanks for what he was doing and for the
news he had provided. The Tsar and the Patriarch praise Roussel 'and in
future will entrust to you those matters of state about which earlier you
spoke secretly with me'.[90] As soon as 7 October 1631 Roussel sent
Wassermann to Moscow again, with a letter. This told of Gustavus
Adolphus's victories 'against our common foe', most eloquently vaunted
the King's military genius, and returned to the project for an attack on the
Rzeczpospolita from Silesia and for a treaty with the Tsar 'for friendly
alliance with my lord the King'.[91] Wassermann left Moscow with a letter

[88]  Christian Wassermann was a gentleman-in-waiting to Gustavus Adolphus (Wejle,
      *Sveriges politik*, p. 34), one of those Swedish court officials (like Lazar Mavius) who were
      put at Roussel's disposal by the King and who later, in 1633, returned to their previous
      state service.
[89]  *TsGADA, Dela shvedskie*, 1631, stb.10, *l.* 7.
[90]  Ibid., *l.* 14. It is also said that the letter which Roussel asked to be extracted from
      Talleyrand's papers had been found, in accordance with the description he gave of it, and
      was being sent to him via Wassermann (ibid., *l.* 13).
[91]  *TsGADA, Dela shvedskie*, 1631, *stb.* 10, *ll.* 23–31, 47–53. Wassermann brought detailed
      information about the situation in Smolensk and about the political struggle in the
      Rzeczpospolita, various 'printed news-sheets' (leaflets, newspapers), a letter from Lew
      Sapieha to Roussel and other materials which described the preparations for war with
      Muscovy and the internal situation in the Rzeczpospolita.

from the Tsar and a rich reward to Roussel on 9 December 1631.[92]

After this there is an interruption in the materials in the Embassies Department concerning their dealings with Roussel. The next roll tells us of Roussel's departure from Moscow in 20 June 1632 (the date of his arrival there is not known). From Swedish sources we know that at the end of 1631 a fierce struggle began between Roussel, on the one hand, and Axel Oxenstjerna and Johan Skytte, on the other. The occasion for their attack was the failure of the mission of l'Admiral and Des Grèves to the Zaporozhian Cossacks. With a view to smoothing the diplomatic conflict and at the same time discrediting the King's agent and his policy, the Chancellor, and later the Council of State as well, declared officially that Roussel had exceeded the powers granted him by Gustavus Adolphus.[93] In response, Roussel took the bold step of open struggle: he decided to make the whole affair public and disgrace his adversaries. In January 1632 he printed in Riga, in Latin, German and Polish, the text of his credentials and the plenary powers given him by Gustavus Adolphus to negotiate with the Polish–Lithuanian magnates and the Zaporozhian Cossacks. But this did not help him. He was accused of leaving out in the credentials a reservation which restricted his powers.[94] However, this did not bring Roussel to a halt. He sent his printed materials to the Polish nobles in Warsaw, by hand of his agent Lazar Mavius. This mission proved to be a real bomb, with immense resonance both in the Rzeczpospolita and abroad. At first Mavius was arrested in Warsaw, but then, by the advice of King Sigismund himself, he was allowed to appear before an assembly of nobles, specially selected, of course, who put on a loyal demonstration of support for Sigismund III and the constitution of the Rzeczpospolita and threatened to hang Mavius, who found safety only in the house of the Crown Marshal. If Roussel's task had been to ensure the peaceful election of Gustavus Adolphus to the throne of Poland, then he ruined everything by his action. But his task actually was (as we recall), by parading Gustavus Adolphus's hopes of election, to promote as speedy as possible a commencement of war between Muscovy and the Rzeczpospolita, and so he had not ruined anything at all.[95] But even by using such extraordinary methods he was unable to defend himself from Axel Oxenstjerna. On the contrary, the Chancellor took steps to discredit and eliminate him finally.

---

[92] Ibid., *ll.* 63–66.    [93] Wejle, *Sveriges politik*, p. 26; Norrman, *Gustav*, p. 106.

[94] A year later, in a letter of 23 March 1633 to the Council of State, Oxenstjerna censures Skytte for not preventing the printing of Roussel's letters and appreciating what he was up to, but finds an excuse for him in that he thought Roussel must have secret instructions from the King (Wejle, *Sveriges politik*, p. 25).

[95] In Norrman's words, Gustavus Adolphus's written instructions ordered Roussel to concern himself with the problems of the Polish succession, but his oral instructions were to inflame Russo–Polish antagonisms and bring about war between Muscovy and the Rzeczpospolita (in accordance with Monier's task) (Norrman, *Gustav*, pp. 37–38).

Unfortunately, we know nothing of Roussel's dealings with Gustavus Adolphus after their first meeting in November 1630.[96] Considering how many couriers Roussel sent to Russia and Poland, we can have no doubt that there were also reliable persons at his disposal whom he could dispatch to Germany, to the King's headquarters. In his letters to Moscow we notice echoes of exchanges with Gustavus Adolphus. We can confidently assume that such an energetic man would have found ways and means of keeping up some kind of communication with the King. In Gustavus Adolphus's papers, however, not a single letter from Roussel has survived, nor the draft of any reply thereto. Either the King himself destroyed all such correspondence or someone else removed it after his death.

All that we know is that it was only in appearance that internal German affairs occupied Gustavus Adolphus to the exclusion of everything else. With the offensive of spring 1632 he was again, although in the midst of his struggle with Wallenstein, taken up with his earlier Eastern concerns. Behind his moves this way and that in Germany the outlines of a larger, world-wide policy emerged. It was impossible to put off any longer settlement of the Polish problem, especially as in February 1632 an official alliance, defensive and offensive, directed against Gustavus Adolphus, was concluded between the Emperor and the King of Spain – an alliance that it was open for the Polish King to join. Special embassies strove to draw Sigismund III into this alliance, and all Europe hung upon their results.[97] Without formally joining the alliance, the Rzeczpospolita renewed its permission to the Habsburg powers to recruit troops on its territory. Wallenstein negotiated with Crown Prince Wladyslaw. The vojvoda Lubomirski promised to lead his forces into battle, along with Wallenstein, either against György Rákóczi[98] or against Gustavus Adolphus.[99] Skytte had already in January 1632 reported to Gustavus Adolphus and the Council of State on the growing threat of a breach by the Rzeczpospolita of its truce with Sweden.[100] In April 1632 Sigismund III died and the Polish throne was vacant. The Muscovite government had still not begun war with the Rzeczpospolita and the intimidating effect on the latter of Moscow's celebrations of the Swedes' victory in Germany might eventually fade.

As early as March 1632 Gustavus Adolphus wrote to Chancellor Oxenstjerna that, as before, he had no ambition to acquire the Polish

[96] See *supra*, p. 79.
[97] Arlanibaeus, Ph., *Theatrum Europaeum*, Vol. II, Frankfurt-am-Main, 2nd edition, 1679, p. 576; *Le soldat suédois*, pp. 430–433, 589–590 [pp. 296–298, 404–408].
[98] The Prince of Transylvania who succeeded Bethlen Gábor when he died in 1629.
[99] Norrman, *Gustav*, p. 106.    [100] Ibid.

Crown, but had to think about it for political reasons.[101] A little earlier he seemed even to be trying, for the first time, to change course. On a quite trivial pretext he suddenly decided to transfer part of his forces back into North-Eastern Germany, to join up with Banér. While on the move he changed his mind, apparently under pressure from Chancellor Oxenstjerna, who then paid an urgent visit to him at Frankfurt-am-Main. Lengthy secret talks took place between the King and his Chancellor.[102] By analogy with the similar secret talks that were held a few months later and about which we know more, we can presume that the Chancellor was insisting on a further advance in Germany and no return to the Polish frontier. This time, the King submitted. Who knows how many times the name of Roussel was uttered in those conversations, with the matter of his failed embassy to the Zaporozhians? Oxenstjerna dealt his final blow to Roussel, however, only in April 1632. It is not known whether it was Lazar Mavius's escapade in Warsaw that served as sufficient basis for his demand that Roussel be dismissed or whether the King was shown false evidence against Roussel. The second possibility is the more probable.[103] In any case, on 6 May 1632, at Freysingen in Bavaria, Gustavus Adolphus was obliged to sign a letter to Johan Skytte ordering him to dismiss Jacques Roussel, but to treat him in a friendly way.[104] That proviso shows that the King was only yielding to pressure, that he did not believe in

---

[101] *Rikskansleren Axel Oxenstjernas skrifter och brefvexling*, Vol. II, p. 738.

[102] *Le soldat suédois*, p. 325 [pp. 221–224].

[103] In 1634 the Dutchman Isaak Massa presented to the Russian government a denunciation of Roussel. Analysis of the text shows that Massa derived his biographical facts to a considerable extent from conversations with Roussel himself, merely decorating them with malicious commentary. Roussel's dismissal is explained here by the allegation that 'there came to the King's knowledge some handwritten letters which Jacques Roussel had sent through third parties to the Kaiser's general Wallenstein and also secretly to the Kaiser' (*TsGADA, Dela gollandskie*, 1634, *stb.* 1, *l.* 13). Roussel apparently spoke of this in 1634 as the delation that led to his dismissal. Significantly, it was with very similar accusations that the Swedish government tried later to discredit Roussel with the Muscovites: Roussel was a secret Catholic (a Jesuit), had betrayed the Russo-Swedish negotiations to the Poles, and so on. But, however we may judge Roussel as a whole, his fervent hatred of Catholicism, confirmed by deeds throughout his life, is not open to doubt. We know that Massa was in the secret service of the Swedish government, from whom, perhaps, he received the information referred to. The denunciation was written after Massa's departure from Russia, from 'the Swedish frontier' on 3 April, possibly when he met Christian Wassermann, who had been sent to Russia with the task of slandering Roussel at any cost. From the proceedings of the Swedish Council of State it is clear that all the efforts to collect proof of Roussel's links with Catholics and Jesuits, all the tricks of the secret investigation, resulted in material that was worse than dubious (*Svensk riksrådets protokoll*, Vol. IV, 1634, pp. 50, 56, 87 *et seq.*, 224). Eventually the Council of State itself expressed hope that Isaak Massa would, when he arrived, 'reveal to us the secret of Roussel' (ibid., pp. 100, 23 April 1634).

[104] Wejle, *Sveriges politik*, p. 33. The view (Paul, *Gustav Adolf*, p.44) that on 6 May Gustavus Adolphus ordered Roussel to be 'arrested' is refuted by this phrase about friendly treatment.

Roussel's guilt, and, perhaps, that he counted on using his services again, unofficially, in the future.

Roussel did not yet know he had been dismissed when he travelled from Riga to Moscow (evidently in May), but he must have sensed that a crisis was approaching in his struggle with the Chancellor, and he was going to Moscow to arm himself for that struggle. Although he visited Moscow as a private person ('not as an ambassador') he was given when he left on 20 June 1632 an official letter from the Tsar for transmission to Gustavus Adolphus. This was a diplomatic note supporting Roussel and his activity. It began with the statement that the Tsar and the Patriarch had been visited by 'the ambassador of Your Royal Majesty, Jacques Roussel', i.e, an unreserved recognition of his competence. Later this letter accords high value to his work: 'And he serves us both with great and hearty zeal, without any deceit, and wishes for and seeks all good and close unity and reinforcement between us, and he intends all harm to come upon our common foe, the Polish King Sigismund, and promotes the common cause in Poland of Our Majesty the Tsar and Your Royal Majesty, which cause is advantageous to both of us.' Further on, the Russian government casts into the scale in Roussel's favour not only its formal agreement to Gustavus Adolphus taking the Polish throne but also its diplomatic influence on other states to the same effect. It states that, for the sake of friendship and close alliance with the King of Sweden, it has sent embassies to the Turkish Sultan Murad IV and the Crimean Khan Jan-Bek Giray to urge them 'to write to Poland that they wish you, our friend, Your Royal Majesty, to have the Polish Kingship, that nobody but Your Royal Majesty be elected, neither the Crown Prince or any other'. Finally, the letter conveys the promise that was most important to Gustavus Adolphus: 'And we are ready for war on the Polish King in this present year 1632 [in the draft, 'in the summer' has been deleted].'

Thereafter come expressions of friendship and love, wishes for a prosperous reign and victory over enemies, hopes 'to be in firm friendship and love, in good relations and in close unbreakable alliance for ever, and to fight together against our common foe.' At the end of this important foreign-policy document the Russian government again links Roussel's name inseparably with the Swedo–Russian alliance and the agreed plan for a combined offensive against the Rzeczpospolita. It is clear from the context that dismissal of Roussel would be seen as the Swedish King's repudiation of the line he had been following hitherto. 'And your ambassador Jacques Roussel, having been rewarded by us for his service and zeal, has been allowed to return to Your Royal Majesty, to concern himself further with our common affairs of state as he has done up to now.'[105]

[105] TsGADA, Dela shvedskie, 1632, stb. 4, ll. 1–5.

Roussel proposed to go from Riga to Stockholm and, evidently, to present the Council of State with this weighty document. But he seems to have received information, while still in Riga, which convinced him that even the Tsar's letter would not protect him and enable him to overcome the Chancellor's power in the Council. In any case, after setting sail with his retinue from Riga for Stockholm on 1 July, he eluded the vigilance of the Livonian authorities, changed course and arrived at Lübeck, which became his new base.[106] He did not decide to go to Gustavus Adolphus at once but his messenger was able to cross Germany quickly. We have some grounds for assuming that this messenger was Lazar Mavius: he had previously been in the service of the Swedish state, perhaps even in the King's retinue ('royal service'), and was only temporarily attached to Roussel.[107] He may have seen the King personally after reaching his camp near Nuremberg in the first days of July.

As we recall, Gustavus Adolphus's first impulse to return to the north-east was checked. He did not receive until May 1632 the Russian government's reply to the proposals in writing which he had sent as far back as August 1631. He could not, of course, know that his letter had taken more than three months to reach Moscow and that Mikhail Fedorovich's reply dated 19 January 1632 had been mysteriously held up on its way to him.[108] It may be that he sent the trade project[109] to Möller on 16 April with the idea of testing the state of communications, to remind Moscow by means of this letter – in itself inoffensive to the Chancellor – that he was awaiting an answer to his important military proposals.

The Tsar's letter of 19 January was held back by the Chancellor for several months and delivered to Gustavus Adolphus in Augsburg only on or about 20 May.[110] The King, who, as he said himself, had wished for nothing so much as to receive this letter of the Tsar's earlier, wrote his reply on 23 May.

---

[106] According to information received, the archives of the city of Lübeck contain a special file concerning the visit and activity there of Jacques Roussel. It would appear that this file has not yet been consulted by any researcher.

[107] *Svensk riksrådets protokoll*, Vol.IV, p. 100. Mavius subsequently returned to Sweden's state service.

[108] One of the reasons that induced Gustavus Adolphus to choose Johan Möller as Sweden's resident agent in Moscow was Möller's promise so to organise correspondence between the King and Moscow that it took no longer than a month for a letter to reach its addressee. In practice this was quite feasible, but it was prevented from happening by the intermediaries. Roussel's couriers (and he himself) travelled from Riga to Moscow in ten days and sometimes even faster. Communication between Riga and Germany by sea took very little time, and the Swedish courier service within Germany was well organised.

[109] See *supra*, footnote 46.    [110] Norrman, *Gustav*, pp. 128–129.

This reply should have become the decisive document in the development of the Swedo–Russian alliance, strengthening the *entente* that had already been achieved. But Gustavus Adolphus was obliged to take into account the Chancellor's active opposition to his plans. The document that emerged was curt and extremely cautious, with reservations, but, all the same, it continued and confirmed the King's line. The text of this letter was sent, on the day it was written, to Mainz, to Chancellor Axel Oxenstjerna, with the request that he make any formal corrections needed and then forward it to Russia.[111] The point was, of course, not so much for Oxenstjerna to see to the formal aspect of the letter, as to ascertain the Chancellor's reaction to the King's firm resolution to begin a war with the Rzeczpospolita in alliance with Russia, using as pretext the advancement of his candidature to the Polish–Lithuanian throne. Chancellor Oxenstjerna resorted to his previous tactic: he said nothing. Gustavus Adolphus thus received neither a reply to his letter to the Chancellor nor the latter's corrections to his draft letter to Tsar Mikhail Fedorovich.[112] A month passed, and then Gustavus Adolphus acted with decision. On 25 June 1632 he signed his letter to the Tsar and sent it off without the Chancellor's sanction – possibly by the Russian courier Menin.[113] His impatience was due to the onset of summer, when the Muscovite government had promised to begin the war, and the approach of the elections to the Kingship in Poland.

Almost simultaneously, on 21 and 25 June 1632, in his camp outside Nuremberg, the King signed two important documents: instructions for the envoys he was sending to the Rzeczpospolita for the election meeting of the Sejm, and his letter to the Tsar in Moscow.

On 20 June Gustavus Adolphus had written to Johan Skytte, the governor of Livonia, ordering him to back with money and by other means the campaign of the Polish–Lithuanian dissidents led by Radziwill in support of the Swedish King's candidature to the Polish throne. It is particularly noteworthy that Skytte was instructed to prepare to give armed support to this campaign, using Swedish troops who were stationed in Prussia.[114] In his instructions to his envoys Sten Bielke and Johan Nicodemi (with whom were to be associated the Burgomaster of Riga, Ulrich, who acted as Gustavus Adolphus's go-between with Radziwill), the King proposed that an open threat of war be issued to the Poles, if they did not voluntarily elect him King. Among their arguments for electing Gustavus Adolphus, the envoys were to point to the Swedish

---

[111] *Rikskansleren Axel Oxenstjernas skrifter och brefvexling*, Vol. II, Part 1, p.802.
[112] Norrman, *Gustav*, p. 129.
[113] At the same time, on 26 June 1632, Gustavus Adolphus sent a letter to Möller, evidently by the same courier.   [114] Wejle, *Sveriges politik*, p. 41.

King's military might and to his influence on the Tsar, which was sufficiently great to persuade the latter to call off the war he was preparing against the Rzeczpospolita. 'Of two evils – the burden of the Polish Crown on his [Gustavus Adolphus's] head, and the war that would be inevitable if one of Sigismund's sons was elected – he chose the former, as being the lesser evil.' True, the envoys were, formally, to threaten war on Sweden's part only when the term of the Swedo–Polish truce ran out, which meant in two years' time, but they were also, along with this, to point to the possibility in the immediate future of invasion of Poland by the Russians, the Tatars and the Turks. Gustavus Adolphus could not, of course, expect to be elected; he knew that Wladyslaw, Sigismund's son, had a better chance, but he instructed his envoys to intensify the conflict as much as they could, so as to disrupt the elections and leave the Rzeczpospolita in maximum internal disorder.[115]

Four days after giving these instructions Gustavus Adolphus signed his letter to Moscow, in which he fully revealed his intentions.[116]

Actually, this was not one letter but two. Attached to the main letter was a letter from the King to Patriarch Philaret (also dated 25 June 1632, Nuremberg). It replied to Philaret's letter to the King of 3 March 1632. In this letter, Gustavus Adolphus thanks the Patriarch for rejoicing at the fact that 'Almighty God has given Our Royal Majesty victory over our common foes', and for his wishes for more victories, and himself expresses his wish for prosperity and strength 'to the great Russian Tsardom, for the hindrance of our common foes, the Papists', and further strengthening of Russo–Swedish friendship – 'to the terror and ruin of our common foes'. As we see, this is the tone appropriate to a close alliance.

About the specifically military aspect of this alliance, 'the war that His Majesty the Tsar wants to wage on German soil', Gustavus Adolphus writes in his main letter, addressed to the Tsar.[117] This begins by explaining that Gustavus Adolphus had received only a few days earlier Mikhail Fedorovich's letter of 19 January, blaming for this the distance to be covered, the winter weather and other hindrances and delaying factors, and assuring the Tsar that if his letter had arrived earlier, the King would already have contributed, by advice and action, to fulfilment of the Tsar's designs. Then Gustavus Adolphus again welcomes warmly

[115] Ibid., pp. 42–55; cf. Norrman, *Gustav*, ch. IV – 'Det polska konungvalet 1632', pp. 153–299.
[116] It was published in a collection of Sweden's treaties with foreign powers – *Sveriges traktater med främmande makter, utg. af O. S. Rydberg och C. Hallendorff*, Part 1, Stockholm, 1903, p. 783 *et seq.* In the 'Swedish files' of the Embassies Department in Moscow there are two variants of a translation of this letter. The quotations that follow are taken from this translation.
[117] *TsGADA, Dela shvedskie*, 1632, *stb.* 5, *ll.* 13–21.

the Tsar's intention to raise troops in Germany and emphasises that 'the Poles, enemies of Your Majesty the Tsar, will suffer great harm and loss if your forces act from this side, in Germany, and enter Upper Poland'. But whereas, before, Gustavus Adolphus had hinted that he was ready to break the Swedo–Polish truce unilaterally, he was now more cautious, undoubtedly making here a concession to Oxenstjerna's position. Until the term of the truce ran out he would not be able to facilitate implementation of the plan with his troops. However, he argues, since the Poles, in violation of the truce, have allowed his enemies the Catholic League to recruit soldiers on their territory, he can, 'on that account', allow the Tsar to recruit soldiers, to fight the Poles, in the states under his occupation. To observe absolute secrecy and ensure complete success for the enterprise, the King proposes the following procedure. The officials whom the Tsar will send to Germany should, for the time being, not be named as envoys of the Tsar, but should act in the name of the Swedish King and, in conjunction with his commanders, recruit and assemble troops as though for the Swedish service. When this process has been completed, Gustavus Adolphus will order the troops concerned to give their allegiance and service to the Tsar. They will then go forward in the Tsar's name and the whole plan will be accomplished in the name, by the will and in the interests of Muscovy's ruler. Sweden's participation will be expressed not only in permission to raise and form this army: Gustavus Adolphus is ready to do all, 'and more', that is conceivable before the truce with Poland expires. In particular, his generals will 'advise and help' the Tsar's plenipotentiaries, 'so that Your Majesty's project may begin and end with complete success'. The King does not openly say here that he will personally direct this enterprise (as he had earlier promised to do), but this intention is clearly apparent from the whole tone of the letter, which offers a sort of personal guarantee to Moscow by Gustavus Adolphus that their design will succeed.

On the practical side, Gustavus Adolphus asks that two embassies be prepared as soon as possible. One is to be sent to Stettin (where he received the Russian envoys in 1631 and whither he may have intended to return), for recruitment and equipment of the army mentioned earlier. The King's strategic plan had been changed slightly: whereas previously he thought that the blow at Upper Poland should be struck from Silesia, now, apparently because of the unfavourable military-political situation in Silesia, which was occupied by an Imperial corps under Schaffgotsch, he indicates Pomerania and Brandenburg as a more suitable base for the operation. After arriving at Stettin, 'with money', the Tsar's representatives can discuss with the Swedish commanders how to hire experienced professional soldiers, choose officers of good quality and buy equipment, and also work out with them the plan for invading Poland from Pomerania and Brandenburg. Maintaining a 'distinguished army' with guns, ammunition and powder will require (apart from additional expenses) 100,000 each month, but, of course, large sums will have to be laid out immediately, for the purchase of weapons, swords, military equipment and uniforms, 'without which there can be no army.' As we see, everything is set out concretely and precisely: this is a real war-plan.

Gustavus Adolphus asks that a second embassy be sent to him in order that, at the same time, a Russo–Swedish political treaty may be signed, aimed against the Rzeczpospolita. He points out that his aid to the Tsar will inevitably bring upon him the anger and vengeance of the Poles. Consequently, he asks and hopes that the Tsar will form an alliance with him by which Muscovy undertakes not to make peace with the Rzeczpospolita without his counsel and approval and without including in such a peace 'Our Royal Majesty and Our Royal lands and states'. If this idea seems 'agreeable and good' to the Tsar, let him send ambassadors 'with full power', so that 'everything to do with this alliance may be discussed and accomplished'.[118]

Comparing this letter with the instructions to the envoys sent to the Rzeczpospolita at the same time, we see in outline the King's fully defined political course in relation to the Polish question. This is a programme for resolute and immediate action, even though all precautions are taken. These documents are, in essence, quite sufficient to explain why Gustavus Adolphus returned four months later to Saxony, situated not far from the Polish frontier, to the area from which he had begun his campaign a year earlier.

The King's letters reached Moscow on 20 August 1632.[119] We can assume, though, that the Russian government had learnt what was in these letters, or had received an oral reply from Gustavus Adolphus already at the beginning of August. This assumption is supported by a fragment of a file preserved in the archives of the Embassies Department which refers to the extraordinarily rapid arrival in Moscow, at that time, of a courier from Jacques Roussel, namely, that same Lazar Mavius to whom only the most responsible missions were entrusted and who had already had to risk his head in the service of Roussel, or, more correctly, of Gustavus Adolphus through Roussel. We have no direct knowledge of what it was that Mavius communicated to Moscow, as we possess only

[118] Ibid., *stb.* 5, *ll.* 2–12.
[119] On the following day, 21 August, Johan Möller, Sweden's representative in Moscow, died, evidently from some excitement (ibid., *stb.* 7, *l.* 3). His duties were a long time performed by his widow, Catharina Stopia, 'the first woman diplomat in the history of Sweden' (Norrman, *Gustav*, p. 131).

fragments of Prince Cherkasskii's answer to Roussel, dispatched with Mavius on about 21 or 22 August. From these fragments, however, we can see that it was something of extraordinary importance. If we are correct in our supposition that Roussel had sent Mavius to Gustavus Adolphus from Lübeck (or, perhaps, a few days earlier, from Riga), the entire journey to Nuremberg, back to Lübeck, and from Lübeck to Moscow was accomplished by Mavius in six weeks.[120] He could have handed the King the letter from Mikhail Fedorovich, dated 20 June, which had been given to Roussel, and received instructions orally from Gustavus Adolphus, if the latter had decided to make further use, unofficially, of Roussel's services for dealings with the Russian government. In Prince Cherkasskii's words, Roussel conveyed, through his courier and secretary, Mavius, 'matters greatly needful for the service of our great sovereign His Majesty the Tsar', these matters were reported to the Tsar and the Patriarch, and now 'these matters are known to them'. Further on, the answer begins: 'And on the 3rd day of August in this year 1632 His Majesty the Tsar and his father the Most Holy Patriarch sent to our common enemy,[121] to the Polish Crown Prince Wladyslaw and to the Pol . . .' Clearly, Roussel had communicated something from which followed the necessity or the possibility of immediately beginning military operations. This could have been either news of preparations for the speedy election of Wladyslaw, or news of Gustavus Adolphus's final agreement to all the conditions that had been discussed for a military alliance against the Rzeczpospolita. The latter seems the more probable in the light of other words of Cherkasskii's in his letter to Roussel: and you also ordered 'that your messenger set off without delay with the best and rapid treaty'.[122] This means that Mavius was to take back from Moscow a draft treaty that would be concluded between Muscovy and Sweden simultaneously with the beginning of military operations.

And so the Russian army set out from Moscow on 3 August 1632. The advance guard was commanded by Alexander Leslie junior. The Smolensk War had begun. Undoubtably, receipt of Gustavus Adolphus's reply served as the final signal which was all that Moscow was waiting for, and without which, at least, active operations would not have begun, even if the army had already reached the frontier of the Rzeczpospolita. As we know, the Russian army, on the contrary, launched already in September–October a vigorous and highly successful offensive.[123] Thus, the offensive

[120] In calculating and comparing the dates we take into account the difference between O.S. and N.S.
[121] Consequently, the letter was meant to be sent to Gustavus Adolphus.
[122] *TsGADA, Dela shvedskie*, 1632, stb. 7, *ll.* 1–3.
[123] Already on 30 July 1632 Johan Möller had written to Gustavus Adolphus that the Russians would hardly begin the war before the end of the year. He presumed that even

was, to a certain degree, fulfilment of Muscovy's duty to Sweden as an ally. The whole army was enthusiastic about this alliance. 'It is reported', Skytte informed Gustavus Adolphus on 18 September 'that the soldiers say that their Tsar relies on Your Royal Majesty more than on anyone, after God.'[124]

Mavius was not allowed to leave Moscow until Gustavus Adolphus's own letter arrived. He was released the day after it came. He took to Roussel the news that the war had begun, and the draft treaty. This was truly the high point of Roussel's activity.[125] In Prince Cherkasskii's letter Roussel is thanked by the Tsar and the Patriarch for his 'work', is asked to try to continue to send them news, and is promised that 'in the future they will reward you in lordly fashion for your service'. But, what is most important, Mavius had to convey to Roussel personally 'what he has been instructed to tell you about these matters of state'.[126] This certainly meant agreement to the project of a Swedo–Russian treaty. On 13 September Roussel, having received at Lübeck 'the letter and reply' from Moscow, sent there a new courier, whose name, apparently, was Jean De Vergier.[127] Along with several important pieces of information, which prove that Roussel was well informed about Gustavus Adolphus's affairs, De Vergier took to Moscow the text of the Russo–Swedish treaty which was to be included, without any changes, in the mandate of the 'Great Embassy' sent to the King of Sweden.[128]

Preparations for this embassy had begun in Moscow as early as June 1632,[129] evidently while Roussel was there. It was then, too, as we see from the draft of the Tsar's letter of 20 June and Roussel's letter of 13 September 1632, that the strategic plan was adopted for beginning the war at the end of summer.[130] In initiating warlike operations the Russian government undoubtedly pursued not military ends alone but also the

if the Russian army received the order to advance before the middle of August, it would go no further than to the frontier (*Akty i pis'ma k istorii baltiiskogo voprosa*, Vol. II, No. 55, pp. 134–135). But four days later the army advanced from Moscow to Mozhaisk, and on 10 September it was ordered to proceed to Viazma, and soon crossed the frontier.

[124]  Norrman, *Gustav*, p. 133. This testimony helps us to understand the reaction in the army when it became clear that Sweden was *not* marching against Poland.

[125]  The Swedish Council of State accused Roussel in 1634 of 'boasting that he alone caused the Polish War' (*Svenska riksrådets protokoll*, Vol. IV, p. 306).

[126]  *TsGADA, Dela shvedskie*, 1632, stb. 7, *l.* 3.

[127]  In the papers of the Embassies Department his name is written variously as *Deverzher*, *Verzhi* and *Verzhe*.

[128]  For more on the 'Great Embassy' see Chapter 5.

[129]  Norrman, *Gustav*, p. 127.

[130]  As has been mentioned, in the draft for the Tsar's letter the word 'summer' has been deleted. Roussel recalls the decision 'to strike at the enemy immediately after the corn has been threshed, and so will be available for sustenance for the forces of Your Majesty the Tsar, and this will do . . . great harm to all the land of Lithuania and deprive the enemy of all his power' (*TsGADA, Dela shvedskie*, 1632, *stb.* 8, *l.* 11).

aim of bringing pressure to bear on the Swedish ally: a successful beginning of the war by Russia would face Sweden with the danger of ceasing to matter, and would stimulate its government to hasten to conclude the treaty formally, accepting the Russian conditions. That was how they calculated in Moscow, and this was the plan, to all appearances, that Roussel himself put forward. The march on Smolensk was conceived as a first act, as a demonstration, after which it would be necessary to wait for the treaty with Sweden and the attack on the Rzeczpospolita from the west. Dispatch of the 'Great Embassy' was to take place soon after hostilities had begun. The Russian government did not accept Gustavus Adolphus's proposal of two embassies, one for recruiting an army in Germany, the other for concluding the treaty. Separating the former from the latter was seen, evidently, as too risky (and there was indeed a risk of spending a huge sum of money without any guarantee of compensation in territory). It was decided to prepare one embassy only, supplying it with both money for raising an army and powers for concluding a treaty. Twenty-five days after the army set out from Moscow, on 28 August 1632, credentials were signed for an embassy of thirty-two persons,[131] headed by the boyars Boris Ivanovich Pushkin and Grigorii Gorikhvostov and the secretary Mikhail Neverov. On 19 September Skytte was officially notified of the impending arrival of an embassy from Russia, and immediately wrote to Gustavus Adolphus about this.[132] Thereafter, however, a long delay occurred before the embassy set out, and there can be only one explanation for this – they were waiting for the draft Russo-German treaty sent with Mavius to Roussel to be returned by him. They thought it necessary first to reach final agreement on the draft unofficially with Gustavus Adolphus's 'great ambassador', as everyone still referred to Roussel, and only then to begin the journey of the official embassy. In the first days of October the mandate, the credentials, everything needed for the embassy lay ready, but the embassy started to move only after De Vergier's arrival, on 31 October. The text brought by De Vergier was at the last minute hastily transcribed and attached to the embassy's mandate.[133] Thus, in September/October the Russian army's drive on Smolensk was delayed,

---

[131]  The embassy was originally intended to number seventy, but Möller advised against this large number. Even as many as thirty was quite unusual, and caused Skytte to fear incurring unbearable expense for the upkeep of the embassy while it was in Livonia, as he wrote to Gustavus Adolphus on 19 September 1632.

[132]  Norrman, *Gustav*, p. 132.

[133]  *TsGADA, Dela shvedskie*, 1632, *stb.* 6, *ll.* 154–155 and 171–175. E. Stashevskii published in the appendices to his book *Ocherki po istorii tsarstvovaniia Mikhaila Fedorovicha* (Kiev, 1919) the text of this mandate (No. XVII) and also a fragment 'From the reply of J. De Vergier to the sovereigns' (No. XVIII).

and it was held back later in expectation of formal conclusion of the treaty with Sweden (which, from the purely military standpoint, had bad consequences, as the Poles were able to use the time to fortify Smolensk).

The mandate of the 'Great Embassy' contains, first of all, a detailed history of Russo–Polish antagonisms since the time of Boris Godunov, and motives for the war which had begun. This is followed by the various considerations which are to be the basis for the Russo–Swedish treaty of alliance. The first of these is a mutual undertaking of non-aggression (to keep the previously prevailing peace 'without any wrongdoing', 'unchanged for all time').[134]

The second is a mutual undertaking to stand together 'against our common foes' the sons of Sigismund III (Wladyslaw and Kazimir).[135] The two rulers promise 'with all their strength and mind and heart' to help each other in the matter of Poland – 'with men, with money, and with all means that may lead to the destruction of the enemy: and if it be not possible for one of them to overcome the enemy, the other will send men to the side that is in need, at the first news of such need, out of friendship, and will not expect any payment for that, only so that, by

---

[134] *TsGADA, Dela shvedskie*, 1632, stb. 6, *l.* 145. The Russian government remained extremely suspicious of Sweden and even of Gustavus Adolphus himself. In a special memorandum to the ambassadors they are ordered to find out secretly whether Gustavus Adolphus has had secret dealings with Sigismund III or, after his death, with the Sejm, 'and whether certain princes want to help the Polish King against Muscovy' (ibid., *l.* 167).

[135] The idea of 'common foes' was extended indirectly to include the German Emperor as well. The ambassadors were to say that the recent embassies from Poland and the Emperor were not admitted to Moscow because the Tsar and the Patriarch knew that 'the Polish King is at one with the Kaiser in friendship and purpose. And since the Swedish King has gone to war against the Kaiser on account of his wrongdoings, and the Polish King, violating his oath [on the truce with Sweden] ... has sent away many Polish and Lithuanian men to help the Kaiser', and they, as is known, have fought against the Swedish King's troops along with the Emperor's men. The embassy from the Rzeczpospolita was sent with the cunning plan to cede to the Muscovite ruler cities which formerly belonged to him but are now under the Polish King, and having thereby stopped the Russian offensive, 'with all their might to send many Polish and Lithuanian men to help the Kaiser against the Swedish King, and stand together with the Kaiser and the Pope, and strengthen and spread their accursed Popish faith' (ibid., *l.* 75). From this, on the one hand, there emerges the enmity of Muscovy to the Emperor and the Pope: with the former the Tsar 'will have no relations, for the Kaiser is a foe to all Orthodox Christians' and is at war with the Swedish King: and with the Roman Pope also, because 'the Pope is a foe to all Orthodox Christians and wants no good among Christians' (ibid., *l.* 163). On the other hand, what emerges from the statement is the inevitability and necessity for the Swedish King of going to war against the Rzeczpospolita. The cunning plan of the Polish embassy is brought to the knowledge of the Swedish King so that he may 'launch his enterprise against the Polish and Lithuanian cities without waiting upon the will of their present ruler' (ibid., *l.* 175). It is not difficult to discern that the simultaneous appearance of Imperial and Polish embassies on the Russian frontier was being used for diplomatic pressure – to raise the bogey of a possible Russo–Polish *rapprochement* on the basis of the disputed western lands being returned to Russia.

their friendship, the common foe may be the more speedily destroyed'.[136]

The third is that neither side is to conclude a separate peace or truce: 'not to conclude any new truce or peace without agreement', 'war against the common foe to be begun, carried on and ended with agreement by both sides'.

The fourth is that, at the end of the war there is to be a 'a just and good division and drawing of frontiers with the Poles in conformity with the dignity and convenience of His Majesty the Tsar'. There are to be returned to Muscovy 'those lands which have always from time immemorial belonged to our sovereign His Majesty the Tsar' and 'which were ceded during the years of the truce to the Crown of Poland and the Grand Duchy of Lithuania' – meaning all the territory to the east of the Dvina, the cities ('with adjoining districts and areas') of Smolensk, Belaia, Dorogobuzh, Roslavl, Monastyrevsk, Chernigov, Starodub, Popova Gora, Novgorod-Severskii, Pochep, Trubchevsk, Serpeisk, Nevel, Sebezh, Krasnyi, Polotsk and Kiev. The western frontier of Russia is to run 'from Polotsk down the river Dvina 20 versts to Riga, and from that place [to a point] on the river Niemen 20 versts above Gorodek [Grodno], and from that place along the Niemen to the river Dnieper [at a point] 100 versts below Kiev, and then down that river to the Black Sea'. On this approximate basis 'a true frontier between the two states' is to be drawn later. While hostilities are in progress the allies 'are obliged to help each other'. The Swedish King will, with all his forces, help the Tsar to conquer Polotsk, Smolensk, Kiev and other nearby places which lie on his side of this line, while the Tsar will, with all his forces, help the Swedish King to conquer Vilna and other places on the other side of the line. If the troops of one of the allies, 'in pursuit of the enemy', should enter territories which the treaty has allotted to the other, it undertakes not to lay claim to these territories, but to hand them over ('to waive its rights', 'without any delay or hesitation'), 'not to take anything from them except the spoils of war', which unavoidably fall to the soldiers. In the event of victory for his arms, Gustavus Adolphus is not to promise the Rzeczpospolita, either before or during his coronation, to keep those places which by right and by this treaty belong to Muscovy.

The fifth is that Muscovy will, accordingly, help Gustavus Adolphus

---

[136] Ibid., *ll.* 171–173. Here the Muscovite government is putting forward a sort of maximum programme as a counter to Gustavus Adolphus's draft which it had accepted, by which it was obliged to pay for the Swedish troops sent against the Rzeczpospolita from the west. However, as we see from the ambassadors' questions in writing (ibid., *ll.* 71–72), they received supplementary oral instructions in case the Swedes should revert to the previous draft and their previous arguments about the impossibility of openly breaking the Swedish–Polish truce. Perhaps the ambassadors were also told, in this event, to haggle further, since the Russian offensive had already changed the situation substantially but, nevertheless, they were given a large sum of money to take with them (according to Skytte: see Norrman, *Gustav*, p. 132).

'to obtain the Kingship of Poland and Lithuania'. Thereby the Tsar will 'reward His Royal Majesty for his friendship and love' in helping the recovery by Muscovy of the ancient Russian lands. The Tsar has already written to Turkey and the Crimea, as well as to Poland and Lithuania, that he supports Gustavus Adolphus's candidature to the Polish throne and seeks their support for it. As a condition of this support Gustavus Adolphus is to be obliged, when he has mounted the Polish throne, to remain in close alliance with the Tsar, as hitherto – 'as before in friendship and love, in perpetual treaty and union'. On his part, the King proposes (through Roussel) 'to promote and constitute a firm, perpetual, continuing peace between the two monarchs . . . and to strengthen their unity, so that each shall help the other; if one of the allies is being defeated, the other will give it support'.

This close friendly alliance between Russia and Sweden is to be binding also on the successors of the monarchs who signed it. The fixity of Russia's western frontier is to be compensated for, in the draft sent by Roussel, by the prospect of 'provision, through the union of our rulers, for the extension of your realm eastward', i.e., of freedom for Russia's expansion to the East.[137]

We know that the outlines of this international agreement had been sketched in roughly long before the embassy of Pushkin and his companions was sent off. Negotiations were carried out through Roussel from 1630, and also through Monier and Möller.[138] The draft was thoroughly considered by the rulers of Muscovy, headed by Patriarch Philaret, and it made a truly remarkable impression. True, O.L. Vainshtein expresses surprise at the readiness of the Tsar and the Patriarch 'to sign so disadvantageous an agreement'.[139] When he says that an outlet to the

---

[137] On all this see *TsGADA, Dela shvedskie*, 1632, stb. 6, *ll.* 136–175.

[138] They had long known in Moscow, through Möller, that Gustavus Adolphus was trying to get possession of Livonia and Prussia, and, through Roussel, that he claimed the Crown of Poland. On his part, Gustavus Adolphus had long known, for example, of Russia's claims to Smolensk, Chernigov, Zaporozhe and Byelorussia (the governments of Polotsk, Vitebsk, Mstislavsk and part of Minsk, which made up about half of the territory of the Grand Duchy of Lithuania) (Norrman, *Gustav*, p. 74). Rumours of these negotiations had spread already by the beginning of 1632 among the inhabitants of Poland and Lithuania. In March 1632 an immigrant from Lithuania, Kornei Krukovskii, told the governor of Vyazma: 'In Poland and in Lithuania the rumour runs that your ruler Mikhail Fedorovich, the Tsar of All Russia, has agreed with the Swedish King that your sovereign shall take Lithuanian and Polish cities, while the Swedish King will advance against the Poles and Lithuanians up to the river Bereza [to the river Berezina – which reflects a variant somewhat less favourable to Russia than what had been agreed and included in the mandate – B.F.P.], and they say that when your ruler's soldiers enter Lithuania, German soldiers will enter from the Swedish side at the same time' (*Akty moskovskogo gosudarstva*, Vol. I, 1890, No. 330, p. 347). As we see, the rumours current among the population conveyed quite accurately the content of the secret negotiations.

[139] Vainshtein, *Rossiia*, p. 138.

Baltic Sea was more important for Russia than one to the Black Sea, that it was inexpedient to hand over the lion's share of the Polish–Lithuanian state to the Swedish King, and so on, the author is looking at the seventeenth century through the prism of Peter the Great's epoch, being unaware that in the seventeenth century the principal task facing Russia in the sphere of foreign policy was not yet recovery of the Baltic coastland but recovery of the Russian, Byelorussian and Ukrainian lands to the west. In the years under review Muscovy was trying to secure a stable western frontier after re-uniting the extensive territories which had been torn from it in earlier times. Only in the eighteenth century did Russia's economic development bring to the forefront a new task, struggle for an outlet to the Baltic Sea. Almost all of the seventeenth century was devoted to struggle to accomplish a quite different task, which was certainly more progressive at that time, namely, that which was clearly set forth in this foreign-policy document of Patriarch Philaret's government. Russia was, according to the draft summarised above, to receive more than it gained thirty-five years later, as a result of bitter fighting, by the truce of Andrusovo (1667). True, part of Western Byelorussia and a substantial part of Right-Bank Ukraine were to be left behind the frontier. But even this limited fulfilment of the very difficult historical task of re-uniting with Muscovy those Russian, Ukrainian and Byelorussian lands would have constituted, at that time, an outstanding success. Moreover, this draft was based on the idea that it was possible to replace the traditionally hostile relations between Russia and Poland with friendly relations, as allies, founded on mutual aid. The thinking of the Russian statesmen penetrated much more deeply than appears at first glance. They undoubtedly knew (through Roussel) that Radziwill and the other Polish and Lithuanian magnates were disposed to favour the election of Gustavus Adolphus only on condition that he returned to Poland not only Livonia and Prussia but also Silesia, torn from Poland long before by the German emperors.[140] Gustavus Adolphus alone was able, through his victories over the Emperor, to accomplish this most important historical task for Poland.[141] Simultaneous shifting of the eastern and western frontiers of the Polish state, its transference on to its ancient territory to the west, while liberating the alien lands it had seized to the east, could

---

[140] See Paul, *Gustav*, Vol. III, p. 43.

[141] To be sure, the Imperial commander Wallenstein offered, through General Schaffgotsch, who was then occupying Silesia, to cede it to Poland in exchange for a military alliance against Sweden (Irmer, G., *Verhandlungen Schwedens und seiner Verbündeten mit Wallenstein und dem Kaiser von 1632–1634*, Vol. III, Leipzig, 1891, p. 439). However, a similar offer had been made as far back as 1619, and not fulfilled, though the Rzeczpospolita had, on this consideration, sent a substantial number of Zaporozhian Cossacks to help the Emperor against Bohemia.

have created the basis for lasting peaceful neighbourly relations with Russia. The Patriarch and his colleagues were looking at Gustavus Adolphus not so much in his capacity as King of Sweden as in the role of future head of this friendly Poland.

The 'Great Embassy' of Pushkin and his companions was ordered to go to Stockholm with exceptional speed and there demand to be sent at once to meet Gustavus Adolphus in Germany. Besides the official letters, they carried a personal message from Patriarch Philaret to the King (dated 11 October 1632) which expressed hope, in very friendly tones, for the alliance between him and the Tsar to be strengthened – 'and that in the future you may stand together against your enemies'.[142] The embassy left Novgorod on 22 November 1632.

At about that time, on 27 November, another document was sent off from Moscow – a letter from the Tsar and the Patriarch to Jacques Roussel.[143] This letter, sent with De Vergier, was a reply to the letter of 13 September he had brought at the end of October and to his oral communications.

De Vergier had brought to Moscow a great deal of information about 'the Kaiser's war and all the surrounding wars', and about all the important events in the states of Europe. Included were not only the events of the war in Germany but also the revolt of Montmorency and Gaston of Orléans in France, the despotism of Strafford in England, and so on. There was particularly detailed news concerning the election struggle in the Rzeczpospolita and that state's plans and preparations for war against Muscovy.[144] This information, of an absolutely secret nature, had been obtained by Roussel from Christian of Anhalt, the son of a prominent German Protestant prince, whom circumstances had obliged to seek a career outside the war with Emperor Ferdinand II and who had agreed to take command of the mercenary *lansquenets* of the Polish Crown Prince Wladyslaw. Roussel was able, making use of his own Evangelical position in religion, to persuade Christian not only to decline this appointment but also to offer his services to the opposite camp, to Muscovy. Central to Roussel's letter and to De Vergier's memorandum is an argument for the appointment as leader of the foreign soldiers

---

[142] *TsGADA, Dela shvedskie*, 1632, stb. 6, *ll.* 179–185.

[143] Almost all the text of the draft of this letter is corrected, and in parts re-written, in the handwriting of Patriarch Philaret.

[144] De Vergier also brought the extensive selection from foreign newspapers mentioned earlier. How carefully this material was studied by Moscow's ruling circles and the Embassies Department is evident from the fact that as early as 2 November 1632 De Vergier presented to the Embassies Department an amplification and elucidation, in writing, of some of the news from abroad, possibly at the request of Prince Cherkasskii (*TsGADA, Dela shvedskie*, 1632, *stb.* 8, *ll.* 30–32).

recruited by the Russians of this outstanding commander and military expert, who was also a kinsman of Gustavus Adolphus, the Prince of Orange and a number of other German princes.

Roussel told the Tsar that if his advice was not accepted, 'without this Prince, he will not now be able to accomplish that assembling of troops of which he spoke'. In their reply the Tsar and the Patriarch expressed, regarding that point, their high valuations of Roussel's success, but said that it was too late to make Christian of Anhalt commander of the foreign troops in the army sent against Smolensk. However, Roussel could convey to him a 'gracious word' from the Tsar and the Patriarch and, if he agreed to serve on the German frontier of Poland, also a sort of advance payment: a 'little something' of a reward (from the characteristic turn of phrase, this was written by the Patriarch himself), in the form of sables to the value of 1,000 rubles. In other words, Christian of Anhalt was taken into the Russian service, but, so to speak, posted to the reserve.[145] Another of Roussel's requests was fully satisfied. He recommended for the Russian army (or, more correctly, released 'temporarily' from his own service) a 'well-tried and clever' engineer named David Nicole, who had distinguished himself in the defence of the principal Huguenot fortresses (Montauban, Nérac, etc.) in France in the 1620s. Roussel hints at Nicole's participation in those clandestine actions in Smolensk and Polotsk about which he had written earlier and which must inevitably lead to the fall of those fortresses. The Russian government's decision was most favourable. On his arrival in Moscow, Nicole was at once enrolled as chief military engineer of Russia's army, with the high salary of 50 rubles per month, and took charge of all the fortification and siege works of the Smolensk War.

Roussel writes with great emotion, in his letter to the Tsar and the Patriarch, about the news that Muscovy's war with the Rzeczpospolita has begun, and also about the internal conflict in the latter country. It is impossible, he says, to forecast the outcome of all these events, 'God keeps that secret to Himself – about the great intestine strife which Almighty God has spread in every corner of Christendom and about the great changes in affairs that have taken place since I left Moscow.' While trusting in God, however, it is necessary to make haste to exploit the opportune moment presented by the interregnum and conflict in the

---

[145] This is written in the Patriarch's own hand: 'And when the time comes when his service there will be required by Our Majesty the Tsar, we, the great sovereign, Our Majesty the Tsar, will have word sent to tell him what he must do, how he is to stand and act against our enemy Wladyslaw and his co-thinkers, and we, Our Majesty the Tsar will reward him well for his service and loyalty and for his zeal and enterprise, and will never forget his service, which will be remembered and honoured forever' (ibid., *l.* 55ob.).

Rzeczpospolita.[146] Roussel warns that the Poles, knowing of the Russian army's offensive, will strive as quickly as possible to agree among themselves on the election of one candidate or another, obviously Wladyslaw, so as to close their ranks for resistance. To prevent this happening and to delay the election, Roussel (who had managed to visit Hamburg and return to Lübeck), is going to Küstrin to see the Elector of Brandenburg, who has influence in the Polish elections and has served as go-between for the Polish–Lithuanian dissidents and Gustavus Adolphus, in order to 'put into his mind' the necessity of frustrating the design of the Jesuits in the Rzeczpospolita to have the election take place 'at a time which does not suit us': for this election 'the accursed Jesuits want to bring about, with all their power, before my Lord the King has settled his affairs' in Germany. There can, of course, be no question now of Gustavus Adolphus being elected King of Poland voluntarily, without coercion. 'It seems clear', Roussel acknowledges,

> that God has decided that my Lord the King shall not be elected by a majority of the Poles, and God will not allow him to approach the Polish frontier, there being in the midst of the Kaiser's country such a powerful enemy force as Ferdinand's army, and so it seems that the just God has resolved upon the ruin of the Polish Commonwealth, with its territory divided between Your Majesties, as I told you, great sovereigns, if my lord the King does not obtain that crown by the will and choice of the Poles.[147]

But the circumstance that Gustavus Adolphus was bogged down in the depths of Germany, far from the Polish frontier, also prevented that second variant from coming about. Roussel sees clearly that this is not accidental, but the result of the efforts of a certain political party in Sweden. He describes with great force to the rulers of Muscovy the unseen, intense struggle around Gustavus Adolphus's Russo–Polish policy. He points to the role played by Chancellor Axel Oxenstjerna, by the governor of Livonia, Johan Skytte, and, in general, by those 'Swedes' to whom the King's absence is advantageous. Gustavus Adolphus cannot at present intervene in Poland, 'because the Chancellor hinders him secretly in all his doings', having been since June the *de facto* King and

---

[146] 'If your troops have not yet entered the enemy's country when my envoy arrives in Moscow, it will be most expedient to take advantage of the present situation of interregnum, which God has given us, and the strife among your enemies' (ibid., *l*. 14).

[147] Roussel here reveals the cards of Gustavus Adolphus's Polish policy. In the preceding chapter we showed that all the election propaganda in favour of Gustavus Adolphus in Poland was principally intended as a means of frightening Muscovy with the prospect of his getting elected voluntarily and so impelling it to go to war with the Rzeczpospolita. D. Norrman came to the same conclusion. Not hope of election and not even the desire to create internal divisions was the chief motive of Gustavus Adolphus's interest in the matter of the Polish succession. 'His direct actions regarding Poland were always for him secondary as compared with the negotiations with Russia and his treaty with the Tsar' (Norrman, *Gustav*, p. 150).

not allowing anyone to go either to or from Gustavus Adolphus, 'and because of this he [Gustavus Adolphus] cannot get to the Polish frontier, as he had intended, but has only sent his ambassadors to Warsaw, so as to postpone the election to the Kingship still further, until he can leave the place where he is at present'. The obstacles in the way of the King's plans are not so much the Emperor's troops as 'the King's own people, who have gone mad'. In particular, the extraordinary miserliness and pride of the Swedes, especially their Chancellor, have made Gustavus Adolphus's position difficult by demanding that the German cities swear oaths of allegiance to Sweden and so on, so that they have 'stuck the King fast in that place'. ('I only hope', Roussel adds, 'that the King knows what is at stake and by his own good sense will put things right.') Johan Skytte, 'and a large section of the Swedes with him', want to break up the brotherly friendship that exists between the Swedish King and the Russian Tsar, and 'would with pleasure betray Your Majesty the Tsar and the Russian realm while they can, now that they see that the King is faraway and nobody is watching them'. Consequently, Roussel needs Prince Christian of Anhalt, 'because those who want to break up the brotherly friendship between Your Majesties are boasting that they will take for themselves the money for recruiting the soldiers and betray Your Majesty the Tsar'. Roussel complains of the persecution he has suffered from this party in Sweden. De Vergier adds: 'Moreover, I say to Your Majesty the Tsar that all these Swedes hate the great ambassador [Roussel] because they see his goodwill and activity in the service of Your Majesty and all the Russian realm.' They are no longer paying him the salary laid down by the King, saying that one cannot serve two sovereigns.[148] De Vergier testifies to Roussel's tireless activity, frustrating the designs of the enemies of the King and the Tsar and urging on those who wish them well. He continually dispatches and receives couriers. Seven or eight of these are out in various places at the moment. But Roussel cannot himself get to his King, as the way to him is barred by the Chancellor. Roussel says that he has decided to wait at Küstrin for the Russians' Great Embassy and will go with them to Gustavus Adolphus. He evidently saw this as the only way to break the blockade.[149]

[148] Skytte did not want to let De Vergier go to Russia, and the latter left without permission, after merely giving Skytte not the actual text of Roussel's mandate but some pretended text. In order to return, De Vergier asked to be given some office of dignity, together with a set of horses, since, otherwise, Skytte, after holding him up on the excuse of changing post-horses, would assert his alleged right to examine all De Vergier's papers and take out the letter from the Tsar and the Patriarch to Roussel (*TsGADA, Dela shvedskie*, 1632, *l*. 36). This request was granted, as we see from the file on De Vergier's later visit.

[149] On all foregoing see *TsGADA, Dela shvedskie*, 1632, *stb*. 8, *ll*. 1–26. Besides the questions listed, a number of others are touched on. (1) Roussel returns to the subject of

The reply sent by the Tsar and the Patriarch to Roussel contains unrestrained praise for his loyal service and diligence, for the good he has done. They ask him to continue to look after the interests of Russia, without fear of enemies, of abuse or unpleasantness. This letter almost gives formality to Roussel's transfer to the Russian diplomatic service. He is rewarded for his services with unprecedented generosity. They send him, by hand of De Vergier, sables to the value of 1,000 rubles (apart from the same quantity to be passed on to Christian of Anhalt). In addition, his immodest request to be allowed to buy in Russia, directly from the cultivators, where it is best and cheapest, 50,000 quarters of grain, for seven years, meets with a generous favour from the Tsar – permission to buy at Archangel, in 1633 and 1634, 20,000 quarters each year, 'the rye to be paid for at cost price, without mark-up and no dues be exacted, on account of your service to us'. Furthermore, these apologies follow: 'and do not be offended, Yakov [Jacques]' because the sables have been sent 'meanly' and the permission to levy grain is not as full as was requested – this is due to the immense burden of expenditure that the Treasury has to assume for the needs of the progress of the war, that the boyars M.B. Shein and A.V. Izmailov, with others, have been appointed to commands, that the towns of Dorogobuzh, Serpeisk and Belaia have already been cleared of the enemy, and that the army is heading towards Smolensk.[150]

In the documents quoted Roussel did not depart far from the truth in his account of Gustavus Adolphus's situation. The Swedish King's plans really were bound up with and advanced by Russia's war with Poland, but he was tied down by the war in Germany and by the Chancellor's stubborn unwillingness to free him in time from this preoccupation. Nevertheless, from June 1632 Gustavus Adolphus was continuously

the need, in the Tsar's interest, 'to win over the Zaporozhian Cossacks' and send more messengers to them. De Vergier asks, in particular, that a messenger be sent to Putivl to tell the messenger of 'the great ambassador' (Roussel) who is there that he is not to return without having negotiated with the Cossacks (ibid., *ll.* 26–27). (2) Roussel asks that there be sent to him, by De Vergier, letters to the Kings of France, England, Denmark, to the Venetian Senate, to the States of Holland, to the German Electors, to the Prince of Orange and to the Prince of Transylvania, explaining Muscovy's case for needing to go to war with the Rzeczpospolita, 'because, up to now, these rulers do not know it' (ibid., *l.* 27). (3) Roussel says that the geographer sent to him from Holland can prepare the map of Russia no earlier than in six or seven months (ibid., *l.* 28). (4) Roussel warns against deception by the commanders of the mercenary forces, who keep on their lists soldiers who have died long ago, so that when battle is joined there are fewer soldiers available than had been supposed (ibid., *l.* 28). (5) Roussel proposes to send a 'commissar' who knows several languages to the foreign mercenaries serving with the Russian army (ibid., *l.* 29). (6) Roussel asks to be sent three or four thousand rubles, as his efforts to 'disturb' preparation for the election of the King in the Rzeczpospolita call for much expenditure (ibid., *ll.* 33–34).    [150] Ibid., *ll.* 41–51.

ready to march eastward. He even allowed it to be reported, while he was in camp near Nuremberg, that embassies from Tartary and Muscovy had visited him, to propose that he invade Poland, and he had shown them his well-disciplined and well-trained army of 50,000 men.[151] All that, however, merely reflected his dream. Much more important were the preparatory measures for this forthcoming war which he actually undertook while still near Nuremberg. Not later than 1 July 1632 (i.e., at the time when he sent his letter to Russia) he appointed Field-Marshal Herman Wrangel governor-general of Prussia, with the task of strengthening the armed forces stationed there and also keeping an eye on events in Poland. In Norrman's words, 'there are grounds for thinking that Gustavus Adolphus's decision to send Field-Marshal Herman Wrangel to Prussia was somehow connected with the Swedo–Russian agreement on raising a Russian army in Germany'.[152] In fact, Silesia was at that time not suitable as a base for a Polish war,[153] and Prussia was the only alternative. Wrangel arrived at Elbing at the end of August. There he received fresh instructions from Gustavus Adolphus brought by the ambassador Nicodemi whom the King had sent to the Rzeczpospolita with the task of ensuring postponement of the election and stirring up internal strife among the Poles. The content of these instructions given to Wrangel is not known, 'but probably', Norrman thinks, 'they were connected with the matter of raising a Russian army'.[154]

In September Gustavus Adolphus finally decided to move into North-Eastern Germany, to a point near the Polish border. On 18 September he was again visited, for the purpose of face-to-face conversation, by Chancellor Oxenstjerna. This was a most decisive encounter. The talks were acrimonious. Oxenstjerna demanded that Gustavus Adolphus march on Vienna. On 5 October the King went north with his army. The Chancellor accompanied him until 24 October, then returned to Frankfurt.

On 16 (6) November 1632 Gustavus Adolphus won his last battle, at Lützen in Saxony. Wallenstein's army was destroyed and the best of its commanders were killed. But Gustavus Adolphus also fell in the fighting.

---

[151] *Le soldat suédois*, p. 622 [430].

[152] As evidence Norrman adduces, for example, the fact that 'a report on the German, English and Russian regiments hired by the Russians is present as an enclosure among the letters from Wrangel to Gustavus Adolphus. This report exactly conforms to the data sent by Möller to Gustavus Adolphus and Axel Oxenstjerna on 16 June 1632' (Norrman, *Gustav*, p. 152). Above, we have mentioned that Wrangel had earlier, through Bökman, offered his services to Mikhail Fedorovich as commander of the Russian army in Germany. Since that time he had evidently been engaged in systematic study of the Russian and Polish armed forces.

[153] See *Sveriges Krig 1611–1632*, Vol. VI, 1939, ch. IV, para. 3: *Det schlesiska fältaget*, pp. 268–286.   [154] Norrman, *Gustav*, p. 152.

Although a number of scholars (Diemer, Droysen, Srbik, Wittrock) have studied this battle and the circumstances of the King's death in great detail, the field for speculation is as open as ever: was he killed by an enemy or by one of his own people? The second possibility is the more likely. We are able to refer to a source which has not previously attracted the attention of scholars[155] and which shows that the death of Gustavus Adolphus, and his death in just those circumstances, was not at all unexpected. In the memorandum, mentioned earlier, which De Vergier handed to Prince Cherkasskii on 2 November 1632, it was said, among other things, that the Polish Catholics, seeing the hope aroused among the Protestants by the prospect of Gustavus Adolphus's victory in Germany, had 'plotted in the Sejm' to find means against him. They spread a rumour of the King's death, saying that he had been wounded before Ingolstadt, dying soon afterward, near Nuremberg, and this rumour, circulated both in Poland and Prussia, was so strongly supported that to deny its truth in Poland now put one's life in danger.[156] This forecasting of an event that actually occurred two months later (the information related to a time no later than the beginning of September) is highly significant.

The election of Wladyslaw as King of Poland took place only a few days before the death of Gustavus Adolphus. These two events ruined the entire plan of the Smolensk War and could not fail to discourage the boyar Shein, who knew well all the details of the Swedo–Russian alliance. The 'Great Embassy' of the boyar Pushkin learnt of Gustavus Adolphus's death when they were in Finland, *en route* for Stockholm, and returned to the Russian border, where they received a fresh mandate only on 25 March 1633.[157] The Muscovite government reacted first to the stupefying news by ordering the ambassadors 'to find out the truth about the Swedish King's death, how it happened',[158] because they appreciated all too plainly the possible logic of the matter. Patriarch Philaret ordered a special fast in mourning for Gustavus Adolphus and, according to information received by Skytte, said more than once that the Tsar would willingly have redeemed the Swedish King's life with half his realm.[159] The fateful news found Roussel in Pomerania. According to Skytte, again, he was deeply grieved, put on mourning clothes, hastened to quit Germany and moved to Holland.[160]

---

[155] A critical review of all the sources for this question was the subject of a special report at the International Congress of Historians held at Oslo in 1928: Wittrock, G., 'Die Schlacht bei Lützen (1632). Quellenkritische Bemerkungen', *Historiche Vierteljahrschrift*, 1929, No. 1.    [156] *TsGADA, Dela shvedskie, 1632, stb.* 8, *ll.* 31–32.
[157] *TsGADA, Dela shvedskie, 1632, stb.* 2.    [158] Ibid., *l.* 11.
[159] Norrman, *Gustav*, p. 297.    [160] Ibid., p. 235.

The Swedo–Russian alliance collapsed with the death of Gustavus Adolphus. Pushkin's embassy returned to Moscow in the first days of October 1633.[161]

Norrman came, in his study of these events, to the conclusion that Gustavus Adolphus's policy towards Poland, dictated by his endeavour to find an ally in the war in Germany, so as to weaken the Polish–Lithuanian state, has failed to receive adequate attention, not having been understood either by contemporaries or by historians. In reality, Norrman says with justification, the Swedish King's plan resulted from long reflection and consideration of the experience of the previous two years, when *rapprochement* with Russia was advantageous to him.[162] These conclusions are objective.[163] What has been set forth above should, for its part, help to eliminate this mistake by historians.

[161] For the end of the whole affair see *infra*, Chapter 5.

[162] Norrman, *Gustav*, pp. 134–135.

[163] The report by the West-German historian G. von Rauch on 'Moscow and the European Powers in the XVIIth Century', read at a congress of German historians in 1953, was based, as far as this question was concerned, on works by Soviet historians whose conclusions are close to those set forth above. The author writes of 'the unprecedented possibilities opened up by taking proper account of the Russian factor in the framework of the European system of states'. Proceeding from his experience of war with Russia and with Poland, Gustavus Adolphus 'saw in Russia the natural counterweight to Poland and thereby a potential ally in the fight against the forces of the Counter-Reformation', and 'in a certain sense drew Russia indirectly into the Thirty Years' War' (see Rauch, G. von, 'Moskau und die europäischen Mächte des 17 Jahrhunderts', *Historische Zeitschrift*, 1954, Vol. 178, No. 1, pp. 30–32). One is surprised, though, by the author's one-sided and shallow historico-religious approach to these questions. No less surprising is the fact that Rauch does not know Norrman's book (1943), and of my articles (1945–1947) he knows only one, the first.

# 4    The social and political situation in Germany at the time of Gustavus Adolphus's invasion (1630–1631)

In this chapter we are going to return to Germany in order to study, so to speak, the internal German aspect of the beginnings of the 'Swedish period' of the Thirty Years' War. This period has received, perhaps, more attention than any other in the historiography of the Thirty Years' War, yet it remains in many ways very enigmatic.

The figure of Gustavus Adolphus, 'the King of snow', was surrounded by a haze of legend, almost myth, during his lifetime and, still more, after his death. No bourgeois historian has explained clearly why, out of the many conquerors who appear in the pages of the history of that warlike period, it was this one, who entered Germany, basically, to serve the narrowly greedy will of the Swedish magnates and merchants, who has remained in the people's memory with the features of a positive hero. None of the scholarly and quite prosaic researches of his biographers – and a remarkably large amount has been written about Gustavus Adolphus – has succeeded in wiping away the romantic and heroic patina which has grown over his memory. And in fact, although all his successes and failures in the German campaign have been explained in great detail, there remains something unexplained in the main thing, the dizzyingly easy conquest by the Scandinavian stranger of almost all Germany, and, on the other hand, the ephemeral character of this conquest, which began to get shaky less than a year after the campaign's beginning and, two years after Gustavus Adolphus's death, had become for his heirs an irrecoverable dream. German chauvinist historians refer to this as an example of a 'German miracle'.

Yet the 'miracle' was not the defeat of the Swedes but the previous triumphal march of the 'King of snow'. This too should have been given a scientific explanation. However, historians from the bourgeoisie and the nobility have not looked for this where they should, in the history of the masses of the people of Germany, but have merely focused on the aims and plans of Gustavus Adolphus, his personality, his relations with the German princes, the Imperial officials and the military leaders. Insufficient attention has been paid to the German topical press of that time –

broadsheets, appeals, political pamphlets. These are, of course, not sources for the history of the masses, yet they do provide material for judging what fantastic and conflicting ideas jostled in the minds of Germany's population. On the one hand the Swedes were depicted as the new Northmen, savage Vikings who had fallen upon Europe: on the other, Gustavus Adolphus was proclaimed the man sent from God, the Messiah, the providential liberator of all the oppressed and leader of a forthcoming crusade against Rome, the residence of Antichrist. These messianic expectations associated with Gustavus Adolphus lead us indirectly, of course, into the heart of popular peasant psychology. But these clues have never been followed up. The mysterious halo around Gustavus Adolphus has remained, however, in the memory of historians, providing in the second half of the seventeenth century and, especially, in the eighteenth, opportunities for both Swedish (O. von Dalin and others) and German writers to introduce their own ideals into this image. Some treated Gustavus Adolphus's policy as an ideal example of 'enlightened absolutism', others as ardent combat for the Evangelical faith. The outcome of all this was that romantic image of Gustavus Adolphus which Schiller created in his *History of the Thirty Years' War* and which, in its turn, has set its mark on all subsequent historiography. Schiller's artistic intuition recreated both the reverent rapture and the alarmed apprehensions of contemporaries, but did not understand the reasons for either. His Gustavus Adolphus is that devout hero, that radiant knight, the great 'King of snow' whose life a propitious fate cut short at that moment when its continuation must have been dangerous for Germany, when from a liberator he would have had to become a conqueror.[1]

A whole pleiad of Protestant historians has sought to interpret Gustavus Adolphus as exclusively a religious figure, a fighter for Protestantism.[2] Some of them have raised the question whether it would not have been better for Germany if Gustavus Adolphus had succeeded in conquering the country: would Germany, in that case, have avoided its decline in the second half of the seventeenth century and the first half

---

[1] Schiller, F., *Istoriia tridtsatiletnei voiny, Sobranie sochinenii v 7–ii tomakh*, Vol. V, Moscow, 1957 [*Geschichte des Dreissigjährigen Krieges*, 1791–1793]: cf. his dramatic trilogy *Wallenstein* in *Sobranie*, Vol. II, Moscow, 1955 [*Wallenstein*, 1798–1799].

[2] For example, Moser, F. S., *Gustav Adolph der Beschützer protestantischer Religion und deutschen Freiheit*, Leipzig, 1832; Arndt, E.-M., *Schwedische Geschichte*, Leipzig, 1839; Lamparter, E., *Gustav Adolf, König von Schweden, der Befreier des evangelischen Deutschtums*, Barmen, 1892; Fletcher, C. R. L., *Gustavus Adolphus and the Struggle of Protestantism for Existence*, New York, 1890; Schubert, H. von, *Feiern wir Gustav Adolf mit Recht als evangelischen Glaubenschelden?*, Halle, 1904; Treitschke, H. von, *Gustav Adolf und Deutschlands Freiheit*, Leipzig, 1895; Freytag, G., *Bilder aus der deutschen Vergangenheit*, Vol. 3, Leipzig, 1903–1905; etc.

of the eighteenth?[3] Since the facts, in particular the rather unceremonious way in which Gustavus Adolphus sometimes treated Protestant princes, do not agree very well with this purely 'confessional' presentation of the Swedish King, Ranke and his followers (the school of 'political historians') pointed to the interaction of political and religious motives,[4] and some even rejected any religious motivation, seeing only a purely secular, military-political basis for Gustavus Adolphus's entire German campaign, his striving for the Imperial Crown, the logic of the military struggle, and so on.[5] Other scholars have focused attention on the economic motives of Gustavus Adolphus's policy.[6] There was also a small number of German Catholic historians and admirers of the Habsburg Empire who tried to eradicate 'Schiller's mistake', to show that Gustavus Adolphus was neither a hero nor a liberator, that he was just another foreign conqueror in Germany, an adventurer driven by boundless ambition merely hidden behind the mask of religion.[7] This point of view, however, could not obtain wide acceptance – it merely revolted against the exaltation, 'humiliating' for Germany, of a foreign conqueror, but did not explain the source of this exaltation, and still less how it was that

---

[3] Moltke, H. von, *Gesammelte Schriften und Denkwürdigkeiten*, Vol. II, Berlin, 1892, pp. 185–187; Lenz, M., *Gustav Adolf, dem Befreier, zum Gedächtnis*; idem, *Schweden und Deutschland in 17 Jahrhundert*, in *Kleine Historische Schriften*, 2nd edition, Munich and Berlin, 1913; Schäfer, D., *Zum Gedächtnis Gustav Adolfs*, in *Aufsätze, Vorträge und Reden*, Vol. I, Jena, 1913.

[4] Ranke, L. von, *Geschichte Wallensteins*, Leipzig, 1869; Kahnis, K. F. A., *Der innere Gang des deutschen Protestantismus*, Parts I–II, Leipzig, 1874; Gutjahr, E., *König Gustav II Adolfs von Schweden Beweggründe zur Teilnahme am deutschen Kriege*, Leipzig, 1894; Kretzschmar, J., *Gustav Adolfs Pläne und Ziele in Deutschland und die Herzöge zu Braunschweig und Lüneburg*, Quellen und Darstellungen zur Geschhichte Niedersachsens, Vol. 17, 1904; Paul, J., *Gustav Adolf*, Vols. I–III, Leipzig, 1927–1932. Of Swedish historians see: Ahnlund, N., *Gustav Adolf den Store*, Stockholm, 1932 [English translation by Michael Roberts, *Gustav Adolf the Great*, Princeton, 1940 – Trans.]; Wittrock, G., *Gustav II Adolf*, in *Sveriges historia till våra dagar*, utgiven av E. Hildebrand och L. Stavenow, 6 Vols., Stockholm, 1927.

[5] Droysen, G., *Gustav Adolf*, Vols. I–II, Leipzig, 1869–1870; Bär, M., *Die Politik Pommerns während des Dreissigjährigen Krieges*, in *Publikationen aus den K. Preussischen Staatsarchiven*, Vol. 34, 1896; Schulz, H., *Wallenstein und die Zeit des Dreissigjährigen Krieges*, in *Monographien zur Weltgeshichte*, Vol. III, Bielefeld, 1898; Ritter, M., *Deutsche Geschichte in Zeitalter der Gegenreformation und des Dreissigjährigen Krieges (1555–1648)*, Vol. III, 1908.

[6] For example, Bothe, F., 'Die wirtschaftspolitischen Absichten Gustav Adolfs und seines Kanzlers in Deutschland', *Frankfurter Historische Forschungen*, No. 4, Frankfurt, 1910. Cf. Schäfer, D., *Zum gedächtnis*.

[7] Schmidt, M. J., *Neuere Geschichte der Deutschen*, Vienna, 1785–1793; Gfrörer, A. F., *Geschichte Gustav Adolphs*, Stuttgart, 1837; Barthold, F. W., *Geschichte des grossen Deutschen Krieges vom Tode Gustav Adolfs ab*, Vol. I, Stuttgart, 1842; Janssen, J., *Gustav Adolf in Deutschland*, 1865; idem, *Schiller als Historiker*, 2nd edition, Freiburg, 1879.

an 'ambitious adventurer' achieved his spectacular conquests in Germany.[8]

Basically there is no Marxist historical writing devoted specifically to Gustavus Adolphus. Franz Mehring's attempt to give a rebuff to the idealist uproar raised by the bourgeois press in connection with the 400th anniversary of Gustavus Adolphus's birthday, though interesting in its polemical aspect, was not based on independent study of the sources and was weak methodologically. Mehring, too, treats Gustavus Adophus as merely a foreign conqueror in Germany, a 'forerunner of today's imperialism', admiration for whom is not appropriate for the German working class.[9]

This way of presenting the question remained traditional in social-democratic historiography.

It is quite true that Gustavus Adolphus was a conqueror, that the impetus for his expedition to Germany was the endeavour of Sweden's ruling classes to establish their rule over the countries fronting on the Baltic Sea. But it is not true that Sweden was the only predator in this struggle. The policy of the Habsburgs and the activity of Wallenstein on the Baltic Sea pursued the same aim and directly threatened the independence and sovereignty of Sweden. Gustavus Adolphus's attempt to strike at the very heart of the ultra-reactionary Habsburg Empire thus responded to a genuine need for the Swedish state to avert this mortal danger. But what is most important is to understand that Gustavus Adolphus could, with his comparatively small army, have achieved nothing in Germany had he not been supported by not only external but also some internal German forces (as we shall see, to some extent independently of his will).

As regards the external forces, it has been shown above that inclusion of Muscovy in the field of vision of 'universal history' at once facilitates solution of a number of mysterious, obscure problems concerning Gustavus Adolphus's German campaign. By following that line, that is to say, by paying serious attention to the state of affairs in Eastern Europe, above all the history of the Russo–Polish conflict in 1632–1634, we can find the explanation also of other riddles of the 'zigzag lightning', the Swedish army's raid into the depths of Germany and its impetuous return to its initial starting point.

---

[8] Of recent writing on Gustavus Adolphus see, e.g., Roberts, M., *Gustavus Adolphus: A History of Sweden (1611–1632)*, Vols. I–II, London, 1953, 1958, and also these articles: Ekman, E., 'Three decades of research on Gustavus Adolphus', *Journal of Modern History*, Vol. 38, No. 3, 1955; Roberts, M., 'Gustavus Adolphus and the Art of War', *Historical Studies*, Vol. I, 1958; idem, 'The Political Objectives of Gustavus Adolphus in Germany, 1630-1632', *Transactions of the Royal Historical Society*, 5th series, Vol. 7, London, 1957.    [9] Mehring, F., *Gustav Adolf*, Berlin, 1894.

Here what is needed is to explain what the forces were, within Germany, that facilitated the Swedish King's task in making that raid and why he did not consider it possible to base himself seriously on these forces, but preferred to turn back. This aspect of the matter is no less important for refuting the falsifications of the bourgeois historians. As has been said, the latter, while making great efforts to settle the question of Gustavus Adolphus's policy in Germany, and that of the opposing policy of the German princes and ruling circles, have not taken a single step towards clarifying the main problem, the chief mystery, namely, the reasons for the miraculous fl;ight of 'the King of snow', which surrounded him with unprecedented sympathies and legends, and the reasons for the simultaneously maturing military and moral collapse which were averted only by his strange death during the battle of Lützen in 1632.

We can answer these questions only by starting from the conception put forward by Friedrich Engels. The main point in this conception is that Engels links the question of the Thirty Years' War with the question of the fate of the German peasantry and sees the fundamental importance of the war for the fate of Germany in the fact that it broke the capacity of the German peasantry, and, with them, of all the progressive forces in German society, to resist advancing feudal reaction. At the time of the Thirty Years' War menacing attempts by these social forces to fight against the prevailing order had already been made, and thirty years were needed to break these forces. During the Thirty Years' War, Engels writes,

for a whole generation Germany was overrun in all directions by the most licentious soldiery known to history. Everywhere was burning, plundering, rape and murder. The peasant suffered most where, apart from the great armies, the smaller independent bands, or rather the freebooters, operated uncontrolled, and upon their own account. The devastation and depopulation were beyond all bounds. When peace came, Germany lay on the ground helpless, downtrodden, cut to pieces, bleeding: but, once again, the most pitiable, miserable of all was the peasant.[10]

Engels saw as one of the main consequences of the war that 'serfdom was now general'. 'The German peasant, like the whole of Germany,' Engels goes on, 'had reached his lowest point of degradation. The peasant, like the whole of Germany, had become so powerless that all self-help failed him, and deliverance could only come from without.'[11]

These hopes for 'deliverance from without' intermingled with the last attempts at 'self-help' by the weakened peasantry, began to appear already during the Thirty Years' War. The political structure of the

---

[10] Marx, K., and Engels, F., *Sochineniia*, p. 341 [F. Engels, 'The Mark' (1882), appendix to *The Peasant War in Germany*, Moscow, 1956, p. 177].

[11] Ibid., p. 342 [ibid., p. 178].

Empire, its fragmented character, made such feelings more plausible than anywhere else. Owing to economic and political decentralisation the formation of the German nation was much delayed. National consciousness was but weakly developed. Many Germans as yet made no clear distinction between the German nation and nations speaking other Germanic languages – the Dutch, the Swedes, the Danes. The Austrian Habsburgs who headed the empire were members of the college of Electors in their capacity as 'Kings of Bohemia'. In what way could a Swedish King be worse in the eyes of many Germans than an Austro–Czech King, or, in the eyes of the Czechs, say, why should he be worse as ruler over them than an Austrian? Only if we take into account these features of the Empire can we understand how the hopes of the oppressed classes and nationalities could rally to Gustavus Adolphus once he had entered Germany as the enemy of their enemy.

Whether these hopes proved illusory is another matter. However, the early death of Gustavus Adolphus prevented a final collapse of these illusions, though they had already been deeply shaken.

The international struggle ultimately turned out to be inseparable from the class struggle. Whoever opposed the main bastion of reaction in Europe, the Empire, even if he had been drawn to this merely by the territorial, commercial and strategic interests of his own state, could count on success only if he was supported by forces stronger than his own, forces that were combating that reaction.

Gustavus Adolphus was brought into Germany by the logic of Sweden's struggle to secure monopolistic domination of the Baltic Sea. But it was one thing to want, another to be able to. With all his foreign subsidies, Gustavus Adolphus might have remained a factor of far from first-rate magnitude in German affairs, and perhaps would have been quickly thrown out of Germany by the Imperial army, if a number of circumstances had not endowed him – partly through his own initiative, but to a much greater degree independently of his will – with the halo of liberator in the eyes of the Germans. And it was not the logic of the Swedish struggle for the Baltic but the logic of the class struggle in Germany that carried the Swedish conqueror, like a following wind, across the great spaces of the Empire.

At the source of this transformation lay a fact of which Gustavus Adolphus himself was hardly aware, or anyone in his circle either. The core of his army was made up of personally free peasants. There is no need to recall here that the history of feudalism followed a distinctive path in the Scandinavian countries: no developed form of serfdom ever existed there. This army, the core of which consisted of free peasants, was an absolutely unusual phenomenon in continental Europe of the seventeenth century. In order, though, to appreciate fully its effect on men's minds one has to remember that it appeared in Germany at the time of the process called the 'second enserfment' of the peasantry. However risky the analogy, a comparison suggests itself with those distant times of the early Middle Ages when the enserfed peasantry of Europe sometimes rose to greet the invading free barbarians, the Norsemen, and supported their incursions, because they looked on them as liberators – until, of course, the moment when they themselves experienced the Vikings' violence and devastation. In the Germany of the early 1630s, however, it was not a matter of the contrast between the intensifyingly servile condition of the local population and free, armed strangers. The Swedish army had been in other countries where serfdom prevailed without evoking the same political consequences there. We need to consider the distinctiveness of this particular moment in the development of the class struggle in Germany. By the time the Swedish invasion took place in the period which can be called the prologue to the all-European war, the 'Bohemian' and 'Danish' periods of the Thirty Years' War, the German peasantry had accumulated considerable experience of struggle and defeat.[12] A critical stage had been reached. Several large-scale and innumerable small-scale spontaneous peasant revolts had already made manifest the upsurge of peasant pressure. All these revolts, even though they sometimes succeeded in spreading as widely as, for instance, the Upper Austrian rising of 1626, graphically exposing thereby the relative feebleness of the forces of 'order', were nevertheless put down sooner or later by the civil or military authorities. But the 'Danish' period showed that through the 'upper circles' of society there ran a deep and irremovable division and that the conflict in the 'upper circles' on how it was necessary to crush the revolutionary movement of the masses duly facilitated the unleashing of these spontaneous actions. In fact, Wallenstein's system – if one can give the name 'system' to an unbridled, bloody, ruinous trampling down of the German people by the centralised Imperial and Catholic army – although it performed to some considerable degree the domestic political task of subduing the people everywhere that they tried to lift their heads, clashed with the 'system' of decentralisation, meaning the independent authority of the princes, and had to give way. Wallenstein was dismissed. True, the Imperial and Catholic army continued, under Tilly's command, to pacify Germany in the same spirit, with the scythe of death and expropriation, but its political weight was no longer the same. Although the princes had got the better of Wallenstein they were unable to implement what we have called 'the princes' plan' for accomplishing

[12] Porshnev refers here to his own Chapter 2 on 'Germany'.

the internal German social task:[13] to involve in their internecine disputes neighbouring powers that were sufficiently strong for their armies to crush, in passing, the revolutionary forces of the German people. Or, more precisely, the princes did take that path, but were far from having attained their goal. After the forces of the Danish King had been defeated, the Protestant party conspired with the King of Sweden, and the Catholic party, especially Maximilian of Bavaria, with the King of France.

But all this was still embryonic and as yet served not to suppress the social danger but, on the contrary, to unsettle the 'upper circles' and provide the 'lower orders' with opportunities for activity.

Who could lead the spontaneous upsurge of the masses? In seventeenth-century Germany there was no bourgeois party, not even one like the burghers' party of Luther in the period of the Reformation and the Peasant War. The development of Germany's burgher estate followed a downward rather than an upward line in the sixteenth century. Nor was there a popular party like Münzer's. But when the peasants and the plebeian elements in the towns started to move, they felt their powerlessness for lack of a common political leadership, and groped around in search of it. Since there were no national leaders, the search was, willy-nilly, directed outward, for a foreign leader. The rumour of the arrival on German soil of Gustavus Adolphus, who was, on the one hand, the leader of an army of free peasants and, on the other, the adversary of the Imperial army under Wallenstein which stood for the most frightful oppression and torment of the people, had a rousing effect on the broadest masses in Germany. Their hearts beat more boldly and were filled with hope. Among the people there was talk of a Messiah, of a man sent from God.

These were the contradictory possibilities that opened up before Gustavus Adolphus as soon as he set foot in Germany. He had to choose. To become an ally, even a collaborator in the policy of the German princes, to employ his Swedish soldiers in waging war on the German peasants and, at this price, to obtain the political, military and financial support of many princes, would, of course, have been the line incomparably closer to the outlook of the monarch of the Swedish nobility. Subjectively, to take this option was clearly and indisputably right for him. At the same time, though, he could, in the best case, become the ally of only one of the contending princely parties, the Protestant one, and be faced with the undefined position of some of the Catholic princes and authorities and with the inescapable prospect of war with the Imperial and Catholic army all over the great expanse of Germany, where even territorial gains were dangerous, since, as they grew, they required the installation of more and

[13] As with n. 12.

more garrisons. Who could add to his insufficient forces? The potential of all the Protestant princes put together was far from adequate to ensure victory over the enemy, and in any case could hardly be fully mobilised in time. The power of the popular upsurge, though, was so great that it would be enough to join with it and open its sluices, and such a flood would burst forth as would drown the enemy. Arguing not like a monarch of the nobility but as a commander accustomed to seeking the real way to real victory, Gustavus Adolphus could not ignore that line.

This was an epoch when often it was not leaders who ruled events but events that ruled leaders. Thus, a few decades earlier, the simple logic of struggle led Prince William of Orange, who was profoundly averse to the spirit of revolution, to become leader of the revolt of the Netherlands against Spain, a leader of the masses, of the bourgeois revolution. And, a decade and a half later, Oliver Cromwell, who was essentially no revolutionary but a practical military commander, proceeding from the single task of finding real forces with which to wage war to victory against the King, once that war had begun, was obliged to become eventually the leader of the Independents, of the English bourgeois revolution.

But Gustavus Adolphus became neither William of Orange nor Oliver Cromwell. The reason for that was that a bourgeois revolution was impossible in Germany in the seventeenth century, though it *had* been possible there a century earlier, in the sixteenth. The development of the German burghers was, at that time, downward, not upward. There was a burgher opposition but it was weak and was concentrated almost exclusively in the Hansa towns. That semi-revolutionary bloc of the bourgeoisie with a section of the gentry which had come about in the Netherlands and in England, and on which William of Orange and Oliver Cromwell directly relied, did not exist in Germany. The Swedish King would have had to assume direct leadership of a peasant war, and that ran counter to his whole nature as a nobleman, all his education and mode of thought, even though as a commander, moved by the inspiration and excitement of war, he could not fail to perceive the tremendous force which was straining to meet him.

This was the fundamental contradiction which explains the surprising fate of Gustavus Adolphus in the last year of his life.

It is not easy for an historian to study the socio-political circumstances within Germany in which the Swedish army found itself operating. In the numerous stout works by bourgeois historians about Gustavus Adolphus and Wallenstein, the Emperor Ferdinand II and the German princes, this aspect of the question is almost completely ignored or distorted. Among the sources, if we do not speak of unpublished documents and broadsheets and pamphlets that are difficult to access, we are obliged to rely principally on the various 'histories' of the Thirty Years' War written by contemporaries who were either observers of or direct participants in its events. These are, of course, all extremely tendentious and amount largely to political propaganda coming from one or other of the contending sides.[14] Nevertheless, echoes of reality are ineradicable in them: they tell us, directly or indirectly of truths which later historians have tried to ignore. Valuable fragments telling of the social aspect of the Swedish campaign in Germany we have found especially in Chemnitz's work[15] (though Pufendorf[16] largely follows Chemnitz, he already effected a certain 'purge' from Chemnitz's data of what he considered excessive realities), in Burge,[17] and, especially, in the anonymous work, mentioned earlier,[18] entitled *Le soldat suédois descript les actes guerriers . . . de son Roy*, published, in French, in Rouen in 1634.[19]

This last-mentioned work has proved particularly useful, possibly just because it bears a plainly propagandist nature and, as it were, tries to distort the facts before the reader's eyes. It was written for the purpose of winning sympathy in France with Sweden and the Swedish army in Germany, in the interests of strengthening the Swedo–French alliance. The author, who conceals his name from the reader, was a certain Spanheim, but his material was prepared for him by one of the leading wielders of the propaganda weapon under Gustavus Adolphus, C.L. Rasche, who wrote some important works of a military-publicistic nature to make propaganda in Germany for the Swedish cause. *Le soldat suédois* begins with these words: 'The war now being fought between the Emperor and the King of Sweden has divided Christendom into two factions, and there are few persons who look upon it with indifference, and are neither "Imperialists" nor "Swedes" '. These words express excellently the all-European importance of the events that were being played out in the heart of Germany. Some, the writer goes on, rejoice, while others mourn at the way this war is going, but all equally are amazed that so great a body [i.e. the Empire – B.F.P.] swollen with such forces and such successes, should have suffered such a hard shock in so short a time and by means so little obvious. Some seek the explanation for this in the righteousness of the cause that the King of Sweden fought for, others in mistakes made by the

[14] Cf. Droysen, G., 'Quellenkritik der deutschen Geschichte des 17-ten Jahrhunderts', *Forschungen zur deutschen Geschichte*, Vol. IV, Göttingen, 1864.

[15] Chemnitz, B. P., *Königlichen-schwedischen in Teutschland geführten Kriegs*, Vols. I–II (1630–1636), Stettin, 1648.

[16] Pufendorf, S., *Commentariorum de rebus Suecicis libri XXVI, ab expeditione Gustavi Adolphi regis in Germaniam ad abdicationem usque Christinae*, Ultrajecti [Utrecht], 1686.

[17] Burgi, P. B., *gennensis, De bello suecico commentarii . . .*, Leodii, 1633.

[18] See Chapter 3, p. 122, and n. 35.

[19] *Le soldat suédois descript les actes guerriers, merveilles de nostre temps, plus que très-généreuses et très-héroiques . . . de son Roy*, Rouen, 1634.

Imperialists, in the people's despair, or in the usual alternations of prosperity, which have their cycles and begin to decline when they can no longer rise. In short, they talk very differently according to their respective inclinations or passions.[20]

Clearly, one alone of the explanations listed here, namely, that which sees the reason for the Swedish successes in 'the people's despair' in Germany can be directly related to 'passions', to revolutionary passions. The writer, therefore, leads us with his very first words into that range of opinions which he is going to combat, despite their being widely held. He will not go along with this highly disloyal (especially for France, where popular revolts were always seething) explanation of the Swedes' successes, namely the despair and struggle of the masses in Germany. He counterposes to this explanation, which he sees as incorrect, what is for him the only true one, 'the righteousness of the cause that the King of Sweden fought for'. The 'just and noble' motives that impelled Gustavus Adolphus to invade Germany are given much attention.

Later on in this work we come upon a passage where the author nevertheless lets himself mention that in their propaganda in Germany, addressed to the German people, the Swedes made use of precisely that conception which he repudiates here. He is speaking of the triumphal march of the Swedish army towards Vienna which could not be checked either by the military and diplomatic efforts of the enemy or by their propaganda directed against Gustavus Adolphus. 'In short,' says *Le soldat suédois*,

everything seemed to bend before the onslaught of his arms. The Imperialists were pleased then to put about the story that the King had Lapps in his army, who cast spells on those they fought against so that it was impossible to resist them. This they supported with many old tales about how those people knew how to call up winds and storms and to make themselves arbiters of good luck and bad.

The Swedes, on their part, carried on an active counter-propaganda, exposing the silliness of these inventions and opposing them with the thesis 'that the Imperialists should seek the reasons for their defeats in their own acts of violence and brigandage, in the people's despair, and in a just curse which followed them everywhere, on account of the barbarities and cruelties they committed throughout the Empire'.[21]

As we shall see, Swedish propaganda in Germany explained the

---

[20] Ibid., pp. 1–2 [ditto].

[21] Ibid., pp. 125–127 [pp. 86–87]. The author lets out the truth similarly in another place, too. He speaks of the organisation in Vienna of a procession of all the children in the city, offering up piteous prayers for Heaven to grant victory to the Imperial army, and remarks: 'This spectacle evoked commiseration in some, but in others murmurings that they [the Imperialists] had got themselves by their own will into these desperate difficulties through their unbearable acts of violence' (ibid., p. 247 [p. 168]). We doubtless glimpse here a frequent theme in Swedish propaganda of that period.

successes of the Swedish army and the failures of the Imperial forces at the beginning in a way that was broadly correct – by the social atmosphere which prevailed in Germany, by the frightful terror with which the Imperial and Catholic army strove to crush the rising movement of the German masses. Merely two years were needed for this truth to be repudiated by those who had acknowledged it in the heat of the war. The history of Gustavus Adolphus's campaign written by 'the Swedish soldier' (Spanheim and Rasche) was the first account of that campaign to be published. And it was already subjected to the task of falsifying the truth. But that truth was nevertheless too fresh; it shows, here and there, through the cloak deliberately thrown over it by the author.

Later historical works dealing with Gustavus Adolphus's campaign contain incomparably fewer of these precious fragments of the truth about that aspect of the campaign which interests us. But, taken together, they enable us, if not to light up this question, at least to perceive some of its outlines. In the works of historians written in the nineteenth and twentieth centuries we can also find scattered but sometimes important facts. Future researchers will undoubtedly be able to assemble more fully all the evidence from the sources.

Gustavus Adolphus's conquest of Pomerania is impossible to explain from a purely military standpoint. The King had not yet conquered the whole of Pomerania when its Duke, Bogislaw XIV, surrendered to him, explaining this action among other things, in a letter to the Emperor, by 'the barbarities and cruelties of the Imperial soldiers'. They did not forgive Bogislaw in Vienna, despite all his excuses, considering that he had favoured the Swedish invasion, and they ordered the Imperial troops in Pomerania to act even more harshly than before. The Imperialists made frequent raids into the outskirts of Stettin, burning and devastating villages, buildings and mills, and inflicting all sorts of cruelties on the population, who fled from them into the forests. 'All this', writes *Le soldat suédois*, 'served only to make the Emperor's name more hated and that of the King of Sweden more agreeable in the country and among the subjects of Bogislaw.'[22] Thus, from the very outset Gustavus Adolphus appeared in Germany, whether he liked it or not, in the role of defender of peasants oppressed by the Imperialists.

The social contradictions in Pomerania at the time of the Swedish landing were extremely acute. The 'second edition' of serfdom was being vigorously pressed in Pomerania. This process had, of course, begun in the first decades of the sixteenth century. In the words of the German historian Spahn, the agrarian system in Pomerania became 'morbid' (and

---

[22] Ibid., pp. 17–18 [p. 13].

more so the further east) under Bogislaw X (who died in 1523). 'But from about 1600', he goes on, 'the peasants in Pomerania became if not slaves, then at least unfree, having to perform personal services and corvée . . . In the Rügen area alone did some vestiges of an independent peasantry survive.'[23] In short, during the first three decades of the seventeenth century the bulk of the Pomeranian peasants were made serfs. It is easy to imagine how acute the social contradictions in that region were. Furthermore, just at that time another process painful for the peasants was at its height: owing to the poor income to be got from cultivation, the nobles were urgently going over to wool production, and a section of the peasantry were driven from their holdings. 'Sheep were eating up men.'

The urban population gained nothing from these changes in agriculture. No industry for working with wool developed, as this material was mostly exported. Apart from the ports, such as Stralsund, which enjoyed the fruits of a certain improvement in Hanseatic trade in the first decades of the seventeenth century, the other towns underwent that 'regression to natural economy' which was happening almost everywhere in Germany. The curtailment of craft production resulted in unemployment and increased poverty of the lower strata of the urban population, with consequent straining of social contradictions.

The class struggle of the lower orders was clothed in the religious outward form of fanatical devotion to Protestantism, in opposition, to a large extent, to the neutral attitude towards religious questions adopted by the authorities both spiritual and temporal. The rich Lutheran clergy of Pomerania were not at all disposed to sacrifice their wealth for the defence of their faith, and consequently were always for compromise with the Emperor's policy and against straining relations with the Catholic upper circles of the Empire. The merchants of the port towns were not, of course, guided in their activity by the interests of Protestantism – Bogislaw XIV, the head of the Pomeranian nobility, who had inherited three parts of the country previously separated, followed an openly pro-Imperial and, consequently, pro-Catholic policy. In opposition to all this, only the 'common people' were seized with fanatical willingness to fight for Protestantism, only the masses, says Spahn, 'more short-sighted', 'more subject to fanatical enthusiasm for religious struggle', were ready to sacrifice everything for the cause of faith, 'seeing clearly that their earthly possessions were in any case lying as so much booty for the Imperial troops' whom Bogislaw XIV had admitted into Pomerania to maintain order.[24]

---

[23] Spahn, M., 'Auswärtige Politik und innere Lage des Herzogtums Pommern von 1627–1630 in ihrem Zusammenhange', *Historisches Jahrbuch . . . des Görres-Gesellschaft*, Vol. 19, No. 1, 1898, p. 59.     [24] Ibid., pp. 74–75.

This is the background against which we have to look at Gustavus Adolphus's appearance in Pomerania in the summer of 1630. All aspirations, social and religious alike, reached out to him. Only in the light of this background can we understand the correspondence, preceding the Swedish landing, between two of the principal Pomeranian towns, Wolgast and Stralsund, about the possibility of resisting the excesses of the Imperialist troops with the help of the Swedes who had offered their services from across the sea. The ruling group in Stralsund favoured this move, but the town council of Wolgast, while also leaning to the side of the Swedes, nevertheless advised against it, because it could have fatal consequences for all the privileged estates in Pomerania. The town councillors of Wolgast explained this quite definitely: if they were to invite in the Swedes to resist the Imperialists, 'a domestic revolt (*innerliche Empörung*) would break our necks'.[25]

Not everyone saw the matter so clearly. The 'upper circles' of Pomerania could hope that their Swedish counterparts would not allow events to take such a turn.

Spahn, a typical representative of the Prussian historical school, made his study of the internal and external situation in Pomerania in 1627–1630 in order to find an explanation for the irresolute policy of Bogislaw XIV. After careful investigation of the country's central administrative apparatus and of its financial potentialities, he came to the conclusion that the objective prerequisites for a firm and independent policy did exist for Bogislaw XIV. Therefore, it was only the subjective factor that prevented this. Spahn concludes his study with the trivial, idealistic statement that the whole trouble came down to the personal characteristics of the last Pomeranian duke. The fall of the Duchy of Pomerania was to be explained by the fact that it lacked at that moment a sufficiently great ruler, someone like 'the Great Elector', who would have used his absolute power and the country's resources to pursue a firm foreign policy.

There is a grain of truth in this. Pomerania was overrun first by the Imperialist and then by Swedish troops owing to a certain 'subjective' position taken up by its ruling 'upper circles'. Undoubtedly, Bogislaw XIV himself, or, more correctly, Bogislaw XIV carrying out the will of the Pomeranian nobility, determined his own fate. In order to put down his peasants he first called to his aid the ravaging Imperialist hordes, and then, when they had become the *de facto* masters of Pomerania, in an attempt to neutralise them, but without allowing the peasants to throw off the bridle, he sought, apparently, to bring in to help him a foreign intervention force, the Swedes – and in the end, was deprived of his

---

[25] Bär, M., *Die Politik Pommerns*.

power. The Pomeranian peasants themselves welcomed the invasion by the Swedes, seeing in them, above all, the enemies of their enemies, the Imperialists, the defenders of their Protestant faith and, we must also suppose, representatives of a country where there was no serfdom.

To Bogislaw nothing was left but, without even waiting for the military *dénouement*, to surrender to this conjunction of the forces of his subjects with those of the conquerors from across the sea.

While there can be no doubt that the Swedes, having ousted the Imperialists, thereby considerably eased the position of the Pomeranian peasantry, it remains quite unresearched and unclear whether they satisfied to any degree the aspirations of that peasantry in the socio-economic sphere. One can only speculate that the peasants probably utilised the appearance of this unexpected ally in order, *de facto*, to achieve some sort of improvement in their situation, that the Pomeranian landlords had to make some concessions (many noblemen fled with Bogislaw) and that the armed free peasants from Sweden saw nothing unnatural in the Pomeranian peasants' fight for freedom. Indirect confirmation is provided by the fact that, during the whole time that the Swedish army was in Pomerania, according to the careful formulation of 'the Swedish soldier', 'the entire country was favourable' to it, even when Gustavus Adolphus carried out a rather burdensome mobilisation of the peasants to build fortifications.[26] But we can also speculate that the King of the Swedish nobility must have felt very awkward and subject to inward waverings as a result of this complicated situation. The contradictoriness, even unnaturalness, of his position helps us to understand more fully all the reasons for his protracted, more than year-long, 'marking time' in his Pomeranian bridgehead.

Already some three or four months after the Swedish landing, according to something said by 'the Swedish soldier' which, though tossed out in passing, is important, throughout North-Eastern Germany 'fear of the Imperial name had changed to hatred, and the people began everywhere to attack those guests who had bullied them for so long'.[27] The presence of the Swedish army in Germany unleashed a popular movement, giving it courage. This turn of events naturally had a sharply cooling effect on the sympathies of the German princes with the Swedish King. Instead of the alliance with all the Protestant princes which he had expected, Gustavus Adolphus found himself isolated and faced with increasing alienation, which came to a head in the decision of the Leipzig congress of Protestants in February 1631 to observe neutrality. All historians affirm that the Imperial forces which were operating in

[26] *Le soldat suédois*, pp. 28–38 [p. 20].    [27] Ibid.

Pomerania under the command of Torquato Conti would all have perished from hunger, cold and, especially, from the vengeance of the infuriated population if they had not been given refuge, in Küstrin and Frankfurt-am-Oder, by Georg Wilhelm, the Elector of Brandenburg.[28] It is generally agreed that the Dukes of Mecklenburg did not at once recover Mecklenburg, which Wallenstein had taken from them (although the Diet at Regensburg had confirmed their rights) only because the leaders of the Protestants, the Electors of Brandenburg and Saxony, categorically forbade them to call on their subjects to revolt.[29] As we shall see, the Protestant princes preferred, as a rule, to ally with the Emperor and Catholicism rather than promote further activisation of their subjects, and for this reason recoiled from Gustavus Adolphus.

For his part Gustavus Adolphus did all he could to stop seeming to the feudal, and especially the Protestant, upper circles in Germany the incendiary and accomplice of a popular uprising. As we know, he conducted patient and persistent friendly negotiations for an alliance with the Electors of Saxony and Brandenburg.[30] Renouncing his former intractability with the French ambassador, Charnacé, in January 1631 he authorised his generals Horn and Banér to sign a treaty with him at Bärwalde – not merely from financial necessity, as is commonly alleged (he had, not long before, proudly offered to pay a subsidy to France, though this was, of course, not seriously meant).[31] On the one hand the treaty of Bärwalde made up for the inadequacy of allies for Gustavus Adolphus in Germany, while, on the other, it proclaimed the purpose of the alliance to be 'the restoration of German liberties', meaning defence of the princes' interests, and demonstrated the King's complete loyalty not only to the Protestant princes but even to the Catholic ones as well.

But losing the support of the people would have meant for Gustavus Adolphus risking all he had gained. We are struck by the efforts of the

---

[28] See, e.g., Schlosser, F., *Vsemirnaia Istoriia*, St Petersburg, 1871, p. 331 [*Weltgeschichte*].
[29] For more detail on this see Grotefend, O., *Mecklenburg unter Wallenstein und die Wiedereroberung des Landes durch die Herzöge*, Marburg, 1901 (Dissertation).
[30] See Helbig, K. G., *Gustav Adolf und die Kurfürsten von Sachsen und Brandenburg 1630–1632*, Leipzig, 1854; Kretzschmar, J., 'Allianzverhandlungen Gustav Adolfs mit Kurbrandenburg in Mai und Juni 1631', *Forschungen zur brandenb.-preuss. Geschichte*, Vol. 17, 1904; Boëthius, B., 'Aktstycker rörande Salvius underhandlingar med Brandenburg i September 1631', *Svensk Historisk Tidskrift*, 1913. On dealings with the West-German princes see Boëthius, B., *Svenskarne i de nedersachsiska och westfaliska Kustländerna juli 1630–november 1632 till belysning of Gustav II Adolfs tyski politik*, Uppsala, 1912.
[31] The Swedish historian Weibull has shown, by examining the whole history of the Swedo–French negotiations and Charnacé's prolonged attempts to clinch this treaty, that France was the more interested party than Sweden (Weibull, L., *De diplomatiska förbindelserna mellan Sverige och Frankrike 1629–1631*, Lund, 1899; idem, 'Gustave Adolphe et Richelieu', *Revue historique*, Vol. 174, No. 2, 1934). Paul takes the same view: Paul, *Gustav Adolf*, Vol. II, pp. 143–144.

Swedish commanders from the very beginning and all through the subsequent campaign to rely on a kind of 'middle' or 'third' force, namely, the cities. Gustavus Adolphus paid exceptional attention to the liberties and the needs of the German cities and received municipal representatives with ceremony. One of the King's very first acts in Germany was to grant immense privileges to Stralsund, making it almost a free city.[32]

However, the cities, meaning the urban patriciate and burghers, were in themselves by no means a decisive political force. The burghers could become such a force only if they put themselves at the head of the elemental struggle of the broad masses and united with it. Magdeburg tried to rise in a revolutionary spirit, and so became almost the centre of the entire revolutionary opposition in Germany, and its monstrous destruction proved to be an event of all-German significance, claiming the attention of all the publicists and newspapers, and all contemporaries, near and far. We must go into that event in greater detail.

German scholars have written a great deal, several dozen books and articles, on the destruction of Magdeburg in May 1631. Here are the main stages in the historiography of this question. Down to the 1840s the generally accepted view was that Tilly bore responsibility for the destruction of Magdeburg. Protestant historians cited this event as an example of the enormities committed by the Catholic reaction.

In the 1840s and 1850s the Austrian historian Majláth, and in his wake a number of other Catholic historians – Heisig, Bensen, Klopp, Kretschmann – rejected, on the basis of much source material, the charge against Tilly and maintained the thesis that it was not the Imperialists but the burghers of Magdeburg themselves, in alliance with the Swedish commander, who had given the city over to fire and destruction. Protestant historians – Kutscheit, Opel – launched a counter-attack based also on examination of sources, and in 1863 there emerged from their camp a major work by G. Droysen. This, however, did not attempt to rehabilitate the rejected view concerning Tilly's guilt but expounded a careful thesis to the effect that the sources point directly to the guilt of the Imperial general Pappenheim for one local fire only, and that it is not possible to establish who was responsible for the burning of the entire city.[33] In 1874 there appeared a two-volume monograph by K. Wittich

[32] See Carlson, W., *Gustav Adolf och Stralsund 1628–Juli 1630*, Uppsala, 1912. Also Langer, H., 'Stralsunds Entscheidung, 1628', *Greifswald-Stralsunder Jahrbuch*, Vol. 4, Schwerin, 1964; idem, 'Die Rolle Stralsunds bei der Vorbereitung und beim Beginn der schwedischen Agression in Deutschland 1630', *Wissenschaftliche Zeitschrift der Ernst-Moritz-Arndt Universität, Geschicht-und-sprechwiss*, Reihe, Greifswald, 1965, Year 14, Nos. 2–3.

[33] Droysen, G., 'Studien über die Belagerung und Zerstörung Magdeburgs 1631', *Forschungen zur deutschen Geschichte*, Vol. 3, Göttingen, 1863; idem, *Gustav Adolf*, Vol. II.

which rejected Droysen's view on Pappenheim's guilt and by thorough analysis of the sources proved that Magdeburg's destruction by fire was planned, so that it should not fall into the hands of the Papists, by a radical faction of the city's burghers and, especially, 'the discontented rabble', on the direct orders of the Swedish commandant of the city, Falkenberg.[34]

After that, the historiography of the problem developed as a dispute between the school of Droysen (Dittmar and others) and the school of Wittich, who himself came forward in the 1880s and 1890s with a series of fresh studies to refute the arguments brought against him. Droysen's pupil, Teitge, when he tried in 1904 to sum up the results of this learned polemic, was obliged to admit that the school of Wittich had the last word, even though he tried to justify an agnostic attitude to the question, as being ultimately insoluble.[35]

It must be said that this very scholarly squabble was somewhat shallow. The dispute came down to a sort of scrupulous judicial inquiry into the narrow question of who actually burnt Magdeburg, on whom lay the immediate criminal responsibility, so to speak. The socio-political aspect of the question was left somewhere far in the background. But what was said on that aspect by Droysen and Wittich is not essentially very contradictory, and can easily be reconciled if we relegate to the background the secondary, criminalistic aspect.

Magdeburg, where a large-scale revolt broke out in 1618 which attracted close attention from contemporaries, was still, in the 'Danish period' of the Thirty Years' War, Droysen says, 'the real centre of the anti-Catholic movement in' the Empire.[36] Although situated quite far from the sea, a long way up the Elbe, Magdeburg was above all a major port. Through it passed a substantial share of the trade of Eastern Germany. The suburbs of the city, spread out along the river-bank, were inhabited almost entirely by persons connected with shipping, trade and the life of a port. We have little information on industry in Magdeburg before its destruction, but we do know, for example, that it exported, especially to the Netherlands, a large quantity of beer that was brewed on the spot.

The city's population in the period that interests us was clearly divided into the three strata distinguished by Engels: patriciate, burghers and plebeians. But the way their forces were combined was rather complex. The patriciate was able to use movements of the plebeians against the burghers so as to strengthen its own position. It held power and, relying

---

[34] Wittich, K., *Magdeburg, Gustav Adolf und Tilly*, Vols. I–II, Berlin, 1874.

[35] Teitge, H., 'Die Frage nach dem Urheber der Zerstörung Magdeburgs 1631', in *Hallesche Abhandlungen zur neueren Geschichte*, herausgeben von G. Droysen, No. 42, Halle, 1904.    [36] Droysen, *Gustav Adolf*, Vol. II, p. 103.

on support from the population of the suburbs, subjected the city's entire policy to the interest of maintaining even under war conditions the previous scale of trade along the Elbe. Naturally, it did not shrink from trying to come to an arrangement with Wallenstein's Imperial and Catholic army. Against the ruling patrician party, linked with the plebeians, fought the burgher opposition, which put forward a strictly Protestant programme and was backed by the Protestant 'administrator' of the Magdeburg diocese, Christian Wilhelm (of the Brandenburg dynasty).

The war and the Edict of Restitution (1629) acutely sharpened social contradictions in Magdeburg. The military operations and the huge tolls imposed along the course of the Elbe by the contending sides reduced the flow of trade on the river. All the 'ship folk' (*Schiffer-knechte*) of Magdeburg – the dockers, boatmen, stevedores and so on – found themselves deprived of means of subsistence. Cases of suicide became frequent among the poor while, on the other hand, the idea spread that 'it's all the same if we all die of hunger'. Hatred for the wealth of the rich grew stronger, and engendered those 'gross excesses' by the common people which the sources mention for the year 1629. The plebeians now turned away from their support of the pro-Catholic city council and, on the contrary, carried out unauthorised actions against the ships of the Imperial and Catholic party. Wallenstein tried to punish Magdeburg, and besieged it, but was as unsuccessful as in the case of Stralsund. During the siege the power of the patrician city council was restricted by representatives of the burgher opposition, sixteen delegates from the city's districts who were, incidentally, in contact with other Hansa towns.

This was why Wallenstein was so alarmed by the arrival of Gustavus Adolphus in Germany. As early as 1627 he uttered his famous remark: 'In the Swedes we shall find a worse enemy than the Turks.' In September 1629 Wallenstein wrote of the danger that Gustavus Adolphus might effect a *rapprochement* with 'certain estates of the Empire such as the Hansa towns and other disaffected elements (*Malcontenten*)'. In November–December 1629 he was expecting a 'general revolt', a 'universal revolt', which might begin with the Hansa towns, headed by Magdeburg.[37]

In December 1629 the burgher opposition brought off a revolution in Magdeburg with the help of delegates who arrived from 'the new confederation' – Lübeck, Hamburg, Bremen, Brunswick and Hildesheim.

As a result of the break-up of the bloc of patricians and plebeians the old city council was swept away with comparative ease and replaced by a new one which represented the burgher party. It remained to clear the

[37] Watson, F., *Wallenstein: Soldier under Saturn*, London, 1938, p. 188; Droysen, *Gustav Adolf*, pp. 109–110.

Imperialists out of the whole territory of the diocese and then to go forward together with the other cities. Thus, at the moment when Gustavus Adolphus stepped on to German soil in June 1630, says Droysen, 'the state of affairs in Magdeburg came close, in real earnest, to a revolutionary explosion'.[38] Gustavus Adolphus hastened to send to Magdeburg his plenipotentiary Stalmann, who not only concluded an alliance between Sweden and Magdeburg and restored the Protestant administrator Christian Wilhelm to his rights, which had been taken away by the Edict of Restitution, but also organised along with him, on 2 August 1630, a sort of mass offensive to liberate the surrounding territory. 'A motley throng', led, as Droysen has it, by 'the city mob',[39] set out from Magdeburg to seize and expel the Imperialists from the small towns, monasteries and villages in the neighbourhood. The peasants who had been oppressed by the Imperialists rose to join the Magdeburgers. An important clue to the social basis of this movement is the commission issued soon after by the administrator, as ruler of the territory: he called directly on the citizens and peasants for continued solidarity and discipline, but the nobles, on the contrary, he addressed extremely sternly, ordering them to send to Magdeburg a certain number of horses and fighting men.

However, this achievement could not be consolidated. To throw the Imperialists out of the region for good, an army was needed. They had to hold out until the Swedes arrived. In the meantime Gustavus Adolphus sent to Magdeburg one of his most outstanding military aides, Falkenberg. The King's war-plan consisted at that time in using Magdeburg, in his own words, as 'the advanced post and base of the whole expedition'. As soon as the Swedish forces arrived in Magdeburg, Hamburg and Lübeck would rise, and, after them, all Germany. The instructions given orally by Gustavus Adolphus to Falkenberg, but at once communicated in writing to Chancellor Oxenstjerna (17 August 1630), gave his task as 'to encourage the administrator and the city; to form some regiments . . . to secure the city' for the Swedes and 'in this way prepare a diversion . . . by means of which we can take control of the Elbe. . .[this diversion] will inspire the disaffected elements (*den Malkontenten Luft gebe*) and support them in denying the Imperialists all forms of payment . . . in short (*in summa*) it will light a torch from which the flames of universal revolt will spread all over Germany.'[40]

It may be that when Gustavus Adolphus spoke of all the disaffected elements (*Malkontenten*) in Germany and of a universal revolt, he had in

---

[38] Droysen, *Adolf*, p. 125.     [39] Ibid., p. 179.
[40] Ibid., p. 184; see *Arkiv till upplysning om svenska krigens historia*, Vol. II, No. 118.

mind, primarily, the Protestant princes together with, at most, the burgher opposition in the great cities: that is, at any rate, how he has been interpreted by historians. But the point is that at that moment, when the burgher opposition was weak, turning to 'the disaffected elements' meant, regardless of subjective intentions, coming face to face, willy-nilly, with the masses, with the movement of the peasants and plebeians, with 'the anger of the low'. Whatever Gustavus Adolphus may have had in mind when, at the beginning of his campaign, he hoped 'to light a torch' for universal revolt in Germany, he actually gave the signal for a movement of the lower orders, a deepening of the class struggle.

In Magdeburg, surrounded by the Imperialist troops of Tilly and Pappenheim, class antagonism showed itself in extreme forms as the city waited for the Swedish army to arrive. In Wittich's view the Swedes, with their 'too far-reaching promises of liberation', promoted excitement among the masses, who were led by 'demagogues', 'fanatical religious preachers' and also by a few of the more 'desperate' representatives of the burghers. Among the latter we see, for example, a merchant who had secretly stored up stocks of powder and weapons in readiness for an uprising, and a ruined brewer who had become an apothecary, 'a restless man', who agitated for the line that 'it would be better not to leave one stone upon another than to submit to the Emperor'.[41]

Whereas the former city council of Magdeburg had been unanimously in favour of negotiating with the Imperialists, in the new council only a substantial section of the elected burghers were a little inclined that way. But the voice of these 'prudent' ones was drowned by the voices of the radical minority or, more correctly, by the voices of the lower orders who had helped to overthrow the old council and were now confident of the speedy arrival of the Swedish liberators. Wittich writes about this period:

Government was not in the hands of the council as such. Along with the executive board of the council, or together with it, the decisive voice belonged, in all matters, to a few resolute men, in so far as these persons addressed themselves directly to the 'common man', wielded strong propaganda influence over him and sought to make him their point of support. These were the leaders of the strictly Swedish party, above whom towered Falkenberg, the Swedish commandant of Magdeburg, and with him the other Swedish officials and officers; then the most determined members of the new council; some fanatical Lutheran preachers; and others, partly direct members of the lower classes, partly persons who had sunk to their level, bankrupt bigwigs from the town's population. It was quite understandable, and this had fatal significance, that in the conditions of socio-political ferment in Magdeburg there should have emerged from the dregs of the people various troublemakers (even the former council had complained,

41 Wittich, *Magdeburg*, Vol. I, pp. 34, 76–78.

long before it was swept away, about 'domination by the mob' in Magdeburg)
who tried, along with Falkenberg and in definite contradiction to the ruling
magistrates, to establish an ochlocracy [rule by the mob – B.F.P.], and politically
paralysed by their terrorism the more noble elements, who had at least a better
right to be in charge of affairs by virtue of their education and their property . . .
The mode of thought according to which 'Magdeburg should be destroyed rather
than surrendered to the Emperor' was undoubtedly typical of this entire category
of persons.[42]

In this way Wittich leads the reader to the conclusion that Magdeburg, at
the critical moment when it was stormed by the Imperialists, was
deliberately destroyed in accordance with a plan and an order from
Falkenberg, in fulfilment of the command not to surrender the city to the
enemy, and making use of the religious fanaticism and social division
among the Magdeburgers. Following Ranke,[43] Wittich compares at
length the fate of Magdeburg in 1631 with that of Moscow in 1812, and
Falkenberg with Rostopchin.[44]

The fallacy in Wittich's conception lies in the fact that, for him, the
Magdeburg masses, the crowd, are merely a weapon, an instrument, a
means in the hands of the heroic strong man Falkenberg, who dies
defending the city but causes it to die along with him. The link between
the 'individual' and the 'crowd' is, in this case, provided by fanatical
preachers from the ranks of the clergy and radical 'demagogues' from
among the burghers. But it is not difficult to take this pyramid standing
on its tip and put it right way up, using Wittich's own material.

Doubtless, when the siege of Magdeburg by the Imperial army began,
the external danger did not bring the population of Magdeburg closer
together but, on the contrary, as the sources show, led to extreme
embitterment of the struggle between the classes. The burghers, of
course, were at first hoping very much for Gustavus Adolphus to arrive
soon, for entry by the Imperialists meant a threat not only to their faith
but also to their possessions, whereas the Swedish army behaved
irreproachably. But the lower orders, too, put their hopes in the coming
of Gustavus Adolphus. And the longer his arrival was delayed, the fiercer
burned the passions of the plebeians, strengthening their hope in the
speedy arrival of 'the man sent from God', who would help to save the
true faith not only from the Catholics but also from its internal foes.
Faced with the activation of the plebeians, who were more and more
siding with the Swedes, the burghers, naturally, inclined more and more
towards the idea of an agreement with the Imperialists who would
establish 'order' in the city, but, because of this, the plebeians attacked

[42] Ibid., p. 82.    [43] Ranke, *Geschichte Wallensteins*, p. 217.
[44] Wittich, *Magdeburg*, Vol. I, pp. 100–102.

the burghers with increasing ferocity. The urban poor marched with such slogans as 'better to give up your body and your life, your blood and your goods, than to take the path of agreement with the enemy'. They were ecstatically devoted to the far-off Swedish King. Rumours of Gustavus Adolphus's approach inflamed the class struggle, as the burghers were now afraid that this might result in triumph for the 'mob', and they worked the more actively for surrender.

Gustavus Adolphus knew, of course, about the situation in Magdeburg. Falkenberg himself, in his letters to the King, voiced insistently his distrust of the overwhelming majority of the burghers, referring to their inclination towards a deal with the Imperialists.[45] If Gustavus Adolphus had reached Magdeburg at that moment and freed it from the agonising siege, he would, willy-nilly, have found himself allied not with the burghers, as he would have wished, but with the 'mob', a possibility highly unattractive to him. That was why, perhaps even without the King realising this, the obstacles in the way of his march on Magdeburg became, in his view, increasingly insurmountable.

The moment when the Imperialists made their decisive onslaught on Magdeburg was also the moment that saw the final explosion of class contradictions in the city. The burghers, says Wittich, 'sought safety in their houses and places of refuge'. From whom? This author's subsequent words make one think that it was not so much from the Imperialists as from the lower orders of Magdeburg whom they had infuriated. Among the common people, he says, 'it was easy to find persons who hated the well-to-do, because they were inclined towards moderation and agreement with those outside the walls, no less than they hated their external foes, and who wanted to doom both equally to destruction and death'. Thus hatred by the poor for the rich made it very easy for the former to 'discover' among the latter 'pro-Imperialist sentiments'. The preachers and radicals exploited this circumstance: 'There is nothing surprising in the fact that the "common man", who had little or nothing to counter these preachings, was soon disposed to call the upper classes "Imperialist scoundrels". . . whose houses ought to be stormed and whose necks should be wrung [as one source has it – B.F.P.]'. 'There is nothing surprising either', Wittich goes on, 'in the fact that this threat was put into effect at the moment when the Imperialists were bursting into the city . . . There is nothing surprising in the fact that their houses fell in upon the citizens who were condemned by the "common people" and hated by them just as they hated the enemy.'[46]

That is what it is really important to know in the history of the fall of

---

[45] Ibid., p. 91.     [46] Ibid., pp. 113–116.

Magdeburg. Whether the fires and explosion resulted from premeditated orders by Falkenberg, whether the wind spread fires across the city, or whether the conflagration started from buildings set on fire by order of the Imperial General Pappenheim is, ultimately, not so important. And it is impossible not to take notice of one of Wittich's arguments: among the smoking ruins of this great rich city, now utterly destroyed, what were saved from the fire were the hovels of the poor – the 'ship-folk' and the fishermen, and also representatives of the 'outcasts', the knackers (*Schinder*) and hangmen (*Diebhenker*).[47]

Immediately after the fall of Magdeburg Gustavus Adolphus endeavoured to divert blame from himself and retain the goodwill of advanced public opinion in Germany. He published a special *Apologia* explaining, with many reasons, why he had not got to Magdeburg, but made no mention of the main cause. He even managed to use this disaster in order to put all the responsibility for it on the Electors of Brandenburg and Saxony and thereby to obtain a moral-political trump card with which to press them hard, as though taking revenge for their having prevented him from marching through their territory and bringing help in time to beleaguered Magdeburg.

In this way Gustavus Adolphus kept his position on the razor's edge: he had not helped any popular-revolutionary actions, yet he retained the sympathy of the revolutionary elements without whom he would have been helpless. After his victory at Breitenfeld the story soon took root that Magdeburg had been burned not by its inhabitants but by the Imperialists, and that Gustavus Adolphus had warmly sympathised with the Magdeburgers during the siege.

Objectively, Gustavus Adolphus's betrayal of Magdeburg was the betrayal of the potential centre of the whole urban, i.e., burgher–plebeian, movement in Germany and, consequently, an irreparable blow to what, even without such a blow, was not the strong side of the social movement as a whole.

It is extremely characteristic that the only ally whom Gustavus Adolphus found among the German princes at this stage, Wilhelm V, Landgrave of Hesse-Cassel, was something of a white blackbird among the princes. By force of complex circumstances he became the political leader of his peasants, who were embittered against the gentry and against the Imperialists. Throughout the Thirty Years' War Hesse was almost the principal arena of the peasant movement and 'the war between the peasants and the soldiers'. It was from Hesse that came Grimmelshausen and his *Simplicissimus*.

[47] Ibid., p. 103.

All this has, unfortunately, been much obscured by German historians, and needs further specialist research of a serious kind, if even a minimum of Marxist order is to be brought into it. In his *Chronological Extracts* Marx paid particular attention to the political history of Hesse in the time of the Thirty Years' War. Basing himself on Schlosser, who in turn relied on von Rommel's *History of Hesse*, Marx noted the very special position in which Wilhelm's father Maurice had found himself during the 'Bohemian' and 'Danish' periods of the Thirty Years' War.[48] The Landgrave of Hesse-Darmstadt,[49] who laid claim to Maurice's territory, made contact with the Imperial commanders and also with the gentry of Hesse-Cassel. More precisely, the gentry of Hesse-Cassel invited, apparently through his mediation, the Imperialist and Catholic hordes of Tilly and Wallenstein to come into their territory because they were unable to cope on their own with their rebellious peasants. Landgrave Maurice opposed this combination not out of love for the peasants but because it was depriving him of his hereditary possessions. Finding himself, however, in conflict with his own gentry, he was forced to assume the role of defender of the peasants. When Wallenstein arrived in Hesse in the wake of his troops and learnt that Maurice was refusing to rob his subjects, through his officials, for the benefit of Wallenstein's soldiers, he authorised his men to take from the country everything they could lay hands on, even to seize the harvest for themselves. The gentry of Hesse, on the other hand, were freed from any form of contribution or military service. Furthermore, so as not to deprive the more 'noble' section of the Hessian gentry of income from their estates and villages, a sort of cynical 'division' of the population was carried out. About a quarter of Hessian subjects, evidently those who bore feudal oppression most submissively, were exempted from the heaviest burdens of war and the soldiers' caprices, while the remaining three-quarters were sacrificed to the unbridled soldiery.

However, the domineering rule of the Imperialist–Catholic troops, instead of subduing the Hessian peasants, gave a fresh impetus to their struggle. As soon as Tilly, in 1626, withdrew the main part of his forces from Hesse, a great peasant revolt broke out there. We are told by the chronicler Latomus, author of one of the 'flysheets' which were published in great numbers during the war, in this case being devoted to the revolt in Upper Austria in 1626, 'after General Tilly had withdrawn most of his infantry, the peasants in Hesse rose in revolt and drove out and killed those soldiers who still remained in some of the towns. Later they began to go from one noblemen's estate to another, plundering

[48] *Arkhiv Marksa i Engel'sa*, Vol. VIII, Moscow, 1946, pp. 204–205.
[49] Hesse was divided into two Landgravates, Hesse-Cassel and Hesse-Darmstadt.

them.'[50] Our information concerning this peasant revolt is very meagre. Another contemporary gives us an even briefer report: 'many peasants revolted in Hesse; they plundered five noblemen's estates, set one on fire, and killed soldiers'.[51]

At first Landgrave Maurice set his hopes on Christian IV of Denmark, but after that King's defeat, the peasants' risings and further cruelties and devastations committed by the Imperialists in Hesse, in 1627 he abdicated in favour of his son, Wilhelm V. He, too, however, was unable to find any alternative to forming a sort of bloc with the peasants. He succeeded in 1627–1631 in preserving only a small part of his territory from the Imperialist forces and the Landgrave of Hesse-Darmstadt. He was even quite impoverished. His last hope of salvation lay in calling for the help of the Swedish King, offering in exchange to provide an army, eager for battle, made up of Hessian peasant volunteers who were ready to perceive the hard-done-by Landgrave as their defender, and the Swedish conqueror as the man sent from God, the Messiah.

Wilhelm V's dealings with Gustavus Adolphus began as early as 1629. In October 1630 a representative of his had talks with the King in Stralsund. In April 1631 Wilhelm V openly asked that Hesse be cleared of Tilly's Catholic-League troops, and sent forward an army 'which was soon reinforced when its ranks were joined by many retired soldiers and peasants embittered against the enemy, who were soon transformed into fighting men'.[52] All the gentry of Hesse opposed him.[53] Tilly moved on Hesse with his main forces in July 1631, threatening frightful punishment if the Landgrave did not surrender at once and dissolve his peasant host. But he was unable to put his threats into effect, because Gustavus Adolphus's warlike preparations obliged him urgently to change his direction of march. This saved the Landgrave of Hesse-Cassel from the intentions of the Emperor and Tilly to 'swallow' him once and for all. *De facto* mutual aid between Gustavus Adolphus and Wilhelm's 'peasant army' had thus already happened. Yet the King put off by every means the formalising of this alliance. In August 1631 the Landgrave came personally to Gustavus Adolphus's camp at Werben to ask for help, 'because he did not feel strong enough to withstand the onslaught of the Imperial army'. This time the King concluded a defensive and offensive alliance with him as commander of the Upper-Rhine Circle and also gave the Landgrave to escort him back to Hesse and thereafter serve under his

[50] Latomus, S., *Eygentlicher und wahrhaftiger Bericht von der Bauernschaft in Oberösterreich*, Frankfurt-am-Main, 1626, p. 11.
[51] Bellus, N., *Österreichischer Lörbeerkranz*, Frankfurt-am-Main, 1627, p. 947
[52] Schlosser, *Vsemirnaia istoriia*, Vol. XIV, 1867, p. 338; cf. *Arkhiv Marksa i Engel'sa*, Vol. VIII, p. 206.
[53] Schlosser, *Vsemirnaia istoriia*, Vol. XIV, p. 338.

command, two regiments from his army and money with which to pay mercenaries. Furious, Tilly sent, to cut him off, a courier with an appeal to his allies, 'to the nobility and estates of Hesse', calling on them not to admit Wilhelm V, an open enemy of the Emperor, 'or otherwise they will make themselves accomplices in his crimes and will bring down on their heads a storm that will crush them and all their posterity'.[54] But the gentry of Hesse did not dare to resist their Landgrave, who now had with him both his own and Swedish troops, while they were unarmed and Tilly was far away, having to fight the Swedish King. Perhaps the Hessian gentry surmised that Gustavus Adolphus would, eventually, curb their peasants no less effectively than Wallenstein or Tilly, and, meanwhile, the peasants' activity could be entirely diverted from domestic class struggle into the channel of war against the Imperialist tormentors.

In order somewhat to make up for the inauspicious impression produced in German ruling circles by his alliance with the Landgrave of Hesse-Cassel, Gustavus Adolphus, having already a forcibly-concluded alliance with the Elector of Brandenburg, hastened to restore Mecklenburg to its expelled Duke and to make an alliance with the Elector of Saxony.[55] This political balance once achieved, he dared at last to face the decisive battle with Tilly's Imperialist army.

A great deal has been written about the battle of Breitenfeld by German and Swedish historians and military specialists. Very detailed plans of the battlefield have been drawn. The location not only of every regiment but almost of every soldier has been established.[56] Yet all this general-staff scholarship collapses like a house of cards when checked against the sources. It suffices to look at the artless account given by 'the Swedish soldier' to discover a totally neglected aspect of the question.

Among the inhabitants of Saxony, he tells us, before the battle of Breitenfeld, stories circulated about signs that had appeared presaging a frightful bloodletting for the enemies of the Christian Church: the waters in the rivers of Saxony were running blood red.[57] This means that an agitation was under way for the Imperialist and Catholic forces to be slaughtered. In fact, conflict with Tilly's soldiers began in Saxony a few days before Breitenfeld, when 200 villages[58] went up in flames, presumably as revenge for actions by the peasants. In other words, a *de facto* alliance

---

[54] *Le soldat suédois*, pp. 79–89 [pp. 50–61].

[55] These alliances have been analysed *supra*, in Chapter 2.

[56] For a summary of these materials see the publication by the Swedish General Staff, *Sveriges Krig 1611–1632*, Vol. IV, Stockholm, 1937, pp. 428–523. See also the Swedish work: Lundkvist, S., 'Slaget vid Breitenfeld 1631', *Historisk Tidskrift*, No. 1, Stockholm, 1963.

[57] *Le soldat suédois*, p. 114 [p. 78].

[58] *Arkhiv Marksa i Engel'sa*, Vol. VIII, p. 208.

against the common enemy which had been formed between the Saxon peasants' movement and the Swedish army forced Elector Johann-Georg to join this alliance out of fear. Also, the battle of Breitenfeld ended otherwise than as military historians have described. Gustavus Adolphus sent all his reserves in pursuit of the fleeing enemy, writes 'the Swedish soldier', and 'the Elector of Saxony also sounded the tocsin throughout the country for the Imperialists to be seized or struck down, and his peasants obeyed him loyally in that matter, having no need of many commands to encourage them. This greatly increased the numbers of the slain, so that not only was the battlefield covered with them, but also all the roads for twelve leagues round about.'[59]

This document can easily be subjected to historical criticism. We know that the Elector of Saxony fled in fear to Eilenburg without waiting for the outcome of the battle of Breitenfeld, so he cannot have given an order for pursuit of the enemy. This 'order' was obviously invented by the narrator so as somewhat to disguise what actually happened – the tocsin sounded throughout the country, the peasants rose and pursued the Imperialists. On the battlefield, writes 'the Swedish soldier' a little later, 'Tilly left 8,000 of his men, not counting the great many who were struck down by the country people as they fled.' Pappenheim said, a few days after the battle, that 18,000 men had been killed as they ran from the battlefield.[60] Even if some of these were cut down by the Swedish cavalry who chased them, it still follows, beyond doubt, that more Imperialists were slaughtered in this 'peasant massacre' after the battle than fell in the battle itself. In the light of these facts the usual notion of the character of the battle is subject to doubt. The battle of Breitenfeld was especially famous for the fact that the Swedes lost no more than 700 men in it. But perhaps this colossal difference is to be explained not so much by the superior quality of the Swedish army (which never subsequently showed itself in the terms of such a coefficient) as by participation in the battle by irregular peasant forces.

One way or another, the battle of Breitenfeld, which is acknowledged to be the most important battle of the Thirty Years' War, has, we see, an aspect which has been totally ignored by historians.

Gustavus Adolphus thought that this battle, which he had put off for so long, would decide the outcome of the entire war. In a speech to his army before the battle, he said 'that he had travelled 200 leagues in order to see this day . . . That a few hours would decide the dispute of many years.' After the victory the further prospect was presented by the King as merely a finishing-off, just the tracking down of the fugitive, defeated

---

[59] *Le soldat suédois*, p. 109 [pp. 74–75].    [60] Ibid., pp. 111–112 [p. 76].

Tilly, 'that old Corporal, to the end of the world'.[61] Historians have long concerned themselves with the question why Gustavus Adolphus went on with the war after Breitenfeld, since he had already achieved Sweden's basic aims. All the territory of North-Eastern Germany lying beside the Baltic had been conquered or placed under Swedish control, the Emperor's flag had been swept from the Baltic sea, and no Catholic army threatened the Swedish conquests.[62] And, indeed, all that followed cannot be treated from the angle of *Swedish* history: the policy of the Swedish oligarchy of nobles and merchants, the policy in the spirit of Chancellor Axel Oxenstjerna, had been fully acccomplished. It was the logic of *German* history, of the class struggle in Germany, that led Gustavus Adolphus on further.

A number of German historians have also discussed this problem: why, after the victory, did Gustavus Adolphus not proceed at once to the Emperor's hereditary domains, i.e., to Bohemia and Austria, which lay immediately to the south of Saxony, where he was, but, instead, to the Rhine, to Western Germany, i.e., avoiding the Habsburgs' family realm? It is quite clear that, after Breitenfeld, he was pursuing not the purely military aim of routing the enemy, but a political aim – a search for allies.[63] But bourgeois historians do not understand, and do not want to understand, that Gustavus Adolphus had to choose between two allies: between the peasants, who were ready to see him as their liberator and saviour, and the princes, whose attitude towards him was extremely guarded.

To march into Bohemia and Austria, where in 1626–1627 peasant wars had blazed and where everything was ready for the struggle to be renewed, meant choosing the former of the two possible allies. The experience of the previous year showed all too plainly that such an alliance arose independently of the will and desire of the Swedish King and despite all his manoeuvres. In Thuringia and Franconia, however, the peasant movement was incomparably weaker. To be sure, even in those regions things were far from quiet. Peasant movements had broken out here and there, in previous years. Nevertheless this was very far from being anything like what had happened in Bohemia and Austria. Gustavus Adolphus may also have considered that entering territory that was inhabited by Catholics would entail the risk of distrust of a Protestant King by the peasant masses, at least unless he himself showed willingness for a *rapprochement* with them. Here Gustavus Adolphus could count a

---

[61] Ibid., pp. 101, 109 [pp. 69, 75].

[62] Paul, J., *Gustav Adolf*, Vol. III: *Von Breitenfeld bis Lützen*, Leipzig, 1932, p. 7.

[63] Wittrock, G., 'Gustav II Adolf', in *Sveriges historia till våra dagar, utgiven av E. Hildebrand och L. Stavenow*, 6 Vols., Stockholm, 1927, p. 364.

little on winning the trust and goodwill of the princes and the estates. To Bohemia, in this disappointing all the expectations of the émigré Czech nobles and also, as we shall see, of the Czech people, he decided to send his newly made ally the Elector of Saxony, a very typical bearer of the princely reactionary spirit – let him sort things out with what revolutionary allies he might obtain, willy-nilly, down there. Meanwhile, Gustavus Adolphus himself would win allies of the opposite kind.

This was, of course, an ostrich-like policy. Gustavus Adolphus could not escape anywhere in Germany from the revolutionary forces which, ultimately, had given him his first decisive victories. The future was to show that the Swedish King could indeed not evade this fateful problem but could only for a time put off his choice of direction for his military advance and political line after Breitenfeld.

Directly after the battle he addressed an appeal to all the states, princes and cities of the Empire – but not to the people! – calling on them to render no aid to his enemies and promising 'liberty and peace to Germany'. On arriving at Erfurt Gustavus Adolphus issued a reassuring proclamation, referring to the example offered by his good relations with the Electors of Saxony and Brandenburg and promising equal treatment of Catholics and Evangelicals. The edict issued by the King at Würzburg (26 October 1631) again strikes one by its orientation exclusively on the princes and estates who had been offended by the Emperor. Even the atrocities committed by the Imperialists on the population of Saxony, mentioned in the edict, are condemned only as violations of the 'constitution' of the Empire. Here too Gustavus Adolphus refers to the promise he had given to France that he would be as friendly as possible to the princes who were members of the Catholic League. He was waging war only against the Emperor, not against the Empire and its established structure. As though to confirm this thesis in practice, Gustavus Adolphus concerned himself meticulously, on the way, with petty administrative questions, rights of municipalities and so on, without carrying out even the slightest serious reforms. Moreover, he very conspicuously combated armed peasants whenever he encountered them, in this white-hot period of 'war between peasants and soldiers'. But here what matters to us is not that façade shown to the princes which was what Gustavus Adolphus's triumphal march from Saxony to the Rhine amounted to, but something much more fundamental, though usually left in the dark, namely, the Swedo–Saxon army's campaign in Bohemia.

Entrusting this expedition – from Saxony through Lusatia into Bohemia and Silesia – to the Elector of Saxony meant, from the outset, betraying the popular movement which spontaneously rose up to meet the Swedes. Johann-Georg was a sworn enemy of that movement. He was too much afraid of it at home in Saxony. It was typical that, as soon as Gustavus Adolphus had left the area where the battle of Breitenfeld was fought, the Elector not only released the besieged Imperialists from Leipzig, but took most of them into his army. These were men of whom 'the Swedish soldier' writes: 'Among others captured were the commissary Valmerode and many other such vultures in various places who had extorted and plundered all over the country, squeezing huge contributions out of the people.'[64] These experienced monsters were not merely saved from death by the Elector of Saxony but were included in his army. He wanted no further upsurge of the struggle of the Saxon peasants but, on the contrary, sought to curb and suppress that brief outburst which the Swedes had promoted. With this began a whole series of betrayals of the Swedes by him, culminating in the Peace of Prague in 1635.

The commanders of the Imperial armed forces studied both the military plan and the political sentiments of their opponent. The Imperialist generals Götz and Tiefenbach, who were covering the road into Bohemia, carried out a counter-action. They invaded Lusatia, devastating the countryside, towns and villages and then, committing dreadful atrocities, broke into Saxony. The Elector did not hesitate over the dilemma whether to stir up his peasants against the Imperialists or to let the Imperialists suppress and tyrannise over them. He preferred the latter choice and willingly let himself be persuaded to 'pardon Tilly's offences' by the plenipotentiary sent to him by the Emperor and the King of Spain. They were unable, though, to persuade him openly to betray Gustavus Adolphus. The victor of Breitenfeld was still close by, he might turn round and start all over again, so there was nothing for the Elector to do but to honour his obligations and proceed with the Saxon army through Lusatia to Prague. The government in Vienna understood this and, apparently not without some influence from Wallenstein, who was manoeuvring between the two camps, came to a deal which was obvious to all contemporaries. Götz and Tiefenbach were ordered not only to retreat from Saxony but also to 'cleanse' Lusatia, leaving it at the disposal of the Saxons. What was taking place here was a sort of class-political collaboration, a kind of mutual aid by the 'adversaries' against a common foe. The Saxon Elector could not fail to be afraid that uprisings by the restless Lusatian peasants would endanger his men and threaten his communications when he advanced further, so the forces of Götz and Tiefenbach, as they withdrew, 'cleansed' Lusatia and so prevented that danger from emerging. 'They made their withdrawal felt by the poor inhabitants, by their devastations and extortions, driving

---

[64] *Le soldat suédois*, p. 111 [p. 76].

away all the cattle and everywhere leaving grievous signs of their passage.'[65]

But Lusatia was only a transit area. The problem of Bohemia was incomparably more complex. A 'mutual understanding' between Saxon and Imperial policy can also be observed where Bohemia was concerned. Wallenstein entered into direct dealings with the Elector and his commander-in-chief, Arnim. On the one hand, Wallenstein, deeply angry with the Emperor because of his dismissal, and living in Bohemia as its uncrowned ruler, informed Gustavus Adolphus that, while seeking nothing for himself, he was ready, along with him, to overthrow the Austro–Spanish dynasty and exile Ferdinand II to somewhere in Italy. He even put forward a concrete plan for joint military action. On the other hand, it was not out of the question that a deal could be struck between Vienna and the Elector of Saxony if only Wallenstein and Arnim could succeed in detaching him from his alliance with Gustavus Adolphus. But these were all unreal plans, since the Elector, arriving with his army as liberator, at the frontier of Bohemia, was already no longer master of events as they developed, and lacked the power to direct them as he intended. He found himself in Bohemia in the same situation as Gustavus Adolphus had been when he was in North-Eastern Germany. The slightest, even merely symbolic, actions against the Imperialists were enough to unleash the popular forces.

We need to go back a few years if we are to appreciate what those forces were.

Bourgeois historians traditionally reiterate the idea that the Czech peasants took no part in the struggle in 1618–1620 and so helped to cause the loss of Bohemia's national independence. The facts, however, tell the opposite story. In the summer of 1620, not long before the battle of the White Mountain, several thousand Czech serf-peasants assembled on the outskirts of Tabor. They demanded that they be freed from bondage and that the outrages committed by the soldiers be stopped.[66] Bohemia was undone not by the peasants but by the gentry who, at the critical moment, refused to abolish serfdom when a peasant movement was flaring up.

Historiographical tradition has made so much of the catastrophe at the White Mountain that the idea is widespread that, after the battle, Czech resistance to the Habsburg–Catholic feudal-reactionary onslaught came to an end. In fact it went on increasing right up to 1632.

During the 1620s the rising struggle of the Czech people was directed against four principal forms of oppression. First, against serfdom, which was intensified further by a largely new set of landlords. Second, against

[65] Ibid., p. 153 [p. 104].
[66] Arlanibaeus, Ph., *Theatrum Europaeum*, Vol. I, Frankfurt-am-Main, 1679, p. 353; Khevenhüller, F. C., *Annales Ferdinandei*, Vol. IX, Leipzig, 1724, p. 1002.

the burden of taxes. Third, against military garrisons and guard-posts, the most immediate expression of foreign domination. Fourth, against Catholic reaction and religious persecution. The last point, concerning religion, occludes all the rest, to an exaggerated extent, though it was certainly very important. The fight to maintain their faith, in the face of Catholic missionaries and Jesuits who employed every method in order to 'convert' the Czechs to Catholicism, became indeed, in no small measure, the banner of resistance by the Czech people to their oppressors.

Those nobles and citizens who did not wish to accept Catholicism could emigrate. The peasants were tied to their fields by need and to their lords by serfdom. On the spot, in the heart of Bohemia, a stubborn day-to-day struggle was waged, costing the lives of many oppressors and missionaries. Sometimes peasants would 'convert' to Catholicism with ostentatious ease, so as secretly to preserve their old faith, sometimes they were forced by harsh coercion, troops being called in to put down their resistance. At Netvorice near Prague, over several years the peasants resisted the missionaries, hiding from them in the woods. Battues were organised to round them up and eventually their flocks and herds were seized, whereupon, armed with pitchforks and stakes, they burst into the town and slaughtered their own animals. Paul Michna himself, one of the largest of the new landlords of Bohemia after Wallenstein, arrived with substantial forces and by a bloody repression completed the 'conversion'. At Rozmital, in order to discover who were the instigators of resistance, some of the peasants were thrown into prison, and the rest fled into the forest. 'Never mind', the Jesuit Kotschel said, reassuringly, 'let us wait for winter: the frost will force them to return home, and then we'll catch them!'

Particularly strong resistance was put up by the peasants in the East and North-East of Bohemia. On the border with Lusatia it proved impossible to convert them to Catholicism until the middle of the century. Wallenstein, whose principal estates lay in North Bohemia, around Jicin and Friedland, despite thousands of tricks played by the Jesuits whom he invited there – spectacles, wonders, and so on – and despite arrest and breaking on the wheel for those peasants caught attending Evangelical meetings, despite the outrages committed by his soldiers, succeeded only in causing many of his villages to be half depopulated, while accomplishing hardly any conversions. Visionaries and prophets appeared among the people. Their theme was: it cannot be that God has abandoned his people, He is simply testing their loyalty and steadfastness.

There were many cases of armed rebellion by the peasants in the Czech lands, against the landlords, the tax collectors and the military garrisons. Denis writes of the 'long and monotonous history of these serf revolts'.[67] The unbearable burden of feudal-serf exploitation and the extortion of taxes, which was often effected by threats to burn the peasants' homes, resulted all through the 1620s in ever-renewed risings.

Immediately after the battle of the White Mountain the threat of a peasant revolt began to grow so obvious that the Emperor had to maintain garrisons in Bohemia. Already in December 1620 the Emperor's governor of Bohemia, Prince Liechtenstein, reported to him that there were peasant disturbances in the Rakowec area and other places. In May 1621 the Imperialist soldiers on the Lanskroun estate asked for help against a force of about a thousand peasants. At the same time there were reports of peasant risings in the country round Hradec. In June 1621 the village headman reported to Prague that in the neighbourhood of Velvary the peasants had killed a number of the Emperor's soldiers. In 1620–1621, during the revolt of the Valasi people, hundreds of peasants fell in battle against the troops of Cardinal Dietrichstein. Subsequently the 'Valasi territory' long remained one of the principal areas of popular anti-feudal activity.[68]

In 1623 several thousand peasants, headed by a knight who had suffered from the confiscations, went into action against the feudal–Catholic forces in the Krivolat forests and tried to drive the Germans out of Krivolat, but were beaten.[69] In that year the peasants were so restive that, fearing an all-Bohemia revolt (since 'they did not trust the peasants and feared a rising', says Gindely), the government in Vienna put Imperialist troops into many Bohemian towns.[70] This measure proved, however, to be double-edged. The guard-posts and levies so kindled the anger of the Czechs that in 1624, at the special request of the governor, Liechtenstein, the soldiers were withdrawn from most of the cities and towns of Bohemia.[71] But that, in turn, facilitated a new upsurge of popular struggle. In 1625 there was a whole wave of serious peasant movements. In the Kourim district several thousand peasants successfully besieged and captured Kourim town, then advanced into the Hradec region, captured several castles there, killed noblemen and, in general, says Pelzel, 'raged just like the Taborites in former times'.[72]

A rebellion of many villages occurred on Von Wartenberg's estate: the peasants put forward their demands, then laid siege to his castle, smashed down the gates and, bursting in, killed both him and his wife.

[67] Denis, E., *La Bohême depuis la Montagne Blanche*, Vol. I, Paris, 1903, p. 95.
[68] *Istoriia Chekhoslovakii*, Vol. I, Moscow, 1956, p. 264.
[69] Khevenhüller, *Annales*, Vol. IX, p. 742. [Page 742 covers 1619, and the whole volume goes up only to 1622. Vol. X deals with 1623, but its p. 742 covers events in 1625. This reference is inaccurate, therefore – Trans.]
[70] Gindely, A., *Geschichte der Gegenreformation in Böhmen*, Leipzig, 1894, p. 373.
[71] Ibid., p. 376.
[72] Pelzel, F. M., *Geschichte der Böhmen*, Vol. II, Prague, 1782, p. 751.

Almost simultaneously with the movement in Kourim a revolt began in North Bohemia, on Wallenstein's estates, in the area of Friedland and Liberec. Hardly had they been put down when 600 peasants rose in the Nove Mesto area and on the property of the Jesuit college in Litomerice district.[73] These events greatly alarmed Wallenstein. At that moment there were not many troops in Bohemia, but the towns could not be left without garrisons, so, by order of the Emperor, additional forces were again sent in. They suppressed the peasant movements, including those on Wallenstein's land.[74]

But in 1626 peasant risings had not ceased in Bohemia. This is apparently to be explained by co-operation with the peasant war that was developing at that time in Upper Austria. On the one hand, the Bohemian movement had a revolutionary effect on the Austrian peasantry. Already at the beginning of the Upper Austrian troubles, Ranpeck, the secretary of Maximilian of Bavaria, had written to his master about the dangerousness of this movement, especially because 'the peasants of Upper Austria have the idea of linking up with the Bohemian peasants and rebels, and munitions are being received from there'.[75] Count Martinitz was convinced that the Upper Austrian peasants had an agreement with the Bohemians.[76] There is no doubt that many of the Czech peasants who had been beaten in 1625 crossed the border to fight under the banner of the Austrian peasants' leader Stefan Fadinger.

On the other hand, the Upper Austrian rising affected, in its turn, a new upsurge of struggle in Bohemia. In July 1626 a number of preachers were arrested there who were calling on the peasants to rise and who had already succeeded in assembling several hundred armed peasants. At that time Ranpeck wrote to Khevenhüller: 'There is bad news about the peasants in Bohemia and the Palatinate: they too are preparing to rise in great numbers . . . If the *Oberennser* [Upper Austrian – B. F. P.] peasants succeed we can expect, without any doubt, that revolt will begin.'[77] Several sources testify to the ferment, the 'rebel propaganda' among the Bohemian peasants and the revolts that broke out, now here, now there: 'Not only in one place', says Carafa, 'but also near Kuttenberg [Kutna Hora], and on the border with Saxony threatening signs were already appearing. In one place the revolt was still clandestine, in another it blazed up openly'.[78] Major peasant disturbances occurred in 1627. We

[73] Svatek, J., *Die Bauernrebellionen*, Vienna, 1879, pp. 166–167.
[74] Gindely, *Geschichte*, pp. 405–409.
[75] Czerny, A., *Bilder aus der Zeit der Bauernunruhen in Oberösterreich, 1626, 1632, 1648*, Linz, 1876, p. 53.
[76] Gindely, *Geschichte*, p. 409.    [77] Czerny, *Bilder*, pp. 81–82.
[78] Carafa, C., *Commentarii de Germania sacra restaurata*, Cologne, 1639, p. 256.

know of a revolt in the lordship of Konopiste, on the estate of Count Michna. From there the trouble spread to his possessions in the Caslav and Kourim areas. The peasants, who here numbered 8,000, seized a small town, some monasteries and some castles, including Michna's own, and he himself had a narrow escape. The peasants carried the heads of the lords before them, on stakes. During these disturbances a clergyman named Matous Ulicky called on the peasants to follow the example of the Czechs of olden days, meaning the fifteenth century, and deal with the Papists 'in Zizka's way'. This revolt was put down by the troops who had been brought in and its leaders were quartered.[79] On Wallenstein's lands there were disturbances at the Jesuits' estate at Ticin. The entire north-eastern part of Bohemia, where Wallenstein's lands were spread out, was gripped by revolt, right up to Friedland itself.[80]

Repression could not break the will of the Czech people. In 1628 the curve of the peasants' struggle in Bohemia rose even higher. A huge revolt blazed up in the Hradec region, where about 4,000 peasants rebelled on the Opocno and Trckovsko estates. They destroyed estates and castles and captured the town of Nove Mesto. The peasants of Opocno tried to act in combination with those of Moravia and Silesia.[81] This revolt was put down by specially summoned troops. Five hundred peasants fell in battle, while those who were taken prisoner were brought to Prague, where their noses were cut off and their backs branded.

In the following year, 1629, the inhabitants of Rovensko began a movement when a certain Jesuit called in soldiers to convert them. Roused by the tocsin, the peasants of the neighbourhood forced the troops to withdraw, and they lynched the Jesuit. The rebels, whose numbers quickly grew, marched on Turnov, where they inspired such terror that Wallenstein himself fled to Prague. Unable to force the town's walls, the rebels nevertheless refused to heed threats and refused to retreat. 'What we have begun we shall not give up', they said. 'We are fighting for freedom!' Eventually they were defeated in battle, many died, and their leaders were broken on the wheel.[82] In 1630 the peasants' guerilla war in Bohemia assumed a still more permanent character, especially in the Riesengebirge [Krkonose] and the Erzgebirge. The rising lasted a whole year, and not only in these mountains but in other places as well.[83]

All these facts, which unfortunately are far from exhaustive, testify to the steady rise of the revolutionary upsurge in Bohemia. They enable us

---

[79] Gindely, *Geschichte*, p. 412; *Istoriia Chekhoslovakii*, Vol. I, p. 264.
[80] Pescheck, C. A., *Die Geschichte der Gegenreformation in Böhmen*, Vol. II, Leipzig, 1843, p. 305.     [81] *Istoriia Chekhoslovakii*, Vol. I, p. 264.
[82] Denis, *La Bohême*, pp. 95–96.     [83] Ibid., p. 144.

to imagine the condition of the masses in Bohemia at the moment when the Saxon army entered. Thousands of peasants had hidden in the forests, while others were fighting, arms in hand. Struggle was going on in the towns as well. In Prague alone several hundred preachers who were accused of inciting the people against the Emperor and the Church had hidden themselves in the vaults of the White Bastion. 'With every movement beyond the frontier a thrill of joy aroused people's spirits and the governors feared an uprising.'[84] When Gustavus Adolphus appeared on the political horizon all the oppressed hailed in him the long-awaited man sent from God, the liberator and avenger. The King himself, immediately on landing in Germany, ordered that communication be established with the 'faithful Bohemians'. At that time he did not realise to whom he was appealing. If he himself had entered Bohemia with his army, he would not have met any forces that could oppose him – they were hardly in a position to fight. 'It would have been enough, seemingly,' says Denis, 'in order to unite, in a unanimous effort at salvation, this people whose conscience had been outraged, whose heart has been trampled on and whose vital interests had been damaged, to raise the banner of Hus and Zizka.'[85]

But that was the problem, that neither the Saxon Elector and his commander-in-chief, Arnim, nor the Bohemian aristocrats at their headquarters – Thurn, Bubna, Kinsky, Trcka and the rest – nor those wider circles of the Protestant noble-and-bourgeois émigrés, who had concentrated several regiments of volunteers on the borders of Bohemia, were in any circumstances going to raise the banner of Hus and Zizka, the banner of popular anti-feudal struggle. No, they thirsted to extinguish the blazing flame of that struggle. In Denis's view, the Elector and Arnim decided to send their army into Bohemia as 'a measure of conservation' – as the best way of maintaining the purely political character of the war and not letting it become social-revolutionary.[86] Only two months were needed for this to become obvious. It can be confidently affirmed that the entry of the Swedo–Saxon army into Bohemia acted as a signal for a real revolt for popular liberation. How much, for example, is said in the few words written about this by 'the Swedish soldier': 'the peasants of Bohemia, seeing that they were supported by the Saxons, rose up in several places against the Emperor's men who had oppressed and bullied them for so long. All of these whom they caught paid for themselves and for their comrades.'[87] In 1631 important peasant risings took place in the Zatec, Slanec, Litomerice and Hradec regions, where many castles and

---

[84] Ibid., p. 95.   [85] Ibid., p. 144.
[86] Ibid., p. 142.   [87] Le soldat suédois, pp. 176–177 [p. 120].

202 Muscovy and Sweden in the Thirty Years' War

fortresses of the new landlords and many Catholic monasteries were demolished.[88]

In the towns, too, risings greeted the liberators. The town of Eger (Chleb), for example, was taken by the Saxons thanks to a rising of the citizens, who broke open the gates and admitted the besieging army.[89] Typical were the events which took place in Prague when, in November 1631, the Saxon army approached its walls. Wallenstein was there, with Martinitz, Harrach, Maradas, the commander-in-chief of the armed forces in Bohemia, Michna, the head of the Czech Catholic nobility and other leaders of the Imperial and Catholic party in Bohemia, and they prepared to defend the city, dispersing their troops and, for the first time since 1620, arming the citizens. The inhabitants were alarmed by the frightful excesses of the Saxons and also feared punishment if they showed cowardice in the defence. 'Yet', says 'the Swedish soldier', 'all this was insufficient to make the people of Prague submit to their masters' orders, whether it was fear of the enemy, impatience with the yoke they had borne for years, or hope of a better regime coming in that predominated in their thinking. In any case, they opposed to all the arguments of the Imperial officers their own weakness and that of the city' – excuses for refusing to defend Prague. The atmosphere which was created within the city's walls compelled Wallenstein and the other leaders hastily to quit the place with their troops and administrative officers. The inhabitants of Prague, says 'the Swedish soldier' disapprovingly, 'being left without head or bridle', asked the Saxon command to guarantee that no excesses by the soldiers would be allowed, and let into the city only a small part of the army, the rest having to go to Budejowice and Pilsen.

Exactly eleven years after its fall, Prague was free again. Old Count Thurn, leader of the anti-Habsburg movement of the Bohemian nobles in 1618–1620, who had come with the Elector of Saxony, was reinstalled in his castle, which had been seized by Count Michna. But the people of Prague evidently understood their liberation as not meaning merely restoration of the former, pre-war situation. Not in vain does 'the Swedish soldier' speak in the passage quoted above, about their 'hope of a better regime coming in'. There were some social movements of which our source speaks obscurely: 'With this change in the situation there was some murmuring and disturbance among the populace of Prague, who were still resentful of the treatment they had suffered in recent years. A number of bad characters wanted to attack the monasteries, more with a view to plundering them than for reasons of conscience' (as the author

---

[88] *Istoriia Chekhoslovakii*, Vol. I, p. 264.    [89] *Le soldat suédois*, p. 238 [p. 163].

points out to reassure his French readers), but the Saxons were able to 'establish order'.[90] As we see, the Saxons' role was ambiguous in the highest degree. They had succeeded only thanks to the Czechs' rebellions. 'They were helped by the country people', 'the Swedish soldier' relates, 'who drove the Imperial garrisons out of Postelberg, Ferit, Brustwald and Auguditz.' Many other towns 'surrendered without haggling'. 'This great facility which the Saxons met with everywhere'[91] was due, of course, to the mighty national-revolutionary upsurge of the Czech people. The Imperialists had to fight Czechs more than Saxons. Here, for example, is an episode from the story of how a raid by the Emperor's Croat cavalry was warded off:

These Croats, tireless at plundering, having set themselves to cross the river Moldau [Vltava] at a point seven leagues from Prague and ravage the neighbourhood of Pilsen, the peasants, alarmed, sounded the the tocsin, assembled to the number of 600, found means to hole the Croats' boats and chased them from every side, so that, finding themselves surrounded by local people who knew all the paths, they were mercilessly slaughtered ... But a few were able to tell the news of all this to their comrades.[92]

Sometimes the peasants' participation in the struggle was more clandestine, but it is not difficult to perceive features of guerilla war in this account, for example: '[Generals] Aldringer and Gallas were ordered to enter Bohemia from the Upper Palatinate in order to reassure those places that were still loyal to the Emperor, but they encountered insurmountable obstacles – the paths occupied, the woods cut down, and a shortage of victuals everywhere, so that they had to turn back.'[93]

All these are, of course, only isolated details. Historians have hitherto written incomparably more about the national catastrophe at the White Mountain in 1620 than about the remarkable *revanche* of 1631, which was prepared by the growth of the peasant movement in Bohemia in the 1620s. This is connected with the circumstance that it was short-lived. On the one hand the mobilisation of the forces of Imperialist and Catholic reaction, and, on the other, the betrayal by the Saxon command and the Bohemian émigrés soon ruined this brilliant success of the Czech people.

Nevertheless, in the book by Denis, for example, who approached these events in Czech history with a certain degree of conscientiousness and democratic sympathy, we find a few bright pages about them, even though they are, unfortunately, too much concerned with the religious aspect. Here are a few extracts.

[90] Ibid., pp. 173–176 [pp. 118–120].    [91] Ibid., p. 170 [p. 185].
[92] Ibid., p. 285 [pp. 195–196].    [93] *Le soldat suédois*, pp. 201–202 [p. 138].

As the Saxons advanced, all the towns had opened their gates without resistance. Arnim entered Prague on 20 November. The country was in complete anarchy. Everywhere the former masters were evicting the usurpers and the persecutors fleeing, pursued by their victims. The mob's fury was directed above all against the priests . . . Almost the entire North and North-East rose up, to the cry of 'Death to the Papists!' This movement spread right down into the south of Bohemia . . . On Slavata's estate the peasants attacked some Jesuits who had thought to find safe refuge there, and massacred them. In the neighbourhood of Budejowice, Klatovy and other places the Catholics were in very great danger . . . Military precautions were taken to safeguard Pilsen and Hradec Kralove [which were still in Imperialist hands – B.F.P.] from a coup by the rebels. The teeth of the governors who were at Budejowice [whither they had fled from Prague – B.F.P.] chattered, and 'in view of the revolt of the populace in many places', they begged to be allowed to return to Vienna. In the towns the poor people, whose unimportance had saved them [from conversion to Catholicism – B.F.P.] and who had been less decimated by emigration [than the upper classes – B.F.P.] called for re-establishment of the national religion. In Prague the Imperial authorities had hardly left when the mob of craftsmen and winegrowers from the neighbourhood swept through the city, breaking into the houses of suspects. As in the time of the priest John [Hus – B.F.P.] and Zizka, the democratic forces of town and country shook hands.

Subsequent events proved that here were serious factors of resistance. When, at the last moment, faced with the Imperialists' advance, the Saxon generals allowed the Bohemian lords to organise the defence for themselves, the peasants arrived by hundreds to rally round the representatives of the national nobility, and fought bravely. Many towns that were threatened by the army of the League refused to yield and obliged it to retreat. The old Hussite spirit was not yet dead and, from some standpoints, the moment would certainly have been much more favourable than in 1618 to unleash a real popular insurrection.

Of course, Denis goes on, it would not have been easy 'to transform these disorderly forces into a real army and to weld into an invincible will to liberation these tumultuous and momentary desires for vengeance. One word alone would have wrought that miracle – abolition of serfdom. Nobody thought of it.'

The author is right, of course, that neither the landlords who had emigrated and had returned with short-sighted aspirations, nor the Saxons, were able to tolerate a really liberating movement of the Czech masses. It would have been different, we will add, if Gustavus Adolphus's army had been in Bohemia, an army the core of which still consisted of men from a country where there was no serfdom. What, for them, would have been the sense of opposing an anti-serfdom movement? But the Czech émigrés and the Saxon conquerors were, though 'good Protestants' and enthusiasts for 'the national idea', also serfowners.

Denis goes on:

The historian Paul Skala, a very good Protestant, feels only terror and disgust at 'this mob from the outskirts, this populace from the fields'. Most of the émigrés shared these feelings, stunned as they were by all this uproar, and wounded in their delicacy by these furious acts of violence. They suffered the punishment of their offences: they had demanded exclusive privileges, disdained the mob, and now that it was this mob alone that could defend them they stammered as, frightened and disgusted, they stood before it.[94]

Vienna was extremely alarmed by the state of affairs in Bohemia. The main attention of the Austrian court was fixed upon the events there, not upon Gustavus Adolphus's triumphal march through Thuringia and Franconia to the Rhine. Where were they to find troops to subdue Bohemia?

Despite the return of Gallas's corps from Italy the Imperial army was weak and dispersed. Tilly and Pappenheim were tied up in various places by Gustavus Adolphus, his allies and generals. However, this 'military stroll', in which the King avoided major engagements, made it possible for part of the Imperial forces to be detached and sent to Bohemia. As we have seen, though, Gallas and Aldringer were not able even to enter Bohemia. In their search for armed forces, the Imperialist politicians turned their gaze towards Lorraine. The Lorraine army set out at the Emperor's call, intending, on the way, to trample down Hesse, which, as we recall, was one of the centres of the peasant movement. The social objective of the Lorrainers' campaign is indicated by the fact that in their atrocities they outdid all others: 'there was no sort of barbarity and excess which they failed to perpetrate even in friendly country, and on those whom they were supposed to be protecting, for they were not content to consume or carry off all they could, but also took pleasure in reducing to ashes and making useless whatever they were obliged to leave behind'.[95] However, Gustavus Adolphus beat the Lorrainers en route and they did not get to Bohemia. As we see, the Swedish King was still, even without wishing it, the ally of the revolutionary popular forces!

To suppress lost and rebellious Bohemia only one means was left – to ask Wallenstein to repeat the 'miracle' of creating almost from nothing a ferocious anti-popular Imperialist army. The Emperor, let us emphasise, humbled himself before Wallenstein and agreed to all his ultimatums, not owing to the military operations of Gustavus Adolphus but owing to the events that were taking place in Bohemia. This was obvious to contemporaries. 'The Swedish soldier' goes on, immediately after his words quoted above about the peasant uprisings in many parts of Bohemia: 'The Emperor's Council, seeing this storm break over Bohemia, considered that they could find no instrument more powerful than Wallenstein to counter it',[96] and so they turned to him, in his retirement, with the request that he again resume command of all the armed forces of

---

[94] Denis, *La Bohême*, pp. 146–148.     [95] *Le soldat suédois*, p. 232 [p. 159].
[96] Ibid., p. 177 [p. 120].

the Empire. All hopes were focused on Wallenstein not because he was a particularly outstanding commander – we know that throughout his political career he never won a single major battle[97] – but because he personified the regime of military dictatorship, the ruthless enforcement on the people of unrestrained coercion. Furthermore, Wallenstein's personal interest, since, after the White Mountain, he had become the biggest feudal landowner in Bohemia and Moravia, and had already, as we have seen, had experience of putting down the peasantry on his estates, required the liquidation at all costs of the successes of the Czech people, which threatened him with the loss of all his possessions.

In accordance with the conditions on which, after prolonged appeals by the Emperor's emissaries, Wallenstein at last agreed, in April 1632, to accept appointment as generalissimo of all the Imperial (and also the Spanish) forces, he required that as soon as Bohemia was conquered, a garrison of 12,000 men be installed in Prague, as being 'necessary to keep the Bohemians in obedience',[98] while the rest of his army could be used in other parts of the Empire.

When we have looked at the social background, the return of Wallenstein from disgrace, which is reduced by most bourgeois historians to a matter of intrigues and the personal characteristics of Wallenstein, the Emperor, various court personages, and so on, the reason thus becomes clear and all the tinsel falls away. In turn, the unprecedented 'humiliation' of the Emperor, obliged, by the capitulation concluded with Wallenstein, not only to grant all his demands but also to hand over some fundamental rights of governmental power, helps us to estimate the decisive importance of the social background for the history of the Thirty Years' War.

Here we must cut short our consideration of the socio-political situation in which Gustavus Adolphus fought his campaign. The events of the following year, 1632, would call for further investigation. We have examined only the opening of the drama. It reached its climax a few months later. Here it is enough to say that Gustavus Adolphus tried carefully to 'avoid' the popular movement which sprang up spontaneously to meet him. He gave thorough proof of his devotion to the interests of the princes and nobles, crushing the peasant movement in Bavaria, sending part of his army to effect a bloody repression of peasant risings in Franconia, Swabia and by Lake Constance. Eventually, when he approached Austria, the question faced him point-blank. To meet him, a

---

[97] Watson (see Watson, *Wallenstein*, p. 169) says that Wallenstein acquired the reputation, among soldiers, of invincibility but politicians called him a 'general without victories'. Watson justifies both opinions by the fact that Wallenstein was predominantly a master of defence and in that role never suffered defeat.

[98] *Le soldat suédois*, p. 245 [p. 168].

fresh revolt of the peasants of Upper Austria had broken out,[99] and he must choose between victory over the Emperor in alliance with these peasants or renunciation of his hope of winning the Imperial Crown. Formally, he accepted the alliance offered to him by the peasants' leaders, but in practice he betrayed them, by retreating and letting Wallenstein drown the revolt in blood. That pre-determined his downfall. Having undermined the trust of the princes and nobles which he had won with difficulty, but having failed to make use of the support offered him by the popular movement, Gustavus Adolphus now lacked any basis in the Empire, unless we allow for the beginnings of a 'gentlemen's' agreement with Wallenstein. The catastrophe culminated, after the King's death, in the rout of the Swedish interventionists at Nördlingen. Wallenstein, no longer needed now that the socio-political crisis was past, was removed from the scene.

[99] Czerny, *Bilder*; Samokhina, N. N., *Krestianskie vosstaniia v Verkhnei Avstrii v kontse XVI-seredine XVIIv.*, Moscow, 1952, pp. 547–567 (Dissertation).

# 5    Russia's 'Great Embassy' to Sweden in 1633: Death of the leaders, death of the alliance

The 'Great Embassy' from Moscow to Stockholm, headed by the Boyar B.I. Pushkin, was mentioned in passing in Chapter 3. However, it definitely calls for separate and very detailed analysis. Sources concerning the embassy have been preserved in both Russian and Swedish archive collections. They have been mentioned by G.V. Forsten,[1] O.L. Vainshtein[2] and A.A. Arzymatov.[3] Among Swedish authors, Wejle, Ahnlund, Paul, Norrman and others have made passing reference to them. The present writer's general conception concerning the development of Russo–Swedish relations was set forth at the XI International Congress of Historians held at Stockholm in 1960[4] and essentially the same view was expressed by his Swedish co-*rapporteur*, W. Tham.[5]

As the reader will recall, the so-called Smolensk War between multi-national Muscovy and the multi-national Polish–Lithuanian state proved to be inseparably linked with Sweden's war in Germany. The Russo–Swedish negotiations on a military-political alliance were going very well until the death of Gustavus Adolphus on 16 (6) November 1632. The embassy of B.I. Pushkin, G.I. Gorikhvostov and M.V. Neverov marked a turning-point that was tragic for both sides in the history of the conflict concerning the Russo–Swedish alliance. The tragedy is emphasised so to speak, by the fact that it was optimistically entitled in Moscow at the outset, with great optimism, the 'Great Embassy'.

The reader will recall that the embassy of Pushkin and his companions was prepared long before the news of Gustavus Adolphus's death was

[1] Forsten, G. V., *Baltiiskii vopros v XVI–XVII stoletiiakh*, Vol. II, St. Petersburg, 1894, pp. 435–441.

[2] Vainshtein, O. L., *Rossiia i Tridtsatiletniaia voina, 1618–1648gg.*, Moscow and Leningrad, 1947, pp. 137–145.

[3] Arzymatov, A. A., 'K voprosu o russko-shvedskikh otnosheniiakh v 1618–1648gg. (po materialam TsGADA', in the book *Skandinavskii sbornik*, Vol. I, Tallinn, 1956, pp. 80–82.

[4] Porchnev, B. F., 'Les rapports politiques de l'Europe occidentale et de l'Europe orientale à l'époque de la guerre de trente ans', *Rapports du XIe congrès international des sciences historiques*, Stockholm, 21–28 août 1960, IV.

[5] Cf. Tham, W., *Den svenska utrikespolitikens historia*, Vol. I, Part II, (1560–1648), Stockholm, 1960.

received. A survey of the sources has to begin with that distant stage. It consisted mainly of Prince I.B. Cherkasskii's negotiations with the Swedes through two channels, the governor of Livonia, J. Skytte,[6] and De Vergier, Jacques Roussel's representative.[7]

It is not clear from the relevant roll in the Embassies Department records when exactly, the decision was taken to send an embassy to Sweden. Mention is made in the first documents dated 22 July 1632, of a magnificent embassy of thirty-two persons as something already decided on. The embassy's credentials are dated 28 August. For some reason, however (did De Vergier not arrive?), the embassy was delayed, and only on 1 October 1632 was an order sent by the Tsar and the Patriarch to the clerks of the Embassies Department to prepare fresh credentials and other documents, which was done by 11 October 1632.

Of particular interest is the lengthy mandate which, apparently, was further added to during the talks with De Vergier. We have already described its content.[8] A source of the greatest interest is that part of the mandate which contains the official conception of the history of Muscovy since the death of Ivan the Terrible. The story of the 'Time Of Troubles' is presented here in that treatment by the Russian Court which was destined to become canonical. Through it runs the red thread of Polish–Lithuanian intervention and the hostility which subsequently ensued between liberated Muscovy and the Rzeczpospolita. Hostility to the German Emperor is revealed as purely derivative, due to Emperor Ferdinand II's conduct as ally to the Polish–Lithuanian King Sigismund III and, along with this, as enemy to the Swedish King Gustavus Adolphus. Later comes detailed explanation of how the Russo–Polish Smolensk War happened, with references to everything that had already been written about this in Russo–Swedish diplomatic correspondence. The Tsar having already begun operations, the Swedish King is called on not to delay his attack. In that connexion the Swedes are reminded, as of something that had already been agreed, that if Gustavus Adolphus captures any Polish–Lithuanian towns: 'on this side' (i.e., on the Muscovite side of the river Dvina), he is to 'give them up' to the Tsar, 'but those towns . . . he takes on that side of the river' are to remain with His Royal Majesty of Sweden. For his part, the Tsar has already exerted pressure on Sultan Murad IV, on the Crimean Khan Jan-Bek Giray, and on his supporters in Poland and Lithuania, for Gustavus Adolphus to be proclaimed King of Poland.

This plan for reorganising Eastern Europe was closely connected in the

[6] Golitsyn, N. V., *K istorii russko-shvedskikh otnoshenii i naseleniia pogranichnykh so Shvetsiei oblastei (1634–1648)*, Moscow, 1903.
[7] *TsGADA, Dela shvedskie*, 1632, stb. 8; 1633, stb. 5.    [8] See *supra*, pp. 151–155.

mandate with a certain conception of the existing international situation of Muscovy. Along with the traditional evaluations of relations with England, France, Denmark and Holland, and along with the sharp formulation about absence of relations with, and hostility to the German Emperor and the Pope, as enemies of all true Christians, much attention is given to Muscovy's position among the states and peoples of Asia. Here particular emphasis is laid on friendly co-operation with the neighbouring Muslim states – Turkey, Persia and the Crimea. Importance is assigned to the submission to the Tsar's will of very extensive territories and peoples far to the east of Moscow:

The Greater Nogais and Kazyi's *ulus*, and the Circassians and Kumyks of the mountains are all subject to the will of the Tsar's Majesty, and serve the sovereign as before, and have never been out of favour with the Tsar. In Siberia many towns have been built, and all manner of service people and settlers have been welcomed with rewards in money and food, and great fields have been cultivated, and there live service people and settlers in calm and quiet, serving His Majesty the Tsar, and the Siberian peoples render much tribute, in sables, foxes, squirrels and other furs.

A surprisingly wide survey is made of the whole Eurasian world with which Muscovy was involved in one way or another. Only the states of the Far East remained outside the field of vision. But their affairs are not of direct concern here.

Obviously inserted into the mandate are extracts from De Vergier's project.[9] The second of these is added after the signature of the secretary to the council, Ivan Gavrenev. It is headed: 'On the secret treaty and strengthening relations with the King.' Here we see, decoded, the mutual military obligations. If one of the allies: 'is beaten back', the other is required to 'support' him. Here too, is further definition of the future frontier of Muscovy (it is to run along the western Dvina, the Niemen and the Dnieper, from its exit into the Black Sea), and the idea that after the new frontiers have been established on the territory of the Polish–Lithuanian state, Sweden will guarantee complete freedom for Muscovy to expand its possessions *eastward*. The treaty of alliance and friendship is to be binding not only on the sovereigns signing it, but also on their successors.[10]

As mentioned above, all this had been agreed earlier through Jacques Roussel's secret diplomatic agent. He was the initiator and deviser both of most of the details and of the formulations in these secret annexes to the mandate, and in the additions included in the main text. What Jacques Roussel's own motives and political ideas were, we have examined in

[9] *TsGADA, Dela shvedskie*, 1632, *stb.* 8, *ll.* 154–155.    [10] Ibid., *ll.* 174–175.

another context.[11] Nevertheless, there can be no doubt that he would have been unable by means of any hypnosis to impose his conceptions on the leaders of two powerful states unless he had divined and given concrete form to their own conceptions and profound interests.

In the mandate of the 'Great Embassy' of Pushkin and his companions, alarm is also sounded regarding Sweden's loyalty to its duty as ally. Of course, the prospect of obtaining the Crown of Poland and Lithuania and the western half of the Polish–Lithuanian state was an important incentive for Gustavus Adolphus to be faithful to this alliance. But they knew in Moscow that he was hunting in Germany for another even more tempting crown, that of the Empire. And they knew too, that in Sweden a section of the oligarchy was opposed to the King's acquisition of any foreign crowns, which would make him too independent. The mandate definitely foresees the possibility of a Swedo–Polish agreement. On the one hand, information is selected at this point, to be passed on to the Swedes, about the complete unity and indissolubility of the policies of the German Emperor and the Polish King. On the other hand, in concluding the treaty, both sovereigns must swear that they: 'will not make any new truce or peace, without mutual agreement, with their common foes, the Polish Crown Prince Wladyslaw, or his brother Kazimir or any of their brothers who may be wearing the Crown of Poland or Lithuania.'[12] Finally, the ambassadors are instructed, during their time in Sweden and Germany, to investigate secretly, among other things, whether there have been any dealings by Gustavus Adolphus with King Sigismund III or, after his death, with the Sejm.

The supplement to the mandate also includes a diplomatic counter-threat. The intention of the embassy from the Archbishop of Gniezno which was not received in Moscow, was said to be to propose that in return for the Russian cities seized by Poland being given back to Muscovy, the Russo–Polish war should be called off and the entire Polish–Lithuanian army be sent to help the Emperor against the Swedes.[13] Did Muscovy really have this information or was it just speculation? In any case, this prognosis was subsequently confirmed. Here it is being put forward merely as a means of pressure on the Swedish side. This was a subtle and clever move – not just to counter with this threat any move towards Swedo–Polish reconciliation, but also to impel Gustavus Adolphus not to get too carried away with war against the Emperor, but to hasten to fall upon Poland. Moscow could free his hands to do that.

On 11 October 1632, the following documents were signed: the

[11] Porshnev, B. F., *Frantsiia, Angliiskaia revoliutsiia i evropeiskaia politika v seredine XVIIv.*, Moscow, 1970, pp. 339–354.
[12] *TsGADA, Dela shvedskie*, 1632, stb. 6, *l.* 154.    [13] Ibid., *l.* 75.

ambassadors' credentials; a letter to the Danish King Christian IV, in case the ambassadors should happen to traverse his dominions; a similar letter to the German princes and cities; an accompanying letter from Patriarch Philaret to Gustavus Adolphus, in which, concealing his true role, he merely expresses his rejoicing over the alliance between his son and the Swedish King.[14] The ambassadors were supplied with model drafts for the letters on which the Tsar and the King were to take their oaths, i.e., the draft treaty for an alliance on the conditions set out above.[15]

The roll contains some interesting questions put by the ambassadors about points unclear to them, which had been formulated most probably before the final composition of the mandate with the annexes mentioned above. These questions essentially relate to the unclear nature of the mandate with regard to Gustavus Adolphus's previous projects. What if, as before, he refers to his being tied up with the war against the Emperor and if he again restricts his proposal to hiring troops with the Tsar's money and sending them from the west against the Polish–Lithuanian state? And if the ambassadors insist that it is incumbent on him ('a matter of duty') to invade the Polish–Lithuanian state in aid of the Tsar, he may answer that when he was fighting Poland, the Tsar likewise ought to have sent his commanders with troops there – what are they to say in reply? There are no answers to these questions in the roll, but the questions evidently related to a past stage in negotiations, and the 'Great Embassy' was charged with tasks of a higher political order.

The 'Great Embassy' left Moscow at the end of October 1632. It stopped when it reached Novgorod owing to illness of the son of the ambassador Gorikhvostov, and resumed its journey on 22 November. On 3 December, a courier was sent to Moscow from Oreshek with messages of secondary importance concerned with the journey, and on 14 December the courier left Moscow with the reply.

In one of their subsequent letters, the ambassadors inform Moscow of their questions regarding the aspects of the affair that were worrying them most. From the son of the governor of Hudiksvall whom they met on their journey, they learnt that after the death of King Sigismund III, his sons sent envoys to Gustavus Adolphus in Germany giving him his full title in the letters they brought and abandoning in his favour the dynastic dispute over the Crown of Sweden. These ambassadors bore an invitation to Gustavus Adolphus to come to Poland for the funeral of his cousin Sigismund III and the coronation of Crown Prince Wladyslaw. The Swedish King had replied to Wladyslaw in writing in a brotherly way, that he could not attend owing to his war with the Emperor, and sent

[14] *TsGADA, Dela shvedskie, 1632, stb. 6, ll.* 176–191.    [15] Ibid., *ll.* 193–236.

to him as ambassador a Swedish magnate named Stenbolk[16] with three companions, who left Sweden for Poland via Riga three weeks before Christmas, that is, at the beginning of December 1632. However, it was not known whether these ambassadors had been given any particular instructions.[17] This news was later confirmed from the Swedish side.[18] It could not fail to intensify Moscow's anxious misgivings.

But misfortune was on its way from an unexpected quarter. On 5 January 1633, before they reached Stockholm and whilst they were still in Finland, the ambassadors learnt of the death of Gustavus Adolphus. They broke off their journey, and a courier was sent to Moscow with details of the Swedes' victory at Lützen bought with 'the King's precious heart's blood'.[19]

On 25 January 1633, an instruction signed by the Tsar was sent to the ambassadors ordering them to return home, clarifying on the way the circumstances of the Swedish King's death and the probable prospects of war or peace in Germany. Already on 11 February however, a new order was sent to the ambassadors. They were to go to Sweden after all to meet the new monarch.

By that time Pushkin, Gorikhvostov and Neverov had already met a representative of the Swedish government sent to them from Stockholm. He told them in detail about the battle of Lützen and about the oath sworn by the Swedish magnates to the King's daughter Christina. The King's widow had gone to Germany and would not return with his coffin until the opening of navigation in the Baltic in the spring. The Riksdag which was about to assemble in Stockholm would send embassies to all the states that were Sweden's allies, to request confirmation of previous treaties and alliances directed against the Emperor. The Muscovite ambassadors expressed a desire for a continuation of the previous joint policy aimed against the Polish King, the Emperor and the Pope, who threatened Sweden, and told of the successes of Russian arms in the war with the Polish–Lithuanian state. This news the Swedish plenipotentiary immediately conveyed to Stockholm.[20]

There also reached the Russian ambassadors at the New Year a courier from Johan Skytte, the governor of Livonia, bringing documents about the decisions adopted by the Polish Sejm, which evidently concerned the election of King Wladyslaw IV. In view of the importance of this matter, the courier was sent off to Moscow with his papers.[21] Then Pushkin and his companions received from the capital yet another new order. They were to return to Novgorod the Great and there await instructions. This order was sent twice from Moscow, first, on 25 February, and then again

[16] Probably Stenbock.     [17] *TsGADA, Dela shvedskie*, 1633, *stb.* 2, *ll.* 22–25.
[18] Ibid., *ll.* 27, 30.     [19] Ibid., *ll.* 2–3.     [20] Ibid., *ll.* 26–33.     [21] Ibid., *ll.* 37–39.

on 4 March. It was followed by a demand that the ambassadors immediately send back to Moscow both their mandate and the model treaties, keeping nothing back, as a fresh mandate was being prepared. The point here was that the previous mandate had been oriented not only on Gustavus Adolphus when he was in Germany, but also on the group at the Swedish court in Stockholm around Queen Maria Eleonora. In Moscow they had no confidence in the circle around Christina in Stockholm, and Chancellor Oxenstjerna, who had been with the King in Germany. The news they had received of the forthcoming coronation of Christina obliged them to change their orientation. However, the new mandate, which was signed on 25 March 1633, was addressed to the two Queens: Maria Eleonora and Christina. They probably hoped in Moscow that, under the regency of Maria Eleonora, there would be established in Stockholm a 'regime of two monarchs', something like the relations between Patriarch Philaret and his son the Tsar.

the ambassadors now had to go forward 'not delaying' and 'without stopping'. When they were received by the King's widow and daughter, Pushkin and his companions were to express condolence in unambiguous terms, emphasising 'that King Gustavus Adolphus was killed in battle by the soldiers of the enemy, the Emperor', and:

that against the common foes of our great sovereign Majesty the Tsar and His Royal Majesty, against the heretics of the Roman faith, the Papists and the Jesuits, their wrong-doings and persecutions, and for your faith, His Royal Majesty stood forth in his valour, firmly and courageously, and won many a victory over them, and in that war, for his sovereign nature and his faith and for all the people of the German states to have justice, he yielded and laid down his royal life.[22]

The immediate diplomatic task of the 'Great Embassy' amounted almost to a single proposition: to obtain confirmation by oaths on both sides for the permanent peace of Stolbovo. To this there was only one addition: the rulers of Sweden were to bind themselves not only to maintain peace between the two states, but also to fight alongside Moscow against their common foes, in particular the Polish King Wladyslaw and the Polish–Lithuanian state, and not to make peace without mutual agreement, that is, to refrain from concluding any separate peace. An oath-taking would ensure international publicity for this agreement.[23] Only after the Swedish rulers had confirmed by oath the sincerity of their intentions could 'the great ambassadors' turn to the history of the Russo–Polish conflict which had been included already in their first mandate. Added here was the history of the Russo–Swedish negotiations beginning with the arrival of Monier and Bönhardt in 1629. The Swedish revelations of

[22] Ibid., *ll.* 59, 80–81.     [23] Ibid., *ll.* 62, 85–108.

the 'evil intent' of the Polish King, the Emperor and the Pope, against Sweden, Denmark, Muscovy and other states were reproduced, revelations which had impelled the Muscovite government not to wait for the truce to expire but to begin war against the Rzeczpospolita on 3 August 1632. Following this came the lists of Russian cities already recovered and those that were still held by the enemy, and an appeal to the Queen and Crown Princess of Sweden, remembering Gustavus Adolphus's alliance with Mikhail Fedorovich, to go to war with Wladyslaw and not to conclude a separate peace.[24]

Evidently, though, the ambassadors' chief task was now to discover the true political situation in Sweden, Germany and Poland. A very detailed list of questions was drawn up concerning the military-political situation in Germany after Gustavus Adolphus's death. With whom, and to what ends did he, in his will, call on his successor to wage war? Had he ordered the Swedes to make peace with the Emperor after his death, and if so, on what conditions? If the war was to continue, which side had the advantage? Who was helping the Swedish army and how? Where was the Swedish army? Where and with what result was the last battle fought? Where was the Emperor and who was in command of his army?

Another set of questions related to Sweden's internal situation. Was support for Maria Eleonora and Christina unanimous? Or was there the possibility of 'dissension and disagreement' (about which the embassy had already heard during their journey), and under these Queens who in fact 'of those noblemen close to the throne, or of the Council men', would 'rule and govern'?

What especially worried the Russian government though, putting aside these 'direct heirs', was the possibility of a claim to the Swedish throne by the Polish line of the Vasa dynasty. On the back of several pages a special instruction was written, telling the ambassadors what to do if, by the time they arrived in Stockholm, somebody else turned out to have been already confirmed in possession of Sweden's throne. The mandate was filled with alarm. If no direct seizure of the Swedish Crown from weak women's hands by the sons of Sigismund III had taken place, they are to find out whether there have been any ambassadors, envoys or communications from the Poles 'and in particular, whether in their communications any mischief is being plotted, or any plan aimed against Muscovy'. This Pushkin, Gorikhvostov and Neverov were to discover 'with all diligence' and 'thoroughly'.

Thus, two dangers had arisen simultaneously – of a reconciliation between Sweden and the Emperor, and of a *rapprochement* with the

---

[24] Ibid., *ll.* 120–158.

Polish–Lithuanian state directed against Muscovy. Therein could be discerned the outlines of an alliance between three states for war with Russia. If the Swedes, having ended their war in Germany, were to free the Emperor's hands, he would at once intensify his political, financial and military support for the Polish–Lithuanian state which was suffering disasters on its eastern and southern frontiers: 'Are the Polish Crown Prince Wladyslaw and his brothers talking with the Emperor at present and if so, what about? And will the Emperor help Crown Prince Wladyslaw and his brothers against Muscovy in some way, and if so, how? With men or with money?'

In the thinking of the Muscovite politicians – perhaps Prince I.B. Cherkasskii – a terrible historical experience was being contemplated, as we see, namely, a Polish and Swedish intervention, backed from afar by the Empire. And yet other allies might join in this attack: 'And the ambassadors are to discover whether other states are having fresh discussions with the Polish Crown Prince and his brothers, and if so, what about? And do any of these states want to help the Poles against Muscovy, and if so, how do they mean to help? With men or with money?'[25] The prospect of a whole hostile coalition was in the air. This must be remembered when we consider the conclusion, in the following year, of Muscovy's peace with the Polish–Lithuanian state on the river Polyanovka, after the Patriarch's death.

As regards the instructions on how to reply to certain questions, in the second mandate there was only one substantial addition to what was contained in the first. With the Turkish Sultan there is not only friendship: 'the Turkish Sultan wants to go to war along with His Majesty the Tsar against their common foe, the Polish King'. It was also stated that ambassadors from the Tsar were being sent at once to Denmark and Holland.[26]

Attached later were letters from both the Tsar and the Patriarch separately to Maria Eleonora and Christina. Here the theme was again taken up that Gustavus Adolphus had died in courageous and victorious struggle 'against our common foes – the heretics of the Roman faith', both for his own state and faith and 'for all the peoples of the Evangelical faith in the German states'.[27] In the annexed examples of oath-documents it was said of the death of Gustavus Adolphus: 'The Emperor's men killed him in battle, those enemies of all Christendom.'[28]

While on the road, the 'great ambassadors' sent Moscow information on the decisions of the Swedish Riksdag to continue with the war in Germany, where Chancellor Oxenstjerna and the Elector of Saxony were

[25] Ibid., *ll*. 158–169.    [26] Ibid., *ll*. 171–174.    [27] Ibid., *ll*. 183–193.
[28] Ibid., *ll*. 219–249.

leading the fight against the Imperialists. On all these letters we note the presence of minutes which show that they had received attention at the highest level: 'The sovereign and the Most Holy Sovereign-Patriarch have heard this.'[29]

There is a letter in the Swedish archives from the highest official in Narva, Nils Asserson, which is dated 23 March 1633, and which is addressed to the Queen and the Council of State in Stockholm. The governor of Novgorod has written to him that a Russian embassy is on its way to Sweden. The ambassadors are accompanied by forty-two persons. From Narva they will be taken to Stockholm by sea, but navigation will not be open earlier than the end of April or the beginning of May. However, the governor of Novgorod writes that the ambassadors think it necessary to remain in Novgorod for four or five weeks so that a ship can be got ready for them by that time. The ambassadors will be met at the frontier, and Asserson himself undertakes to provide a fitting reception and the best accommodation.[30]

The 'Great Embassy' arrived in Stockholm on 4 June 1633. From this point on we possess parallel sources from the Russian and the Swedish archives. In a report of 8 June the ambassadors describe their ceremonial entry into the Swedish capital. In another message they convey the Swedish political news. The most important item for Moscow was that the child Christina had finally been chosen Queen and that the country's rulers under her would be Gabriel Oxenstjerna, Jakob De la Gardie, Karl Karlsson and Per Banér, while 'Queen Maria Eleonora will have no sovereignty in affairs of state, and nobody mentions her name anywhere'.[31] This was a clear and unambiguous sign that there was *not* to be continuation of Gustavus Adolphus's policy!

Later the ambassadors reported that Chancellor Axel Oxenstjerna was at that time in Germany. Enclosed was a printed pamphlet (a 'news book') in German about current international affairs, including a visit to the Swedish Chancellor by an ambassador sent from Poland. Pushkin and his companions checked this alarming news through several channels. From some well-informed citizen of Stockholm they learnt that in fact, after Gustavus Adolphus's death in Germany, an envoy from King Wladyslaw went to the Swedish Chancellor and the Swedish army to ask Sweden not to break the truce with Poland before its time was up. The details and results of these talks were not known, but another Polish ambassador was now on his way from Danzig to Stockholm to continue or reinforce them.

[29] Ibid., *ll.* 334–337.
[30] *Svenska Riksarkivet, Stockholm, Muscovita, Best,* N. 229, RGS, N. 631. *Protokoll Vid Konferenser med Ryska Beskicknigar Till Sverige, 1633.*
[31] *TsGADA, Dela shvedskie,* 1633, *stb.* 2, *ll.* 345–355.

Pushkin and his companions at once sought unofficially ('by way of conversation') explanations from the official who had been attached to them ('the escort'), and this man, evidently following instructions, confirmed the story about a Polish ambassador coming to the Swedish capital. He also said that the government had ordered that when the ambassador arrived at the Livonian frontier, he was to be asked 'for what purpose' he was coming, and if his purpose was to seek a *rapprochement* between Sweden and Poland, he was not to be admitted. If, however, his purpose was to convey congratulations to the Queen and to talk about observation of the truce, 'they will let him come to Stockholm and his embassy will be listened to'.[32]

Worried about all this, the Russian ambassadors took a secret decision to get ahead of their rival 'to carry out their embassy and obtain the reply before the arrival of the Polish envoy'. Accordingly, they requested through their 'escort', that their audience be granted soon. However, the dignitaries concerned replied through the escort and extremely vaguely, that they would be received 'after Whitsun', without mentioning any precise day. From the queries that the ambassadors put to Moscow as to how they should act in the event of failure to agree on the part of the Swedes, it is clear that they had lost hope of getting included in the Russo–Swedish oath-taking the bilateral undertaking about war and peace with the Polish–Lithuanian state.[33]

These reports by the ambassadors signified that the long campaign by Patriarch Philaret had failed. The second mandate to 'the great ambassadors', which was drawn up after the news of Gustavus Adolphus's death had been received, already leaves the impression that the Patriarch had been, or was being sidelined. With the ambassadors' dispatches from Stockholm, something odd happened which cannot but attract an historian's attention. Sent in the first half of June, they reached Moscow only on 17 August. The courier cannot have been two-and-a-half months on the road. The diplomatic bag must either have been intercepted, or deliberately delayed. And the instructions composed in reply were signed only on 14 September, a mere fortnight before the Patriarch's death. Some complicated struggle was going on in the Kremlin. But we can trace only the nature and the fate of the information which was poured into Moscow through various channels, or was actively sought by Moscow from the time of Gustavus Adolphus's death, and the changes in the international situation which took place in that connexion.

One of our sources consists of the regular reports of news from Europe sent by the governors of Novgorod. At the end of January and the

---

[32] Ibid., *ll*. 348–349.     [33] Ibid., *ll*. 350–351.

beginning of February 1633, questioning of Russian and foreign merchants who came over the frontier gave frequent confirmation of the news that the King of Sweden had been killed. It was reported that command of his army had passed to the Duke of Weimar, who was betrothed to Princess Christina and so might become King of Sweden. The governors of Novgorod also passed on rumours about the possibility of peace being made between the Swedes and the Imperialists.[34] On the back we read a minute stating that the Tsar and the Patriarch have heard this and have ordered that the story be checked and the sovereigns written to when this has been done. An order to this effect was sent to Novgorod on 11 February.[35]

An extremely important channel of information and communication was constituted by dealings with the Swedish governor of Livonia, Johan Skytte, who was in Riga. It must be observed that control of this information was wholly monopolised by Prince Cherkasskii who may not even have reported everything to the Patriarch. Of interest is a letter found in the Ducal archives at Jelgava [Mitau, Courland], from Cherkasskii to Skytte, 'governor of Livonia, Karelia and Ingria', dated 30 January 1633. It continues an earlier correspondence which has not come down to us. The letter is in reply to news of the death of Gustavus Adolphus and reproduces the official formulas of condolence, as sent with the ambassadors to Stockholm. More important, we find here developed the idea of arranging direct correspondence between Prince Cherkasskii and Skytte (to which Skytte had already agreed), 'when a direct agent is available who can be trusted with these matters'.[36] Skytte's answer from Yuriev [Dorpat] we find in the records of the Embassies Department. On 22 February 1633, his courier Schwengel arrived in Moscow with credentials and a plentiful supply of information, both written and oral. It was proposed that Schwengel be employed for further exchanges of information until a permanent agent in Moscow was appointed in place of the late Johan Möller. But this was immediately followed by a query as to whether the Muscovite government would regard as a suitable candidate for that post, one Melchior Bökman, 'who is now in Moscow'. The information about foreign politics brought by the courier can be divided into three main groups – the situation in Sweden, in the Polish–Lithuanian state, and in Germany. In Sweden the courier reported: 'it is firmly declared and confirmed that on the throne there will be not a man, but a queen such as England had in Elizabeth'. All Sigismund III's claims to the Swedish throne had been rejected, although Wladyslaw IV was ingratiating himself with the Swedish magnates in the hope of coming to

[34] *TsGADA, Dela shvedskie,* 1633, *stb.* 1, *ll.* 1–9.    [35] Ibid., *ll.* 10–11.
[36] Golitsyn, *K istorii,* pp. 7–9.

Sweden and marrying Christina. The most important items of news about the Polish–Lithuanian state were: the Sejm's official report of the election of Wladyslaw IV; the printed 'glorification' of him by the Church; secret reports by word of mouth about a decision to send against Muscovy, when summer came, the Zaporozhian Cossacks, representatives of whom had already gone to the Sejm for negotiations and who intended not merely to do great damage but 'also to break into Moscow itself and plunder it'. The Tsar was advised to take protective measures in good time. News about the course of the war in Germany was very full: the disposition of the Swedish forces; Silesia's complete defection from the Emperor; the attack on him by the troops of the Transylvanian prince Yuri (György) Rákóczi. In a German newspaper brought by the courier, besides news from Paris about the residences of the Cardinal and the King, the disgracing of the Duc de Longueville and the death of Marshal Schomberg, there was an abundance of descriptions of military operations in all parts of the Empire. The Swedish troops and those of the Elector of Saxony had captured towns and were pursuing the Imperialists. To help the latter, a detachment of Cossacks had been sent in from Poland and they had clashed with Swedish, Saxon and Brandenburg troops. The Elector of Saxony had sworn to avenge the death of Gustavus Adolphus and had placed half of the army under the command of Bernard of Weimar and with the other half, and accompanied by General Arnim, had gone into Bohemia, to Prague. An interesting detail: Wallenstein, sent by the Emperor to put down the rebel Czech peasants, had encountered resistance: 'yes, it seems that the Duke of Friedland's Bohemian peasants do not want him to live among them and for that they are to be flogged to death'. The Swedish Chancellor Oxenstjerna had gone to Stettin.

The fundamental conclusion to be drawn from the international situation which Skytte put to Cherkasskii and the Muscovite court was that the death of the Swedish King ought not to mean that 'the main thing is ended'.[37]

As for Melchior Bökman, the candidate for the role of permanent Swedish agent (resident) in Moscow, he failed to retain this appointment. At the start he sent by his man to the Embassies Department foreign news under forty-one headings together with five secret items addressed to the Tsar and the Patriarch and also was received by Prince Cherkasskii who passed on to the sovereigns what Bökman had told him. The text of this information is missing from the roll. Melchior Bökman was given the reply that he should continue to seek out useful news and send it to the sovereigns for which he would receive recompense, 'according to his work and service'. But this time the service he rendered did not secure his

[37] *TsGADA, Dela shvedskie*, 1632 (error for 1633), *stb.* 5, *ll.* 69–82.

appointment to the Tsar's service as agent for Swedish affairs, which included the purchase of grain. It may be that, generally, this was not thought a convenient moment for appointing a permanent agent.[38]

We do not know what Cherkasskii replied to Skytte. The courier Schwengel did not visit Moscow again and his role as go-between for Skytte and Cherkasskii was taken over by Martin Beijer. He had already played that role in Moscow and reappeared in the first days of June. Beijer brought a letter from Skytte dated 2 May. Skytte confirmed receipt of two letters from Cherkasskii, one of 30 January, brought by Beijer, the other of 8 March, brought by Schwengel. He thanked Cherkasskii for a generous gift sent by Schwengel, that of two 'forties' of sables. The reply was delayed because Skytte had waited for the return of his courier (evidently this Beijer) from Poland where he had visited the Sejm in Cracow.

Besides the oral information and the newspapers brought by Beijer, Skytte offers a summary of international problems in the following main propositions. The Polish–Lithuanian state will shortly initiate talks about peace with both Sweden and Russia, but only so as to deceive both states until it has assembled sufficient forces large enough to devastate Muscovy: 'and both the Russian people and we Swedes can remember that from many examples'. Both states must be on their guard and put no trust in these peace moves. The Swedish Riksdag has rejected, for now and forever, the claims of Sigismund III's sons to the Swedish Crown, and this is confirmed by a document which is enclosed. The newspapers also enclosed ('news books') report that Chancellor Axel Oxenstjerna is successfully carrying on the war in Germany. Skytte was well informed about the embassy of Pushkin and Gorikhvostov sent to Stockholm and wrote that as a member of the Council of State he was interested in the success of their negotiations and the strengthening of Russo–Swedish friendship.

In this interesting missive of Skytte's are many protestations that he is an active champion of the Russo–Swedish alliance. He is moved by the friendship, faithful unto death, between Gustavus Adolphus and Mikhail Fedorovich: 'And I know how to spread and fame it abroad'. He is in favour of 'maintaining the good relations which we have initiated for the good and benefit of both states, and we should be in communication with each other'.[39] Skytte repeats several times a request that his news be conveyed to the Tsar and Patriarch, treating Prince Cherkasskii as no more than a go-between. Perhaps he already knew something about the disagreements between uncle and nephew.[40]

The missive could be interpreted either as a far-reaching offer of

---

[38] Ibid., 1633, *stb.* 13.    [39] Ibid., *stb.* 8, *ll.* 4–16.

[40] Between the Patriarch and Prince Cherkasskii, whose mother was the Patriarch's sister (Editor) [i.e. the editor of the Russian original – Trans.].

Skytte's services to Muscovite diplomacy, or as double dealing. The published proceedings of the Swedish Council of State, where Skytte was soon to speak quite differently, show that the second interpretation is the correct one.[41]

The roll contains fragments of drafts from which it is clear that the final text of the reply was sent off by Cherkasskii only after Skytte's next move, his sending to Moscow of his nephew Håkan. This looked like an attempt to impose on the Muscovite court acceptance of his offer of personal service. As we shall see, the Patriarch tried energetically to make use of this possibility, but was evidently sidelined by the more cautious Cherkasskii. Håkan Skytte arrived in Moscow in July 1633. With him there came the Crimean envoy Nurali and his companions who had been to Sweden. Although Håkan Skytte was not an ambassador or envoy, and there was, consequently, no obligation to arrange to meet him before he entered Moscow, the Patriarch insisted that on this occasion the rules of diplomacy should be breached. There is a personal minute in his handwriting: 'arrange a small reception for the sake of Johan Skytte'. Later however, we note in the file a momentary victory for the other line, that of caution. Håkan Skytte was kept in Moscow in conditions of fairly strict isolation.[42] But he brought important messages from his uncle and from the Swedish government. The Patriarch took an unusually active part in preparing the answers to both.

The reply to Johan Skytte sent in the name of Prince Cherkasskii was composed as an important state document and was undoubtedly dictated, for the most part, by the Patriarch himself. Here, incidentally, a special fragment explains to Skytte the mistakes he has made in the titles of the Tsar and the Patriarch. In the letter sent by the hand of Håkan Skytte on the progress of the Russo–Polish war, detailed information is given on the operations from the very beginning, on the taking of twelve towns, and on how the siege of Smolensk is going. Johan Skytte is told that all the information, written and oral, sent *via* Beijer has been imparted to the Tsar and the Patriarch. They talk to him almost as to an agent of the Russian government. The Tsar and the Patriarch 'praise' him for having 'served [them] and shown zeal in their affairs', including his supplying to them of what they needed to know about Polish–Lithuanian and German matters. They praise especially his expression of readiness to continue 'to show zeal and industry':

And you Johan, will continue to serve the great sovereigns . . . About the Swedish monarchy, about what is happening between the Swedish army and the Kaiser's army and about Polish and Lithuanian affairs, what their cunning intentions for

[41] *Svenska Riksrådets protokoll*, Vol. III, Stockholm, 1885, p. 288.
[42] *TsGADA, Dela shvedskie*, 1633, *stb*. 9, *l*. 22.

the future are, about all these things you have amicably written and told everything. These things are needed by the Great Sovereign Our Majesty the Tsar and by his father the Great Sovereign the Most Holy Patriarch.

The Tsar and the Patriarch are pleased with the news of the military successes of Oxenstjerna in Germany and ask God to continue granting victory to Swedish arms 'over their common foes, over the accursed Papist Jesuits so that they may be utterly destroyed and eradicated'.[43] This was evidently written in September 1633. On 21 September, ten days before the Patriarch's death, Håkan Skytte had a farewell audience with the Tsar. He was given the Tsar's letter to Christina, but the personally composed letter to her from the Patriarch was apparently withheld from him at the last moment. It remained lying in the Embassies Department. The Patriarch was still in good health, but just then had been manifestly sidelined from state affairs. More will be said about that later. Meanwhile, we need to go back in time once more in order to learn of the other channels of Russo–Swedish contact during the stay of the 'Great Embassy' in Stockholm.

The Swedish magnates sent the courier Markus Stenman and the envoy Hans Berenson to Moscow with the official announcement of Gustavus Adophus's death. The former had the Swedish magnates' letter of 9 March, the latter their letter of 8 March. However, the latter travelled with his retinue more slowly than the former. The courier reached Moscow on 7 May, the envoy not until 11 June. In the intervening month the atmosphere in Moscow had had time to alter somewhat.

Stenman brought a letter signed by twelve of the most prominent Swedish magnates – De la Gardie, Gyllenhjelm, Gabriel Oxenstjerna and others. From inertia, the letter expounds a conception entirely inherited from Gustavus Adolphus. The magnates recall with gratitude the Russian grain subsidies for the conduct of the war in Germany. Today, after the King's death, say the magnates, they have even greater reasons than before to go on with this war, the blame for which lies with the Emperor, the Polish King and the Papists. They assume that the Tsar too, as before, is interested in 'crushing and sinking the Kaiser and the Papists, the persecutors of the Evangelical and of the ancient Greek faiths'. Consequently, they ask that, as before, he will help them in the war by means of grain subsidies. Sweden is hastening the dispatch of the 2,000 cuirasses purchased for the Russo–Polish war and will render as much other aid as it can.[44]

Stenman also brought information about the Riksdag's decision to continue the war in Germany, the transfer of command of the Swedish army to Chancellor Axel Oxenstjerna, the proclamation of Queen

[43] Ibid., *stb*. 8, *ll*. 17–37.    [44] Ibid., *stb*. 6, *ll*. 9–16.

Christina and the declaration that it was treasonous even to talk of giving
the Swedish Crown to Wladyslaw or his brothers. Of particular interest
to Moscow was the news that Radziwill, the Hetman of Lithuania, had
sent to Sweden, on behalf of Wladyslaw, a proposal for a ten year truce
and a request that the Polish–Lithuanian troops be allowed to pass
through Livonia in their campaign against Muscovy. Sweden however,
had rejected these proposals.[45] Was this not an invention for the purpose
of exerting diplomatic pressure?

The envoy Hans Berenson arrived before Moscow literally the day
after the arrival of Martin Beijer with his news from the governor of
Livonia. It was undoubtedly for this reason that Berenson was kept
waiting outside the capital for two days and nights and, when he was
admitted, was lodged with his retinue in particularly bleak conditions.
However, there had been no hint of this in the instructions given only a
few days earlier to the escorting officials: to extend 'honour and protection'
to the envoy with the utmost courtesy. Evidently, the information
supplied by Beijer gave a trump card to those leaders of foreign policy in
Moscow who were already no longer counting on continuation of the
previous line. The escort with the Swedish embassy was given a special
order not to let them leave their lodging and to watch closely that neither
foreigners nor Russians 'approach and talk with them about anything',
'and if any man comes to their lodging and tries to talk with the envoy or
his people, he is to be arrested and taken to the Embassies Department.
This is to be done quietly so that the envoy and his people do not notice
it.' Then we find the reason for this strictness. The escort is ordered to
discover, by all possible means, from the envoy, the interpreter and the
retinue, whether ambassadors from the Polish–Lithuanian state had been
in Sweden, and if so, how long were they there? Why did they come and
with what did they leave? And was peace or war expected between
Sweden and Poland?

On a formal pretext Berenson was refused an audience with the Tsar.
On 18 June, the boyars heard what he had to say and accepted from him
the letter signed by the Swedish magnates. In both the speeches made and
the written text, apology was offered for so late an official communication
concerning the death of Gustavus Adolphus. The Swedish magnates
gave an absurd explanation for this lateness – 'their grief'. Probably the
ship of Swedish diplomacy had at first listed strongly to the side opposite
to Gustavus Adolphus's policy, and only in March had it steadied. (As we
shall see, however, only to rock later on). The accession to the throne of
Christina, 'the direct heiress', 'the beloved daughter', was now treated as

[45] Ibid., *ll.* 4–7.

the symbol of complete continuity between Gustavus Adolphus's policy and the line of the oligarchy now in power. What is most surprising in this message and in the accompanying speech, is the repeated and emphatic repetition of the formula about Gustavus Adolphus having died in the fight 'for the Evangelical and for the ancient Greek faiths'. The Papists are tirelessly and by means of all sorts of intrigues trying to crush and eradicate the Evangelical and the ancient Greek faiths and to spread their own accursed Papist faith. Gustavus Adolphus fought for and defended both of these two faiths against the Emperor, the Polish King and all the Catholics and also defended the great possessions and state of the Russian Tsar. The Catholics, headed by the German Emperor and the Polish King, strove to break through to the Baltic Sea, 'they wanted first to conquer the great Kingdom of Sweden and then the great possessions and state of Your Majesty the Tsar, and to crush the Evangelical and the ancient Greek faiths and install instead their accursed Popish darkness'. The Swedish Riksdag wishes to continue with constancy 'the task that they are carrying out in Germany'.[46]

This favourable swerve in Swedish policy apparently offered a big opportunity for the Patriarch. He had been silent for some time, the reason for this being, we may suppose, the manoeuvres of groups at the Muscovite court. On 6 July, there was an official conference between the Tsar and the Patriarch in the latter's audience chamber at which it was decided and announced that the letter of reply to the Swedish envoy, nominally from the boyars but in fact avoiding them and Prince Cherkasskii, would be handed over in the Embassies Department by the Council secretary Ivan Griazev. The letter, dated 5 July, was given to Berenson on 9 July. In it, on the one hand, the 'confessional' conception in the Swedish message was repudiated. Nothing was said about Gustavus Adolphus dying for the two faiths. On the contrary, it was frankly stated that he 'fought for your faith' and died 'for his faith and truth and for all the people of the German states'. On the other hand, however, the political aspect was eagerly emphasised. Gustavus Adolphus fought 'against the common foes of His Majesty the Tsar and of His Royal Majesty'. The Russian Tsar accepts the idea of Christina as the direct continuator of her father's policy and wishes to be in the same 'firm friendship and love and kindness, with exchange of counsel', as with Gustavus Adolphus. The statement that the previous permanent peace of Stolbovo needed to be 'renewed and confirmed' has been corrected in the Patriarch's own hand, to 'confirmed and consolidated', that is, to be made a firmer alliance. Later comes a significant gesture. The request already

[46] Ibid., *stb*. 7, *ll*. 1–111.

made by Stenman for further permission to buy grain in Archangel for the Swedish government on the same conditions as before, is granted in full. He is permitted to buy in the current year, the same amount as in the previous year – 50,000 quarters (this was the last permission of that sort!). And then, the desire of the Tsar and the Patriarch to maintain with Christina the same alliance as they had with her father is repeated again and again.[47]

In fact, however, this optimistic document was already a blank shot. Not long before, a Swedish courier to the envoy Berenson had arrived on the Russian frontier and asked that he be driven to Moscow with all possible speed, travelling 'night and day'. On 7 July, the Patriarch and the Tsar, alarmed, gave permission and on 10 July, Berenson himself left Moscow presumably to meet the courier.[48] It is not hard to realise what had happened. Negotiations had begun in Stockholm with the 'Great Embassy', and engagements undertaken in Moscow at the same time might tie the hands of the Council of State.

One more channel of communication existed for the Patriarch. It was the principal one, namely Jacques Roussel and his agents. One of the latter, Jean De Vergier had been to Moscow on his behalf, as we remember, and now appeared again at Pskov on 25 April 1633. With him was a 'man' named Mark Brandenburg and also a fellow traveller of whom it is hard to find any trace in the files of the Embassies Department but who is sometimes called Thomas and sometimes Mathis. The report of the governor of Pskov stated that in December of the previous year, De Vergier had driven across the frontier in a *troika* pulled by excellent horses bought for him, and in Pskov there remained a letter from the Tsar ordering that when this Jean De Vergier, or anyone sent by him, should appear, he was to be allowed to proceed to Moscow without hindrance. De Vergier reached Moscow on 8 May. That same day he was received by Prince Cherkasskii, handed over Roussel's letter for the Tsar and the Patriarch, and conveyed what else he had to convey by word of mouth. All this was secret and not kept in the files, as Cherkasskii talked with De Vergier in the Treasury with only a French interpreter present, 'and nothing was told of this to the Embassies Department'. One can only guess, from the reply sent by the Tsar and the Patriarch, that Roussel was now trying to take upon himself the realisation of a direct link 'at the highest level' between young Christina and the Muscovite throne. In this reply, all that is omitted is the word 'ambassador' or 'agent' of 'Her Royal Majesty Queen Christina of Sweden'.

So far as the record was concerned one problem remained, namely

---

[47]  Ibid., *ll.* 117–158.    [48]  Ibid., *ll.* 163–164.

Roussel's wish to re-visit Moscow. This favour was at once granted to him. The letter addressed to him on 12 July 1633 was corrected in several places by the Patriarch personally. Come, certainly, said the letter, and when you come 'we shall welcome you, Jacques, for your services past and present to us the Great Sovereigns. [Added in the Patriarch's hand: 'and your services to King Gustavus Adolphus'.] Our princely eyes desire to behold you and to welcome you with our princely reward [inserted in the Patriarch's hand: 'as before, and higher than before'], and you may trust in our princely favour and reward and come to us in Moscow without fear.'[49]

That same day, 12 July, letters from the Tsar were dispatched to Archangel, Vologda and Iaroslavl about the admission to Moscow and supply of fodder and escorts to Roussel who was coming by sea from Holland with his men (deleted: with noblemen).[50] But the letter was too late. Without waiting for a reply, Roussel left for Russia in a ship belonging to a Dutch merchant and arrived at Archangel on 18 July. On board with him was the well-known intermediary between Holland and Russia, Isaak Massa. Roussel's retinue consisted of six noblemen, two of whom were French, Pierre de Roquevire and Maurice de Paquevire, the others being Anton Keijser, Andre Müller, Jan Fribit and Jan Sanderis. The local authorities at Archangel decided to risk receiving Roussel with honour, supplying him and his retinue with appropriate food and showing other marks of respect.

For reasons unknown to us, Roussel asked permission to send ahead to Moscow his secretary, Anton Keijser, with a letter, whilst he himself along with Massa, his noblemen and his servants, would come by water. Keijser reached Moscow on 11 August. He was received by Prince Cherkasskii in the Treasury and quickly sent off with the sovereigns' letter to meet Roussel. The text of this letter is not in the file. Moreover, everything is now mysteriously interrupted. There is nothing about Roussel's arrival in Moscow, nor about his subsequent doings. All the documents have been removed by some hand. There can be no doubt that Roussel arrived in Moscow not later than September 1633, and that he was among Philaret's most trusted men right down to the end of the Patriarch's life. After the Patriarch's death on 1 October 1633, Roussel stayed on in Moscow for five months more, trying to engage in complex intrigues, Isaak Massa was later to report. In the records of the Embassies Department, however, every trace of him has been destroyed and his name is mentioned only in connection with his departure from Moscow for Turkey on 4 March 1634. Again he took with him a retinue and a rich

[49] Ibid., *stb.* 5, *ll.* 1–14.    [50] Ibid., *ll.* 19–20.

reward in money.[51] About that time the disarmed army of the boyar Shein returned to Moscow from Smolensk.

The more we study these files, the more definitely do we hold to the conclusion that in those months the Patriarch was making more and more vigorous efforts to pick up the reins of foreign policy, but the Embassies Department clearly perceived that his line of military alliance with Sweden against Poland had failed, and influenced Prince Cherkasskii accordingly. Several times they deprived the all-powerful Patriarch of the means to intervene directly in diplomacy. Probably connected with such an episode is the otherwise inexplicable revocation of the intended appointment to Sweden of a permanent agent, one Franzbekov. It appears that he was very close to the Patriarch, from whose hands he had received baptism into the Orthodox Church in 1625. The order for Franzbekov to go to Sweden was issued in the Tsar's name on 22 March 1633, and by 19 April all the relevant letters had been signed including an accompanying letter to Pushkin and Gorikhvostov.[52] It is not clear from the documents why the agent's departure did not then take place. (Nevertheless, at the end of 1634 Franzbekov did become Russia's permanent agent in Sweden.) Perhaps it was because there was no suitable candidate for Sweden's corresponding post in Moscow? But a different explanation seems more probable. The appearance in Stockholm of a permanent plenipotentiary resident would have created a diplomatic channel parallel with that of the 'Great Embassy'. In which case the Patriarch would have had that parallel channel in his own hands, and this had to be cut off by some means.

We know of yet another attempt by the Patriarch to free himself from control by the machinery of state. We do not know exactly when this happened, but he devised a code for secret correspondence with confidants of his in foreign countries: 'He wrote in his own sovereign and prelatic hand on all his state and diplomatic affairs, or it happened that in some states their ambassadors and envoys or their agents wrote to him about such great matters of state of theirs and wrote to him in secret writing so that it would not be understood in those countries'. The enclosed alphabet of 'secret writing', inscribed in the Patriarch's own hand, which it was ordered should be kept strictly secret, is not very complicated. The code devised by the Patriarch consists merely in changing the order of the Slavonic letters, writing some the wrong way round, leaving others incomplete, or adding unnecessary strokes to them.[53] It has been supposed that a second copy of this alphabet was with Franzbekov in Sweden in 1635, but it is more likely that the Patriarch devised it for

[51] TsGADA, Dela vengerskie, 1634, March.    [52] TsGADA, Dela shvedskie, 1633, stb. 4.
[53] See Zapiski imp. Arkheograficheskogo obshchestva, 1853, Vol. V, Section II, pp. 124–127.

Franzbekov in March–April 1633. What is most interesting though, is that the Patriarch was compelled to hand over his copy of the alphabet to the Council secretary Ivan Griazev on 8 August 1633. This looks like a direct victory for the Embassies Department over the attempts to practise personal diplomacy made by the 'Great Sovereign' whose plan in the field of major policy had already failed.

Perhaps this conflict at court also explains the long delay in the arrival, or simply in the registration, of the dispatches sent to Moscow from Stockholm by Pushkin, Gorikhvostov and Neverov. On 17 August, however, these dispatches suddenly reached the Patriarch and we find under that date a hastily written note to the effect that the ambassadors must be sent a reply. This was apparently written by the secretary at the Patriarch's reception.[54] At about this time there is traceable yet another dash by the Patriarch towards authoritative and active guidance of policy. It was the last such attempt, lasting a little over a month. It was ended by the return to Moscow, empty handed, of the 'Great Embassy'.

Instructions dated 14 September were sent in reply to the ambassadors' report. This was a fortnight before the Patriarch's death. For practical purposes the message was useless, since the ambassadors were already on their way home. They left Rugodiv (Narva) on 6 September. The gist of the instructions was that as a last resort the ambassadors could abandon the demand for an oath-taking and, in general, reduce the matter to two points: ratification of the peace of Stolbovo by mere signature on the part of the Swedish magnates, and a written undertaking by them concerning the alliance against Poland with a pledge not to conclude a separate peace. Should these two points be rejected the ambassadors are to inform Moscow and wait in the Swedish capital for fresh orders. Later, however, a directive appears, in the Patriarch's handwriting, for the situation if the Swedes agree to the first point but reject the second. Of the few texts by Filaret Nikitich that have come down to us, this is one of the longest:

And if the Councillors affirm the former permanent treaty with their signatures and seals, albeit without a formal oath, it would also be good to write this in their affirmation with signatures and seals: why they do not want to include a clause committing them to act in concert, according to the former treaty, against King Wladyslaw and his brothers and the Poles and Lithuanians, so that we may know and be sure about that. If they will confirm with their signatures and seals both [points] set out above, you will return with these documents to us in Moscow, but if they will not confirm either of them with their signatures and seals, you are to report this to us . . . and await our orders in Stockholm.

As we see, the Muscovite demands have been reduced to the minimum but the Patriarch is still full of deluded hope that the Swedes will find it necessary to accept them. This document was written earlier than Saturday 14 September, as it is followed by a postscript in the Patriarch's writing meant for the secretary or for Prince Cherkasskii: 'I want to talk to you about this before Mass on Saturday, the feast of the Exaltation of the Cross.'[55] Two days later on 16 September, one of the ambassadors, G.N. Gorikhvostov, galloped into Moscow bringing a brief report on the results of the embassy. The report is minuted: 'The Tsar and the Most Holy Sovereign Patriarch have heard this.'

What had happened in Stockholm? The negotiations began on 8 June. A summary of the Russian proposals and documents compiled by the Swedish side, together with the first exchange of views, is dated 22 June. From the beginning the chief plenipotentiary of the Swedish Council of State was Per Banér, although his colleagues changed later. The Russian ambassadors immediately put forward the main points already known to us: ratification of the Treaty of Stolbovo by oath-taking on the part of the ambassadors in Stockholm and Moscow, and conclusion of a new alliance against the Polish–Lithuanian King who called himself ruler of Muscovy and Sweden and was, for that reason, their common foe. This new alliance was to be expressed, above all, in an undertaking by both Sweden and Russia not to make a separate peace with the Polish–Lithuanian state under any circumstances whatsoever. The Swedish delegation replied agreeing to the first point and even expressed their readiness to send an embassy to Moscow at once, in order that the oath-taking might be performed simultaneously in both capitals. On the second point, however, they required elucidation. The Muscovites' answer followed, signed by the secretary M.V. Neverov. Standing together against Wladyslaw and his brothers and against the Polish–Lithuanian state as a whole meant that Sweden would have no dealings or negotiations with them without first informing the Tsar, and the Tsar would not make peace with them without warning the Swedish Council of State. In other words, only joint peace negotiations with the Polish–Lithuanian state could be advantageous to both powers. This, however, assumed joint military operations, and so long as Sweden had not begun hostilities, the Tsar remained justified in either continuing the war or making peace with the Polish–Lithuanian state. In the text of the embassy report signed by Pushkin and Gorikhvostov this was later expressed thus: 'And while the Swedish side is not at war with all its power against the Polish King and his brothers and the Poles and Lithuania, his Majesty the Tsar is free for his part, either to wage war against the Poles or to make peace with them without informing the Kingdom of Sweden.'[56]

[55] Ibid., *ll.* 355–364.    [56] Ibid., *l.* 399.

Here resounds the threat of a separate peace! However, the Russian embassy went on, Sweden too could be included in this peace treaty. The rest of the reply was devoted to detailed discussion of the possible procedure for mutual oath-taking, and even for its repetition in the future after Christina had come of age. Account had to be taken of the need to await the arrival in Sweden of the remains of Gustavus Adolphus soldered in a tin coffin, and to attend his funeral.[57] The stay of the 'Great Embassy' in Sweden was indeed being protracted, and from 11 August the negotiations were transferred to the port of Nyköping where the funeral ship docked and whither the entire Swedish government moved for the ceremony.

There would be no point in describing step by step, and day by day, the course taken by the negotiations, although we have very full sources for them. First, from the Swedish side, we possess the proceedings published long ago of the sessions of the Council of State, where we find reports of the debates on the Russian proposals on 31 July and 15, 16, 20, 21, 22 and 24 August 1633. Secondly, all the matters connected with the visit of the Russian embassy are reflected in the corresponding unpublished file kept in the State Archives in Stockholm, a microfilm of which is held in the Central State Archive of Ancient Documents in Moscow. Here also are special documents which the two sides exchanged during the negotiations and the general review presented to the Council of State by the Swedish plenipotentiaries at the end. From the Russian side, in the corresponding roll of the Embassies Department, there are, first, a brief *exposé* sent to Moscow by Pushkin and Gorikhvostov as soon as they reached Narva and, second, the formal report of the embassy, which unfortunately is not quite complete, having apparently been written in haste and in summary fashion. But all these plentiful documents are poor in content. The 'Great Embassy' revealed its programme almost immediately, at the second meeting with the Swedes. This programme was not identical with either the first mandate or the second. Either the ambassadors took their cue from the situation they found themselves in, or else they were given additional orders which are not reflected in the roll. From the outset the Swedish delegation also took up a position which did not subsequently alter. Therefore, although the embassy lasted a long time, it is more expedient not to describe its work chronologically, but systematically.

In principle, the problem of ratifying the 1617 Treaty of Stolbovo was not a matter for dispute. It would be tedious to delve into the lengthy drafts and counter-drafts concerning the procedure for reciprocal oath-taking. To this group of discussions which are not important for our

[57] *Svenska Riksarkivet, Stockholm, Muscovitica*, N. 631, 1633, 22 June, pp. 1–4.

subject must also be assigned the mutual reproaches and corrections related to the observation of protocol in writing the titles of the monarchs on either side, though this, it seems, evoked very acute feelings. In general the Swedes agreed without difficulty to the desirability of such normal diplomatic procedure as the renewal of an inter-state treaty of perpetual peace at the beginning of a new reign. However, one circumstance in this connection affected the second subject of the negotiations, namely the Polish question. The Russian ambassadors emphasised that the treaty of Stolbovo included an article directed against the Polish–Lithuanian state and treating Sweden and Muscovy as allies against a common foe. This was the case,[58] and not for nothing did the embassy's report have attached to it as documentary proof the relevant extract from the treaty of 1617.[59] The Swedish plenipotentiaries, however, presented at the negotiations their own version of the Treaty of Stolbovo, in which, according to the Russian ambassadors, 'extra articles were included, while the Polish article was omitted'.[60] The Russian ambassadors recalled the entire history of the question, reminded their interlocutors of the situation in 1609 when, at the signing of the Treaty of Vyborg between Tsar Vasily Ivanovich Shuiskii and the Swedish King Charles IX, the 'Polish Article' was agreed upon, stating that Muscovy and Sweden 'stand together against the Polish King and his successors'. The ambassadors affirmed that this 'Polish article' was not rescinded by the Treaty of Stolbovo, but on the contrary, was confirmed and this was what underlay the counsels which Gustavus Adolphus and Mikhail Fedorovich had exchanged and as a result of which the Tsar had sent against the Polish King 'his all-powerful army' which had already achieved so many successes for Russian arms.[61]

Thus, already, the question of ratifying the Treaty of Stolbovo proved to hang mainly on the 'Polish Article'. And in the second half of the negotiations, the Swedish side's position amounted to a wish to put off the signing of an anti-Polish alliance for two years, during which time they would undertake no obligations. Through all the documents we can perceive traces of complete confidence, on the part of the Swedes, that it would not suit Muscovy to make peace and so it would go on with the war regardless, even without allies. But this futile confidence of the Swedish statesmen was to be undone. It was of course, not short-sightedness that made them step over the precipice. On the contrary, they had fallen over

[58] See Lyzhin, N. P., *Stolbovskii dogovor i peregovory emu predshestvovavshie*, St Petersburg, 1857; Shaskolskii, I. P., *Stolbovskii mir 1617g. i torgovye otnosheniia Rossii so shvedskim gosudarstvom*, Moscow and Leningrad, 1964.
[59] *TsGADA*, *Dela shvedskie*, 1632, stb. 6, *ll.* 406–408.    [60] Ibid., *l.* 381.
[61] Ibid., *l.* 369.

the precipice and for that very reason shut their eyes, cultivating subjective illusions. True, at the session of the Council of State held on 15 August, a sober voice was heard saying that they ought to keep the Russians in hope as: 'otherwise in desperation, they may make peace with Poland'.[62] But the Russians required not hope but real obligations, and the members of the Council of State tried to forget their misgivings and to believe in their own fantasy according to which the Russians would not consider peace with Poland as anything other than highly undesirable. They possibly had in mind the maintenance by Wladyslaw IV of his claim to the throne of Muscovy.

After their first meeting, the Swedish plenipotentiaries put this question to the Russians: On what conditions was the Russo–Swedish military alliance against Poland to be conceived? 'How was this war to be begun and how ended?'[63] As we know, the first mandate given to Pushkin and Gorikhvostov contained a detailed elaboration of these conditions. Now, however, the ambassadors did not mention them. Essentially, their answer amounted to a single point: the military alliance was to consist of both sides waging war against the Polish–Lithuanian state, and neither Sweden nor Muscovy entering into negotiations or making peace with the common foe except by agreement one with the other. In other words, both sides were to bind themselves not to conclude a separate peace. The Swedish side indicated agreement in principle to this, so that Sweden bound itself to this obligation in the future war and gave assurances that it would begin that war, but only in two years' time. The Russian ambassadors tried to counter this procrastination with a plainly stated threat: so long as Sweden had not begun military operations against the Polish–Lithuanian state, the Tsar would be within his rights should he not wish to go on with the war, if he were to make peace with that state.

But the trouble was that the Swedish politicians blindly refused to believe in the reality of this threat. True, at one of the meetings they asked on what conditions Moscow would be ready to make peace with Poland. Not getting any answer, however, they felt reassured. They even put forward a counter-threat. In Gustavus Adolphus's time the Polish King had tried, and was still trying, to persuade Sweden to replace the truce of Altmark by a treaty of peace. He was promoting this idea through the mediation of the Kings of France, England and Denmark and the Dutch States and through other high personages. However, the Swedish Council of State had rejected all these attempts in conformity with the will of the late King 'for the sake of his friendship with the Tsar's

---

[62] *Svenska Riksrådets protokoll*, Vol. III, p. 164.
[63] *Svenska Riksarkivet, Stockholm, Muscovitica*, N. 631; 1633, 22 June, p. 2; *TsGADA, Dela shvedskie*, 1632, stb. 6, *l.* 367.

Majesty'. If, contrary to expectations, the Tsar should wish to enter into peace negotiations with the Poles before the Swedo–Polish truce expired, he should not be surprised if, in the interests of their country, the Swedish government were to try to start negotiations with the Poles about peace.[64] But this was not at all an effective chess move, for once Muscovy had decided on making peace with the Polish–Lithuanian state, it would be a matter of indifference to the Russians whether that state was or was not at war with Sweden.

In their preliminary report sent from Reval, Pushkin, Gorikhvostov and Neverov wrote: 'We note sovereigns, their desire that although the Swedish side will not for a long time go to war against the Poles, your Sovereign Majesty is not to make peace with them without having informed the Kingdom of Sweden.'[65]

To this end, Sweden is to render 'aid' to Muscovy by allowing mercenaries to pass through its territory and helping with the purchase of munitions and the selection of commanders. The Russian ambassadors, however, agreed to give the undertaking not to make a separate peace only on one of two conditions. Either Sweden should at once break the truce and go to war against the Polish–Lithuanian state, and it was hinted that there was a juridical justification for breaking the truce since Wladyslaw was calling himself King of Sweden. Or else the Swedish government must provide the Tsar, at its own expense, with 5,000 soldiers and other aid for the continuance of the war against the Poles. It was implied that this would amount to the same as Sweden going to war, if not *de jure* then *de facto*. But both variants for breaking the truce were rejected again and again by Sweden's Council of State. They proposed that the 5,000 soldiers be hired with Russian money, not Swedish.

Each time they justified their attitude by considerations of an ethical nature: the inviolability of word once given. For this reason, they said, Gustavus Adolphus himself had never broken the truce of Altmark: 'we must act in this way towards friend and foe alike'.[66] But the entire history of diplomacy bears witness to the fact that such obstacles are overcome when necessary either without any pretexts, or more often, by putting the blame on the other side. As we see, the Russian ambassadors hinted at a completely proper pretext. But this time the formal obstacle to war revealed the toughness of granite. The Swedish government took shelter behind the utter and absolute impossibility of breaking the truce and,

---

[64] The Swedish reply, on behalf of Christina, 1 July 1633: see *Svenska Riksarkivet, Stockholm, Muscovitica*, N. 631.

[65] *TsGADA, Dela shvedskie*, 1632, stb. 6, *ll.* 367–368.

[66] *Svenska Riksarkivet, Stockholm, Muscovitica*, N. 631: report on negotiations with the Russian embassy, 26 June to 26 August 1633.

consequently, the necessity of putting its decision off for two years.

A historian with a broad view will never say that the whole outcome of the Thirty Years' War, the fate of Europe for many years, hung on this rather accidental fact. It was no more than a tiny grain in a huge scale, the balance of which was wavering before it began to tip one way. The Russo–Swedish military alliance against the Polish–Lithuanian state did not collapse because the Swedes stayed true to the letter of the truce (and distorted the letter of the peace of Stolbovo), but on the contrary, because history had already doomed that alliance.

At that moment the Swedish statesmen sincerely believed that all they were doing was postponing the alliance for a couple of years. This theme is apparent in all the Swedish documents, including the debates in the Council of State.[67] To a certain extent, even the 'great ambassadors' accepted the idea that such a two-year postponement was possible. In their written reply of 16 July, they formulated third and fourth points in this spirit: if at that time all their demands were unacceptable, and the Tsar's Majesty was pleased to go on with the Polish war, then let the Swedish government send an embassy to Moscow to discuss how best, in two years' time, to implement the Swedo–Russian alliance.[68]

It must be remembered that the negotiations were concerned not with some spectacular project, but with an alliance which, in practice, existed in objective reality. Both sides understood that perfectly well, even though each side emphasised only what in the alliance served its own state's interest. At the session of the Council of State and in Per Banér's reply to the Russian ambassadors on 16 August, it was said that the hard war that the Swedish army was waging in Germany was equivalent to indirect aid to the Tsar, since the Poles were not receiving any help whatsoever from the Emperor. Indeed, they were still obliged to divide their forces because they feared that one day the Swedes would invade from Silesia. In that connexion, in the official letter on behalf of Christina, it was said that the requested 5,000 soldiers would best be kept, at Sweden's cost, in Silesia so that Wladyslaw would feel a constant menace of invasion from the west and the need to split his forces between the frontiers on opposite sides of his country.[69] On their part, the Russian ambassadors recalled that the German Emperor was very much interested in reconciliation between Russia and Poland. 'If the Tsar had not launched this war, half of the Polish army would be helping the Emperor,

---

[67] *Svenska Riksrådets protokoll*, Vol. III, pp. 147, 163–164, 168–169, 174–175, 294–307.

[68] *Svenska Riksarkivet, Stockholm, Muscovitica*, N. 631; report on negotiations with the Russian embassy, 26 June to 26 August 1633.

[69] See ibid. and also the letter from Queen Christina at Nyköping to the Tsar, 26 August 1633, and to the Patriarch on the same day. Cf. *Svenska Riksrådets protokoll*, Vol. III, p. 295; *TsGADA, Dela shvedskie*, 1632, *stb.* 6, *ll.* 391–395.

and the other half would be in Livonia.'[70] And neither side was departing from the truth in these statements. Mutual aid between Sweden and Muscovy was objectively happening, and the minimum programme for the 'Great Embassy' amounted to this – either to reinforce the mutual aid with reciprocal undertakings, or (the line of Prince Cherkasskii) to break free from it altogether.

The Swedish Council of State could not grasp the actual course of history, including the internal socio-political situation in Russia during the Smolensk War. It could not know that the existing situation could not be kept the same for two years. It sought in every way not to refuse negotiations about the alliance, but to prolong them. To this end, it was decided, on 31 July, to begin preparations for sending a Swedish embassy to Russia. As soon as the 'Great Embassy' left Stockholm, the Swedish embassy to Moscow would set out on its journey.

Pushkin, Gorikhvostov and Neverov sought every diplomatic means to oppose prolongation of the talks. They understood better than the Swedes how much depended in Moscow on what they brought back with them. Apparently, at the final stage they deliberately began to strain relations so as to force the other side to hasten their decision. The concluding meetings of the two sides on 20, 22 and 24 August, passed in a very tense atmosphere and were, to a large extent, occupied with purely diplomatic fencing – disputes about the titles of the two monarchs and about procedure and the texts of the documents. But the Swedish side did not budge an inch. They imitated the tactics of the Russian embassy and charged the atmosphere in their turn. Among other things, accusations against Roussel were put about that he was a swindler, a braggart, claiming 'that he alone was the cause of the renewed Russo–Polish war'.[71] That was a prick of the rapier at the Patriarch personally. On 26 August, Pushkin, Gorikhvostov and Neverov attended a farewell reception at the Royal Palace in Nyköping. They were handed a letter in reply from the Queen regarding those points that had been agreed on and saying that a Swedish embassy would be sent as soon as possible to Moscow to discuss the remaining points. As soon as possible! In fact, many months were to pass.

Meanwhile, the failure of the 'Great Embassy' had had a very violent sequel in Moscow. We have already mentioned that soon after they reached Narva on 4 September, the ambassadors had sent to Moscow a preliminary report on their mission. As preserved in the Embassies Department, this report has strange gaps where the political rumours from Stockholm were being quoted. It may be that these passages

---

[70] *Svenska Riksrådets protokoll*, Vol. III, p. 295.
[71] *Svenska Riksarkivet, Stockholm, Muscovitica*, N. 631: reports and proceedings of 20, 22, 24 and 26 August 1633.

concerned Jacques Roussel. The document was sent to Moscow on, or soon after 20 September, and the 'Great Embassy' arrived in the capital bringing fuller documentation in the first days of October. Between the earlier date and this one, a drama was played out in the Kremlin. In the morning of 1 October 1633, the Patriarch died suddenly. We have a source for the inner life of the Tsar's court in the seventeenth century called the 'engagements books' of the sovereigns. If Filaret Nikitich had been ill for some time, this diary would have recorded the Tsar's visits to his father, just as it mentions all previous meetings between the two sovereigns. Such meetings are logged in the first ten days of September. Thus, on 3 September, the Tsar and the Patriarch received the Swedish ambassador, and on 8 September, Mikhail Fedorovich was host to the Patriarch and several boyars. Subsequently, the Tsar visited his father only on the actual day he died, in the morning after Mass. And immediately 'at the last hour of noon', that is at 11a.m., the Patriarch's death was announced. That everything happened at a rush we are told in a document quoted by the Patriarch's biographer: 'The sudden death of Filaret Nikitich gave rise to many unpleasant and seditious remarks.'[72] This is shown even more clearly by the urgency with which the consequent political decisions were taken, including the immediate offer of peace to the Polish–Lithuanian state.

This does not mean that the *coup d'état* at court was due solely to Moscow's receipt of the report of the 'Great Embassy'. All through August and the first half of September, signs were evident of a political struggle under way at court, some of which have been mentioned above. The Russian troops suffered a major defeat before besieged Smolensk on 4 September. This did not become known in Moscow until 10 September when additional recruits were sent to help the boyar M.B. Shein.

But let us go back to Stockholm. Before the 'Great Embassy' had left, there arrived, having been sent on 4 August, from Germany, an anxious message from Chancellor Axel Oxenstjerna insisting on a change in the line being followed by Swedish diplomacy. Earlier, for example, in February 1633, Oxenstjerna had written more than once to the Council of State about the need to hold back from an alliance with the Russians, even while urging them to go on with their war against the Rzeczpospolita. As we have seen, the Council of State carried out his recommendations to the letter. But those were the first months after the death of Gustavus Adolphus when Oxenstjerna had not yet established his own view of the military and political situation and was being guided by the inertia of his previous opposition to the King's policy. Only gradually did he grasp all

[72] Smirnov, A. P., *Sviateishii patriarkh Filaret Nikitich Moskovskii i vseia Rossiia*, Moscow, 1874, p. 216.

aspects of the great war being waged in the middle of Europe. And a moment came when he was seized with alarm at the thought that the Russo–Polish war might stop. He looked into the heart of the matter, at what Gustavus Adolphus had seen by virtue of the position he held. And so in August, and still more categorically in a letter of 5 October, Oxenstjerna informed Stockholm that he had changed his mind. The Poles might indeed make peace with the Russians on any conditions at all, so as to free their hands to recover Prussia and Livonia from the Swedes. Therefore, it was necessary to resume negotiations about an alliance with Muscovy, so that the latter should in no circumstances call off the Russo–Polish war.[73]

The Council of State discussed the question of sending an embassy to Russia on 9 October, 20 November and 18 December 1633. Clearly, they did not realise in Stockholm that they needed to hurry, but they referred to the fact that it was in any case impossible to make the journey in the autumn, owing to the condition of the roads.

The proceedings of the debate in the Council of State on 18 December reveal a wide range of differences. At one pole was Tott's view. The King of Poland had *de facto* renounced his claims on Sweden, so should they not return to him everything they had taken from him and transform the truce into a permanent peace, so as to concentrate all their forces on the war in Germany? Johan Skytte supported Tott. Alliance with Russia would only make more difficult the achievement of peace with Poland which was so necessary for the prosecution of the German war. The opposite view was represented by Fleming, De la Gardie and Gabriel Gustavsson. Poland willingly maintains the state of truce with us so long as it is burdened with care regarding Russia, but as soon as that situation ceases to be, it will turn on us. War with Poland would come, it was inevitable: 'Therefore, our security in relation to Poland consists in Russia's success.' The Russian ally must be helped, and care taken not to let Poland grow stronger than Sweden, 'just as the King of France sees to that where the House of Austria is concerned'. If Poland got Prussia back it would be twice as strong. So that this should not happen, alliance with Russia was needed, and needed precisely because the war was being fought in Germany. If things were not to go very well in Germany and then there came a clash with Poland, Denmark would not hesitate to form a war-coalition against Sweden and the situation would become catastrophic. Accordingly, there should be talks with Russia. Alliance with Russia would make it easier to get peace with Poland. Sweden would keep everything it had previously taken from Poland, while Russia would

---

[73] See *Handlingar rörande Skandinaviens historia*, Vol. 27, Stockholm, 1847, p. 167; Wejle, C., *Sveriges Politik mot Polen 1630–1635*, Uppsala, 1901, pp. 84–85.

obtain the Smolensk region and its other lands.[74]

This second view prevailed, but it was paralysed. First, by the position previously taken that in no circumstances should the truce with the Polish–Lithuanian state be broken before its term expired, and second, by the mission assigned to the embassy above all to 'discredit' Jacques Roussel in Moscow and have him exiled to Siberia. But that meant discrediting the dealings between Gustavus Adolphus and the Patriarch, in other words, all the preparatory work for the Swedo–Russian alliance! Consequently, dispatch of the embassy to Moscow was held up.

On 17 January 1634, the Council of State wrote to Chancellor Oxenstjerna about this 'weighty and important problem' of the alliance proposed by the Tsar. First, the arguments against the alliance were set forth. This unreliable friend would, at the first opportunity, take back by force or cunning the lands and provinces annexed from it and now subject to the Swedish Crown. The truce with Poland could be prolonged at will 'without any need to inform the Russians or obtain their consent'. But there were many more arguments in favour of alliance with Russia. Ten points were enumerated:

1. War with Poland was unavoidable anyway and the truce would be no guarantee against it.
2. If Russia were to fall, that would entail grave danger for Sweden.
3. If the Swedes refused to form the alliance 'Russia may, in desperation, decide to make peace with the Poles and join with them against us'.
4. In which case Denmark would join them.
5. If Sweden's fortunes in Germany were to take a turn for the bad (which God forbid!), the Poles and Danes would not fail to attack Sweden, which meant that it would be better to have Russia as a fighting ally than to allow a situation to develop in which that state remained aside, watching the attack on Sweden.
6. Sweden's position would be strengthened in the territories it had taken from both Poland and Russia.
7. The rise of Poland would be hindered.
8. It would be easier to establish trade relations with Persia through Russia.
9. 'Even if Russia will not be a loyal friend, it will for a time nevertheless, not be an enemy to us.'
10. If military operations were not carried on in one and the same province of Poland, the alliance could be made secure and the allies could help each other.

Proceeding from these ten propositions, the Council of State found it

---

[74] *Svenska Riksrådets protokoll*, Vol. III, pp. 287–289.

advantageous, in principle, to form an alliance with Russia against Poland for a period of eight to ten years. One of the conditions should be that, after the truce with Poland expired, Sweden would go to war with that country and then neither Sweden nor Muscovy would have the right to make a separate truce or peace and each would have to inform the other and obtain its consent before entering into any negotiations with the enemy. In the Council's opinion, war with Poland would be twice as burdensome for Sweden as for Russia. The Poles would have to be threatened through Prussia and Livonia and, in order to make impossible mutual aid between Poland and the Emperor, also through Silesia. Consequently, Russia would have to contribute a certain sum of money to finance Sweden's war. The other conditions for taking this important political step affecting the fate of 'the fatherland as a whole', were to be considered at a special assembly in February of representatives of the nobility, clergy and towns of Sweden.[75] Chancellor Oxenstjerna replied to this letter from Magdeburg on 4 March 1634. In his reply too, the arguments against alliance with Russia were set forth first, and then the arguments for.

Alliance with the Russian neighbour, Oxenstjerna admitted, might eventually lead to mutual accusations, ill will and, in the end, war. 'This is all the more to be feared from our neighbour, who is by nature arrogant and bold and judges every matter from the standpoint of its own advantage.' The Russians might not honour their obligations if it suited them better not to.

But the arguments for alliance were much stronger. The reasons for war with Poland were insurmountable and the Poles would begin war at the first breathing space or when Sweden was first in difficulties, whatever promises they had made. Alliance would bind Russia and it would be unable to harm Sweden even if it wanted to. Thus, there was hope of keeping the Russian government from making peace with Poland, which Poland was trying by every means to bring about as it would have preferred to be interfering in Sweden's affairs during the Queen's minority. To keep track of the Russian court's loyalty it was necessary to have there a serious and intelligent agent, someone who 'would know everything better than the Russians themselves' and who would expose the Poles' intrigues. Referring to Gustavus Adolphus's experience, Oxenstjerna emphasised the interest that Sweden had in making an alliance with Russia. Muscovy should be obliged to continue the war against Wladyslaw, and Sweden should undertake to enter that war immediately when the truce of Altmark expired (that is, in July 1635). Neither party must negotiate for peace or a truce without the knowledge

[75] *Handlingar rörande Skandinaviens historia*, Vol. 28, Stockholm, 1847, pp. 11–14.

and agreement of the other. Neither Sweden nor Russia must make a separate peace or truce. Demands to be put to the enemy would be agreed when the time came but meanwhile, the minimum could be stipulated. These were as follows. Sweden insists that Wladyslaw IV and his brothers renounce their claim to the Swedish throne and also to the lands, fortresses and ports taken from Poland by Sweden which are now under Swedish rule. The Polish King is also to renounce his claim to the Muscovite throne and return to Russia the lands around Smolensk and Novgorod-Severskii. It will be left to Russia's discretion whether or not it is to be included in the new treaty between Sweden and Poland which was proposed to the late Gustavus Adolphus by France, England, Brandenburg and Holland. Muscovy must render substantial financial help to the Swedish Crown, since the Swedes will draw upon themselves the major part of the enemy's forces and invade the least vulnerable part of Poland. While the Russians are attacking the enemy in Lithuania, the Swedes will be attacking him in Livonia, Lithuania and Prussia and sending an army into Upper Poland through Germany or Silesia. But, Oxenstjerna adds, however important the point about a Russian financial subsidy may be, the alliance should not be broken off on that account. Muscovy must allow Sweden to carry on trade with Persia across its territory, sharing in the profits of this trade. But any difficulty on that point should not hinder conclusion of the alliance, either. The term of the future Russo–Swedish alliance should be from four to twelve years, or simply until the end of the war with Poland. As for the procedure for signing the treaty, Sweden might (for the sake of speed and keeping the initiative) be the first to sign both documents without waiting for the signature of the Tsar.[76] So solidly and circumstantially did the Chancellor prepare for the political designs of Gustavus Adolphus to be resurrected and put into effect. But neither he nor the members of the Council of State took account of the court *coup d'état* and the socio-political situation in Muscovy. While the Swedish statesmen were re-writing, re-thinking and preparing their embassy, history had swerved in quite a different direction.

Analysis of the subsequent events in the 'Swedish period' of the Thirty Years' War falls outside the framework of the present study. At this point however, running ahead, we must show the conclusion to all this history which has served, so to speak, as a factual verification of the view I have expressed regarding the decisive importance of the Polish problem and, in connexion therewith, the Russo–Polish conflict, for the outcome of the Swedes' campaign in Germany.

Resulting from his failure to understand in time the profound designs of Gustavus Adolphus, the ambiguity of Oxenstjerna's policy, together

[76] Ibid., Vol. 29, pp. 268–276.

with the attitude of the Swedish Council of State, were among the reasons that impelled the Muscovite government to terminate the Smolensk War with the Polish–Lithuanian state and, in June 1634, to conclude it with the peace treaty of Polyanovka. The catastrophic significance for Sweden of this event was not long in making itself felt. The series of defeats suffered by the Swedish army in Germany beginning with Nördlingen, were due not to the genius of Wallenstein, not to the 'German miracle', and not to betrayal by the fortunes of war, but to the fact that at the moment of highest tension in the conflict in Germany in the second half of 1634 and the first half of 1635, Sweden was forced to concentrate some of its forces on the Polish frontier. Freed from war with Russia (and then from war with Turkey), Wladyslaw IV began preparing in 1634, in alliance with Denmark, for renewed war with Sweden. It is generally accepted that Sweden lost the war in Germany 1634–1635 through lack of reserves. But Sweden did have reserves at that time, only they were partly in Sweden, kept there against the possibility of war with Poland, partly in Livonia and Prussia, that is, on the Polish frontier, and partly on the Russian frontier. It was not only impossible to transfer any troops to the German theatre of war, but several regiments had to be taken from there and sent to the border of Poland.

Thus, the failure of the Swedish campaign in Germany was a direct consequence of the ending of the Smolensk War. The Swedes were saved by Richelieu. In June 1635, France entered the Thirty Years' War openly and took on the Emperor's main forces. This enabled Sweden to concentrate its main forces against the Rzeczpospolita, to conclude with that state in September 1635 the Treaty of Stuhmsdorf, and after that to return to active participation in the war in Germany.

# Index

Abelin (Abelinus), J. Ph., *see* Arlanibaeus, Ph.

Ahnlund, Nils, 69, 80, 106, 208

Aldringer, General Johann von, 203, 205

Aleksei Mikhailovich, Tsar, 53, 133

Altmark, truce of (1629), 9–10, 15, 21, 25, 32, 34, 48, 64, 69, 72, 81, 86, 234, 240

Amsterdam, *see* Netherlands 7

Andrusovo, truce of (1667), 156

Archangel
  as grain port and market, 43, 49, 51–3, 56–7, 61, 74, 128, 161, 226
  Roussel arrives in, 227
  violence against foreigners in, 62

Aristov, A., 38, 55, 77, 84–5, 101–3, 129, 138

Arlanibaeus, Ph. (J.Ph. Abelin), 66, 102

Arnim, General Hans Georg von, 3, 117, 196, 201, 220

Arnoldin (Imperial envoy to Muscovy), 134n

Arzymatov, A.A., 208

Asserson, Nils, 217

Augsburg, peace of (1555), x, xii

Austria, 122, 193, 199, 207

*Balashovshchina* (peasant-Cossack rising, 1633–4), xvii

Banér, Johan, 143

Banér, Per, 217, 230, 235

Baron, Benjamin, 73, 130–1, 133n

Bärwalde, treaty of (1631), 86, 180

Bavaria, 206

Beckman (Swedish envoy), 46

Beijer, Martin, 221–2, 224

Belaia, 161

Bensen, H.W., 181

Berenson, Hans, 223–4, 226

Berlin, siege of (1631), 100, 102

Bernard, Duke of Weimar, 219

Bethlen Gábor, ruler of Transylvania
  death, 35, 71, 79, 142n

embassy to Moscow, 35
  Muscovy proposes alliance with, 30
  and Ottomans, 18–19, 30
  and Polish Crown 80–1, 94
  prepared to cede Ukraine, 94
  relations with Gustav Adolf, 20, 30, 70
  Roussel's mission to, 19–20, 79–80

Bielke, Sten, 146

Bogislaw XIV, Duke of Pomerania, 98, 176–9

Bohemia
  class struggle and peasant revolts in. 125, 196–204, 220
  Gustav Adolf avoids, 193–4
  Swedo-Saxon campaign in, 194–6, 202–5

Bökman, Johan, 127

Bökman, Melchior, 127n, 162n, 219–20

Bönhardt, J., 7, 14, 26–7, 30–1, 34, 74n, 214

Boris Godunov, Tsar, x–xi, 153

Bormosov (Muscovite envoy to Turkey), 133n

Brandenburg, 3, 19, 98–100, 148
  *see also* Georg-Wilhelm, Elector of Brandenburg

Brandenburg, Mark, 226

Breitenfeld, battle of (1631), 98, 104, 109, 111, 115–18, 188, 191–4

Bremen (Swedish statthalter at Reval), 12, 25–6

Bremen (town), 183

Brunswick, 183

Brussels congress (1626), 2

Bubna, Count of, 201

Burg, A. (Dutch envoy), 54, 57n

Burgus (Burge), P.H., 66, 86n, 102, 174

Byelorussia, 93–4, 133, 155n, 156

Cantacuzene, Foma, 7, 12, 29

Carafa, C., 199

Carlisle, Charles Howard, 1st Earl of, 112n

243

Nurali (Crimean envoy), 222
Nuremberg, 162
Nyenskans, 125n
Nykerke, Joost, 39, 54

Opel, J.O., 181
Orlik, Adam, 134
Osman II, Ottoman Sultan, 12, 23, 29
Ottoman Empire (Turkey)
  attempts to bring into anti-Empire
    coalition, 17–19
  conflict with Spain for control of
    Mediterranean, xx
  Gustav Adolf attempts collaboration
    with, 70, 99
  and Gustav Adolf's candidature for
    Polish throne, 155
  and Muscovite threat to Poland, 7
  Muscovy negotiates for alliance with, 23,
    29–31, 74, 114, 132–3
  Muscovy offers payments to, 44
  peace with Poland, 70
  and Prussia, 2
  relations with France, 17–19
  and Smolensk War, 133
  as threat to Holy Roman Empire, x, 35
Oxenstjerna, Axel (Swedish Chancellor)
  agrees to truce of Altmark, 32
  and Baron, 131n
  and Breitenfeld victory, 193
  commands Swedish army, 223
  conflict with Roussel, 141, 143–4, 159–60
  continues war against Empire, 216, 221,
    223
  converted to favour alliance with
    Muscovy, 237–41
  differences with Gustav Adolf, 108n,
    109, 116, 121–5, 127, 146, 148,
    159–60, 162
  fails to understand Gustav Adolf's grand
    design, 241
  in Germany and Stettin, 217, 220
  and grain speculation, 38, 50
  and Gustav Adolf's attitude to Poland,
    73, 82
  and Gustav Adolf's candidature for
    Polish throne, 81–2
  and Gustav Adolf's policy on
    Magdeburg, 184
  and Gustav Adolf's policy to draw
    Muscovy into war against Poland,
    88–92, 96n, 103–4, 115–16, 121–2
  hopes for Polish–Muscovy conflict, 107–8
  informs Gustav Adolf about
    Poland–Lithuania, 106n

Muscovy lacks confidence in, 214
obstructs access to Gustav Adolf, 132,
    160
opposes mission to Cossacks, 95
optimism, 61
and Polish war, 5, 121–3
and Prussian customs duties, 113n
and Roussel's missions, 81, 88, 90, 109n,
    124, 133n
sends embassy to Moscow, 26
on supply of troops and Muscovite
    payments, 129n
and Swedish anti-Empire stance, 35
visits Gustav Adolf in Germany, 143,
    162
Oxenstjerna, Gabriel, 50, 217, 223

Pappenheim, Gottfried Heinrich, Count zu,
    98, 182, 185, 188, 192, 205
Paquevire, Maurice de, 227
Paul, J., 106, 125, 208
peasants and peasantry
  at Breitenfeld, 192–3
  in Austria, 199, 207
  in Germany, 169, 171
  Gustav Adolf's attitude to, 206–7
  in Pomerania, 177, 176, 179
  revolt in Hesse, 189–91, 205
  in Saxony, 194–5
  in Swedish army, 170–1
  unrest in Bohemia, 196–205, 220
Pelzel, F.M., 198
Philip IV, King of Spain, 142, 195
Plemiannikov, Fedor, 38, 55, 77, 84–5,
    101–3, 138
  death, 103n, 129
Pogozhev, Dementii, 62
Poland–Lithuania (Rzeczpospolita)
  attempts to negotiate with Muscovy,
    134–5
  Baltic coastal possessions, 9
  dealings with Gustav Adolf after
    Sigismund's death, 212–13
  French hostility to, 16–19
  and grain trade, 42
  and 'Great Embassy', 232–5
  Gustav Adolf plans offensive against,
    110–11, 115–16, 161–2
  Gustav Adolf presses Muscovy to attack,
    82–3, 87–9, 103, 106–7, 109, 114–15,
    121
  Gustav Adolf's attitude to, 69–70
  and Gustav Adolf's campaign in
    Germany, 99
  and Gustav Adolf's candidature for